First in Violence, Deepest in Dirt

First in Violence, Deepest in Dirt

HOMICIDE IN CHICAGO

1875-1920

JEFFREY S. ADLER

HARVARD UNIVERSITY PRESS
Cambridge, Massachusetts
London, England
2006

Printed in the United States of America

Library of Congress Cataloging-in-Publication Data
Adler, Jeffrey S.
First in violence, deepest in dirt : homicide in Chicago, 1875–1920 /
Jeffrey S. Adler.
p.   cm.
Includes bibliographical references and index.
ISBN 0-674-02149-5 (alk. paper)
1. Homicide—Illinois—Chicago—Case studies. 2. Murder—Illinois—
Chicago—Case studies. 3. Chicago (Ill.)—Social conditions. I. Title.

HV6534.C4A35 2006

364.1520973'1109034—dc22   2005052778

Contents

First in Violence, Deepest in Dirt

C hicago," journalist Lincoln Steffens reported in 1903, was "first in violence, deepest in dirt."[1] Again and again, observers reached similar conclusions, at least about local violence, often asserting that "Chicago leads America in homicides" or that it was the "murder capital of the world."[2] "No other city in the United States," its police superintendent conceded in 1913, "is more open to the depredations of criminals than Chicago."[3] During the opening decades of the twentieth century, Chicago did indeed experience more homicides than any other urban center in the nation.[4] Furthermore, its homicide rate—that is, the number of homicides per 100,000 residents—far exceeded that of other big cities; only southern and a few smaller western cities had higher levels of bloodshed. But despite Chicago's distinctive record for violence, the Illinois metropolis also symbolized America's progress, vigor, and industrial might, with its phoenixlike rebirth from the Great Fire of 1871 and its hosting the

Columbian Exposition of 1893. In addition, Chicago achieved renown as a booming commercial and manufacturing center and as an important hub for education, the arts, and Progressive reform. This book examines homicide in Chicago during the age of industry, exploring the relationship between violence and urban life from 1875 to 1920. Well before the reign of Al Capone, the Beer Wars, and the St. Valentine's Day Massacre (all of which occurred after 1920), Chicago stood apart from its peers in violent crime.

Homicide is a "social event."[5] It is the product of social relations, and it is shaped and influenced by social conditions. Although every killing in Chicago between 1875 and 1920 was bound up in intensely personal, deeply emotional circumstances, in the aggregate the violence formed clear, larger patterns. Broad-based pressures triggered hundreds of similar explosions of homicidal behavior, even if each particular act of violence erupted from a unique chain of events. Moreover, the larger trends in homicide shifted over time, simultaneously reflecting and revealing the social and cultural sources of conflict and the ways in which urbanization affected interpersonal violence.

Chicago homicides changed in two ways between 1875 and 1920. First, the rate at which Chicagoans slaughtered one another fluctuated over time. Some periods were significantly more violent than others. Rates of homicide, measured in a way that controls for population increases, ebbed and flowed in response to changing urban conditions. Second, the form, or nature, of lethal violence shifted dramatically. Not only did Chicagoans kill at different levels during some periods, they also committed homicide in different ways and for different reasons in some periods than in others. The choice of victim, the location of the violence, the triggering incident, the backgrounds of the participants, the relationship between the victim and the killer, the instrument of death, and even the number of shots fired or punches thrown changed between 1875 and 1920. Simply put, the sparks that generated murderous behavior shifted as Chicago grew.

A note of explanation about the narrative style is in order. Although a rich, interdisciplinary scholarship on violence and related themes informs my argument, the body of this book focuses on the killers, their victims, and the social world in which they lived and fought. As much as possible, the actors speak for themselves and explain their motivations, behavior, and observations. Rarely did Chicagoans simply "lose control" and engage in random acts of violence. Contrary to the fears of some early twentieth-century sociologists, the scale and anonymity of urban life did not overwhelm Chicagoans or produce irrational explosions of violence.[6] Nor did local residents somehow "snap" and shoot, stab, or pummel the first person they encountered. Even the most seemingly impulsive and spontaneous murders typically made sense—at least at the time of the violence—to the killers and often to the victims and bystanders. Although many assailants regretted their actions, they generally killed with purpose. Furthermore, the participants in Chicago homicides between 1875 and 1920, especially the killers but frequently dying victims as well, were often eager to explain their actions. In suicide notes, conversations with friends, interviews with journalists, police interrogations, court testimony, clemency petitions, and other records, barroom brawlers, wife killers, and other homicidal Chicagoans insisted that violence was a logical response to the pressures and tensions they encountered. Given their life circumstances and values, assailants believed that they had to kill—or at least fight. In order to understand trends in violent behavior, I have attempted to explain why vicious, murderous behavior seemed rational to the killers themselves and understandable (if not defensible) to witnesses. The participants' explanations, though often self-serving, one-sided, and distorted, reveal the stresses that transformed some Chicagoans into killers. Because this book focuses on the social world of the assailants and their victims, the narrative remains grounded in late nineteenth- and early twentieth-century Chicago; the citations identify the modern scholarly perspectives that have influenced my ideas on violence and urban life in industrial America.

Likewise, the theoretical foundations of my analysis are imbedded in the narrative and discussed in the endnotes. Many theoretical perspectives influenced my treatment of homicide, though Norbert Elias's work proved to be particularly important. Writing during the 1930s Elias, a German sociologist, offered a model for explaining long-term trends in aggressive behavior. He argued that the rise of European court culture since the Middle Ages, along with the expansion of state institutions and the emergence of powerful bureaucracies, transformed social conventions. The elite, he noted, launched civilizing "offensives," or "missions," intended to extend their influence and establish cultural hegemony. These efforts sought to elevate standards of comportment, and as social interdependence increased, the middle and lower layers of European society gradually embraced elite behavioral ideals. Honed over the course of centuries, the new sensibilities encouraged civility and discouraged aggressive, impulsive, disorderly conduct. Political and legal institutions reinforced the emerging cultural and behavioral norms, monopolizing the legitimate use of coercion and criminalizing interpersonal aggression.[7] Ultimately this "civilizing process," as Elias termed it, relied on the development of psychological constraints on aggressive behavior and the internal control of emotional outbursts, though state institutions such as the criminal justice system underscored the lessons for those whose self-restraint flagged.[8] The cumulative weight of external pressures and internal constraints reduced aggressive behavior and violence, according to Elias.

Historians have adapted this model to help explain sweeping shifts in rates of violence, particularly the dramatic decline in European homicide since the Middle Ages.[9] American historians have similarly argued that cultural and economic forces, especially those tied to industrial society, sparked a resocialization process that also inculcated order, self-control, and discipline, thus discouraging the emotional volatility that typically fueled violence.[10] Scholars have offered many variations on Elias's overarching theory, some emphasizing cultural forces and others focusing on economic or institutional forces.[11] These interpretations suggest that social and cultural pressures have reduced aggression and produced a long-term decline in homicide in western European cities and a shorter, but still sharp, decline in homicide in American cities, particularly New York, Boston, and Philadelphia.[12]

Drawing on Elias's theory, as well as recent adaptations of it, this study explores the relationship between homicide and social order—Elias's "civilizing process"—in the great industrial metropolis of America's heartland. It also analyzes the connection between shifts in the level of violence and changes in the form of violence. Between 1875 and 1920 Chicago boomed. The local population grew nearly sevenfold; the city's African-American population rose more than twenty-one-fold; the number of municipal police employees swelled nearly ninefold; and the number of public school teachers jumped more than thirteenfold.[13] The value of manufactured goods in the city in 1920 was more than sixteen times what it was in 1875.[14] During the same period, Chicagoans launched the American settlement house movement, created the American juvenile justice system, led the city planning movement, and established what became known as the Chicago School of urban sociology.[15] If urbanization, industrialization, Victorian values, moral reform crusades, and related social, cultural, economic, and institutional forces inculcated self-control and discouraged aggression, then such a transformation should have been especially pronounced in the city of Cyrus McCormick, Jane Addams, Clarence Darrow, and, of course, Al Capone.

Chapter 1

"So You Refuse to Drink with Me, Do You?"

On June 10, 1897, Albert Burke murdered John Rathgeber during a barroom brawl. The fight erupted as Burke, Rathgeber, and two coworkers guzzled beer in a Chicago saloon across the street from the city's Central police station. The drinkers, three of whom had already visited other local saloons that evening, appeared to have been on "friendly" terms when they began arguing about a work-related matter.[1] But these were tough and unforgiving men. Rathgeber was known for his "gloominess and occasional despondent moods," and Burke possessed a particularly imposing reputation; acquaintances considered him "a man it would not be well to encounter in a fight."[2] Rathgeber knew that Burke was volatile, that he was skilled with a knife, and that he was quick to use the weapon. At 8:30 PM Rathgeber ordered another round of drinks for the group. Burke, however, refused Rathgeber's treat, and the other men immediately "expected there would be trouble" and stepped away from the bar.[3] According to a witness, Rathgeber "imagined the refusal to be a personal slight and took umbrage at it," bellowing, "So you refuse to drink with me, do you?"[4] As Rathgeber moved toward Burke, the latter growled that "he would drink if he felt like it." Burke suddenly produced a pearl-handled pocket knife, and in a flash he severed Rathgeber's jugular vein, inflicted a gash over his eye, and "almost cut out his heart."[5] Within minutes, John Rathgeber was dead, the city's twenty-ninth homicide victim of 1897.[6]

This was a typical late nineteenth-century Chicago homicide. The participants were young, tough, and poor, and they knew each other. The violence punctuated an evening of drinking and occurred in a saloon. The combatants acted aggressively and impulsively, and each man knew the other's reputation and recognized that his adversary would not back down once the conversation became "heated."[7] Finally, only a few words or seemingly trivial actions transformed revelry and camaraderie into brutality and homicidal rage.

Such encounters contributed to Chicago's reputation as a "tough town." Country visitors often arrived in the city expecting trouble, a prophecy that frequently became self-fulfilling. On April 23, 1882, for example, Thomas Kelly, a drunkard, bumped into and then snarled at John Will, an Ohio farmer, on a crowded street. Will, however, "had heard Chicago was a tough place" and "was ready for any emergency."[8] The vigilant but anxious Ohioan "quickly and quietly whipped out his revolver and shot Kelly through the brain."[9] "Well," the shooter defiantly explained, "they told me that people [in Chicago] would cut your throat if you had a dollar, and I thought it was one of them fellers." According to one account, "from reading sermons, or some other source" Will "had come to believe that Chicago citizens were cowboys, and that Chicago was worse than a border town," and he had prepared himself for the dangerous streets of the city, having "loaded up his Smith and Wesson revolver."[10]

Will's fears were not unusual, nor reports of Chicago's toughness isolated. Lincoln Steffens termed the Illinois metropolis "the 'tough'" among cities, a spectacle for the nation," while the Reverend P. S. Henson warned in 1892 that "Chicago is the headquarters of the devil." L. O. Curon concurred, writing in *Chicago, Satan's Sanctum*, "I believe that Chicago is the devil's headquarters." Rudyard Kipling visited Chicago during this period and fled in a panic. "Having seen it," he wrote, "I urgently desire never to see it again. It is inhabited by savages." "In the lower and brutal grades of crime," an 1886 writer averred, "Chicago stands pre-eminent." A journalist for a national magazine reached the same conclusion, observing that "Chicago, in the mind of the country, stands preeminently for violent crime." Upton Sinclair offered an explanation for the untamed, vicious behavior of Chicagoans. "Men who crack the heads of animals all day," he wrote in *The Jungle*, "seem to get into the habit, and to practice on their friends, and even on their families."[11]

Late nineteenth-century Chicago society created men like Albert Burke and John Rathgeber. Economic and demographic forces combined to concentrate enormous numbers of young men in the city and to mire them in poverty. A world of working-class saloons and boardinghouses catered to these newcomers and helped breed a set of class-, age-, and gender-based values that celebrated toughness, ferocity, and impulsiveness, the building blocks of lethal violence. This fluid blend of economic, demographic, and cultural factors sustained the city's reputation for toughness, conditioning newcomers to expect trouble and to respond aggressively, as John Wills did when he fired a bullet into the head of a staggering drunkard.

"Respectable" Chicagoans, however, recoiled in horror at the violent and volatile behavior of these ruffians, and prominent residents struggled to control working-class toughs and to inculcate order in the streets, saloons, and factories of the city. In the short run, their reform efforts sparked a backlash and promoted aggression; young, working-class men rejected middle-class values and venerated toughness. By the end of the century, however, saloons and other settings that nourished these oppositional values were under siege, and a broad range of economic, social, institutional, and legal forces gradually tamped down the world of Albert Burke and John Rathgeber.

Ironically, many of the forces that encouraged saloon brawls and street fights also—over time—discouraged them. Thus, the social and economic pressures of industrial society influenced lethal violence in conflicting ways. On the one hand, they helped forge a subculture of violence in which young, working-class men established and maintained status through acts of brutality and aggression. On the other hand, these forces gradually choked and suffocated the cultural wellsprings of plebeian violence in turn-of-the-century Chicago, and in the process transformed the character of homicide in the city.

Chicago experienced jarring growth during the closing decades of the nineteenth century. On the heels of the Great Fire of 1871, which destroyed 2,100 acres in the heart of the city, Chicago rebounded with dizzying speed and intensity. Between 1875 and 1900 the city's population more than quadrupled, increasing from 400,500 to nearly 1.7 million. By 1890 Chicago was the second largest city in the nation, up from ninth in 1860, fifth in 1870, and fourth in 1880. The number of residents under the age of ten in 1900 was nearly equal to Chicago's total population a twenty-five years earlier, and the city's immigrant population at the end of the century exceeded the total population of every city in the United States except New York and Philadelphia.

More remarkable still, the economic and institutional growth of the city outpaced the population increase, producing what Kipling called the "grotesque ferocity" of Chicago.[12] The number of wage earners in manufacturing quintupled between 1875 and 1900, making the city one of the leading manufacturing centers in the country, and at the end of the century Chicago had two packinghouses with twice as many employees as Andrew Carnegie's renowned Homestead steel plant.[13] The number of cattle slaughtered in Chicago's packing-houses quintupled during the 1880s alone.[14] By 1890, the city led the nation in the production of agricultural tools, tinware, railroad cars, pianos, organs, and furniture, as well as in meatpacking and in foundry and machine shops.[15] Municipal government raced to keep up with the skyrocketing population, the burgeoning economy, and the soaring demands placed on the city's fledgling infrastructure. The police force increased more than sixfold, while the number of teachers in the city's public schools rose more than eightfold during the final quarter of the nineteenth century.[16]

If many residents reveled in Chicago's dynamism and resilience, they also feared the instability that accompanied rapid growth. The Great Fire, for example, had taught middle-class residents contradictory lessons. On the one hand, respectable Chicagoans embraced the triumphal tale of the city's rebirth from its ashes. On the other hand, in the immediate aftermath of the Great Fire, middle-class Chicagoans had captured glimpses of the disorder festering beneath the surface of working-class neighborhoods. Thus, they simultaneously crowed about their city's irrepressible vigor and braced for battle against the criminals, ruffians, and agitators lurking at the edges of their society.[17]

Three bloody clashes between striking workers and law enforcers captured national attention during the closing decades of the century, reinforcing Chicago's reputation for violence and disorder and fueling the anxieties of middle-class residents. The Great Railroad Strike of 1877 plunged the city into turmoil. When the nation's leading railroads slashed wages by 10 percent in response to the depression of the mid-1870s, workers up and down the country's rail network walked off the job, seized depots, destroyed equipment, and disrupted the flow of freight. One of the country's major rail centers, Chicago experienced violent clashes between striking workers and both the local police and the national guard. Enraged workers torched railroad cars; hundreds were injured and many killed in the ensuing riots in and around the city, which local and national observers linked to a radical plot designed to foment class war.[18]

The Haymarket bombing nine years later added to Chicago's reputation for lawlessness. Following a strike at the city's huge McCormick Reaper Works in 1886, almost two hundred policemen gathered to control a small rally organized by local labor leaders to demonstrate support for the eight-hour workday and to protest police attacks on striking workers. From an alley someone hurled a bomb into the police line, creating panic and sparking a flurry of gunfire from the frightened, confused law enforcers. Seven local policemen died and dozens were injured in the incident. The Haymarket bombing solidified Chicago's image as a center of radicalism and as a haven for anarchists, murderous radicals, and toughs.[19]

In 1894, another strike erupted in violence and destruction, this time just outside the city limits. In response to wage cuts, workers at the Pullman Palace Car Company walked off the job. The supporting unions refused to handle Pullman cars, and soon the strike slowed rail traffic nationwide and nearly halted the flow of railroad cars into and out of Chicago. Striking workers derailed freight cars and attacked scabs, while jittery merchants, industrialists, and political leaders summoned private security companies, the local police, the militia, and federal troops to put down the strike. Four died and nearly two dozen were injured in the clashes between the 14,000 law enforcers and the striking workers.

The Railroad Strike of 1877, the Haymarket bombing of 1886, and the Pullman Strike of 1894 did not add appreciably to Chicago's homicide toll, but they affected the city in three ways. First, these encounters contributed to Chicago's reputation for violence. Second, they heightened the anxieties of Chicagoans and increased the resolve of residents and newcomers to be "ready for any emergency."

And third, the disorder of the late nineteenth century produced a powerful counterreaction, as "respectable" Chicagoans struggled to restore law and order.

A sense of panic fueled some of these efforts. Many community leaders believed that both the bloody strikes and the perceived explosion in violent crime represented clear warnings that the "social order of Chicago was inherently unstable" and "might burst into flame at any moment."[20] The local police, Lincoln Steffens noted derisively, "cannot protect itself, to say nothing of handling mobs, riotous strikers, and the rest of that lawlessness which disgraces Chicago."[21] In the chaotic aftermath of the Great Fire, which included a brief crime wave, Chicago's business elite organized to protect the city from the "dangerous class" and supported the imposition of martial law.[22] Still more frantic efforts followed the Railroad Strike of 1877 and the Haymarket bombing of 1886. In 1878 a group calling itself the Chicago Citizen's Association prepared for an anticipated war against the dangerous class by giving the municipal police "a hundred handguns and rifles, four twelve-pounder Napoleon cannons with carriages and caissons, some lighter artillery pieces, one ten-barrel .50-caliber Gatling gun, and thousands of rounds of ammunition."[23] Some merchants and industrialists purchased military-style uniforms and secured rifles for their employees, who might instantly be called upon to preserve law and order, and commercial magnate Marshall Field offered to turn over his delivery wagons to the local police if another riot erupted.[24] Wealthy residents also provided land and buildings for armories, and then, unsure that such fortresses offered adequate protection, turned to Washington and the U.S. Army for additional support; in 1887 powerful Chicagoans flexed their political muscles and convinced federal officials to establish a military garrison just outside the city.[25]

More often, however, the battle against disorder assumed quieter, less martial forms. Business leaders and moral reformers focused their attention on the breeding grounds for violence and social turmoil, such as saloons and working-class neighborhoods. Again and again during the closing decades of the century, proper Chicagoans established anticrime committees, organized law-and-order crusades, and urged tighter restrictions on saloons and other centers of working-class life.[26] During the 1870s a "Law and Order" ticket demanded the enforcement of the city's long-ignored Sunday closing law, and the police often shut down saloons during strikes, believing that drunken young men were the principal culprits in the violence.[27] During the 1880s middle-class Chicagoans established the "Citizens' League for the Suppression of the Sale of Liquor to Minors and Drunkards," which prosecuted "offending saloonkeepers."[28] Police expenditures ballooned by 85 percent in the four years after the Haymarket bombing.[29] By the closing decade of the century, reformers pressured city officials to crack down on prostitution and gambling.[30] Chicagoans' myriad anxieties—about labor violence, street toughs, neglected children, and immigration—dovetailed and inflamed one another in a series of crusades to preserve law and order in the city in the late nineteenth century.

Other reformers shared these concerns but offered gentler prescriptions. Jane Addams and Ellen Starr, for example, established Hull-House in 1889 in order to uplift the poor, and local women's clubs sought to teach newcomers standards of cleanliness and housekeeping that would make them good citizens and productive members of society.[31] Likewise, Chicago's pioneering child savers and juvenile justice reformers hoped to rescue young residents from demon rum, deviant parents, and the moral contagion that supposedly infected working-class sections of the city.[32] In one form or another, some more coercive than others, reformers wanted to inculcate habits of discipline in the poor and foreign-born residents of Chicago.

The pressures of the marketplace and the factory reinforced these efforts. In a city overflowing with people and filled with dangers, public schools and other municipal institutions preached the virtues of self-control and order; teachers compelled children to remain seated and quiet during class, and instructors urged the youngest Chicagoans to cross streets only at intersections and to exercise caution around busy, congested thoroughfares. The regimen of the factory demanded still greater restraint and discipline, as workplace hazards abounded and scientific-management techniques revolutionized manufacturing.[33] Employees in Chicago's packinghouses struggled to keep pace with "disassembly lines," and rapid-fire, simple tasks quickly replaced complex, time-honored skills on the killing floors of the Armour and Swift plants. In 1880, for example, a single worker, the highly skilled "all-round butcher," sometimes with an assistant, undertook the entire slaughtering process. Two decades later, "killing gangs" of 157 men, performing seventy-eight separate tasks thousands of times each day, completed the same procedure. Upton Sinclair described a phase of the hog-slaughtering operation as "a line of dangling hogs a hundred yards in length; and for every yard there was a man, working as if a demon were after him."[34] Workers unable to slit, slash, slice, and split on a pace with the overhead conveyors, or unable to endure the squeals of dying animals and the rivers of blood, were fired and replaced. If nothing else, workers needed discipline and intense focus to maintain their jobs—and to keep their fingers—in Chicago's Packingtown and other manufactories.

Middle-class Chicagoans—including terrified industrialists desperately trying to preserve law and order, well-meaning teachers imparting survival skills to children, caring moral reformers battling the effects of poverty, and employers hoping to transform displaced farmers into steady industrial workers—conveyed overlapping messages that emphasized industry, sobriety, self-control, and discipline. The more heavy-handed crusades typically failed; law-and-order tickets enjoyed scant popularity among Chicago voters, and efforts to rein in grog shops, houses of ill repute, and gambling dens encountered fierce opposition during the late nineteenth century.[35] Subtler campaigns to discourage impulsive, raucous behavior proved to be more effective in gradually changing the behavior of newcomers and workers. But even if most of these crusades enjoyed at best modest success, young working-class men in Chicago heard an increasing chorus singing the virtues of self-control and restraint—and stridently rejected the message, at least when they gathered after work. Perceptions of disorder fueled efforts to remake the Chicago working class, but efforts to remake the Chicago working class indirectly fueled lethal violence during the closing decades of the nineteenth century.

Homicide was a public and shockingly visible activity in late nineteenth-century Chicago. The increase in the death toll from violent crime far outpaced the rate of Chicago's explosive population growth between 1875 and 1890. The number of residents swelled by an impressive 175 percent during this period, while the number of homicides in the city jumped by 413 percent. Even the homicide rate, which controls for population size, increased by 89 percent between 1875 and 1890. Violent crime claimed more lives in Chicago in 1890 alone than it did in the six-year period 1870–1875.[36] Nearly three-fourths of the killings occurred in public space between 1875 and 1890. Homicide was also concentrated in time and disproportionately involved a narrow segment of Chicago society.

Saloons were one of the leading backdrops for lethal violence in late nineteenth-century Chicago, accounting for over one-fifth of the city's homicides between 1875 and 1890.[37] Some local saloons possessed self-fulfilling reputations as "tough dives" and thus attracted the most aggressive and bellicose men in the city. In Fick's Saloon, a journalist observed in 1883, "there is always a big gang of hard characters in the place, and the wonder is that a man is not killed there every day or two." According to the *Chicago Times*, one such murder was indistinguishable from the next. "A party of men drinking in a saloon; a trifling dispute; the gleam of a dagger; and a young man staggers out of the place and dies like a dog in an alley."[38]

Saloon homicides usually involved young, single, poor men. Nearly all such violence erupted between men; they comprised 94 percent of victims and 99 percent of assailants in saloon homicides between 1875 and 1890. The average victim was thirty, and the average assailant was just over twenty-nine. More than 60 percent of the victims and slightly under 50 percent of their assailants were unskilled workers. Most of these men resided in boardinghouses or lived as lodgers in private dwellings; they typically ate many of their meals at local saloons and spent much of their leisure time in such settings as well. Although 48 percent of saloon homicides occurred late at night, at the height of leisure revelry, many also occurred in the morning. Approximately one bar killing in eight, for example, took place at daybreak. Chicago laborers often used a stiff drink at the top of the morning to fortify themselves for work. Others stopped at the neighborhood saloon for breakfast. Similarly, the infamous free lunch offered to bar patrons drew enormous numbers of Chicago workingmen into saloons at midday, and 15 percent of saloon homicides between 1875 and 1890 exploded late in the morning.[39]

Chicago men flocked to saloons—and killed one another there—when they had time on their hands and cash in their pockets. Saturday was the most lethal day in the city's barrooms. Many men cashed their paychecks in local saloons; they poured into barrooms every Saturday afternoon to collect their wages. They remained there to spend their wages. As the workweek wore on and their cash reserves dwindled, working-class Chicagoans spent less time in grog shops and thus fewer of the city's homicides occurred there; nearly one quarter of all saloon homicides occurred on Saturdays, but only 7 percent occurred on Thursdays and 10 percent on Fridays.

More than two-thirds of saloon homicides between 1875 and 1890 resulted from drunken brawls. In crowded barrooms, disagreements easily escalated into what Chicagoans often called "general fights" or "free fights" involving four or more combatants.[40] Twenty-one-year-old Frank Metevier, for example, shot Charles Angel, a thirty-two-year-old coworker at a nearby brickyard, in a typical general fight following a New Year's celebration in William Maxwell's saloon. According to a local crime-beat reporter, Charles Metevier, the killer's brother, and Angel, "who had been drinking considerably, quarreled. Angel struck Metevier with a beer glass. Then the friends of each man tried to help them out. In a short time more than half the people in the place were fighting." While defending his brother, Charles Metevier shot Angel in the left temple.[41]

Drunken brawls, many of which erupted outside of saloons, were by far the leading single motive or cause of homicide between 1875 and 1890. Over a quarter of all Chicago homicides during this period occurred during drunken brawls, more than double the proportion of the second leading cause. They claimed more than twice as many lives as spousal homicides and more than five times as many as robberies.

Although moral reformers and law enforcers argued that beer and whisky inflamed the savage passions of the poor and therefore generated violence, participants offered conflicting opinions. Some killers insisted that demon rum had indeed transformed them into fiends. Patrick Martin, for example, told police investigators in 1875 that he had no recollection of fatally stabbing John Galena in John Healy's "low groggery." "I was so drunk," Martin said, "I didn't know what I was doing." Asked if he "flourished" a knife in the saloon, Martin exclaimed "I might have done so, but don't remember it. I tell you I was too drunk."[42] Pete Monrad, a sailor, acknowledged that he had been "drunk for about a week" when he shot his best friend, Edward Stuart, and a man named Frank Gilroy. According to witnesses, Monrad was "on the border of snakeland" at the time of the shootings.[43]

More often, however, both killers and witnesses denied that drinking triggered the violence, clouded their judgment, or incited uncontrollable behavior. Charles Downey strenuously objected to the notion that alcohol had played a role in the 1884 brawl in which he shot and killed his thirty-year-old brother, William. Admitting to "having taken several drinks during the afternoon," the twenty-nine-year-old killer added that "when I drink I am generally more sober than at other times."[44] At John Flynn's trial, William Miller's testimony rested on similar logic. Miller insisted that at the time of the brawl he witnessed, Peter J. Warren, the victim, "was sober. He was not too sober; he was what I call drunk. He was not too sober or too drunk."[45] Downey and Miller were neither posturing for their peers nor prevaricating; they believed that hard drinking was a normal component of working-class social life and that some provocation other than routine, everyday inebriation had triggered the lethal violence.

Drunken brawls occurred wherever young men consumed alcohol in late nineteenth-century Chicago. Because bottle sales were limited during this period, only 7 percent of drunken-brawl homicides occurred in private residences and boardinghouses. An additional 6 percent took place in brothels, despite the best efforts of madams and their bouncers to maintain order in the city's "disorderly houses." Drunken-brawl homicides between 1875 and 1890 were principally confined to two settings. Slightly over half, not surprisingly, took place in local saloons.[46] An additional 26 percent were committed on nearby streets and alleys. Often general fights spilled out of saloons, and the besotted killer fired the fatal shot, landed the lethal punch, or struck the deadly blow in full view of both bar patrons and pedestrians.[47] Michael McElligot, his brother, and four other men, for example, were drinking together in a local saloon "when a dispute arose. They adjourned to the alley in the rear of the saloon, where it was agreed they would settle their differences in a general fight."[48] Moments later Lawrence Cully shot and killed the twenty-three-year-old McElligot. More often, bartenders evicted wild young men, and the combatants concluded their fight yards from where the conflict began. George Smith and Frank Bamma, both of whom worked in a local livery stable, quarreled in Paul Reichart's Milwaukee Avenue saloon on January 22, 1889. After "Bamma struck Smith with a stovepoker," the bartender "interposed and, separating the men, sent one out the front door and the other out through the rear door."[49] The men quickly resumed their battle, and Bamma stabbed Smith in the chest with a pocketknife. Late nineteenth-century saloonkeepers and bartenders, in short, displaced as much as they discouraged violence, and lethal brawls often shifted only a few feet, moving from the semipublic world of the saloon to the open streets of the city.[50] Whether they erupted in crowded bars or congested streets, drunken-brawl homicides were public spectacles, giving these fights a visibility that made them seem to be occurring in ever-increasing waves.

Drunken-brawl homicides reflected the rhythms of working-class leisure activities. Between 1875 and 1890, these lethal fights usually occurred late at night and on weekends. A fifth of them occurred between 6:00 PM and 9:00 PM, and nearly half took place between 9:00 PM and 1:00 AM.[51] Similarly, drunken-brawl homicides were clustered on weekends. Almost a quarter occurred on Saturdays, and another quarter took place on Sundays. Late Saturday evening, from 9:00 PM to 1:00 AM, produced the highest death toll, with this four-hour span of the week accounting for 20 percent of all drunken-brawl homicides. Because most Chicagoans did not work on Sundays, the greatest number of lethal drunken brawls took place on that day. In 1880 the *Chicago Times* pronounced Sunday "the day of human sacrifice among the lower classes."[52]

Even by comparison with other Chicago killers during this era, the brawlers tended to be young. The average killer in a drunken brawl between 1875 and 1890 was twenty-eight years old, nearly two and a half years younger than the overall average for Chicago killers. The victims in Chicago drunken-brawl homicides were young as well;

on average they were just six months older than their assailants. In fact, second only to the assailants in labor violence, drunken brawlers were the youngest killers in late nineteenth-century Chicago. Drinking, even excessive drinking, was not confined to the young in late nineteenth-century Chicago, though drunken brawling was a young man's activity.

Drunken brawlers were also poor. Unskilled laborers comprised one-fifth of Chicago's workforce between 1875 and 1890, but they made up approximately half of all Chicago's killers and were almost two-thirds of the assailants in the city's drunken-brawl homicides.[53] Their victims had similarly low skill levels. Just as older men avoided lethal brawls, slightly wealthier, more skilled Chicagoans either kept out of drunken brawls or managed to escape without killing or being killed. Age and skill level, however, worked together, as did skill level and personal demeanor. All things being equal, young men would have been least skilled, having spent less time in the workplace and having acquired fewer skills or contacts that enhanced occupational stability. The aggressive behavior that embroiled these Chicagoans in lethal drunken brawls probably flared in other settings as well and slowed their occupational mobility, reinforcing the correlation between age and class status. In short, Chicago's drunken-brawl killers lived at the margins of society and were too green, too wild, and too rebellious to secure financial or social stability.

Deadly drunken brawls tended to be closed affairs, rarely crossing social boundaries. Although data on the ethnic backgrounds of brawlers are fragmentary, surviving evidence suggests that Irish immigrants and their children were overrepresented among Chicago's brawlers.[54] Covering the 1878 coroner's inquest on Hugh McConville, a *Chicago Tribune* reporter described the killer, Jeremiah Connelly, as a "product of generations of ignorance, starvation, neglect. Pour whisky into an orang-outang [*sic*], and he would in all likelihood behave as this wild Irishman has done." A *Chicago Daily*

News crime-beat writer portrayed Mike Moriarty, a twenty-eight-year-old killer, in similarly unmistakable terms. "He is a perfect type of the 'dead tough' young man. His nose is almost lost between high cheek-bones and his small eyes glower beneath scowling brows." Class, ethnicity, and age overlapped; men killed their peers, which is not surprising since young, poor, foreign-born men moved in relatively narrow social, occupational, and residential circles. Chicagoans such as Jeremiah Connelly and Mike Moriarty seldom visited upscale wine rooms and rarely shared the pails of beer they consumed in local alleys with high-born clerks or even with those who spoke in another language or with a different accent. Michael Haggerty died in a typical drunken brawl in 1890. According to an account of the homicide in the *Chicago Times*, "the participants in the fight were James G. Connerton, a well-known tough who has earned the title 'Bad Jimmie,' and Michael Haggerty, alias 'Bull' Haggerty, alias Doc Haggerty, a gambler who has long been regarded as one of the most desperate rough-and-tumble fighters in Chicago." "The murders of Chicago," another journalist concluded, "are generally personal matters between the savages."[55]

Chicago's drunken brawlers also knew their fellow combatants, narrowing the demographic, social, and cultural world of lethal violence still more. One drunken-brawl killer in eight described his victim as a "good friend." Patrick Furlong immediately regretted shooting and killing his "good friend" Edward Leach. After each man had consumed three drinks in a local saloon, "I suppose we both got a little angry," the killer told the police after firing two bullets into his friend's midsection.[56] Similarly, Henry Lehr and F. R. Williams were "fast friends" until a dispute arose about the dice game that determined who would purchase the next round of drinks. As the men "came to blows," the bartender threatened to have them arrested "if they fought in the saloon." Banished to the street just outside the barroom, Williams slugged Lehr, who responded by drawing his revolver and fatally shooting his friend in the abdomen.[57] More often, however, drunken brawls exploded between acquaintances. From 1875 to 1890, 56 percent of drunken-brawl killers and victims had been acquainted with one another (but were not friends, relatives, or coworkers) prior to the lethal encounter. In many cases, the men were "regulars" at the neighborhood saloon and knew each other by sight and especially by reputation.[58]

 To outsiders, these brawlers seemed bloodthirsty, irrational, and primitive. Judges, crime-beat reporters, and some policemen viewed local toughs as uncontrollable ruffians who were vicious by nature. In 1878, for example, the stodgy *Chicago Tribune* portrayed one murderer as "a low-browed, dirty libel upon humanity," while the *Chicago Times* explained another homicide by noting that "both parties belong among the lowest of the low and the loss of life would not have been any detriment to other people, to put it mildly." Journalist George Kibbe Turner, writing in *McClure's Magazine* early in the twentieth century, concluded that "these murders were hasty, savage acts of a crude population." The concentration of young, poor, immigrant men in a city experiencing explosive growth and littered with "plague spots of rottenness" produced an epidemic of lethal violence. Describing Chicago in 1907, Turner observed that "a population of hundreds of thousands of rough and unrestrained male laborers, plied, with all possible energy and ingenuity, with alcoholic liquor, can be counted on, with the certainty of a chemical experiment, for one reaction—violent crime." "The loss of life among the savages," he lamented, "is alarming."[59]

Chicago's late nineteenth-century drunken brawls were not inevitable components of life in a big, rapidly growing city. Instead, they reflected the emergence of a coherent set of values that encouraged violent behavior. The impoverished immigrants, the neighborhoods packed with young men, the free-flowing beer, and the unregulated saloons—all factors that many late nineteenth-century Chicagoans associated with violence—did not generate random or irrational acts of savagery. Rather, demographic pressures, alcohol, leisure-time activities, and economic forces combined to produce specific and well-defined acts of violence. These elements blended in a way that created a coherent plebeian culture, one that celebrated toughness and ferocity, venerated aggression and bloodletting, and encouraged young Chicago men to gather in saloons, to drink, to brawl, and especially to drink and brawl. Albert Burke and John Rathgeber, like "Bad Jimmie" Connerton and "Bull" Haggerty, behaved according to the rules and customs of plebeian culture—or at least the version of plebeian culture embraced in the tough saloons of the city.[60]

Population shifts played a crucial role in forging the cultural identities of men like Burke, Rathgeber, Connerton, and Haggerty. During the late nineteenth century Chicago grew by attracting migrants, and men comprised the majority of the newcomers. In 1880, the city had 104 male residents for every 100 female residents; a decade later Chicago had 107 male residents for every 100 female residents. In Chicago's bustling and bursting immigrant neighborhoods, sex ratios were particularly imbalanced; among foreign-born residents, there were 112 males for every 100 females in 1890. Equally important, young men comprised an unusually large share of the newcomers. The local population had 112 men in their late twenties for every 100 women in that age bracket, and Chicago's drunken brawlers were disproportionately drawn from this group.[61] Men between the ages of twenty-five and twenty-nine made up 6 percent of the city's residents but 33 percent of its drunken-brawl killers.[62] In short, young men comprised a large percentage of Chicago's late nineteenth-century population and comprised an even larger proportion of its brawlers.[63]

Not only were the newcomers—and most of the killers—young men, they were also bachelors. As a consequence of shifting labor markets, the age at which young men left their parents' homes rose over the course of the nineteenth century. Across the nation, the average age at marriage for men climbed as well, reaching "a historic high" of over twenty-six in 1890. The proportion of bachelors in American society also hit its high-water mark (until late in the twentieth century) in 1890, and Chicago's migration patterns exaggerated this trend, giving the local population a higher proportion of young, single men than the nation.[64] In 1890 Chicago's bachelor population exceeded the total populations of Minneapolis, Louisville, Omaha, and Kansas City.[65] Among Chicago men in their late twenties, more than half were bachelors.[66] These demographic patterns had unsettling implications for aging bachelors in the city. By the standards of nineteenth-century American society, Chicago men were extraordinarily late in marrying, and the age structure and sex ratios of the city's population meant that prospects for marriage dimmed with each passing year, as the pool of age-appropriate women grew shallower. If marriage was a key component of adulthood, and if family life provided a crucial mechanism for "civilizing" and reining in men's wild behavior, late nineteenth-century Chicago bachelors remained trapped in a kind of protracted adolescence even as they approached their thirties.[67]

Local entrepreneurs, particularly small-scale, neighborhood businessmen, responded to the needs of this group and offered a broad range of leisure activities geared toward bachelors. Boardinghouses multiplied in working-class areas, concentrating the unattached men in space and helping to create a gender-based and age-based social world. The city's sex trades blossomed as well, providing additional diversions for single men. Catering to bachelors and attempting to tap a burgeoning market for cheap entertainment, Chicagoans opened saloons in numbers that mortified the city's already anxious moral reformers. By 1880 Chicago had one licensed saloon for every 53 men—as well as scores of unlicensed saloons (known as "blind pigs") and pool halls that served alcohol.[68] Political corruption and crosscutting ethnic conflicts stymied efforts to regulate these businesses, and with low licensing fees and scant restrictions barrooms sprang up throughout the city but especially in working-class neighborhoods, near factories and boardinghouses.[69] The ratio of residents to saloons reached its nadir during the 1880s, when Chicago boasted more bars than every state in the American South combined.[70] The peak of bachelor society coincided with the peak of saloon business—and vice versa.

While boardinghouses, gambling dens, brothels, and saloons gathered together young, single, poor Chicagoans, a cultural alchemy also occurred in the crowded, dank settings where the city's bachelors spent their leisure time. These social activities and spatial contexts bred feelings of fellowship and celebrated the hard-won, shared experiences at the core of working-class masculine identity. Tired, poor, and frustrated with their prospects for the future, thousands of young men caroused, gambled, drank, strutted, and preened in bars and brothels.

Working conditions molded the worldview that germinated in local saloons—and that ultimately fueled lethal violence. Technological and organizational changes transformed industrial work in late nineteenth-century America. The scale of production increased dramatically, and within a few decades a city of small shops became a metropolis of factories. During the last thirty years of the century, for example, the average number of workers per factory in Chicago's slaughterhouse industry grew by 867 percent, rising from 69 to 667. By the end of the century, packinghouses were the city's largest industrial employer, "accounting for 10 percent of wages and a third of total manufactured goods" produced in the city.[71]

Innovations in manufacturing, particularly the use of assembly lines, also redefined working conditions, sharply reducing the skill level of packinghouse workers. Teams of unskilled and semiskilled laborers rapidly supplanted the highly skilled and well-paid butchers of the middle decades of the century. Aided by scientific-management techniques, the leading packinghouses transformed "butchering into meatcutting," as one historian later put it, significantly reducing dependence on skilled, expensive workers in the process.[72] By the end of the century, most packinghouse workers were unskilled, poorly paid, easily replaced, and frequently unemployed.[73] Unskilled laborers and semiskilled meat cutters found fewer opportunities for advancement and struggled to support themselves and their families. Similar changes occurred throughout Chicago's booming industrial sector. In 1900, for example, more than 28 percent of the city's manufacturing workers reported being unemployed for at least one month of the year.[74]

Large-scale industrialization, and the de-skilling process that accompanied it, had obvious economic effects on Chicago laborers, but it also generated cultural changes that contributed to the city's swelling homicide toll. The transformation of the workplace eroded the cultural status attached to work. Within plebeian society, men possessing high skill levels were respected for the goods they produced and the independence that their skills gave them. They controlled the workplace and, at least in theory, submitted to no one.[75] Those accustomed to relative autonomy, as well as those hoping to acquire such stature, found themselves scrambling to find work during the closing decades of the century.[76] As a result, work-based sources of status were increasingly beyond the reach of most Chicago wage earners. Demographic changes compounded this crisis as wave after wave of young men poured into the city and heightened competition for work, for housing, and for women to marry. These economic and demographic shifts stalled the progression of young men from adolescence to adulthood—both economically and socially. Losing status in the workplace, struggling to marry, and thus encountering barriers to the transition to full-fledged adulthood, large numbers of aging, working-class bachelors had difficulty attaining respectability in plebeian society. Nor did middle-class homilies preaching the virtues of industry, sobriety, thrift, and self-control resonate with single men who were crammed into boardinghouses and unable to escape poverty. In short, economic pressures and demographic forces blended to erode traditional sources of working-class cultural status.

As a consequence of this collision of class-, gender-, and age-based pressures, the working-class bachelors of Chicago searched for other ways to gain the respect of their peers, and in the saloons, gambling dens, and boardinghouses where these men congregated, a masculine, honor-based culture flourished.[77] Status and achievement were not internally derived in plebeian society. Rather, they were conferred by peers and thus established in public settings, where behavior could be observed and judged. Poor young men battled for respect in bars and during leisure-time activities. In such public settings, they stridently rejected the discipline and hierarchy of the factory. Drawing on a well-established antiauthoritarian tradition, working-class Chicagoans inverted the middle-class emphasis on self-control, personal restraint, and civility, all of which they considered signs of weakness, dependence, and submission.[78] Within working-class bars and boardinghouses, refusing to conform to the demands of polite society became a source of pride and a badge of defiance. Just as restraint served as a marker of middle-class respectability, volatility and public demonstrations of toughness became sources of plebeian respectability.[79] The city's working class also embraced an exaggerated version of masculine identity; at a time when young middle-class men affirmed their sense of "manliness" with athletic challenges, working-class Chicagoans demonstrated their masculinity through displays of aggression and ferocity.[80] A distorted set of bachelor norms also blossomed; if young men are typically prone to engaging in reckless, wild, flamboyant behavior to impress one another and to capture the attention of young women, in this particular setting, with its surfeit of bachelors, only the most fierce, daring, and explosive conduct commanded attention.[81] Most important, honor had to be established or defended at the expense of a peer. Status, in other words, rested on a man's ability to cow, intimidate, and dominate other men; and, as other sources of status proved unattainable, toughness became an increasingly valuable source of social capital.[82]

The man of honor in this social world flouted the grim realities of working-class life, submitted to no man, brooked no disrespect, and refused to back down from a challenge. Such a basis for status, however, was inherently unstable. Reputations were always at risk and had to be defended, and these men constantly sought opportunities to affirm or defend their status before peers.[83] Those atop the hierarchy, and those eager to establish their reputations, manufactured tests of their mettle, lacing leisure activities with rituals that combined revelry with jockeying for status and that blended genuine camaraderie with vicious competition; every public interaction and every jostle represented a potential threat to status and had to be countered immediately, aggressively, and publicly. When a confrontation involved two (or more) men who embraced such a definition of status, each accepted the challenge, making victims instantly assailants and vice versa. The culturally inscribed rules of behavior thus produced cycles of escalating aggression and violence.[84] As a consequence of these cultural norms, brawling—in response to particular cues—became an integral part of plebeian sociability, intertwined with drinking, carousing, and gambling.[85]

Middle-class observers of Chicago's deadly drunken brawls reported again and again that seemingly insignificant, trivial incidents triggered murderous assaults. Police chiefs, coroners, and newspaper editors concluded that vicious fights began "without any provocation," with only the "slightest provocation," or with "slender provocation." For the tough who visited a local saloon in order to maintain his status as the kind of man "it would not be well to encounter in a fight," no provocation was "slight" or "slender."[86] According to the rules of plebeian culture, there were no accidents, no random collisions. As working-class bachelors aged and as their careers stalled, honor and toughness became increasingly important sources of masculine status.[87] And as the cohort of Chicago bachelors ballooned and the de-skilling process unfolded, the cultural pressures to be tougher, to be more aggressive, to appear more independent—to be noticed by peers—grew as well. Challenges to honor, even if they assumed seemingly trivial forms or proved indecipherable to middle-class observers, threatened a poor, aging bachelor's sense of manhood, especially when these challenges were leveled in a crowded working-class bar.[88]

Homicides in late nineteenth-century Chicago often began with exchanges of words. According to the men involved, verbal slights could be overlooked only at the risk of appearing weak, effeminate, and impotent. The stakes were not so high for every working-class Chicagoan, but for the toughest men in local saloons, nothing could be ignored. Some "fighting words" were intensely personal. "Irish Pat" Peterson's 1883 murder, for example, began with a dispute over a card game. Peterson called Charles Watson a "hog," and "the usual quarrel ensued." Similarly, J. F. Whittemore beat to death Paul Fox after the latter suggested that the former was "of canine extraction." In each case, the verbal joust occurred before an audience of peers. Likewise, Henry Dillitsch, a butcher, fatally stabbed his friend Frank Mingel, a laborer in a brewery, in 1887 for being "especially loud" in insisting that brewers were better singers than butchers.[89] Other lethal brawls began with one man calling another, in the presence of peers, an "Irish bastard," a "dummy," a "scab," or a "tow-headed cripple."[90] Twenty-five-year-old Michael McDonough announced in a crowded South Halstead Street saloon that he "didn't like [Frank] Carney's looks," sparking a fatal "pistol duel."[91]

More often, however, the fighting words that triggered lethal brawls were directed toward anyone within earshot. On September 17, 1880, Andrew Anderson burst into Anders Peterson's saloon, "loudly boast-

ing that he could 'lick and cut the guts out of any —— Swede'"; John
Bangson, a young Swedish immigrant, died in the brawl that followed. Also in 1880, Jack McCaffrey, known as a "young man who
when sober is unobjectionable, but when drunk is a quarrelsome and
very offensive loafer," swaggered into another Chicago saloon, tossed
his hat on the floor, and bellowed "he could whip any man in the
place on the drop of his hat." Patrick Bateman died in the ensuing
brawl. Again and again, Chicago toughs postured for their peers by
dropping their hats or daring anyone to knock off their hats, and
then fighting any man who took the challenge. Twenty-seven-year-
old Al Shrosbree offered to "thrash anyone" in the Orpheus Saloon
and died trying to keep his pledge, while Mike Ljiljak met with the
same fate after declaring that if "anybody in this house [saloon]
wants to fight me, come across." Other Chicagoans were even less
discriminating. Daniel McMullen, "a man of great muscular strength
and fond of showing it," promised to "do up" any man living on a
certain block of South Halstead Street. According to his brother,
"Dan ain't afeard o' no man livin' an' he says he don't propose to
run away from no man." John Burke, who lived on South Halstead
Street, "took the words of McMullen as a personal affront" and fatally stabbed him. While these fights appeared to have been spontaneous explosions of irrational violence, the words were familiar, the
cues unambiguous, and the responses predictable. John L. Sullivan,
the "Boston Strong Boy," bare-knuckle boxing champion, and arguably the most revered man in plebeian America during this era, used
the same patter to affirm his legendary toughness and to remind his
adoring fans that he yielded to no one. He strutted into theaters and
music halls across the nation and announced, "My name is John L.
Sullivan, and I can lick any son of a bitch alive! If any of 'em here
doubts it, come on!"[92] The celebration of toughness and fearless-
ness that made Sullivan a symbol of manly defiance and strength
also flared in working-class saloons throughout the city—and the
country.

Drinking rituals were particularly freighted with tests of masculinity and thus sparked many lethal brawls. Something more complicated than inebriation generated drunken fights, for the Irish immigrants who committed homicide in drunken brawls in late nineteenth-century Chicago probably drank as much but killed far less often than they had in Ireland.[93] Treating, the practice where a man bought a drink for another bar patron, was a coded, scripted exercise in which peers navigated their relationships with one another. In theory, buying the next round merely expressed fellowship and generosity. Often, however, the ritual of friendship also entailed an explicit challenge to a man's honor. By offering a treat, a man could exert control over a rival, compelling him to empty his glass in order for it to be refilled, particularly if the men were vying for status and competing for the attention of their peers. John Rathgeber, in fact, baited John Burke into a fight when he offered to refill the "nearly full" glass of his drinking companion. To accept the treat, Burke would have had to guzzle his beer on command, thus ceding control over his actions and therefore his status to Rathgeber. By rejecting the offer, Burke demonstrated his unwillingness to submit, expressed his disrespect for Rathgeber, and affirmed his manly honor. Dozens of lethal brawls began this way in late nineteenth-century Chicago. Just as refusing to accept a treat often produced a brawl, refusing to offer a treat could also signal a slight and an affront to a man's honor.[94]

In a social context in which every act of generosity could represent a challenge, fights abounded. The line separating pure fellowship from deadly competition was ill defined and depended as much on the reactions of the audience as it did on the intentions of the drinkers. And if all of the parties accepted all of the treats, the drinkers would become inebriated, potentially raucous, and less able to decipher the meaning of every personal interaction. Furthermore, if any drinker ran out of cash when it was his turn to treat, his companions might feel snubbed and respond accordingly, triggering the cycle of escalating challenges and, ultimately, violence.

These drinking rituals also routinely embroiled bartenders and saloonkeepers in lethal fights. When a bartender refused to serve a man—either because the drinker was already "on the border of snakeland" and disorderly or because he had no money—then the disappointed patron felt he had been dishonored before his peers, for his credit had been publicly rejected and he was rendered unable to reciprocate for his friends' treating. Angry, drunken, and humiliated drinkers frequently attacked their servers. In 1898, for example, Samuel Blum refused to serve Charles Mulcahy, explaining to Mulcahy, "You don't drink unless you pay." According to a witness, "this remark appeared to anger Mulcahy," who immediately flashed his revolver and shot Blum. Not surprisingly, most bartenders kept firearms within easy reach, which added to the body count from saloon fights.[95]

Jostles and collisions provided unmistakable opportunities for men to demonstrate their manliness and to compel others to submit. In such instances, one man would forcefully impose himself on another and literally claim his place at the bar or spot on the sidewalk; the other would be required to step back and submit or fight to determine who would surrender the space. Some men intentionally bumped potential rivals in order to "call them out." Both challenging another man and responding to a peer's challenge affirmed a man's honor. In other cases, the jostle was accidental and entirely unscripted. But in a setting overflowing with besotted, jittery young men eager to test their courage, misunderstandings frequently turned into homicidal brawls. When twenty-five-year-old John Galena sidled up to the bar in a crowded West Lake Street saloon in 1875, his satchel happened to brush against Pat Martin, who snarled, "Look out how you swing that damned thing round." Galena apologized for his clumsiness; Martin, however, rejected the peace overture and snarled, "You lie, you son of a b——h." He grabbed Galena by the throat, plunged a knife into his chest, and then preened for his attentive audience, driving the weapon into the bar and offering "to stick any son of a b——h who had anything to say." When one "witness began to speak," Martin roared, "Shut up, or I will cut you in two." Simply occupying a man's favorite seat in a saloon could be viewed as an act of provocation (with accepting such a slight seen as an act of submission), and many deadly fights began with confrontations over chairs. On March 18, 1900, for example, Nicholas Thielen killed his "intimate friend" John Sullivan, a nineteen-year-old flagman, when the latter "refused to surrender" a particular chair.[96]

Because plebeian culture placed a premium on explosive, unflinching responses to challenges, Chicago's late nineteenth-century brawlers used any weapons accessible to them. Guns were readily available and inexpensive in the city. For a few dollars anyone could purchase an "American Bulldog" or some other cheap handgun at a local hardware store or pawnshop. Many Chicagoans, especially young ruffians, carried handguns during this era. Nonetheless, drunken brawlers used firearms at a lower rate than other killers between 1875 and 1890: 42 percent of drunken-brawl killers relied on guns, compared with 58 percent of nonbrawl killers. More than other violent Chicagoans, brawlers used knives, relying on the weapon in 28 percent of brawl-related homicides. These men used their fists and blunt instruments—particularly chairs, bottles, and glasses—at slightly higher rates than other killers as well.[97] Some brawlers planned their attacks and secured weapons ahead of time, but most acted in accord with the code of working-class honor: they grabbed whatever weapons they could find and responded immediately to the affront. This probably accounted for the relatively high rate of stabbings and the low rate of shootings.

In part, the reputations of these men demanded such sudden, seemingly impulsive, conduct. Masculine honor was always on display. Peers also provided pressure to strut and perform. After an evening of "riotous revelry" in one of Chicago's most disreputable saloons, Louis and Charles Arado decided literally "to shoot out the lights" and began firing at the "gleaming pendants on the chandelier." The gunfire attracted the attention of two Chicago policemen, who demanded that the Arado brothers put away the revolver and behave themselves. Initially the men agreed, but then the crowd weighed in. Prodded by his peers, Louis Arado approached the patrolmen and bellowed, "I could lick a dozen policemen like you," sparking a volley of punches and a hail of shots, one of which struck and killed Charles Arado, himself an off-duty Chicago police detective.[98] Boisterous audiences encouraged defiant, aggressive behavior.[99]

The crowd relished its role. Andrew Vanders, for example, rushed to the sidewalk to watch Anthony Raggio beat Edward Kelly with a chair and then stab him to death in front of Hank North's saloon on June 17, 1888. At Raggio's trial, Vanders described the "big crowd" that assembled, telling the court, "I got a front seat," and adding that he screamed "Kill him" during the fight. Similarly, a group of nearly fifty men followed John Kinney, a thirty-year-old railroad worker, from a saloon to the sidewalk and saw him kick twenty-five-year-old Harry Waldron to death on November 9, 1880. Waldron was so drunk he could not fight back or even protect himself, yet the audience exhorted Kinney to "give it to him" and "give it to the —— —— —— ——." After murdering the defenseless man, Kinney swaggered back into the barroom. "More than a hundred persons" watched the "unequal contest" in which August Pflaum repeatedly drove a knife into the "prostrate" body of Daniel Markey, who was unarmed. "With the last blow," according to a journalist, Pflaum "left the weapon sticking into his victim." In dozens of brawls, observers howled approvingly as young toughs pummeled and bludgeoned prostrate, often unconscious adversaries. But perhaps more important, an attentive audience of peers likely exaggerated the stakes of these battles, for the recollections and memories of an affair of honor determined a man's reputation.[100] In short, the social, demographic, and cultural forces that concentrated young men in saloons shaped the nature of violence, helping to transform minor disagreements into vicious battles in defense of personal honor.

The particular rules of engagement in plebeian brawls—that is, the Chicago brand of manly honor—valorized brutality. In theory, the code of honor demanded a fair fight, and in theory the audience protected the purity of the contest, insuring, for example, that no combatant gained an unfair advantage. Occasionally brawlers acknowledged such traditions and instructed friends to guarantee that the fighters "got fair play."[101] Typically this was not the case, however. Instead, aggression trumped fairness in the saloons and alleys of late nineteenth-century Chicago. Many toughs insisted that brawls had no rules. Surrounded by a group of young men on a street corner in 1877, seventeen-year-old James Nelson challenged James Holden to a fight. But the "slimly built" twenty-year-old Holden backed down, saying, "I don't want to fight with you; I know you can whip me." Posturing for his buddies, Nelson knocked his victim to the ground. When Holden "got up, Nelson again threw him [to the ground] and punched him still harder, and kicked him several times. Holden asked if it was fair to kick, and Nelson replied, 'Yes, in a rough and tumble, anything is fair,'" and he "knocked down and punched" Holden yet again.[102] Far from insuring fairness, the presence of partisans usually incited brawlers to greater violence.[103] Twenty-year-old Daniel Carroll, a restaurant cook, explained that he had to stab Robert Rowan with a butcher knife during a saloon brawl. "I thought he was going to jump on me. Rowan had friends there, and I knew that if he assaulted me I'd get the worst of it, because if he could not whip me they'd help him. So I just used my knife."[104] Both toughs and their audiences valued ferocity over fairness and volatility over restraint, and the looseness of these rituals of violence encouraged combatants to fight relentlessly.

The young men who frequented Chicago saloons and other public stages in order to establish their manly identities knew the rules or norms of saloon behavior. Although jostles in stores, factories, homes, or backyards may or may not have been acts of aggression, in the roughest bars in Chicago, such as George Dugdale's saloon, known as the "Bucket of Blood," and William's O'Malley's barroom, fondly known as the "mad house," nearly everyone recognized that a jostle or even a menacing glance represented an affront and a challenge.[105] On January 24, 1880, for example, Frank Fuhl and Frank Kandzia prepared to leave a Carpenter Street saloon. As they passed through the door, the men collided with Charles Schank, "who either accidentally or intentionally knocked off Fuhl's hat." According to witnesses, "the latter, for this offense, pitched into Schank." In the melee, Schank drew his pocket knife and fatally stabbed Kandzia in the abdomen.[106] Regardless of Schank's motives, in a crowded working-class saloon in Chicago during the 1880s, a jostle, especially one that dislodged a man's hat, entailed an explicit challenge, one that few patrons believed they could ignore without losing face.

Chicago toughs were impulsive, volatile, and violent, but they did not specifically intend to kill their adversaries.[107] Aggression merely provided the appropriate, expected response in such encounters, and demonstrations of brutality sustained a young man's reputation in the eyes of his peers.[108] Men gained respect by instilling fear in their peers. Put another way, extreme, gratuitous displays of violence were an established means to affirming manly honor; homicide was largely a side effect of the performance, though killing an enemy buoyed a man's reputation. Jerry Milligan, for instance, insisted that he had not intended to kill Denny Mahoney after the latter shoved him in 1881. "I wasn't goin' to be imposed on, so I jest used my gun to defen' myself."[109] Cultural norms, rather than the effects of drink or the ravages of poverty, generated the lion's share of working-class violence.

During the 1880s, Chicago had just the right—that is, the most unstable—mix of combustible elements for such violence: the per-capita concentration of saloons in the city, the proportion of single men, and especially the proportion of older bachelors hit their highest levels. As a result, violence in brawls peaked.[110] But drunken brawls did not become frequent simply because the city had a glut of bachelors or because these men consumed huge volumes of beer. Rather, the concentration of young men made saloons the favored settings in which status was gained and reputations established. Alcohol, fellowship, and the presence of an audience that could confer manly honor combined and nourished one another, making saloons magnets for the poorest and most desperate bachelors and toughs in the city. During the 1880s, drunken brawls were the leading source of local homicides, and Chicago's drunken-brawl homicide rate and the proportion of homicides resulting from drunken brawls reached their high-water marks for the 1875–1920 period.[111]

For all of the ferocity of these aging bachelors, however, and despite the proliferation of tough saloons where they could joust and tussle before admiring audiences, Chicago was not a particularly violent city during the closing decades of the nineteenth century. The rough-hewn culture that flared in local saloons remained confined to a narrow slice of the city's huge population. Aggression was rarely the basis for personal status among wealthier—even just slightly wealthier—Chicagoans or older residents. Levels of domestic homicide were low relative to later decades, and very few Chicagoans were killed during robberies in this period. Similarly, Chicago policemen killed some residents in the closing decades of the century, but both the number and the rate of such killings were modest compared to later periods in the city's history.[112] Group conflict also generated relatively few homicides during the late nineteenth century. Ethnic turmoil and especially racial tensions suffused social life in the city, though bloody group conflict and rioting remained unusual until the twentieth century.

Because brawl violence occurred in public, such homicides were more visible than they were commonplace. In fact, in the decades when Chicago secured its reputation as a "tough town," the city's homicide rate, which fluctuated from 3.2 to 5.2 per 100,000 residents, was only slightly higher than those of the longer-settled cities of New York, Boston, and Philadelphia—and lower than it would later be: over the next hundred years Chicago's homicide rate would increase approximately sevenfold.[113] Men such as Albert Burke and John Rathgeber appeared savage and menacing not only because they reveled in their violent behavior and committed homicide in public settings but also because they brawled and killed one another at a time when Chicagoans were both anxious about social disorder and relatively nonviolent.

The code of manly honor that encouraged brawling also had self-limiting rules. Far from engaging in random acts of violence, working-class toughs acted according to a set of norms that valorized brutality only in specific contexts. Vicious brawlers who abided no disrespect in and around crowded saloons seldom exploded in violent rage in other settings or without an audience of their peers, for ferocity undertaken in isolation failed to enhance reputations or uphold honor. Moreover, because of the public nature of such violence, plebeian rituals were easily derailed. Although submitting in front of peers ceded dominance, friends and bartenders could interrupt the cycle of challenges, and informal rules governing the resumption of the battle proved to be loose. Having demonstrated courage and a willingness to be savage, vicious toughs did not have to reconvene after the gun-wielding saloonkeeper separated the men from one another and, more important, from their audience. Similarly, ruffians did not sacrifice their personal honor if a policeman disrupted the ritual of manly confrontation. As a result, public violence proved to be susceptible to external controls, particularly the intervention of saloonkeepers and law enforcers.

Changes in the arenas of plebeian violence exerted an especially powerful influence on such battles. If middle-class screeds did not directly discourage brawlers (and, in fact, added to the cachet of their fights), crusades to control saloons and public disorder gradually diminished the audiences for brawls, thus robbing the activity of its social lifeblood. After the 1880s, the ratio of residents to saloons in the city grew, and the saloon business flagged. By the first decade of the twentieth century, higher licensing fees and other forms of regulation had slowed the rate of saloon growth.[114] In 1880 Chicago had a licensed saloon for every 160 residents; fifteen years later, the figure was one saloon for every 232 residents; and in 1910, the number of residents per licensed saloon had surged to 307—a 92 percent increase in three decades.[115] This change in turn reduced the audiences before which toughs performed. Attacks on the ancillary activities connected to saloons contributed to the erosion as well. Relying on newly created lower courts, police raids, and legal injunctions, local officials regulated brothels, gambling halls, and other side businesses that attracted patrons to saloons. Even the free lunches that lured workingmen into local barrooms waned during the early twentieth century, further constricting the flow of young men into Chicago's saloons.[116]

Changes in the bottling and distribution of alcohol also drove down the city's drunken-brawl homicide rate.[117] Bottle sales and new delivery options permitted Chicagoans to drink at home, far from the tangle of young men bumping and jostling one another and isolated from the bloodthirsty crowds that prodded local toughs to defend their manly honor. Even if residents maintained impressive levels of alcohol consumption, drinking lost part of its social function and its cultural significance.

New competition for local consumers and for workingmen's dollars ate away at saloon life as well, further diminishing the crowds that undergirded the city's violent bachelor subculture. At the turn of the century, young men poured into nickelodeons and dance halls, where impressing young women—rather than dominating one's peers—shaped social interactions. Spectator sports, which blossomed in Chicago during this period, also competed with the local bars and provided more passive outlets for manly competition. Amusement parks became popular, and the city opened its first public beaches early in the century, both of which drew young men away from bars, provided new ways for residents to socialize, and sapped plebeian brawling of its social context. Even the cycling craze and the automobile mania of the era weakened the honor-based culture that spurred young men to fight.[118] Taken together, these leisure-time activities competed with saloons and offered young men other ways to define their status and to establish a sense of masculine identity.

The new leisure-time activities, like the factories of the era, required greater self-control and personal discipline than had their earlier counterparts. As the scale and complexity of commercialized leisure grew, consumers were compelled to stand in lines, sit quietly, defer to ushers and other authority figures, and refrain from disturbing other patrons, depending on the particular form of entertainment. Such increasingly rigid standards of comportment conflicted with older rules of plebeian sociability and inculcated discipline and self-control into the rising cohort of young Chicago men.

Economic forces reinforced this process. Although factory workers resisted the behavioral demands of the industrial setting, the hectoring of foremen, the threat of unemployment, and the dangers of the mechanized workplace discouraged volatile, impulsive conduct.[119] Simply put, the rhythms of industrial work dovetailed with the rules of commercialized leisure activities and cobbled away at the rough edges of plebeian, masculine identity.

Demographic changes contributed to this transformation as well. Sex ratios became better balanced by the turn of the century and, along with new fads in leisure, prompted Chicago bachelors to spend less time with their peers. During the final decade of the nineteenth century, the surplus of men in Chicago fell by more than 50 per-cent.[120] The age of marriage and the proportion of bachelors in the local population also fell, further reducing the popularity of rituals in which young men sought status by impressing, intimidating, and pummeling one another.[121] As working-class Chicagoans spent more time in heterosocial activities, as they married, and as they increasingly embraced ideas about companionate marriage, bachelors became adults and the cultural foundations of masculine identity shifted. Chicago had fewer aging bachelors trapped between adolescence and adulthood and desperate to affirm their sense of manhood, fewer rough dives where aggressive behavior was expected and where fawning crowds conferred status on brawlers, and as a result the city had fewer drunken brawls.

With fewer brawls, Chicago's drunken-brawl homicide rate plummeted. Between 1880 and 1920, it dropped by more than 77 percent (see Figure 1, page 42). Similarly, as Figure 2 (page 43) indicates, the proportion of the city's homicides that occurred as a product of drunken brawls fell by 85 percent during the same period.[122] The leading single cause of homicide throughout the last quarter of the nineteenth century, drunken-brawl homicide dropped to the eighth leading cause by 1920, trailing fatal lovers' quarrels, botched robberies in which the victims killed their assailants, and five other kinds of violent encounters.

The sharp drop in lethal drunken brawls transformed the character of Chicago violence. Because brawling reflected a particular set of cultural values, as working-class leisure activities and cultural norms changed, the nature of lethal violence shifted accordingly. When homicide moved out of saloons, away from brawls, and apart from the cultural world of local toughs, the backgrounds of killers and victims changed as well. For the 1875–1920 period, the proportion of victims in their twenties, the proportion of Chicagoans clubbed to death, and

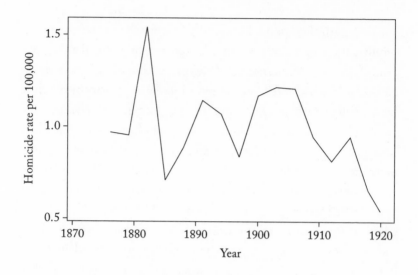

FIGURE I   *Drunken-brawl homicide rate*
            (three-year averages; source: see Appendix)

the proportion of residents who killed acquaintances peaked during the early 1880s. Likewise, the proportion of killers who were un-skilled workers peaked during the late 1880s, as did the proportion of homicides committed with knives and the proportion of victims who died at the hands of friends. With the relative decline of brawling, Chicago killers became older, relatively wealthier, and more highly skilled, and were more likely to use firearms. Just as violence from brawls contracted, so too did other activities connected with the strutting, preening, swaggering, impulsive world of late nineteenth-century plebeian masculinity; along with the rate of drunken-brawl homicide, the rates of death from accidents and from acute and chronic alcoholism dropped.[123]

Neither brawling nor drunken toughs disappeared from the city, of course; ruffians for whom ferocity defined status continued to live in Chicago and to prowl the saloons of the levee district. But without the demographic, institutional, and economic pressures that com-

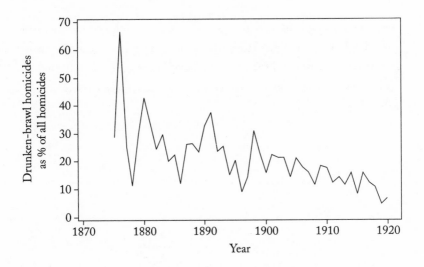

FIGURE 2   *Proportion of drunken-brawl homicides to all homicides*
(source: see Appendix)

bined to create a kind of cultural critical mass during the late nineteenth century, the level of brawl violence dropped and remained low.
Newcomers, particularly from southern and eastern Europe, poured
into the city, and many defined masculinity in ways that venerated
peer violence.[124] The lower proportion of bachelors in society, the
shrinking number of tough saloons, and the increasing behavioral
demands of both work and leisure, however, discouraged volatility
and aggressiveness. In short, the violent rituals of plebeian honor
gradually succumbed to the cultural, economic, and demographic
pressures of industrial society, and deadly brawls over jostles or treating, such as Albert Burke's murder of John Rathgeber, became rare in
Chicago.

Despite these trends, however, levels of lethal violence in the city
did not fall at the turn of the century. Although drunken-brawl
deaths in particular and plebeian violence in general decreased, Chicago's homicide rate surged. The forces that first sustained and then

discouraged plebeian violence did not reduce violence as much as they displaced it. During the early twentieth century other forms of homicide increased rapidly, and the city's homicide rate swelled to twice that of other major urban centers. By 1910, Chicago led the nation in homicide deaths.[125]

Chapter 2

"I Loved My Wife
So I Killed Her"

J oseph Swager murdered his wife, Jennie, on Sunday, December 14, 1913, nearly severing her head with a butcher knife. Immediately afterward, he slashed his own throat in four places with the same weapon. Jennie Swager had left her husband and teenaged son three months earlier and had moved in with relatives, ending an eighteen-year marriage. Increasingly despondent over the separation, Joseph begged his wife "to come home to stay and make our home happy." Jennie reluctantly agreed to meet with him at a busy street corner and consented to continue the conversation in their house. As the couple sat in the dining room of the West Jackson Boulevard home they owned, Joseph revealed that he was desperate to reconcile with his wife and could not face life without her. "I loved her and could give her everything she wanted and tried to reason with her," he said. When Jennie rejected the overture, Joseph said, explaining that "she simply didn't like my companionship," he seized a knife, cut a huge gash in her throat, and then attempted to kill himself.

Though blood poured from his wounds, he failed to sever his jugular vein and recovered from the self-inflicted injuries. "I loved my wife so I killed her," Joseph Swager later lamented.[1] Jennie Swager was Chicago's two hundred thirty-first homicide victim of 1913.[2]

By the beginning of the twentieth century, domestic violence had become the leading cause of homicide in Chicago, having surpassed drunken brawls during the mid-1890s. As the rate of brawl violence tumbled in Chicago, the rate of family violence soared. In fact, domestic violence increased far faster than brawl violence decreased. Between 1875–1879 and 1915–1920, the drunken-brawl homicide rate fell by 16 percent. During the same period, the rate of domestic homicide rose by 312 percent. Spouses comprised the majority of domestic violence victims, and wives accounted for nearly four-fifths of Chicago's 498 spousal homicide deaths between 1875 and 1920. The rate of uxoricide—wife killing—swelled by 263 percent. Over half of the Chicago women who were homicide victims during this period died at the hands of their husbands.[3]

Jennie Swager's murder typified this rapidly increasing form of lethal violence. No longer were the participants in Chicago homicides overwhelmingly young, poor, drunken bachelors who gleefully and impulsively employed violence in public settings in order to impress or intimidate their peers. Instead, the victims of lethal violence were often women in their thirties, and their killers tended to be in their late thirties and of middling economic status; the killers usually struck behind closed doors and attempted suicide after murdering their loved ones. Acutely aware of the surge in uxoricide, the *Chicago Times* termed this violence "Derringer divorce" and "divorce by bullets," while the *Chicago Tribune* expressed alarm at "Chicago's epidemic of crime" that entailed "the getting rid of a wife by a shorter method than that offered by the divorce court."[4]

Turn-of-the-century Chicago was a city of paradoxes. "Its bad," Theodore Dreiser observed, "was so deliciously bad, its good so very good." Likewise, English journalist George W. Steevens described Chicago as both "queen and guttersnipe of cities." Teeming, vice-ridden slums festered in the shadows of the opulent palaces constructed for the Columbian Exposition of 1893; local government gained notoriety for being both a backwater of political corruption and a leader in Progressive reform; visitors termed Chicago "the most beautiful and the most squalid" city in the nation; and residents became more violent in private just as they demonstrated increasing restraint and self-control in public.[5]

Chicago grew rapidly but not necessarily chaotically. Between 1890 and 1910 the local population more than doubled, exceeding 2 million residents by 1908. During this period the city attracted migrants from throughout the United States and large waves of newcomers from abroad. Gradually the sources of immigration to Chicago—and the United States more generally—shifted from northern and western Europe and toward southern and eastern Europe. Industrial development increased even faster than the city's population. Between 1890 and 1910, the value of the manufactured goods produced in Chicago rose by 181 percent.[6] The scale of production surged as well, and the average number of workers per factory, which ballooned during the decades after the Civil War, maintained its ascent, rising by 60 percent during the turn-of-the-century period.[7] Although the streets of the city became more congested, the tenements more crowded, the extremes in wealth more pronounced, and local society more riven along ethnic, religious, racial, and linguistic lines, countervailing forces blunted many of the worst effects of rapid growth and social change. For example, despite the overcrowding, the inadequate sanitation, and the mountains of filth and garbage heaped in local streets and alleys, life expectancy from birth increased by 52 percent and Chicago's death rate decreased by 21 percent.[8] Moreover, the swirling mix of newcomers generated menacing social tensions but little group violence, Chicago's nineteenth-century reputation for public disorder notwithstanding. The city of the Great Railroad Strike of 1877 and the Haymarket bombing of 1886 suffered from no major riots during the quarter-century after the Pullman Strike of 1894.[9] Blistering growth did not produce disorder in Chicago, but increasing social order did not reduce violence in the city.

The institutional and demographic pressures that discouraged plebeian violence transformed the nature of homicide more than they reduced lethal violence. Such forces, in fact, contributed to a rising tide of domestic violence in turn-of-the-century Chicago. During the final decades of the nineteenth century, law enforcers, factory foremen, schoolteachers, and the operators of leisure-time activities demanded greater levels of self-control and personal restraint. These efforts slowly but inexorably inculcated self-discipline in working-class Chicagoans and gradually weakened the ethic of honor and the bachelor subculture that had celebrated toughness and fueled plebeian violence, thereby contributing to the reduction of drunkenness and brawling violence. As sex ratios evened and a higher proportion of Chicago men married and established families, social life—including violent behavior—moved away from saloons and into homes.

Cultural forces reinforced this process, entangling a new group of Chicagoans in a storm of conflicting social pressures. Just as the world of commercialized leisure and consumption venerated materialism and upward mobility, domestic harmony and family life became increasingly important sources of masculine respectability, even for many working-class Chicagoans. But the new foundations of masculine status exposed different pressure points, or cultural fault lines. If Chicago men felt less inclined to prove their toughness in local bars, they experienced greater stress at home and with their loved ones. In short, the locus of masculine violence changed. Chicago killers continued to use violence to bolster their sense of masculinity, though the masculine ideals that they coveted shifted during the closing decades of the nineteenth century. While the opinions of peers sparked the brawls of the 1870s and 1880s, inner, more private emotional turmoil generated the wife killing of later decades. Joseph Swager, for instance, vowed to provide his wife with "everything she wanted" and resorted to violence when he failed to persuade her to "come home to stay and make our home happy."

Domestic homicide in Chicago changed in two significant ways during the closing decades of the nineteenth century and the opening decades of the twentieth century. First, as social, demographic, institutional, and cultural forces focused emotional conflict on family life, the level of family violence surged. Second, these pressures also redefined the nature of domestic homicide, producing changes in the social-economic backgrounds of family killers, the kinds of circumstances and incidents that triggered domestic violence, the weapons employed, and the postviolence behavior of killers. Wife killing, in short, underwent far-reaching shifts as the city changed.

At the same time that public life was becoming more disciplined, private life was becoming more violent. Between the late 1870s and the early 1910s, Chicagoans rioted less, brawled less, and were arrested for disorderly conduct less; yet the city's homicide rate nearly tripled.[10] Early twentieth-century Chicagoans killed one another at nearly five times the rate of Newark and Milwaukee residents, more than twenty times the rate of city dwellers in Germany, and more than thirty times the rate of Londoners.[11] "Human life is the cheapest thing in Chicago," a local observer reported in 1908.[12]

During the 1870s and the 1880s, domestic homicide occurred at low levels in Chicago. Such violence accounted for less than 12 percent of the city's homicides during the late 1870s, whereas drunken brawls produced over 28 percent of Chicago homicides.[13] Demographic factors contributed to this pattern. With a low proportion of married men in the population in this period, it is not surprising that spouses, children, and other relatives would make up a modest share of homicide victims. But cultural factors were more important than demographics. As long as young men used demonstrations of public toughness directed against friends and acquaintances to establish their social status, peers would remain the principal targets for violent behavior. For every spousal homicide during the late 1870s, there were five homicides between acquaintances and nearly three homicides between friends.

Domestic homicide was relatively uncommon in Chicago during the late 1870s and the 1880s, though local men sometimes murdered their loved ones. Aggressive young bachelors who reveled in displays of brutality occasionally killed their siblings, parents, or other relatives. Moreover, such men did not instantly abandon violence when they married, even if they married relatively late. Deeply ingrained habits followed these Chicagoans as they formed households and gradually changed their social orbits. Not surprisingly, wife killers during this period looked and behaved very much like brawlers, though they were older and better off economically. Between 1875 and 1890, the average age of Chicago wife killers was thirty-eight, compared with twenty-eight for brawlers. The difference reflected the stages of the life cycle; simply put, married men in late nineteenth-century Chicago were older than bachelors. Similarly, both wife killers and brawlers were clustered at the bottom rungs of the city's occupational ladder, though the former enjoyed slightly higher standing. Approximately half of wife killers were unskilled, compared with nearly two-thirds of brawlers. The age difference between the two groups probably accounted for the higher occupational status of wife killers; an additional decade in the work force enabled many men to gain experience, forge contacts, hone their skills, and advance from unskilled to semiskilled positions. In short, the Chicagoans who graduated from bachelorhood and the culture of the saloon carried their aggressive behavior with them when they married and entered middle age.

More important, late nineteenth-century uxoricide sprang from the behavioral norms of plebeian culture. Like their younger friends who engaged in brawling, wife killers of the late 1870s and 1880s were impulsive and volatile. Furthermore, they typically interpreted disagreements with their spouses as challenges to their identity as men and as heads of households.[14] They responded with explosions of brutality.

According to contemporaries, these men were "rage" killers. Murderous husbands themselves often used this term. For example, Thomas Walsh, a twenty-eight-year-old day laborer from Ireland with a long history of wife beating, explained that he "got crazy with rage" when he found his wife, Elizabeth, drunk on February 19, 1883, and "took down the strap and began beating her." Similarly, Frank Nolan insisted that "a blind rage seemed to seize me, and before I knew it I had shot her" (his wife). Witnesses to domestic violence frequently used the same term to describe the explosive behavior of wife killers. Paul Pollner, observers reported, was "in a rage" when he shot and killed Agnes Pollner in 1882; Frank Slaby "flew into a rage" seconds before he crushed his wife's skull with an ax. Nearly half of the wife killers in Chicago between 1875 and 1890 described themselves, or were described by witnesses, as having acted with uncontrollable "rage."[15]

Rage killers differed from other men who committed uxoricide. They tended to be older than other murdering husbands; their average age was close to forty, compared with just over thirty-six for those not described as being enraged. Rage killers were also poorer than other wife killers. Between 1875 and 1890 64 percent of rage killers were unskilled workers, compared with 29 percent of wife killers who did not act in rage. In addition, Irish immigrants were overrepresented among rage killers.[16]

These men acted impulsively, murdering their spouses wherever and whenever they were overtaken with rage. The details of their crimes underscored this volatility. Nearly a third of rage killers struck in the kitchen or the dining room, compared with one-sixth of other wife killers. A cross glance, an odd inflection, a disrespectful word, or a discordant comment during dinner triggered rage murders. Albert and Theresa Becker quarreled in their parlor after dinner. "Both of us were very angry," the thirty-five-year-old packinghouse butcher noted in his confession. According to him, Theresa "picked up a plate from the parlor table and threw it at me." Enraged, Albert "hurled the hatchet at her. It struck her square in the middle of the forehead." Moreover, rage killers often employed any weapon at hand—fists, belts, and blunt instruments, particularly the legs of chairs and tables. Forty-year-old Benjamin Gates, for example, bludgeoned to death his thirty-two-year-old wife, Annie, with a leg of their dining room table. Nonenraged killers, by contrast, were more inclined to use firearms.[17]

Rage killers also stood apart from other wife killers in their brutality. Frequently drunken at the time of the lethal attack, they typically rained blow after blow on their spouses, often continuing the assault long after their wives had lost consciousness. Nearly 60 percent of rage killers slashed, punched, or shot their spouses three or more times, compared with 32 percent of nonenraged killers. One enraged husband fired three shots at his wife and then announced, "I only wish I had shot her six times." Steve Page stabbed his wife sixteen times, and William Schultz "crushed his wife's skull with a hammer and then stabbed her seven times." Edward Koehler, a Chicago policeman, transformed his forty-five-year-old wife's body into a bloody mass of bruises and welts. The coroner's physician found Effie Koehler's "jaw out of place and face scratched; left eye discolored; three ribs on the right side broken, and body below right breast discolored and skin lacerated." Dr. Joseph Springer noted, "If the woman had fallen from the roof of a three-story building, she couldn't have been hurt any worse." Rage killers sought to inflict pain and suffering on their wives, even after the women had died. Forty-year-old Louis Buskin gloated to a local policeman regarding his assault on his wife, Sarah, that "I cut off a piece of her nose afterward, so that she will remember me if she comes to."[18]

The sparks that set off these violent explosions were firmly grounded in plebeian notions of masculinity and reflected an unstable interaction between gender identity and class identity. Chicago husbands lapsed into rages in response to perceived challenges to patriarchal authority and prerogatives. Certain fears, words, or actions typically ignited the violence.

Jealousy often triggered the rage of late nineteenth-century Chicago wife killers. This was the specific cause or spark in nearly half of rage uxoricides, compared with one-third of wife killings not accompanied by rage.[19] Convinced of their wives' infidelity, jealous men who killed often hid in bushes or peered around corners when they left their spouse alone. In the weeks leading up to her 1880 murder, Livia Zimmerman's husband, Simon, "used to crawl up the stairs on his hands and knees at night, with a cocked revolver, and hunt all about the house for hidden men." Similarly, Patrick Ford, a night watchman, observed "every move his wife made, even keeping a lookout through the shutters when she went into the street to get milk." Finally, "mad with rage," Ford fired four bullets at his wife, striking her in the breast and the abdomen.[20]

Such violence flowed naturally from notions of plebeian masculinity. If bachelors preened, strutted, brawled, and killed to impress peers and cow potential competitors, it is not surprising that former bachelors viewed their wives in proprietary terms and that they would respond to fears of sexual betrayal with explosions of violent rage.[21] They viewed infidelity as an assault of their hard-won reputations, and their ferocity and brutality represented both a visceral response and a culturally conditioned prescription for defending their masculine honor.[22]

Any perceived challenge to patriarchal authority could trigger a rage killing. Many lethal beatings began with disputes over the preparation of meals. Upon finding "his supper not ready" on Christmas Eve of 1885, Thomas King, a thirty-eight-year-old Irish laborer, beat his wife to death with a chair. "I knocked her down and pounded her until she didn't feel so frisky," the defiant King explained.[23] Rage uxoricides frequently began when wives failed to submit to their husbands' demands.[24] One man explicitly asked his wife "if in the future she would obey him. She replied no, and thereupon drawing a revolver, he fired at her twice." Another Chicago man flew into a homicidal rage when his wife refused to share the "comic supplement of a Sunday newspaper." Frederick Pflugradt, a hardware merchant, grabbed "his paper," threw it to the floor, and roared, "I'll teach you to oppose me." Neighbors then heard "a cry of pain and the sound of a descending strap."[25] For men who came of age in a cultural world in which they gained status by dominating others and in which they lost status if they could not compel another person to submit, minor domestic disputes easily and rapidly escalated into violence, just as trivial violations of drinking etiquette and incidental jostles triggered deadly saloon brawls.

Like their counterparts in saloons, late nineteenth-century rage killers believed that their actions were justified or, at the very least, understandable. "How could you commit this terrible crime?" one woman asked her brother after finding his wife's corpse in 1885. "Well, I did it, and there's no use crying about it," the killer answered. James Nolan told the policeman investigating his wife's 1892 death, "Of course I am sorry I committed the crime, but it can't be helped now. At least she's paid for her unfaithfulness." He then added, for good measure, "I think she deserved it." Thomas Walsh said of his wife, Lizzie, "I did not mean to kill her, but thought when she got sober in the morning the beating would have a good effect." Even from jail cells, rage killers typically remained defiant.[26]

For most rage killers, uxoricide represented the culmination of a long-standing pattern of wife beating. The majority of these men had beaten their wives prior to the final battle.[27] Put differently, husbands who engaged in rage killings had significantly higher rates of wife beating than husbands who engaged in nonrage killings. Moreover, rage killing and abuse were related: they reflected similar attitudes toward women, toward patriarchal authority, and toward emotional restraint. Just as rage killings were particularly common in Chicago between 1875 and 1890, so too were uxoricides in which a pattern of abuse preceded the final encounter. During this period, 86 percent of rage killers had a history of wife beating, compared with 44 percent of nonenraged killers.

Accustomed to hearing the cries of abused women, neighbors expressed scant surprise when rage turned into homicide. Often they had heard the screams for years and had intervened as much as they thought advisable.[28] One woman, for example, admitted that she had learned to ignore her neighbor's screams for help because she was "too much afraid of Walsh [the abusive husband] to invade his premises." After an 1885 wife killing, the residents who lived next door to the victim admitted that they "knew the woman was in danger for her life, but say they had learned from past experience never to interfere with their neighbors' family jars." Many concerned neighbors became inured to the cries of abused wives. On July 4, 1881, Mrs. Patrick Clancy had heard her neighbor, Catherine Cunningham, sob "'Oh Jim! Don't, don't, don't.' Then all was still." Clancy told the police that "she thought nothing of the occurrence, as it was a common thing for James to beat his wife." For his part, the forty-two-year-old husband "admitted having beaten her often, but thought that he and she had lived together as happily as other couples in the neighborhood." Likewise, neighbors reported that Annie Thomas's "screams and pleadings for mercy could be heard almost every night." Alice Painter's cries shot through the neighborhood "about five times a week." So frequent were her "cries of anguish" that on the night of Painter's murder, neighbors went "to bed, thinking nothing of the affair, for similar disturbances had frequently occurred." Although neighbors heard Paulina Merry screaming, "Please don't kill me! Let me alone! Don't kill me," they ignored the sounds of Chris Merry beating his wife to death with a poker. According to those who heard the woman's cries of pain, "no attention was paid to this, as Merry, it is said, was in the habit of beating his wife."[29] During the late nineteenth century, rage killers saw violence as normative masculine behavior; by reining in ill-behaved women, wife beaters maintained domestic stability and bolstered the gender hierarchy at the core of their conception of family life.

Rage killers proved to be remarkably focused in their homicidal attacks. These men exploded in seemingly uncontrollable rage, yet they managed to target specific parts of their victims' bodies. Rage killers disproportionately shot, stabbed, bludgeoned, and hammered their wives' breasts, revealing the intensity of gender conflict in late nineteenth-century working-class households. Over one-third—35 percent—of rage killers assaulted their wives' breasts, nearly double the proportion of nonenraged killers. Nor were these homicidal men simply firing, pounding, or slashing at their wives' torsos; the target was unmistakable. When Agnes Pollner refused to "obey" her husband, Paul Pollner shot her twice, "one in the right breast and one in the left breast." Likewise, fifty-four-year-old Carl Nitz stabbed his twenty-six-year-old wife five times in the left breast and then shot her in the head and neck; forty-five-year-old William Schultz plunged a knife into his wife's breast seven times. On September 5, 1889, John E. Johnson, a fifty-seven-year-old Swedish carpenter, threw his wife Josephine to the floor, tore "open her dress at the neck, partly opened her corsage [sic], and was plunging a knife into her left breast as often as his strength and dexterity would permit."[30] Typically older, poorer, more often drunken, and more often driven by jealousy than other wife killers, these men were particularly desperate to maintain patriarchal authority, especially quick to assert their dominance over their wives, and unusually insecure about their status as men and as heads of households.[31] Just as aging bachelors and poor workers felt greater pressure to dominate those around them in local bars, middle-aged, poor, married men appear to have been particularly anxious to dominate those around them in local homes.

But with a huge cohort of men marrying late and embracing the rough-hewn, bellicose value system nurtured in Chicago saloons, why was the uxoricide rate so low during this period? The lion's share of the Chicago men who came of age in the era of barroom brawling, bare-knuckle boxing, and exaggerated honor were married by the late nineteenth century; in 1890 only 30 percent of local men over the age of twenty-five remained single.[32] Furthermore, abusive husbands behaved very much like brawlers, complete with trademark volatility, obsession with dominating those around them, and unabashed ferocity. Yet Chicago's uxoricide rate in 1890 hovered at approximately one-third its drunken-brawl homicide rate.[33] If the behavioral norms of the saloon infused the conduct of working-class men during the late nineteenth century, and if the overwhelming majority of the city's aging, brawling bachelors had married, why was uxoricide relatively uncommon during this period?

Domestic violence lacked one of the core elements of brawl violence: an audience. Local toughs swaggered and scowled, jostled and tussled to impress their peers, and appreciative audiences heaped praise on vicious fighters and goaded timid men into more aggressive behavior. Working-class Chicagoans during this period demonstrated little compunction in beating their wives, and they sometimes boasted about it and nearly always felt justified in doing it.[34] But wife beating represented a more defensive form of violence than brawling; men believed that they were the aggrieved parties, that their wives' behavior made the thrashing necessary.[35] One wife killer, for example, had earlier lamented to a friend, "That woman of mine has been raising the ——. I have a good mind to beat her brains out." Another explained, "I have had to lick her lots of times before I could get her to cook my meals."[36] Insubordinate, "disobedient," or unfaithful wives could humiliate their husbands, though the men gained little status when they bludgeoned their spouses. There was no audience to affirm their manliness, only terrified children and anxious neighborhood women desperate to intervene. As a rule, a working-class man would not violate the sanctity of another man's home during a domestic affray.[37] Neither women nor children conferred status on a man, and thus a wife beater's only audience proved unable to bolster his flagging status, repair his wounded ego, or enhance his reputation.[38] Chicago husbands were often abusive and brutal, and levels of wife beating, though impossible to calculate with precision, were undoubtedly grotesquely high. Without a fawning audience of supportive peers, however, most Chicago wife beaters stopped short of landing a lethal blow. The norms of plebeian masculinity encouraged men to be violent, but denied them glory when they assaulted their loved ones.

Changes in the informal rules of working-class society affected wife killing during the late nineteenth and early twentieth centuries, and the cultural, demographic, and institutional pressures that discouraged brawling violence also reduced rage uxoricides. As volatility and aggression lost their cachet within plebeian circles, relatively fewer Chicago husbands murdered their wives in explosions of rage. During the 1880s, 41 percent of uxoricides were rage killings. By the 1910s, the figure had fallen below 21 percent. In short, characteristic forms of plebeian violence—brawl homicide and rage uxoricide—faded as the nineteenth century drew to a close.

Although rage killings decreased and jealousy-inspired murders became less common, domestic homicide increased sharply in turn-of-

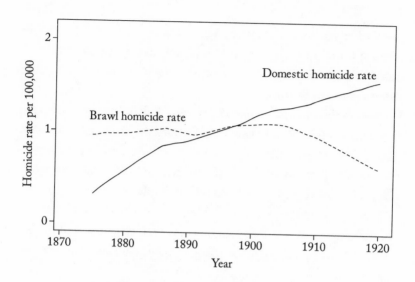

FIGURE 3   *Smoothed homicide rates for brawls and domestic violence
(source: see Appendix; LOWESS technique used for smoothing)*

the-century Chicago (see Figure 3). Between the late 1870s and the late 1910s, the city's domestic homicide rate nearly quintupled, while the city's wife-killing homicide rate more than tripled. Rage killings did not disappear, but they became less frequent. Instead, uxoricide assumed different forms and involved different groups of Chicagoans as changing cultural norms generated new social pressures and produced new sparks for domestic homicide.

Demographic data provide clues about what may have sparked violence in Chicago homes. Turn-of-the-century wife killers were not young newlyweds fresh from the volatile world of bachelors, bars, and brothels. To the contrary, family killers were older than other Chicago murderers. For the period 1890–1910, the average age of a domestic killer in Chicago was thirty-seven and the average age of a wife killer was thirty-nine, compared with thirty-one for all Chicago killers.[39] Between the periods 1875–1890 and 1890–1910 the average age of the residents who murdered loved ones increased, rising by

nearly five years for all domestic killers and by one year for wife killers. Far from being wild young men chafing at the new constraints of
family life, turn-of-the-century murdering husbands were in their
late thirties and forties.

The socioeconomic status of domestic killers shifted during the
late nineteenth and early twentieth centuries. Family killers became
relatively wealthier. Between 1875–1890 and 1890–1910, the proportion of unskilled domestic murderers dropped by 26 percent, while
the proportion of semiskilled and skilled family killers rose by 30 percent and 21 percent respectively.[40] Thus, the men who committed domestic homicide were increasingly concentrated in the middle and
even upper tier of Chicago's working class, just as they were increasingly clustered in their middle years.

German immigrants committed a disproportionate share of family
homicide, particularly at the turn of the century. These residents
were one of the least violent groups of Chicago residents, with a homicide rate roughly half that of the overall city. But when German
Chicagoans killed, they often targeted loved ones.[41] Between 1890
and 1910, 20 percent of all Chicago homicide victims died at the hand
of relatives, though 41 percent of German victims were killed by relatives. German immigration to the city peaked during the 1880s and
then fell sharply, and thus the percentage of German residents plummeted over time, dropping by more than 51 percent between 1890 and
1910.[42] The proportion of homicides committed by German immigrants decreased at a similar rate, though Germans remained overrepresented among family killers through the first decades of the
twentieth century. In part, the ethnic concentration dovetailed with
changes in the socioeconomic status of Chicago killers. Irish immigrants, for example, committed a small and rapidly decreasing
proportion of the city's family homicides. Furthermore, as rage uxoricides became less common and as unskilled workers committed
fewer wife murders, the proportion of domestic homicides commit-

ted by Irish Chicagoans plunged. By contrast, German men remained overrepresented among wife killers and among skilled workers in the city through the first decade of the twentieth century.[43] In fact, more than two-thirds of German wife killers held semiskilled and skilled occupations between 1890 and 1910. Shifts in the occupational and ethnic backgrounds of Chicago family killers suggest that the pressures buffeting semiskilled or skilled workmen and the pressures affecting German residents overlapped and contributed significantly to the city's surging rate of domestic homicide.

The actions of Chicago domestic killers after they had committed murder changed as well. The homicide-suicide rate among these killers increased.[44] Between the periods 1875–1890 and 1890–1910, the proportion of family killers who committed or attempted suicide immediately after taking the lives of loved ones rose. The proportion of wife killers who attempted suicide topped 50 percent by the turn-of-the-century period.[45] Once again, the pattern was particularly pronounced for German immigrants who committed uxoricide; by the 1890–1910 period, 62 percent of these men attempted suicide.[46] Similarly, fewer wife killers defended their homicidal behavior as the nineteenth century ended and the twentieth century began.[47] Gilded Age wife killers were typically fiercely confident that their behavior had been appropriate and justified. Their turn-of-the-century counterparts more frequently reaffirmed their love for their victims and attempted to take their own lives.

Weapon use also changed over time. The proportion of wife killers who used their fists to commit uxoricide dropped by 44 percent between 1875–1890 and 1890–1910, and the proportion of uxoricides committed with knives tumbled by 40 percent. Guns filled the gap, with the proportion of wife killings committed with firearms rising from 53 percent to 66 percent. Reflecting the drop in rage uxoricides, turn-of-the-century murdering husbands rarely bludgeoned their spouses to death with chairs, table legs, or other pieces of household furniture hastily employed as lethal weapons. Family homicide, in short, underwent important changes during the closing decades of the nineteenth century and the opening decade of the new century.

Powerful cultural forces transformed family life during the late nineteenth and early twentieth centuries, redefining domestic homicide in the process. First for middle-class city dwellers earlier in the century, but then increasingly for working-class men by the closing decade of the nineteenth century, domestic harmony became a core component of masculine respectability. Chicago men began to invest less energy and time in peer activities and more energy and time in family life.[48] Institutional and legal processes, including the commercialization of leisure, the expansion of heterosocial recreation, and police campaigns to discourage public drinking, fighting, bare-knuckle boxing, disorderly conduct, gambling, and prostitution, reinforced this shift and encouraged emotional restraint, caution, and delayed gratification. Moreover, law enforcers criminalized well-established elements of plebeian masculinity, such as brawling and wife beating, at the same time that religious and social leaders celebrated the virtues of family life and domesticity.[49] Across class lines, private life and domestic harmony gradually replaced public life and male sociability as bases for both emotional fulfillment and masculine status. Chicagoans, like other Americans, embraced the ideal of companionate marriage; and local men, as their homicidal behavior would indicate, coveted their roles as providers—rather than as brawlers and ruffians.

Demographic factors combined with cultural imperatives in making these changes in family life. Just as the decline of the late nineteenth-century bachelor subculture was both a cause and an effect of new patterns of social life, shifts in the structure of family life simultaneously fueled and reflected cultural developments. By the end of the century, sex ratios were better balanced, putting marriage and family life increasingly within the reach of working-class Chicago-ans. This in turn reduced the rate of bachelorhood and the age at marriage. In 1890, for example, 31 percent of Chicago men in their early thirties were unmarried; ten years later, 22 percent of the men in this age group remained bachelors.[50]

The new emphasis on emotional fulfillment and the veneration of domestic harmony, however, had a darker side. Shifting the terrain of masculine status—from the public to the private, from the peer to the family, and from the patriarchal to the companionate—imposed mounting pressures on men, particularly on their expectations for marital stability.[51] During the 1870s and 1880s, Chicago men looked to their peers for affirmation, and thus they were particularly inse-cure and therefore particularly violent in public settings, where they would either garner respect and power or be exposed as weak, subor-dinate, or womanlike. When married men embraced the ideal of companionate marriage, the locus for establishing, protecting, or los-ing status changed, and hence the percentage of homicides that men committed in the home rose rapidly. Between the late 1870s and the late 1890s, the proportion of men's homicides in the home nearly doubled, climbing from 20 percent to 38 percent. As more Chicago husbands embraced the new ideals of manhood and of family life, threats to domestic harmony became assaults on their status as men, and lethal violence moved into the home and became intertwined with pressures for domestic harmony.

The socioeconomic, life-cycle, and age backgrounds of turn-of-the-century wife killers, as well as these killers' words and actions, in-dicate that uxoricide increasingly grew out of challenges to emerging notions of masculine respectability. Between 1890 and 1910, men at the cusp of middle-class status committed the majority of wife mur-ders. Most of the killers had foundered at the edges of middle-class economic standing; they pursued the material and emotional trap-pings of bourgeois life but lacked the income and occupational sta-

bility to achieve their goals. Skilled workers were particularly battered by these pressures and therefore were especially overrepresented
among turn-of-the-century Chicago's domestic killers. De-skilling
added to the financial and emotional woes of the men who murdered
their loved ones. They toiled at the margins of economic stability,
and industrialization eroded their standing.[52] The concentration of
German immigrants among wife killers reflected the clustering of
these residents in some of the occupations most ravaged by the de-
skilling process.[53] The changing organization of local factories, for
example, undercut the status of butchers; not surprisingly, these men,
who were skilled with knives, accustomed to autonomy, and inured to
pain, committed domestic violence at an especially high rate during
the period. In April 1899, the Cook County jail held three German-
born butchers who had slaughtered their wives.[54] In short, wife killers during this period embraced middle-class ideals of masculinity
and family life but lived at the margins of middle-class respectability,
unable to secure the lifestyle and the stability they sought. Moreover,
domestic killers, who tended to be in their late thirties and forties,
had struggled to establish households. As men who came of age in
the heyday of the bachelor subculture, they were also tugged by conflicting value systems. Although these Chicagoans had moved out of
the raucous, impulsive, violent world of bachelor life, plebeian sociability, and violence, they were not firmly ensconced in the domestic,
stable world of middle-class Chicago. Unable to meet their new,
bourgeois expectations, they responded to feelings of failure, insecu-
rity, and inadequacy in the language of plebeian honor.

The triggering incidents in turn-of-the-century domestic homicides revealed the intensity of these cultural pressures. Whereas
Gilded Age killers typically lashed out at "disobedient" wives or exploded in jealous rages, late nineteenth- and early twentieth-century
domestic killers more often attributed their violence to financial setbacks, dashed dreams, failing marriages, and the accompanying feel-

ings of despondence. For example, forty-year-old Charles Andrew shot his wife, Ethel, and himself when "he realized he could not keep her in the style they had grown accustomed to." Peter Haugard, a forty-year-old Danish businessman, killed his wife and children because he could not bear the thought that they might lapse into poverty. "I am entirely out of subsistence, with a wife and five children," Haugard recorded in his 1896 suicide note. "I have tried to get some work in order to support my wife and family, but having failed in this effort . . ." John W. Lehman, a thirty-nine-year-old German immigrant, murdered his three children and then committed suicide because "he thought there was not much of a future in store for his children." But, by all accounts, Lehman was a solid, respectable man. Friends and coworkers described him as "prosperous," "straight, upright, sober, and industrious." Lehman owned a three-story house, and his family "did not know want, or even hardship, and was considered one of the most prosperous in the neighborhood." Unable to afford a home in the country, however, and fearing that his "little ones would probably grow up to the same hardship and toil" he had endured, Lehman shot his children. Forty-year-old Theodore Wasserman, a German immigrant who owned a "cement and reconstruction" business, beat his thirty-five-year-old wife, Freida, to death with a hammer, chloroformed Joseph, their one-year-old son, and then slashed his own wrists and throat and opened the gas jets in their home because he proved "unable to maintain the Sheridan [R]oad standard of living."[55] These men, like dozens of other Chicagoans during this period, believed that they had failed as providers, as husbands, as fathers, and as men, and so they murdered their loved ones. Inner demons, rather than outward triggers (such as obstreperous or unfaithful wives), set off their homicidal actions.

Some Chicagoans resorted to violence when news of their financial problems was about to be made public. For forty-eight-year-old Nels Johnson, it was a foreclosure that triggered a murder and suicide; forty-nine-year-old Jonas Butler poisoned his entire family when his forty-four-year-old wife vowed that "unless he gave her and his children better support, she would appeal to the law."[56] Although these men, like their counterparts of the 1870s and the 1880s, killed rather than face humiliation, turn-of-the-century family murderers defined humiliation in different ways than had earlier killers.

For other men, the cycle of lethal violence began when their wives criticized them for being poor providers, a charge that cut to the core of their identity as men. According to the killers, their spouses "taunted" and mocked them.[57] While many of these men were undoubtedly hypersensitive to perceived attacks on their manliness, some women did indeed impugn their spouses' masculinity. When Victor O'Shea failed his "law examinations," his wife, Amy, told him "she was disappointed in his ability and his success. He did not come up to her standard of a man." At his trial in 1904, his mother-in-law acknowledged that "her daughter had told O'Shea she was ashamed of him." "The young girl's ideas of a home," a journalist noted, "were naturally those of a girl situated as she was." O'Shea's attorney, Clarence Darrow, argued that his client's inability to support his wife properly "made him despondent and led to insanity."[58] Thirty-one-year-old wife killer Emmett Haywood "insisted he was doing his best," but his twenty-eight-year-old wife charged that her husband failed "to support her becomingly." In 1899, when Clara Haywood "threatened to get a divorce" unless Emmett secured suitable employment, the desperate man shot his wife and himself as their children watched.[59]

The Haywood homicide, in which a Chicago husband failed to provide "becomingly" for his family, his wife threatened to "disband" the household, and the man killed the woman when she refused to reconsider, embodied the characteristic elements of turn-of-the-century Chicago uxoricides. The proportion of jealousy-inspired wife killings fell over time, though jealousy remained the leading single trigger. Between 1875 and 1890, men's sexual jealousy generated over 43 percent of the city's uxoricides. By the 1890–1910 period, the proportion had slipped to 38 percent. The percentage of uxoricides that occurred during drunken binges dropped as well, dipping from 23 percent to under 9 percent. Lethal battles over women's refusal to reconcile, however, became an increasingly important spark, rising from 10 percent of wife killings in the earlier period to more than 27 percent in the turn-of-the-century era. Similarly, separation assumed a growing role in domestic violence. The proportion of couples who were living apart at the time of the homicide surged, from 34 percent in the 1875–1890 era to 42 percent in the 1890–1910 period and to 56 percent in the 1910–1920 span. In the majority of the uxoricides involving couples who had separated, the husband murdered his estranged wife when she refused to reconcile.[60]

For turn-of-the-century Chicago wife killers, the preservation of their marriage represented a central element of masculine respectability. Thus, the failure of the marriage signaled their failure as men, especially when financial problems precipitated the domestic crisis.[61] Occupational success and marital stability had become the twin pillars of masculine identity, and failure in one realm often contributed to failure in the other, producing despair and violence. In earlier periods, unsuccessful husbands might have simply deserted their wives and children or they might have measured their self-worth in other ways, such as their toughness. But the emerging standards for masculine behavior discouraged desertion and indifference.

In many cases of uxoricide, the wife had initiated the separation and divorce, thus usurping control over the marriage and overturning the long-established gender hierarchy.[62] At least a few wife killers explicitly refused to cede this power to their wives. In his 1899 suicide note, Henry Emde, a fifty-four-year-old German carpenter, explained, "I did not want to give in at all and let her have her way and make me leave the house."[63] More often, however, these violent husbands expressed desperation. Ironically, just as Chicago men, especially those at the lower edge of middle-class status, were making a greater emotional commitment within marriage, their wives were asserting greater independence and an increasing ability and willingness to dissolve unhappy and abusive relationships.[64]

Turn-of-the-century wife killers were determined to prevent their wives from ending the marriages and pleaded with the women to reconsider, in sharp contrast to the earlier cohort of wife killers, who bellowed rather than begged and crowed rather than cried. Husbands often blamed themselves for the collapse of their marriage and frequently offered frantic, desperate pledges to mend their ways, improve their "habits," stop drinking, or secure better jobs. Daniel McCarthy "promised not to drink anymore"; Henry Lenz guaranteed "good behavior" in the future if his thirty-two-year-old wife, Henrietta, would take him back. Joseph Montag, too, vowed to "behave myself and never drink any more." A fifty-seven-year-old German carpenter, Montag spent three hours begging his wife, Hannah, "to give me another chance and live with me again." He even tried to bribe Hannah, "telling her I would give her $75, nearly all I have in the world." When Lucille Lavelle threatened to leave her unemployed husband and "return to her mother," George Lavelle pleaded for a bit more time. "I can give you a home in three weeks," he promised, "so please wait before you go home." According to the witness to another uxoricide, John Baker sat on the lap of his wife, Augusta, and "began kissing her. 'Won't you come back to me, dearest?'" he begged. When she "shook her head," according to the witness, her husband produced a revolver and pulled the trigger.[65]

In many instances, multiple separations had preceded the homicides, and the men became violent when they failed in their latest attempt to persuade their wives to reconcile. In turn-of-the-century Chicago, women faced the greatest risk of being murdered by their husbands in the minutes, hours, and days immediately after they sep-

arated and refused to return to their spouses.[66] Henry and Henrietta
Lenz had separated seven times during their eight-year marriage.
The thirty-six-year-old German immigrant shot his wife when she
declined to take him back yet again. George Bickering shot his wife,
Lottie, after she refused to reconcile, also for a seventh time. According to an acquaintance, the thirty-five-year-old plumber had "kept
account on a calendar of every time his wife left him, and when he
could stand it no longer he killed her and himself." Women were often murdered just seconds after they rebuffed their husbands. A local
journalist, for example, described the discussion that occurred before Joseph Montag shot Hannah, his wife. "Speaking in German,"
the reporter noted, Montag "asked her if she would return and live
with him. In the same language she emphatically refused his request. Without another word Montag whipped out a revolver and
commenced firing." A similar conversation preceded the murder of
Catherine Arf on October 7, 1908. Moments before William Arf
shot the woman, bystanders heard him wail, "You won't, won't you?
Then I'll kill you."[67]

Far from displaying the self-assured manner of earlier Chicago
wife killers, turn-of-the-century murdering husbands typically affirmed their desperate love for their spouses, even as they slaughtered
them. To be sure, a minority of these men proclaimed that they hated
their wives. "This woman is and has been ten thousand times worse
than the vampires of fiction," noted one wife killer; another, surprised
at how his bleeding spouse clung to life, commented "she was a Tartar, dying as well as living." It is hardly unexpected that some wife
killers admitted that they despised the women they murdered. But
more surprising—and perhaps more revealing—most turn-of-the-
century wife killers insisted that they loved the partners that they had
shot and stabbed. "She left me three times and I tried to get her to
come back to me, for I loved her," Frank Kurtz told a newspaper reporter after he murdered his wife, Ella, in 1894. "I have always loved

her," sobbed Thomas Buckley, a forty-three-year-old blacksmith, after he shot his wife, Lizzie. "I loved her and I wanted to kill myself,"
another murderer lamented. "Cell [Celia] loves me and I love her," a
1901 wife killer recorded in a suicide note. With his seven-year-old
daughter watching, Stanislaus Stepenski, a thirty-nine-year-old Polish immigrant, shot his wife, "stooped and kissed the forehead of the
murdered woman," and then killed himself.[68]

Many of these Chicagoans maintained that they committed uxoricide because they felt devastated that their wives no longer loved
them, thus acknowledging a kind of emotional attachment and dependence rare in earlier periods. Joseph Swager killed his wife after
she revealed she "didn't like my companionship." Likewise, a thirty-
seven-year-old Italian immigrant explained that his wife, Caroline,
"told me this morning that she was done with me, that I was too old.
I couldn't stand it and I killed her." Charles Bauer "became morose"
and killed his wife because she "confessed to him that her affection
for him had died."[69] Lacing expressions of love with acts of lethal
brutality, turn-of-the-century wife killers were desperate, despondent, and overwhelmed with feelings of pain at least as much as feelings of anger.

Men who murdered their children were cut from the same cloth as
those who killed their wives, though the number of child killings was
smaller. Between 1875 and 1920, seventy-nine Chicago children died
at the hands of their fathers, with 94 percent of these homicides
occurring after 1895. Murdering fathers, like murdering husbands,
tended to be middle aged. The average age of the men who killed
their children was forty-one. Homicidal fathers were also concentrated at the upper tier of Chicago's working class; one-third held
skilled positions, many in the occupations undermined by large-scale
factory production. German immigrants were also overrepresented
among both wife killers and child killers: they comprised over a third
of murdering fathers between 1890 and 1910.[70]

The motivations of homicidal fathers echoed those of homicidal husbands. Many murdered their children because they believed themselves to have failed as providers, as fathers, and as men. In the weeks before he killed his daughter, for example, one German immigrant "would sit [for] hours at a time with the little girl on his lap, weeping because he had not been able to earn money to provide for her as he wished to." In other instances, murdering fathers reacted to the dissolution of their marriage by killing their children, insisting that they were "saving" sons and daughters from the pain and humiliation of broken homes—and from the women who had destroyed their home. In November 17, 1900, for example, Peter Johnson poisoned his five-year-old son out of "grief" and "sorrow over the breaking up of his home." Bitterness toward the women divorcing them infused expressions of love and concern for the children. William Meutsch, a forty-four-year-old "man of property," shot his three children in 1908, killing two of them. Meutsch maintained that "I loved the children, but thought it would be better to kill them rather than have them grow up the children of such a woman as their mother." Emil Stech offered the same explanation. After "my wife left me, taking all my furniture and children," he wrote in a suicide note, Stech opened the gas jets in the home and asphyxiated himself and his three children. "I love my children and wanted them, and could not see them raised in the care of my wife, and so I die and take the children with me." Similarly, fifty-seven-year-old Charles Rose insisted that he smothered to death his two-year-old daughter to protect the child from his wife. "I murdered my baby daughter because death was better for her than her mother's treatment," he explained. "I loved my little Beatrice and that's why I killed her."[71]

Just as the emotional burden of failing marriages triggered uxoricide in turn-of-the-century Chicago, these pressures contributed to an increase in fathers killing their children. The rate of child killing by men rose at the end of the nineteenth century and the beginning of the twentieth century. Furthermore, the proportion of child victims killed by men soared. Between 1890 and 1910 Chicago fathers killed twice as many children as Chicago mothers, whereas the mothers had killed twice as many children between 1875 and 1890.[72]

Most of the men who murdered their wives or their children attempted suicide.[73] The homicide-suicide rate remained relatively flat from the mid-1870s until the mid-1890s, but it nearly tripled during the late 1890s, coinciding with the decrease in brawl homicide, the decrease in rage uxoricides, and shifts in masculine ideals. Far from casually justifying their behavior or even boasting about it, turn-of-the-century family killers were despondent and suicidal.

For these Chicagoans, homicide and suicide represented a single act. The killers typically did not murder their loved ones and then attempt suicide out of guilt. Instead, the two acts of violence occurred together, both in time and in motivation. Suicide notes revealed the feelings of hopelessness and helplessness that triggered homicide-suicide.[74] Again and again, the killers explained that death—for their wives, for their children, and for themselves—was the only solution. "If we can't live in peace," Carl Nitz lamented in 1896, "we might as well die." In a 1901 suicide note, John J. Gillen wrote, "God help us, but we cannot live without each other." George Hewitt left a suicide note on his bed pillow that read "I, George Hewitt, do confess that I shot my wife during an argument. This is what happens when a husband is madly in love with his wife. I could not forget or live without her." William Artman contemplated suicide alone, but "then I thought, 'If I am going, you [his wife, Emma] will go too.'"[75] Although many of these men used suicide notes to offer—literally—the last word of explanation and to portray themselves as selfless victims of ill fortune or callous spouses, they did indeed kill their loved ones and themselves in a single act of violence.

Something more than unwavering love, despondence over the collapse of marriages, or even bitterness fueled the murders exploding in

turn-of-the-century Chicago kitchens, parlors, and bedrooms. Men
killed their wives and children in a desperate effort to regain control
of their families and their masculinity. Unable to secure middle-class
economic stability or the domestic harmony they sought, these middle-aged Chicagoans killed their wives and children rather than allowing their spouses to usurp control over them and over the fate of
the family. The violence resulted from a fierce defense of masculine
prerogative and searing emotional pain. Some men, in suicide notes,
comments to friends, or explanations to policemen, acknowledged
that they killed in order to maintain control and dominance, casting
the violence in explicitly proprietary terms.[76] Moments before he cut
his estranged wife's throat and slashed his own, thirty-year-old Frank
Eck told a bystander, "She is my wife. I have come for what belongs
to me." Similarly, in 1895 Charles Keil followed his wife to the home
of her relatives and announced, "I want my wife. I want my wife." He
repeated the demand to his brother-in-law: "she is my wife and I
want her back."[77]

   In committing the murders and murder-suicides, these men aimed
to gain permanent control over their spouses and their family lives.
Daniel McCarthy told an observer that his wife, Addie, "would either live with him or he would kill her." McCarthy later told the police, "I am glad that I shot her so that nobody else should get her." "If
I can't have you," William Grush was reported to have snarled to his
wife, "no one else shall." "You will never belong to another," Stephen
Ference explained just before he shot his wife and himself. According
to a local journalist, "with his last breath he [Ference] said: 'She won't
leave me. She will never belong to another. We will die together.'"[78]
One after another, turn-of-the-century wife murderers vowed to kill
their spouses rather than cede control of the marriages. "Well, if I
can't have you, nobody will," a 1908 killer shouted, while another wife
murderer told the police, "I was crazy about the woman. I made up
my mind to kill her if she wouldn't come back."[79] Likewise, Adolph

Ehrke said, "I shall never let her get the divorce because I love her too much," and Luigi Messori declared his love for his wife but added, "I'd rather see her dead than have her leave me."[80] Describing how her father murdered her mother, one young girl told the police, "Papa walked into the room. He looked white and trembled some when he asked mamma if she was going to get a divorce. When she told him yes he pulled out a pistol and then I and my sister ran."[81]

Turn-of-the-century family killers acted to prevent their wives from challenging their patriarchal authority. But the definition of patriarchal authority shifted during the late nineteenth and early twentieth centuries. Wife killers, for instance, less often resorted to violence to compel their spouses to cook, clean, or even to remain faithful; the proportion of uxoricides triggered by battles over these issues fell over time.[82] Instead, turn-of-the-century family killers shot, choked, stabbed, pounded, bludgeoned, and asphyxiated their wives and other loved ones in order to avoid losing control over their emotional world and to avoid feeling abandoned.[83] Whereas earlier cohorts of Chicago men employed violence to defend an ideal of masculinity grounded in physical exertion—controlling space, forcing peers to submit, and dictating specific actions, such as preparing meals—a later generation killed to maintain control over their private lives and to preserve, in death if necessary, their familial bonds.

In part, these changes in the triggers for domestic homicide reflected ongoing shifts in the definition of masculinity, as Chicago men embraced middle-class notions of companionate marriage, mutuality, personal happiness, and self-worth; but the actions and attitudes of Chicago women played a crucial role in the transformation as well. By the turn of the century they were becoming less submissive. Most early twentieth-century wife killers were separated from their spouses at the time of the violence—and their wives had, as a rule, initiated the separation.[84] Addie McCarthy, for example, left her husband because of his drinking and because he had "slapped her and kicked her, and that she could not stand it any longer. . . . It was time to quit," she concluded.[85] Domestic violence was not new, and in fact the proportion of wife killers who had abused their spouses fell over time.[86] But Chicago women became less willing to endure beatings, stay with men who failed to provide adequately for their families, or remain in unhappy marriages.[87] The women's ability and decision to seize control—to separate or seek a divorce—challenged men's identity in ways that sparked homicidal violence.

As women exercised relatively greater autonomy from their husbands, and as men became more emotionally dependent on their wives, uxoricide surged. In fact, rates of uxoricide and rates of divorce moved together during this period, highlighting men's increasing emotional investment in and violent defense of marriage. Between the late 1880s and the early 1910s, Chicago's uxoricide rate rose by 47 percent and its divorce rate rose by 46 percent.[88] One judge even termed Chicago "the Reno of the middle west," and local newspapers calculated that Cook County led the nation in divorces.[89] More important, women initiated nearly three-fourths of these divorces.[90]

Not only did Illinois's legal system expand women's access to mechanisms of marital dissolution, but local courts and social-welfare institutions offered Chicago women greater protection from abusive and unsupportive husbands and greater claims on marital assets.[91] Although late nineteenth-century judges remained reluctant to "invade the domestic forum, or go behind the curtain," Illinois courts explicitly rejected the notion that a husband had "license to correct" his wife "by personal or physical violence."[92] "To allow the husband to beat his wife into submission, or to correct her delinquencies, would be a return to the barbarisms of the old common law and make the wife the mere vassal or slave of the husband," the Illinois Court of Appeals held in 1888.[93] Local social-welfare institutions provided Chicago women with greater support as well. These institutions typically preferred to preserve families and thus to avoid interfering in domestic conflicts, yet they offered increasing protection for abused wives. In 1885, Chicago women's clubs created the Protective Agency for Women and Children to assist battered women, and in 1911 the Court of Domestic Relations was established with similar goals in mind.[94]

Such efforts proved inadequate. Whipsawed by conflicting cultural currents, the courts and social-welfare institutions did not safeguard women as much they signaled an increasing intolerance of brutish, irresponsible men.[95] More women turned to their parents and siblings for protection than to the courts, and Chicago uxoricides often occurred in the homes of the relatives who sheltered mistreated wives.

Regardless of the precise relationship among changing mores, shifting gender and marital ideals, and emerging Progressive-era institutional development, Chicago women believed that they were entitled to support and to proper "treatment" from their spouses, and they were increasingly willing to leave bad marriages. At the same time these women, in ballooning numbers, fell victim to men desperate to maintain failing unions and frantic to preserve the notions of masculine respectability that family life promised. For example, Frank A. Ethenstadt, a barber, slashed his wife's throat and his own on October 1, 1906, just thirty-five minutes before his wife was scheduled to meet with her attorney and sign a divorce petition.[96] Another wife killer asked his spouse "if she meant to persist in her previously expressed determination to secure a divorce." The woman replied, "Yes, I went down-town today and began proceedings." "Well," the husband retorted, "the case won't ever be tried," and shot her.[97]

As domestic homicide moved out of the world of plebeian culture and toward the margins of middle-class society, family killers embraced some of the behavioral and psychological norms of bourgeois Chicagoans even when they committed murder.[98] Uxoricide, for example, became less impulsive and more calculated. Rage killings fell precipitously; not only did fewer killers or observers use the word to describe the murderers' state of mind, but the behavior associated with rage killing waned as well. Family homicide became increasingly premeditated.

Many turn-of-the-century wife killers announced their intention to murder their spouses, telling friends and acquaintances of their plans. W. J. Meyer confided to the bartender at a local saloon that "he would put them all [his wife and in-laws] out of the way sometime." On the day he committed murder, Meyer finished his drink and remarked, "I am in a hurry to get back, for I've got some work to do." Daniel McCarthy revealed to an acquaintance "that there would be trouble soon," though "no attention was paid to what was considered an idle threat." Others had frequently told their wives they would kill them, though of course many such statements were idle threats uttered in the heat of arguments. Some wife killers, however, committed their threats to writing and sent their spouses letters detailing their murder plans. John Tomachesski, a thirty-eight-year-old German fireman, "sent his wife a letter, informing her he was going to kill her on Sunday."[99] Upon receiving the note, Frances Tomachesski went into hiding, foiling her husband's plan until Monday, when John found, shot, and killed her.

Although most threats were simply intended to frighten women into returning to their husbands, many wife killers planned their murders. Unlike earlier brawlers and rage killers, who committed murder with their hands, glasses, and bottles and who moved in circles in which guns abounded, middle-aged, middling-status wife murderers had to secure weapons for the task. Though 81 percent of estranged wife killers used firearms to kill their spouses, obtaining a revolver could be a daunting task for men who had left the rough-and-tumble world of plebeian society.[100] In 1896 Charles Nelson, a forty-three-year-old Swedish immigrant, worked feverishly to find a gun in order to kill Augusta, his wife of twelve years. Nelson approached a local bartender, Samuel Malineck, and inquired about borrowing a revolver. The bartender, however, proved to be uncooperative and asked Nelson why he needed the weapon. "I want to kill a mad dog," Nelson replied. "Why don't you go to the police and let them shoot it," Malineck suggested. "You will get into trouble if you fire off a revolver in your neighborhood," he added. Determined and increasingly exasperated, Nelson retorted, "I must go to work in a few minutes and I want to kill the dog before people get on the streets." Finally the bartender consented to the loan of the gun, if Nelson left a $2 security deposit. After giving Malineck the $2, Nelson took the gun, rushed home, and shot his wife. As neighbors heard the "sound of the shots" and crowded around the Nelson home, the killer "went straight to the saloon," returned the weapon, and collected his security deposit. More often, the process was simpler, but it still required planning. Like many wife killers, Joseph Regnet purchased a revolver specifically to murder his spouse. Fifty-year-old German-born Joseph Harworth pawned his wedding ring for $2.75 "and bought a cheap revolver" in order to shoot his wife, Bertha, on July 14, 1903, while Dwight Compton sold his horse in order to purchase a weapon. The Chicago policemen who arrived at the scene of uxoricides sometimes noted that the guns used in the murders were new and had never been fired before.[101]

For many of Chicago's murdering husbands, the precrime arrangements proved to be complex. Some killers put their financial affairs in order, often gathering insurance papers and property records.[102] Fritz Roessler visited a notary and revised his will on February 26, 1897. Roessler then causally mentioned to a beer delivery man, "Before you bring in the next keg, my wife and I will be dead." Moments later, the driver heard two shots. Fred Wagner, Peter Johnson, Emil Stech, and Samuel Jackson arranged for the care of their children. On the day before he murdered his wife, wounded his ten-year-

old daughter, Gladys, and his mother-in-law, and committed suicide, Harry L. Summers, accompanied by Gladys, visited an undertaker, John O'Brien. The forty-six-year-old nickel plater, whose wife,
Henrietta, had left him a week earlier, told O'Brien that the woman
was "in a hospital" and that Summers "would need me in a day or
two, as his wife could not live."[103] Other killers left suicide notes that
provided instructions for burial arrangements, for the distribution of
jewelry and other valuables, and for the repayment of loans.[104] Frank
Susanick, a forty-year-old Croatian carpenter who killed his wife and
four children, wrote to Michael Cuculich, "I leave you all my property, all my insurance and union money, if you can get it. I owe Nino
Susanic, my cousin, $20. Please pay it."[105] A perverse caricature of
middle-class behavioral norms, these men carefully planned the murders and even the funerals of their wives and children.

In such murders, the violence was instrumental rather than expressive; these husbands and fathers shot and stabbed to kill, not to injure, inflict suffering, or degrade their victims. Most often they shot
their loved ones, but when they stabbed their wives, turn-of-the-
century killers slashed their victims' throats. Between 1875 and 1890,
43 percent of knife-wielding wife killers stabbed their partners in the
breast and an equal proportion slit their wives' throats. Between 1890
and 1910, the focus of knife attacks on wives changed, with over
68 percent directed at the throat and less than 5 percent at the breast.
In addition, although many wife killers felt that their behavior was
"necessary," few turn-of-the-century murdering husbands argued
that their violent actions were proper or justified, as earlier wife killers had claimed. The new generation of killers tended to be purposeful in a very different way than earlier generations of wife killers.
Turn-of-the-century murdering husbands rarely claimed that they
killed while "disciplining" their spouses. Nor did they mutilate their
wives as often as men had earlier done. Instead, their intention was to
kill and thereby regain emotional control. William Robbel, for exam-

ple, believed that homicide-suicide offered "the only sure way he knew out of his domestic troubles." After Helen, his wife, left him, Robbel planned an ambush and a suicide. He waited for Helen just outside the credit office of Montgomery Ward, where she worked. When she passed near him, Robbel shot her three times, "snatched a bottle of poison from his pocket, swallowed its contents at a gulp and fired three bullets into his body."[106]

Through the start of the new century, violence remained a core component of masculine—particularly working-class masculine—identity in Chicago. As in the 1870s and the 1880s, turn-of-the-century men killed to affirm, defend, and protect their authority and prerogatives as men. But definitions of masculinity shifted during this period, albeit in halting, incomplete ways, and this shift contributed to changes in both the level and the character of domestic homicide. Violence, and especially family homicide, underwent seemingly paradoxical transformations. Chicago became more violent as it became more orderly, and men murdered their wives and children in skyrocketing numbers even as they became more emotionally committed to family life. In addition, murdering husbands and fathers became older, wealthier, less drunken, and less volatile, though they killed their loved ones at soaring rates.

A collision of social, demographic, and cultural forces generated the explosion in family homicide in turn-of-the-century Chicago. Pounded by economic and demographic forces on the one hand and trapped between conflicting value systems on the other, a cohort of Chicago men killed their wives and children at record levels. Just as more Chicagoans sought emotional fulfillment from family life, more husbands and fathers felt unable to meet these expectations, at least judging by the rate of murders in the home.

Both culturally and economically, family-killing men lived at the cusp of middle-class society. Unlike their fathers, these men insisted that they coveted masculine domesticity and abiding emotional bonds with their wives. Yet they had come of age in a world in which men were expected to rule and women were supposed to submit, obey, and defer. Conflicting notions of sentimentality and coercion, mutuality and hierarchy, emotional interdependence and patriarchal dominance suffused the private battles leading to domestic homicide in turn-of-the-century Chicago.[107] Wife killers insisted that they desired the emotional bonds promised by middle-class norms, but they reacted to challenges in the ways of their youth; to affirm their love or to safeguard the bonds of familial affection, they murdered loved ones. If notions of love, affection, and companionate marriage, bolstered by demographic changes, brought middle-class domestic ideals within the reach of many working-class Chicagoans, these dreams remained elusive.

Changes in women's expectations of marriage also unfolded in incomprehensible ways, at least for the Chicago husbands and fathers who murdered their loved ones. While men increasingly defined status in familial terms, women began to exercise greater independence and autonomy. Both men and women had rising expectations for emotional fulfillment from marriage, but they defined these expectations in different, even opposite, ways. For husbands, domestic stability became a core element of masculine respectability; they affirmed their unconditional love for their spouses but seemed more desperate to preserve family stability than to establish egalitarian unions. For women, rising expectations produced an increasing willingness to escape abusive, miserable marriages; the women who were murdered in turn-of-century Chicago typically found their domestic lives wanting—and died trying to escape unhappy marriages. Gender-specific understandings of companionate marriage and emotional satisfaction clashed, boosting the city's uxoricide rate.

While Chicago family killers were caught between middle-class and working-class notions of masculinity and between men's and

women's definitions of domestic harmony, they were also tugged between middle-class economic aspirations and working-class realities in the age of industry.[108] Many wife and child killers struggled
to establish homes, purchase property, and support their families
"properly."[109] But industrialization, particularly the de-skilling process, eroded the economic status of these men. Thus, family killers
were clustered in the upper tier of Chicago's working class, closer to
suburban life than to saloon life. Just as their cultural aspirations became focused on middle-class domestic ideals, their economic for-
tunes became more tenuous. Their expectations rose while their economic standing became more unstable. Furthermore, these men's
emotional burden of providing (or for failing to provide) was rising as
well, both in their own minds and in the minds of their spouses. The
mismatch between expectations and realities, the jarring shift in demographic conditions, and the uneven pace of economic development combined to tear apart families in Chicago during this period.[110]

The words of turn-of-the-century wife killers and child killers reflected these cross-cutting values, aspirations, and realities. Unlike
earlier cohorts of wife killers, turn-of-the-century murdering husbands expressed their love for the victims and their desire to kill and
die rather than endure the emotional pain of separation and divorce.
To be sure, many of these men saw no contradiction between loving
their wives and beating them or between reconciling to preserve the
marital bond and committing murder to prevent divorce. Moreover,
assertions of control and ownership often appeared alongside expressions of affection and devotion. Even if their suicide notes, confes-
sions, and court testimonies were riddled with contradictions, turn-
of-the-century family killers maintained that they acted out of love
and a desire to save the family, in stark contrast to Gilded Age killers,
who defiantly beat and stabbed their spouses, rarely expressed love
or remorse, and demanded deference and obedience. In short, the

language and sentiments of companionate marriage and masculine domesticity filled suicide notes, deathbed declarations, court transcripts, and interviews with police investigators and crime-beat reporters.[111]

The actions of turn-of-the-century family killers also revealed conflicting cultural pressures. The sequence of events leading up to the violence, the particular methods employed to kill, and the actions of the killers after the act indicate an increasing embrace of middle-class values and domestic masculinity, though traces of working-class behavioral norms persisted.[112] By the 1890s battles over the emotional, financial, and legal survival of the marriage, rather than skirmishes over cooking, charges of infidelity, or drunken rages, usually preceded domestic violence; and calculated, premeditated killings took the place of the impulsive, rage beatings of an earlier era, with precise shots to the face and body replacing frantic stabs to the breast. In planning murder, turn-of-the-century men demonstrated a complex blend of middle-class perspectives. Their despondence and their purposeful demeanor were closer to middle-class norms than to the raging, volatile, swaggering conduct of their plebeian, bachelor past. Likewise, their behavior after they slaughtered family members reflected the manners of the parlor at least as much as the code of the saloon. Both the suicide notes and the suicides of turn-of-the-century killers stand in clear contrast to the self-satisfied or nonchalant shrugs and casual justifications of earlier wife killers.

These shifts in the level and the nature of family violence were ironic, for three reasons. First, at least according to the killers themselves, they murdered out of love. Though hardly a paragon of middle-class comportment, Joseph Swager stood apart from earlier wife killers when he wept, "I loved my wife so I killed her," just as other murderers differed from their predecessors when they begged and pleaded with their wives to preserve their families.[113] Second, complex pressures for conformity to middle-class norms contributed to the turn-of-the-century explosion of domestic homicide. As local streets and bars became more orderly, Chicago homes became more violent, and local husbands and fathers became less volatile but more murderous. And third, the increasing embrace of ideals of companionate marriage, as well as the rising rate of wife killing, coincided with a surge in domestic homicide by women.

Chapter 3

"He Got
What He Deserved"

On Saturday, April 8, 1905, Emma Nolan shot and killed her husband, a twenty-eight-year-old agent for a sewing machine company. Barney Nolan had earned a good living, but he had long squandered his salary and his evenings "carousing in saloons" and had failed to support his growing family, forcing Emma to work as a "scrubwoman" and to operate a boarding house. He had also beaten, kicked, and threatened to kill her. "Since our marriage," she lamented, "my life has been a burden." "Finally, when I could stand it no longer, we separated," Emma told the police officers who investigated the shooting. "I would have nothing more to do with him." Emma had looked to the legal system for protection and assistance, filing an arrest warrant in response to the beatings and the threats and securing a court order for child support. Although Barney had abused his wife and had failed to provide for his three young children, he sought a reconciliation and "pleaded with her repeatedly to return and live with him." On the evening of April 8, according to Emma, Barney "broke open the door of my flat" and demanded a reconciliation. She refused, and, like many rejected husbands in turn-of-the-century Chicago, he became violent. Brandishing a carving knife, Barney slashed at his wife, who ran to a closet, found the revolver she had stashed there, and "pulled the trigger as fast as I could." Minutes later the police arrived, and Emma, believing her bleeding, badly injured husband would somehow survive the shooting, declared that "I am only sorry that I did not succeed in killing him. He is a despicable character, better dead than alive." Calm and composed, she explained to police investigators "why she put five bullets into her husband." "A husband is all right when he is willing to support you," she noted, "but mine was not of that sort, and I don't care to have a man who is merely an ornament." Upon learning that her husband had died from the gunshot wounds, Emma announced, "He got what he deserved."[1] Barney Nolan was Chicago's forty-fourth homicide victim of 1905.[2]

Thirteen other women in Chicago committed homicide in 1905, and six of them also killed their husbands. Never before in the city's history had local women been so violent, and thus Emma Nolan's actions typified a growing trend in Chicagoans' gender relations and in the city's violence. Emma had been unwilling to endure a miserable marriage, had refused to submit to abusive treatment, had initiated a separation, had looked to the courts for protection, and had rejected her spouse's increasingly desperate, threat-laced pleas for a reconciliation. In the end, she employed lethal violence to defend herself against her husband.

Perhaps most unsettling to Chicagoans, Emma Nolan, like most other homicidal women in the city, did not conform to the prevailing, "scientific" portrait of a female criminal. Far from being the moral degenerate, the mental defective, or the masculinized deviant described by the leading eugenicists, criminologists, and alienists of the era, Nolan appeared to be a hardworking, respectable woman who embraced mainstream values and who in fact seemed to kill in defense of middle-class behavioral ideals.[3] Homicidal wives and mothers of the early twentieth century lived—and killed—within the boundaries of proper society.

Such violence occurred at the same time that the status of Chicago women was improving, at least relative to previous decades. To be sure, local women remained disproportionately mired in poverty and dependent on their fathers, brothers, or husbands, and each year thousands became ensnared in the city's sex trades.[4] Misogyny also continued to infect the legal system and to contaminate Chicago's social and cultural institutions. Nonetheless, women's access to jobs, political and cultural influence, and levels of legal protection were all increasing in early twentieth-century Chicago. Even their employment prospects in the traditionally male domain of local slaughterhouses improved, with some securing jobs in the "gut-pulling departments" of the city's packing plants.[5] Far more impressive, however, was women's rapid entry into Chicago's white-collar labor force. The number of women working in clerical positions in the city skyrocketed, rising from 8,624 in 1890 to 96,963 in 1920, a 1,024 percent increase.[6] Among bookkeepers and accountants the rate of increase exceeded 800 percent, and among stenographers and typists it topped 2,000 percent.[7] By the late 1910s, women comprised the majority of Chicago's clerical workforce.[8] Store clerks, saleswomen, bookkeepers, and typists were not handsomely paid, though these positions offered women higher wages, more secure employment, and better working conditions than most other sectors of the local labor market.[9]

A smaller group of Chicago women commanded influence at the highest circles of local society during this era. Jane Addams, Florence Kelley, and Julia Lathrop occupied central positions in a wide range of policy debates, and the leaders of Chicago's elite women's clubs participated in nearly every aspect of municipal reform, ranging from beautification campaigns to housing, health, and zoning regulation. Louise de Koven Bowen, for example, served as the president of the

Chicago Women's Club, the president of the Juvenile Protective Association, the president of the Chicago Equal Suffrage Association, and the treasurer of Hull-House, and she led local efforts to restrict the sale of alcohol, to regulate the labor of children, to create a juvenile justice system, to mobilize women in preparation for U.S. participation in the Great War, to investigate racial discrimination in the city, to increase the wages paid to local women in clerical positions, and to promote women's suffrage and political participation.[10] The first cohort of women receiving doctorates from the University of Chicago, including Edith Abbott and Frances Kellor, became prominent policy makers and social activists at the start of the twentieth century and established the institution's prestigious School of Social Service Administration, which quickly became a pillar of the Progressive movement.[11]

Chicago's legal system also became more responsive to the needs of women. For the first time, basic legal assumptions about personal safety and corporate liability, for instance, reflected the participation of women in public life.[12] Local women gained legal remedies against unsupportive husbands, secured greater access to marital resources, and gradually received some legal protection against abusive spouses, as local policy makers and reformers created new layers of the court system to address the needs of wives and children, such as the Court of Domestic Relations and the pioneering Juvenile Court.[13] Although these emerging ideas and institutions retained paternalistic elements, they also provided support and protection for Chicago women.

Just as increasing public order did not reduce men's violence, neither the decrease in disorderly behavior nor improvements in the status of women reduced women's violence during the early decades of the twentieth century. Instead, the level of homicidal violence among Chicago women mushroomed between 1875 and 1920. Women's homicide rate, for example, rose by more than 420 percent between the late 1870s and 1920, far outpacing the overall increase in Chicago violence.[14]

The meteoric increase in women's violence was closely related to the surge of men's violence, especially the rise in uxoricide. Lethal violence by women tracked male-on-female homicide. Cultural pressures, particularly rising and failed expectations for family life, triggered women's violence, just as these forces fueled men's violence. The upturn in wife killing during this period also produced a deadly backlash, as an explosion of husband killing echoed the turn-of-the-century spike in wife killing. Moreover, women's attitudes toward violence changed at the start of the twentieth century. Not only did Chicago women become more homicidal, but they also insisted that they were justified in doing so. In short, shifting assumptions about marriage, respectability, and the "proper use" of a wife sparked a sharp increase in homicide by women.

On August 2, 1920, seventy-eight-year-old William Hubbard became a victim both of the rising tide of violence by women and of this echo effect. At the precise moment when Hubbard stepped into a busy Chicago thoroughfare, Clarence McField chased his wife out of their home, pursued her into the street, and hurled a brick at her. After initially attempting to flee, Jeanette McField stopped, drew a gun, turned toward her husband, pointed the weapon in his direction, and fired repeatedly. At least one of the bullets hit its mark, instantly killing the attacking man. Another bullet, however, grazed Hubbard's scalp. A police officer at the scene of the shooting rushed to the elderly man's aid. Hubbard "bewailed" that he had served in two wars and "had never received a scratch, but 'in his old age [he] had to be shot on State street and by a woman.'"[15]

Chicago women committed 326 homicides between 1875 and 1920, nearly four-fifths of which occurred after the turn of the century (see Figure 4, page 90).[16] Local women committed more homicides

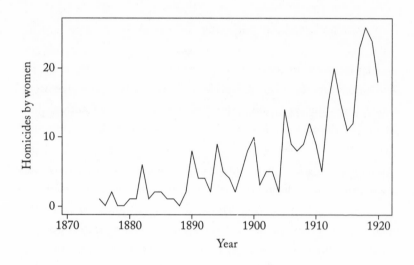

FIGURE 4   *Homicides by women (source: see Appendix)*

in 1918 and 1919 than they had during the twenty years from 1875 through 1894. Two and a half times more Chicagoans died at the hands of local women than were killed in labor violence, despite the city's reputation for bloody strikes and radicalism. Chicago police-men, who were quick to use their service revolvers and still quicker to use their batons, killed fewer victims than homicidal women did between 1875 and 1920. This impressive body count notwithstanding, violence remained a man's activity; local women committed only 6.6 percent of Chicago homicides.

The rate of women's violence in Chicago surged during this pe-riod. The homicide rate for women more than quintupled between the late 1870s and 1920.[17] During the years 1875–1900, women com-mitted 5.2 percent of the city's homicides. By the 1910–1920 period, the figure had risen to 7.3 percent, an increase of 40 percent, though the gap between men's and women's violence remained wide.

Gender roles shaped women's violence in industrial Chicago. Al-though rates of homicide by both men and women rose rapidly dur-

ing the early twentieth century, and although both reflected broader
social, cultural, and demographic currents, women committed lethal
violence in gender-specific ways. For example, even while wife killing
increased in the city, over four-fifths of homicidal men targeted other
men. Chicago women, however, typically crossed sex lines when they
killed. Only 12 percent of the victims of homicidal women were other
women, even though these killers spent much of their time—both
leisure time and work time—with women. Two-thirds of homicidal
women killed men, and children comprised the remaining victims.
Also, despite the increasing participation of women in the workforce,
women's violence in Chicago remained bound up with family life.
Relatives and lovers accounted for nearly 80 percent of women's victims, compared with 27 percent of men's victims, and the figure for
women fluctuated little over time.[18] Put differently, women engaged
in homicidal behavior at one-fifteenth the rate of men, but when
they resorted to violence, they overwhelmingly killed relatives or
suitors. In Chicago between 1875 and 1920, men killed a greater number of loved ones than women, committing 3.8 times as many spousal
homicides and 3.4 times as many (nonspousal) relative homicides,
and killing 7.4 times as many lovers as women. But when women engaged in homicidal behavior, they were 3.5 times more likely than
men to kill a spouse, 3.8 times more likely to kill a (nonspousal) relative, and 1.8 times more likely to kill a lover. Reflecting the same pattern, 77 percent of the homicides committed by women occurred in
the home, compared with 28 percent of those committed by men.

Although the city's homicidal women killed loved ones and disproportionately killed in the home, their violence assumed many
different forms, depending on the relationship of the participants.
Moreover, the level of deadly behavior increased as cultural pressures
mounted. In nearly all cases, the homicides emerged from deep emotional attachments, but the violence directed against husbands, not
surprisingly, differed significantly from that directed against children

or other loved ones. Most of the killings by women appear to have been premeditated. Women typically bought or borrowed weapons and made postmurder arrangements; some even anticipated the arguments that they would offer to policemen, judges, and juries. But the weapons, plans, and explanations depended on the victim. Louise Dimick's preparation for the 1920 murder of her husband proved to be particularly meticulous. Fearing that her nineteen-year-old spouse would leave her, the thirty-five-year-old accountant worked long and hard to ready herself for the murder of Thomas Schweig. She purchased a revolver and spent hours improving her aim: for a month before she killed her spouse, Dimick practiced shooting in a vacant lot adjacent to her rooming house, using "one of Schweig's discarded derby hats as a target."[19]

Chicago women killed sixty-seven (non-newborn) children between 1875 and 1920; these murders accounted for over 20 percent of their homicides. In 97 percent of these deaths, a mother killed her child, making child killing the second largest category of homicide by women, trailing only husband killing. While Chicago men killed nearly fourteen friends and acquaintances for every son or daughter they killed, local women murdered two children for every friend or acquaintance they killed. The rate of mother-on-child homicide also increased after 1900, and it followed the same trajectory and occurred at the same rate as father-on-child homicide, as Figure 5 indicates. Nearly 91 percent of the children murdered by women between 1875 and 1920 were killed after 1900, reflecting the social and cultural pressures that strained early twentieth-century family life.

The Chicago mothers who murdered their non-newborn children were neither social outcasts nor poor women living at the fringes of society. Their circumstances had little in common with the women who committed infanticide. In the overwhelming majority of cases, those who killed their newborn children were either desperately poor

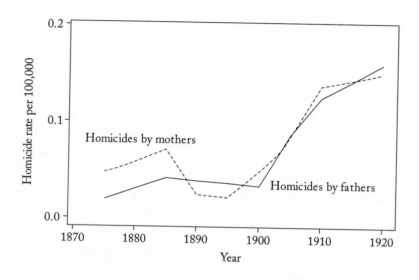

FIGURE 5   *Homicides of children (smoothed, five-year averages; source:*
see Appendix; LOWESS technique used for smoothing)

women who murdered infants they felt themselves unable to support or single women who had been abandoned by the men who fathered the children.[20] Law enforcers usually ignored infanticides, though the killers were identified in a small proportion of these homicides, providing fragmentary evidence about this crime.[21] The average wo- man who committed infanticide was slightly under twenty-eight; three-fourths were under thirty. By comparison, mothers who killed non-newborn children averaged thirty-three years of age; nearly three-fourths were over thirty.[22] In short, very young women strug- gling with the new pressures of parenthood rarely committed filicide (child killing).

Mothers who murdered their non-newborn children, like fathers who murdered their children, were seldom poor. Instead, they came from the middle of Chicago society. Nearly one-third of child- murdering mothers hailed from households headed by a skilled worker, an additional 13 percent were from white-collar households, and only 14 percent came from families headed by an unskilled worker. By contrast, half of the women linked to infanticides were from households headed by unskilled workers. Neither very young nor very poor, mothers who committed filicide were not attempting to marshal scarce family resources for other children.[23] In demographic and socioeconomic terms, these murdering mothers differed from those who committed infanticide but were very similar to fathers who killed their children.

Although mothers and fathers who committed filicide were drawn from the same slices of the Chicago population, they killed their sons and daughters for different reasons and under different circumstances. Broader social and cultural forces shaped patterns of child murder and accounted for the nearly indistinguishable graphs plotted in Figure 5, but the violence unfolded in gender-specific ways. Women, for example, killed younger children than men did. Over 63 percent of the victims of murdering mothers were four years old or under, and the average victim was slightly under five. By contrast, 39 percent of the victims of murdering fathers were four or under, and the average victim was seven years old. Furthermore, homicidal women rarely murdered their entire families; 39 percent killed one child, and 31 percent killed three or more children. Men more often murdered all of their children; 28 percent killed one child, but 57 percent murdered three or more children. Depressed and despondent men, in short, saw no hope for their families and often killed every member of the household, while homicidal women were more selective.

Mothers also killed their children for different reasons than did fathers. Both fathers and mothers typically explained their behavior in copious detail; seldom was filicide a rash or impulsive act. A few women killed out of anger or vengeance, most often murdering stepchildren. Mary Kamis, for example, developed "an insane aversion to her stepson," which led the woman to kill the seven-year-old boy in 1917.[24] But such homicides were rare in turn-of-the-century Chicago, particularly given the spate of stories, fairy tales, and legends of evil stepmothers that fill western literature. Few Chicago women killed their stepchildren or killed in anger or out of revenge.[25]

More often, illness triggered women's child killing. While fathers usually killed their children in response to financial setbacks or failing marriages, mothers killed in response to health crises. Many Chicago women who were guilty of filicide murdered sick children, hoping to spare beloved sons and daughters from years of suffering. Wenzel Bertat, a German immigrant, believed that her one-year-old daughter's health was "so impaired that play with other children would be denied" and feared that the girl would never lead an active, joyful life. "I heard the children playing in the snow outside," Bertat explained, "and looked at my child lying asleep on the couch. For several hours I watched her and she did not stir, so I took out my husband's revolver . . ." Likewise, on October 24, 1917, Catherine Nicholl asphyxiated her children because she was despondent over her son's "incurable disease."[26]

In other cases, the mothers' own illness triggered the filicide. These women resorted to murder out of concern that they would be unable to provide adequate care for their children. "I fear that I am not going to be strong enough properly to care for David," forty-one-year-old Sarah Engelberg explained just before drowning her young son in the bathtub. Despondent over a ten-year battle with tuberculosis, twenty-five-year-old Esther Peterson reached a similar conclusion and asphyxiated her four-year-old son, Vernon. Augusta Klem left a suicide note in which she wrote, "I did this because I am always sick." She added, "I don't want Olga to suffer and I take her with me." Plagued by "ill health" for a year, Antoinette Sitasz locked all of the doors and windows in her home, opened the gas jets, and asphyxiated herself and her four children. According to her husband, the woman was "determined to end the struggle, not only for herself, but for her children, who would otherwise be motherless." In some cases, both the mother and the child suffered from illness. Thirty-three-year-old Agnes Fiala was said to have been "despondent because of ill health, coupled with sensitiveness owing to a deformity to her one year and a half old daughter." Fiala held her daughter, Adeline, in her arms, opened the gas jets, and "cradled" the child until both were dead.[27]

Clearly, many of these women suffered from mental illness, and relatives and friends typically attributed the homicides to "despondence," "melancholy," "nervous troubles," or other afflictions that probably suggested clinical depression.[28] "I think I am crazy," thirty-eight-year-old Myra Conkling wrote to her sister shortly before killing her seven-year-old son. "I realize what a big disappointment I have been to all my friends, my family, and myself, too," Sarah Engelberg penned in her suicide note. Some filicides occurred within months of the birth of the victim, and thus postpartum depression likely played a role in these homicides; again and again in such cases husbands would say that "since the birth of the baby" their wives had been "ill and despondent."[29]

Between 1875 and 1920, 84 percent of murdering mothers in Chicago attempted suicide.[30] These women often left suicide notes in which they insisted that they committed the homicide-suicide as an act of maternal love. Anna Heubraum's suicide note explained, "I knew I had to die, and I loved the children, but I thought it best to take them with me." Similarly, thirty-five-year-old Elizabeth Florin feared that her young daughter, who had "accidentally inhaled gas," would be "unhealthy," so the mother picked up her daughter and, holding her tightly, jumped out of a fifth-story window.[31]

These acts of maternal love, murder, and self-destruction were usually premeditated and carefully planned. Some women bought the gas that they used in the crime. "The purchase of a five-gallon can of kerosene in the morning," a Chicago policeman investigating one homicide-suicide observed, indicated that "the affair was premeditated, as the family uses coal for fuel."[32] Other women sent their children—later to be the victims—out of the house while the mothers composed their suicide note and made the other arrangements.[33] Many mothers who committed homicide-suicide used the hours before their crime to complete, with meticulous care, their final maternal tasks. Some sewed funeral shrouds and bathed and dressed their young children in preparation for their death.[34] Augusta Klem "tidied her home, washed and dressed the baby, and put on her wedding dress" before killing herself and her eighteen-month-old daughter. In her suicide note, Klem told her husband, "You don't have to dress us. Bury us as we are." According to a newspaper reporter, Klem also "laid out the dress clothes of her husband, apparently to have all in readiness for the funeral."[35] Other women put their household in order, leaving precise instructions for the undertaker as well as instructions for the repayment of loans and the distribution of cherished possessions.[36]

Both in the violence itself and in the preparations for the violence, the women in Chicago who killed their children insisted that they were fulfilling their role as loving mothers, who were desperate to protect their children from pain-filled futures.[37] They killed their children in loving ways, eschewing bloody or painful methods. Over three-fourths of murdering mothers asphyxiated their children. According to one newspaper account, for example, thirty-five-year-old Mrs. R. C. Davison "spent all but her last cent to purchase a white suit for her baby's funeral; then took her child upon her knee and rocked him to sleep while two gas jets, opened wide, slowly asphyxiated them."[38] Many women cradled and hugged their children until everyone in the room lost consciousness. Murdering mothers, in fact, relied on gas at twice the proportion as murdering fathers and relied on firearms one-fifth as often. Nor did these women confuse their roles as mothers with their roles as wives. Frantic to escape hopeless situations and to find peace for their sons and daughters and for

themselves, the women who murdered their children in early twentieth-century Chicago did not kill their husbands, even though the
leaking gas that asphyxiated the women and their children could easily have claimed the lives of sleeping husbands as well.[39] Instead,
Chicago's murdering mothers typically opened gas jets at a time
when their husbands were away from home or in closed rooms, often
bathrooms, far from their slumbering spouses.[40] Chicago's murdering
fathers, in contrast, sometimes killed their entire families, including
their wives.[41]

The increasing weight of the cultural pressure for domestic stability and happiness fueled the rising rate of child murder during the
opening decades of the twentieth century.[42] One murdering mother,
for example, killed her child because she felt herself to be losing the
"struggle to give her babies a better home."[43] But Chicago men and
Chicago women defined the struggle for a "better home" in different
ways. Like the men who killed their loved ones in this period, the
women who murdered their children pursued middle-class ideals of
family life and seemed to be haunted by their inability to provide stable, loving, secure homes. Chicago's homicidal fathers believed they
had been unable to fulfill their roles as breadwinners who could support a respectable family. For murdering mothers, the failed dream
was grounded in middle-class notions of the family as a safe haven
for children.[44] When mothers could not protect their children from
harm, some of these women blamed themselves and sacrificed their
children in order to save them from pain and suffering. Homicidal
mothers may have spared the lives of older and hardier children because these offspring seemed better able to survive on their own.[45]

The background of murdering mothers suggest the looming influence of middle-class family ideals. Even though poor Chicagoans
struggled to provide for their children, faced horrific levels of infant
and child mortality, and died from disease at enormous rates, these
residents seldom killed non-newborn sons and daughters. By contrast, child killers were clustered at the lower edge of middle-class so-

cial status, and hence the social and cultural pressures that buffeted these residents played a role in the killing. Murdering mothers' focus on future pain also reflected a middle-class worldview—as opposed to the more fatalistic, presentist orientation that poorer residents tended to have. Fragmentary evidence regarding ethnicity suggests the influence of middle-class values as well. German Chicagoans were significantly overrepresented among murdering mothers, comprising at least 15 percent of the killers.[46] These residents were clustered in the middle ranks of local society. In short, murdering mothers, like murdering fathers, typically came from a lower-middle-class background and killed their sons and daughters when the pressure to establish a safe, stable, and harmonious family life became overwhelming.

Chicago women killed their husbands more often than they killed their children or any other group. Between 1875 and 1920, 103 local men died at the hands of their wives, accounting for approximately one-third of all homicides by women. This figure was triple the number of lovers or acquaintances killed by women in the city and nearly nine times the number of strangers killed by Chicago women. The husband-killing homicide rate also rose sharply. During the late 1870s no local women killed their husbands, but beginning on December 17, 1881, when Alice Brady shot her thirty-five-year-old spouse in a Chicago saloon, the rate of husband killing began to climb. Between the early 1880s and 1920, the husband-killing rate nearly quadrupled.[47]

Husband killing and wife killing followed roughly parallel trajectories. Many of the social, demographic, and especially cultural tensions that contributed to wife killing also fueled husband killing during the late nineteenth and the early twentieth centuries. Comparable groups of Chicagoans were involved in these domestic homicides, and the pressures that contributed to them were similar.[48]

Like their wife-killing counterparts (and like murdering mothers), the Chicago women who killed their husbands were drawn from the middle layers of the population, making them considerably wealthier than most of the city's homicidal residents. Only one husband killer in three came from a household headed by an unskilled worker, and nearly as many murdering wives came from households headed by semiskilled workers. Moreover, 23 percent came from white-collar households. Although husband killers had slightly higher socioeconomic backgrounds than wife killers, in both instances poverty was not related to the violence.

Murdering wives were also relatively older than most Chicago killers. The average age for these women was between thirty-three and thirty-four.[49] Sixty percent were over thirty, and nearly one-quarter were over forty. The husbands who killed their wives during this era were, on average, about four years older than the wives who killed their husbands, reflecting the prevailing practice of men marrying slightly younger women.[50] Thus, even more than the local women who killed their children, those who killed their husbands were not struggling with the pressures of recent marriage, and just as poverty did not spark husband killing, youthful rashness did not produce this violence.[51]

Chicago's husband killers typically explained their motives in unequivocal terms. They killed out of desperation, though they defined desperation in different terms than wife killers or child killers did. Unlike wife killers, husband killers rarely resorted to violence to prevent separation or divorce or because of falling or insecure socioeconomic status; and unlike murdering mothers, illness did not trigger husband killing.

Simply put, Chicago wives killed to protect themselves. Nearly 60 percent of the local women who killed their spouses acted in self-defense; jealousy, the second leading motivator, sparked only 14 percent of husband killings.[52] Between 1890 and 1910, as the rate of uxoricide surged, 68 percent of husband killers acted in self-defense, and the figure remained over 51 percent during the 1910s. In most cases, the homicide followed months or years of physical abuse and threats.[53] Joseph Camilla was a typical victim in turn-of-the-century Chicago. Mary Camilla, an Irish immigrant, told the police a familiar story, explaining that she shot her husband, a fifty-year-old Italian immigrant, in "self-defense." "He threatened my life and whipped me time and again. Last night when he came home I saw that he had been drinking. As soon as he entered the house he began to curse me and threaten to kill me. I did all I could to quiet him," the forty-year-old woman said. "I loved Joe, but I had to shoot him in self-defense." Similarly, Grace Doyle informed police investigators that she shot her husband, Timothy, "in self-defense" because "he has abused me for three years, and I'm all marked up with cuts and bruises he gave me." "I can show knife-wounds inflicted in [sic] my breast," she said. Mary Frank explained, "I only acted in self-defense," as her forty-five-year-old, drunken husband "would surely have killed me had he not received the fatal wounds." "I shot him; I shot him," Mary McDonald admitted. "If I hadn't he would have killed me and his children." Another woman shot her husband in 1912 after he announced, "It is a good time for you to die," and approached her with a razor in his hand. Again and again, husband killers recounted years of physical abuse, repeated episodes in which neighbors interceded to stop beatings, and even cases in which battered wives had reported the violence to the local police and filed assault charges.[54]

Many Chicago women killed their husbands in response to immediate threats to their lives, but others acted to prevent future battering.[55] Grace Doyle defined her action as "self-defense in advance": "If I had not put an end to him this morning, he would have killed me to-morrow." Annie Olsen killed her forty-six-year-old husband on February 8, 1904, after years of threats. "I was so frightened," she later explained, "for he said many times he would cut me up and boil me into potash. He made the threat so often I grew to believe that some day he meant to carry it out." On the night of the homicide, August Olsen, already drunk, repeated the threat. "So when he was asleep," Annie Olsen told the police, "I shot him."[56]

A cycle of escalating frustration, desperation, and violence linked husband killing and wife killing in late nineteenth- and early twentieth-century Chicago. Increasingly unbearable social and cultural pressures contributed to rising levels of uxoricide during this era, and these forces also fueled the soaring rates of husband killing. Feeling helpless and despondent, embittered men attacked their wives in growing numbers during this period, and Chicago women employed greater violence in order to protect themselves.

Early twentieth-century Chicago women shot their abusive husbands only after exhausting other options. Many battered wives sought protection from the police and the courts, as the legal system made greater efforts to discourage domestic violence. At least in the cases that ended in homicide, this strategy failed. Emma Nolan secured a warrant for the arrest of her husband, Barney, after he had thrashed and threatened her, but the police were unable to find him—until he attacked his wife one last time and she killed him.[57] For many women, slow, cumbersome, ineffective legal remedies precipitated the husband killing, as angry men sought to punish the women who had caused their arrest, who had embarrassed them in front of their neighbors, and who had humiliated them during court proceedings.[58] As police detectives gathered in his Larrabee Street home to take him into custody on July 19, 1911, Joseph Lopiscopo whispered to his wife in Italian "that he would shoot" her "when he got out" for "causing his arrest." "I knew that he would carry out the threat and I shot him," the woman informed a policeman as she "cooly handed the smoking weapon" to him.[59] Efforts to provide legal support for battered Chicago wives often failed to protect these women, yet they were sufficient to place the women at greater risk from fiercely defensive and already abusive husbands. As a result, increasing numbers of local wives killed attacking husbands or resorted to "self-defense in advance."

Typically, the police and the courts proved unable to rein in wife beaters, and women who killed their husbands often lacked the support systems that would have made separation or divorce feasible. Husband killers were separated or divorced at half the rate of wife killers.[60] In addition, the women who employed deadly force to defend themselves probably had fewer local relatives than those who separated or secured divorces to escape abusive spouses.[61] Although husband killers were not poor, separation and divorce imposed enormous social and financial burdens on early twentieth-century women, most of whom were also mothers with small children.[62] Some of these Chicagoans were as independent as Emma Nolan, who supported her fractured family "by her own efforts."[63] But more often, separated or divorced women looked to relatives for support and for shelter. Those compelled to remain in violent marriages, and who were unwilling or unable to secure protection from legal institutions, experienced a kind of desperation and social isolation that made violent self-help seem to them the last viable option.[64] Ironically, women in early twentieth-century Chicago who were separated faced increased risk of being murdered by their estranged husbands, while women who remained in abusive marriages more often killed their husbands.[65]

Husband killers acted purposefully, often after resolving never to be beaten again. Most planned the act, and many battered wives procured weapons specifically for self-defense. On August 14, 1899, twenty-three-year-old Mary Jane Wiley pawned a skirt, used the proceeds to purchase a revolver, and shot her twenty-six-year-old husband, Martin. Thirty-year-old Jessie Hopkins borrowed a gun from her father in order to protect herself from her spouse of eight years after "she had been chased by her husband with a revolver and had escaped only by locking herself in a closet." Harriet Burnham hid her revolver in the "bosom of her dress," while other women concealed guns under beds, in kitchen cabinets, in clothing chests, or in other places where the weapons would be accessible when the abuse began anew. "His intention was to kill me, but I got the drop on him," fifty-seven-year-old Kate Snowden told the police captain investigating the death of her ex-husband, Henry Smith. Iva Barnes's preparations proved to be unusually complicated. Planning to kill her husband on September 5, 1916, she obtained a small gun, packed a satchel with clothes so that she could then flee into the night, and arranged to meet her spouse on the street in front of their apartment building, where she intended to shoot him. But after descending the stairs of the building, Iva discovered that she had forgotten to place the weapon in her purse. When James Barnes arrived, she asked him to wait for her, raced upstairs to the apartment, grabbed the gun, returned to the street, and then shot four bullets into her spouse's skull, two of which were fired after he had fallen to the sidewalk.[66]

Like Iva Barnes, most husband killers intended to kill—not frighten, intimidate, or wound—their spouses. Over three-quarters of these women shot their victims.[67] By comparison, two-thirds of wife killers used firearms. Some battered women probably chose guns for their stopping power, as well as the fact that they could compensate for any disadvantage in size and physical strength. But because many wives shot sleeping husbands, knives or even clubs would have accomplished the task; or the women might have opened gas jets and fled to other rooms while their sleeping husbands slowly asphyxiated. Yet only 6 percent of murdering wives used gas for their deed.[68] And only a minority of women whose victims were neither husbands nor lovers relied on guns, using firearms in 39 percent of such homicides. In short, for homicidal women in turn-of-the-century Chicago, situational factors—not an aversion to guns or to bloodshed—determined the instrument of death. Women who killed their husbands chose weapons that insured that the violence would be decisive.

Husband killers used the guns with purpose and precision. They typically squeezed off more rounds than wife killers, no doubt reflecting the emotional toll exacted by years of abuse and the promise of relief and safety. Mary McDonald "emptied every chamber in the pistol" she used to kill her husband, Joseph. "My only idea was to discharge all the bullets," she said. Similarly, Mary Jane Wiley "fired four bullets, all that the revolver contained, into the body of her husband, and while he lay dying on the sidewalk expressed the wish that she had another shot to use on him."[69] Nearly 10 percent of husband killers shot their spouses five or more times, whereas no wife killers fired more than four bullets. Husband killers also tended to be more focused with their aim, even though women had less experience with firearms than their spouses.[70] More than half shot their husbands in the head; by comparison, 43 percent of wife killers using guns targeted their victim's head.[71] Like Mary Jane Wiley, most husband killers fired again and again, making sure the job was done. With her first shot, Wiley's bullet struck her husband in the head, and he crumbled to the ground. Wiley then fired a second bullet into his face, which "tore away a portion of the man's chin," and then she directed a third and a fourth bullet into Martin Wiley's mangled jaw. Other women also felled their spouses with a first, direct shot to the head and then held the weapon against their husbands' disfigured skulls and squeezed off round after round until they emptied the weapon's chambers. "I don't know how many times I fired," Geneva Mitchell admitted, "but I kept firing until there were no more shots left." Unlike the rage-killing men of the late nineteenth century, who often mutilated their wives' breasts, early twentieth-century women killers shot to kill rather than to inflict pain or to degrade their victims.[72]

Husband killers' posthomicide behavior and reactions provide additional evidence of the assertive, purposeful use of lethal violence. Like the women who killed their young children, those who killed

their husbands viewed their actions as the solution to a terrifying
problem. In every other way, however, the reactions differed. For one
thing, homicidal wives rarely took their own lives (fewer than 9 percent attempted suicide); shooting their husbands, after all, resolved
the crisis and eliminated the threat. By contrast, the overwhelming
majority of homicidal mothers immediately attempted suicide; and
more than half of wife killers did so.

Furthermore, women who killed their husbands seldom expressed
remorse and often expressed relief afterward, in stark contrast to
murdering mothers, who characterized their actions as solemn, desperate expressions of love and maternal affection and who usually attempted suicide after killing their children.[73] As the police arrested
Mary Jane Wiley for shooting her husband, she announced, "I hope
he will die." Fearing that her spouse would survive, Harriet Burnham
told the Chicago policeman on the scene, "I only feel sorry I didn't
kill him." Riding in the police wagon as it took her fatally injured
husband, Herbert, to the hospital, Harriet looked down at the bleeding man and said, "Any one who can moan as loud as you can will
never die." Then she exclaimed, "Die, you dog, die." Grace Doyle
"cheerfully" confessed to the police after killing her husband in 1899.
"I killed him and I'm glad of it," she stated. "He got what was coming
to him." For a few women, feelings of joy mingled with the sense of
relief. Jeannette Wall "expressed satisfaction with the shooting of her
husband." Still more pleased was Emma Simpson, who shot her husband six times in a crowded Chicago courtroom. When a stunned
court reporter shouted, "You've killed him," the thirty-seven-year-
old Simpson replied, "I hope so." She added, "He tortured me every
minute of the last four years and he deserved it." Simpson then
"waved and smiled" at a newspaper photographer so he could take
her picture.[74] In view of the physical and emotional abuse that usually preceded the homicides, such reactions were not entirely surprising. But in an age when women who killed those who were not their

spouses or lovers seldom used guns, usually expressed sorrow, and often committed suicide, the decisive actions of Chicago's husband
killers revealed a shift in women's attitudes toward marriage and toward their husbands.

These women were not merely reactive. Their violence represented
more than simply an effect of their husbands' violence, though the
two were related. Late nineteenth-century men battered their wives,
but few of these women killed their abusers. To be sure, the brutish
behavior of Chicago husbands sparked the cycle of violence that often ended with Chicago wives killing their spouses. Yet even though
most of these women believed that their abusive husbands had forced
them to kill, early twentieth-century Chicago wives were also increasingly willing to resist abuse, employ deadly force, and defend
their actions.[75] These two trends—the mounting threat from wife
killers and the growing inclination to resist abusive spouses—occurred simultaneously and were intertwined, and the soaring rate of
husband killing pointed to the increasing assertiveness of women in
Chicago. The words of early twentieth-century husband killers provide more direct evidence of changing attitudes toward domestic violence and patriarchal authority.

Some husband killers described the circumstances triggering the
violence and argued that their spouses had left them no other option,
offering well-conceived, and sometimes well-rehearsed, explanations
to police investigators. For example, after recounting "a tale of continued abuse at the hands of her husband," Mary A. Barker told the
police that she had been "driven" to bash in Thomas Barker's skull
with a stove lid "by her husband's brutal treatment." Even before they
murdered their abusers, many husband killers had contemplated employing lethal self-help and were prepared to defend and to justify
their behavior. When she killed her husband, Belle Benson carried a
purse containing a single item: a newspaper article describing the acquittals of fourteen husband killers. Other women employed legal

terminology from the moment policemen arrived at the crime scene, using phrases such as "self-defense" and "justifiable killing." One battered woman, for example, told the police, "I look upon my act as a morally justifiable killing." Kate Snowden "readily admitted to the [police] captain that she had shot her former husband and stated she was justified."[76] Such language did not suggest deceit or prevarication. Rather, it indicated that these women had wrestled with the morality and the consequences of killing their spouses.

Many early twentieth-century husband killers formulated a specific legal argument to justify their use of deadly force. Defense attorneys played a role in this process and helped to construct or shape their clients' images for policeman, judges, and especially for jurors; but husband killers often explained their conduct to the Chicago policemen who arrived at the scene well before attorneys were involved. These women used their statements to policemen and their courtroom testimony to defend their behavior, just as men who murdered their wives used suicide notes to explain and defend their conduct.

Some husband killers invoked what they called the "'new' unwritten law."[77] The "old" unwritten law, which enjoyed widespread popularity during the nineteenth century and into the early decades of the twentieth century, recognized the "right" of a man justifiably to kill any anyone who despoiled or dishonored his home.[78] More specifically, it permitted and arguably encouraged a man to kill his wife's paramour (and sometimes the woman herself) or any libertine who seduced his daughter or his sister.[79] Most Chicagoans embraced the unwritten law and unabashedly cheered for men who defended their family's honor. In a 1908 trial in which a Chicago man killed his unfaithful wife and wounded her lover, the judge ruled that "the court is of the opinion that a domestic crime of this nature should be dealt with upon a somewhat different basis than in the case of a distinctly anti-social crime."[80] Occasionally women employed this defense as well, claiming the right to kill the scoundrels who seduced, "ruined," and abandoned them.[81] Twenty-five-year-old Pauline Plotka, for example, successfully invoked the unwritten law and gained an acquittal in 1918 after she shot and killed a young physician who promised to marry her, dishonored her, and then jilted her.[82] But this fact did not fit husband killing in early twentieth-century Chicago. The overwhelming majority of the women who looked to the unwritten law did not claim that adultery had occurred, and none of the killers had caught her spouse *in flagrante delicto*. These women, however, invoked a new unwritten law. According to a local journalist, the "new 'unwritten law' has been brought into the limelight by the recent instances of wives charged with the murder of members of their families."[83]

The new unwritten law gave a woman the right to use lethal force in resisting an abusive husband. Some local women specifically invoked this defense, while others employed the logic of the new unwritten law but did not themselves use the phrase, though typically court reporters and attorneys did.[84] In order to secure an acquittal on the grounds of self-defense, a woman had to demonstrate that she had been the victim of wife beating. Having established a history of mistreatment, she was then believed to be legally justified in killing her husband. For example, Jessie Hopkins "anticipated ultimate vindication" for the shooting death of her husband, Harry, a thirty-six-year-old businessman. Harry Hopkins had abused his wife "almost incessantly" during the last few years of their marriage, and on January 1, 1905, the couple quarreled again. Harry "struck her in the face," and Jessie grabbed a gun and shot twice. She immediately told a police lieutenant that "she fired in self-defense." "I knew that when I divulged the story of my wrong treatment, of the suffering that I endured for ten years," Jessie Hopkins said, "that I would be sustained in my action."[85]

The new unwritten law was new in two ways; both shed light on husband killing in early twentieth-century Chicago. First, husband

killers expanded the list of transgressions that permitted private vengeance under the unwritten law. Traditionally, indecent and inap-
propriate behavior toward women—actually, toward the proprietary
interests of their husbands or fathers—justified lethal response. Pro-
ponents of the unwritten law argued that seduction, rape, and moles-
tation were so threatening to the sanctity of the home and family
that men must be allowed to pursue their own brand of private justice.[86] But early twentieth-century husband killers (and their attorneys) insisted that wife beating also belonged on this list of indecent,
heinous offenses that assaulted the moral foundation of family life.
Because companionate ideals eroded the notion that patriarchal authority undergirded marital relations, wife battering, according to
these women, became both improper and a threat to the sanctity of
the home and family.[87]

Second, the women who invoked this argument explicitly claimed
the "rights" of self-defense and personal vengeance, both of which
had been reserved for men. The new unwritten law therefore revised
the old unwritten law in ways that eroded the boundary separating
proper masculine conduct from proper feminine conduct.[88] Wives
who relied on this legal strategy believed that they were justified in
resisting their husbands and using lethal force in doing so. Nor was
this point lost on local jurists. In instructing the jury in Jessie
Hopkins's trial, Judge George Kersten affirmed that "a woman by
marrying does not become the slave or chattel of her husband. She
has a right to kill her husband in self-defense if she is in imminent
danger of bodily harm." Kersten averred that "if a woman is unfortunate enough to marry a brute whose favorite pastime is to mistreat
her, she has the same right as her husband." Other judges endorsed
Kersten's position. Axel Chytraus explained that he also believed that
"a woman has the same right of defense as the man. There is no distinction in her rights," he added, "and there is no distinction between
the rights of the husband and wife as to the other." Judge A. C.

Barnes agreed, noting that "the wife has the same right of self-defense as any other person," as did Judge Richard Tuthill, who argued that "a husband has no right to abuse his wife. Not every case of mistreatment in the home warrants a woman in resorting to extreme measures," he cautioned, "but the wife has the absolute right of defending herself, even to the extent of taking a life. . . . Her rights are co-equal with his."[89] For a local judge to declare from the bench that a woman "has the same right as her husband" and for other judges to support this right of self-defense against husbands signaled a fundamental change in gender and marital relations. Many Chicago women both employed lethal violence against their spouses and invoked this argument, suggesting that such shifting attitudes toward gender relations and marriage contributed to the sharp increase in husband killing during the early twentieth century. In short, Chicago women embraced more egalitarian views of marriage, and both literally and rhetorically, in their homes and in local courtrooms, they claimed the right to use lethal force to defend themselves against husbands who beat them.

If wives and judges recognized the implications of this argument, so too did anxious law enforcers. The new unwritten law enraged local prosecutors, who reminded jurors that an unwritten law was not in fact a law. In his opening statement to the jury in a 1919 husband-killing case, Assistant State's Attorney Edward Prindiville lectured jurors, "You men are representative of all of the forces of law and order. Do you want the law enforced?" In his closing argument in another husband-killing trial, frustrated Assistant State's Attorney Hayden N. Bell chided the jurors, asking if they intended "to join the great army of boob ex-jurors who have acquitted women of murdering their husbands, although they were absolutely guilty." And State's Attorney Maclay Hoyne lamented, "The manner in which women [who] have committed murder in this county have been able to escape punishment has become a scandal."[90]

Local prosecutors feared the effects of the new unwritten law. Some recognized that it chipped away at men's prerogatives as husbands. "What if [Herbert] Burnham did get drunk once in a while?" Assistant State's Attorney John Fleming argued in his opening statement at the trial of Harriet Burnham, who killed her drunken, brutish husband. "You all know a lot of men do it. A glass of beer is the only consolation some men get." J. R. Newcomer, another assistant state's attorney, explicitly defended a man's right to use physical force against his wife if she deserved it. "Like any man of honor," Newcomer said of the murdered man in a 1906 trial of a woman charged with killing her husband, "he was trying to get her to live up to her contract and to behave herself." Besides, the prosecutor added, "if this jury sets the precedent that any woman who is attacked or is beaten by her husband can shoot him, there won't be many husbands left in Chicago six months from now."[91]

Prosecutors focused their concerns on the larger social consequences of this defense strategy, though these men also recognized the potential impact of arming wives with the idea that they could justifiably defend themselves from abusive spouses. State's Attorney Hoyne feared that "the existing belief [is] that a wife may murder her husband in Cook county with impunity." Similarly, Assistant State's Attorney Prindiville worried that the new unwritten law would result in "murderesses [being] turned out on the streets." At stake, he argued, was "law and order."[92]

Jurors, however, disagreed. They embraced both the new unwritten law and the women who killed their abusive husbands. Cook County prosecutors convicted only sixteen of the one hundred three Chicago women who killed their husbands in the city between 1875 and 1920, and nine of the convicted wives were African-American women, for whom such a defense clearly appeared subversive and dangerous.[93] Jurors returned guilty verdicts for only seven of eighty-one white husband killers (8.6 percent), and the judge quickly "remitted" the sentence and released one of the seven.[94] Of the remaining six white women convicted for killing their husbands, two were found to be criminally insane, and two were sentenced to prison terms of one year. Every white woman who killed her husband between August 1905 and October 1918 was exonerated or acquitted, totaling thirty-five consecutive cases.[95] Only two of the eighty-one white husband killers in Chicago from 1875 to 1920 were found guilty and sentenced to prison terms of more than one year.[96] Jurors even acquitted Iva Barnes, the woman who asked her husband to wait for her on the street while she fetched her gun and then shot him four times.[97] Echoing the concerns of local prosecutors, one newspaper reporter expressed horror at the "march of liberated gunwomen from the Criminal Court."[98]

The two white women convicted of murdering their husbands represented the proverbial exceptions that proved the rule. Virginia Troupe, a nineteen-year-old dressmaker from Mississippi, was convicted and sentenced to serve fourteen years at Joliet Penitentiary for the 1905 shooting of her husband. Troupe's personal habits, age, and socioeconomic background hurt her in the trial, for she lacked the dignity and respectability of wealthier and more mature defendants. Far more damaging, however, was the prosecution's assertion that Troupe had been drinking and had killed "not in self-defense, but because she was angry at him [her husband]. They had been quarreling over some man." No one denied that W. C. Troupe was shot while he was attacking his wife, but the assistant state's attorney successfully argued that Virginia Troupe could not claim self-defense if she was being beaten for an appropriate reason—for accepting "the intentions of other men."[99] The prosecutor did not address the authority of the new unwritten law. Instead, he challenged Troupe's attempt to use this affirmative defense and thus won a conviction.

Hilda Exlund, a forty-six-year-old Swedish immigrant, also failed to secure an acquittal and was sentenced to fourteen years in Joliet Penitentiary. Exlund drove a butcher knife five inches into the abdomen of her husband, Frank, after he attacked her with a knife. Edward Prindiville, the assistant state's attorney, argued that this was not a case of self-defense, even though the prosecutor did not dispute the facts leading to the fatal stabbing. Hilda Exlund, he explained, was a woman "of powerful physique," whereas her forty-three-year-old husband was a "small man." Moreover, neighbors and friends testified that Hilda "often cursed" her husband and "had once poured boiling water upon him." In fact, she had been "a husband beater for years." Only a few weeks before the fatal stabbing, neighbors had seen Frank running out of his house with a bloody handkerchief held to his face and wailing, "She tried to kill me."[100] In both the Troupe trial and the Exlund trial, the prosecutor challenged the invocation of the new unwritten law but not its legal authority.

As Virginia Troupe and Hilda Exlund discovered, the jurors who acquitted husband killers were not necessarily endorsing the newfound assertiveness and self-reliance of local women. Furthermore, even the Chicagoans who claimed the new right to self-defense framed their arguments in traditional terms, typically emphasizing the dishonorable, brutish, and unmanly conduct of their husbands and casting themselves as deferential, long-suffering, and respectable wives. "I do not recommend any woman to use a revolver," Jessie Hopkins averred. "But in cases as mine, when a dutiful and devoted wife finds treatment of the most barbarous kind in return for her faithful devotion, she is liable to do anything."[101] Husband killers, and especially their attorneys, also refrained from suggesting that the new unwritten law challenged men's prerogatives. To the contrary, they played on jurors' sense of chivalry and inclination to safeguard fragile, decent women.[102] The "new 'unwritten law,'" one observer concluded, extended "a protective wing over the heads of the weaker sex." Successfully defending Emma Simpson, the woman who shot her husband in a crowded courtroom and then posed for a photographer, Clarence Darrow told jurors, "You've been asked to treat a man and a woman the same—but you can't. No manly man can." Other court observers, including local ministers, court reporters, and a few Cook County judges, recoiled at the way husband killers and their attorneys manipulated the sensibilities of paternalistic jurors and justified murderous behavior. "A gun in her dainty hands," a journalist quipped in reporting another acquittal, "was as deadly as in the calloused paw of the veriest ruffian, but what was a jury of twelve husky, soft-hearted men to do? Send her to the gallows? . . . Unthinkable. So they let her go by the new 'unwritten law.'" Judge Frank Johnston, Jr., attributed the string of acquittals to "mere sentimentality" and proposed adding women to the jury pool in order to combat the new unwritten law and rein in homicidal wives. Judge Marcus Kavanagh bemoaned the "mock sense of chivalry" that enabled "a good-looking woman [to] kill any man she wants," while State's Attorney Hoyne conceded that jurors "bring in a verdict of acquittal whenever a woman charged with murder is fairly good-looking, is able to turn on the flood of tears." A reporter added that "the public bosom must be wrung with lavender-scented details of the woman's past. She loved and was betrayed, trusted and was scorned—both good items." Convicted murderer Hilda Exlund agreed with this assessment. After a jury consisting of married men found her guilty, she erupted, "I suppose if I had been young and beautiful, I would have been turned loose just as other women who have been tried for killing their husbands."[103]

The new unwritten law, however, represented more than merely another winning legal strategy or an artful way to transform killers into sympathetic victims. Such a novel defense of husband killing was largely unnecessary, for Chicago killers seldom landed in prison. Only 22 percent of all homicide cases in the city between 1875 and

1920 ended with a conviction.[104] For cases with women killers, the figure was 16 percent—and just 8 percent for homicides in which the assailant was a white woman.[105] In 1914 a Chicago reporter observed that "women can't be convicted of murder in Cook County," and a state official, writing three years later, reached the same conclusion, noting that "in certain communities a woman can not [*sic*] be convicted of murder."[106] Unless the homicide was particularly grisly or the killer challenged established social mores, as did brawny husband beater Hilda Exlund, conviction was unlikely in turn-of-the-century Chicago.[107] Thus, defense attorneys could have refrained from offering any affirmative defense or they could have relied on the vague, generic self-defense arguments that nearly always persuaded jurors.[108] Put differently, killers and their attorneys need not have formulated a gender-specific defense that, to many observers, both challenged a man's time-honored rights as the head of his household and posed a threat to "law and order."

While husband killers did not offer strident, radical arguments, the new unwritten law and, more important, the violence that it attempted to explain revealed larger changes in gender relations. Both the homicides and the legal argument blended older, familiar assumptions about marriage and family with emerging ideals. The middling, respectable women in their thirties who killed their husbands in early twentieth-century Chicago were not threatening the bedrock of family life, but both their violent behavior and their explanations for it indicate that they embraced more companionate and egalitarian views of marriage than did their nineteenth-century counterparts or the poorer, younger women in the city. Thus, it is not surprising that more mature and slightly wealthier women refused to submit to extreme domestic abuse and killed their spouses. As one Chicago husband killer explained, "I killed him. It would have been all right if he had used me right last night." A local journalist concluded that the woman had killed her husband "because he didn't use her right."[109] At least in the eyes of Chicago women, the definition of the "proper use" of a wife shifted at the start of the new century.[110]

Just as Chicago became more violent as it became more orderly, the women of the city killed their loved ones in greater numbers as they sought stronger emotional bonds with their children and their husbands. The balancing of sex ratios, the waning of the bachelor subculture, the rising popularity of heterosocial leisure activities, the increasing consumption of alcohol in private homes, the ongoing deskilling process in manufacturing, the continuing law enforcement effort to enhance public order, and the growing embrace of companionate marriage ideals combined to venerate family life and to impose overwhelming pressures on Chicago parents and spouses. This swirl of cultural and social torrents hit lower-middle-class Chicagoans particularly hard, fueling an upswing in both marital dissolution and domestic homicide precisely when (and because) these residents struggled to achieve middle-class ideals of family harmony and domestic fulfillment. As fathers and husbands became less secure emotionally and financially, and as mothers and wives expected greater harmony, child murder and husband murder exploded. Husband killers were not the most marginal or "deviant" Chicagoans. Neither were these women indifferent to family life. Rather, early twentieth-century mothers and wives killed their loved ones because they desperately sought emotionally fulfilling family lives.

Chimerical dreams of companionate marriage and domestic harmony contributed to women's homicide in three interrelated ways. First, a modest number of mothers held themselves responsible for safeguarding the health and happiness of their children. These pressures, grotesquely exaggerated by mental illness, produced a rise in child killing. Mothers' desires to protect their children were not new, but the surge in the rate of child killing in Chicago points to the growing weight of such pressures during the early decades of the twentieth century.

Second, gender-specific attitudes and expectations of companionate marriage added to the upturn in husband killing. Both men and women struggled to achieve domestic harmony, but they defined domestic harmony in different ways. These conflicting expectations generated friction and sparked a cycle of escalating tension and violence in Chicago households. With heightened expectations for emotionally fulfilling and egalitarian unions, the women who embraced companionate ideals were more willing to dissolve unhappy marriages than were earlier generations of Chicago wives. But as these women resolved to leave miserable marriages, thus challenging men's notions of masculine authority, local husbands became more homicidal in order to preserve their families—and to reestablish control over their wives. In turn, local women defended themselves against abusive spouses, triggering the sharp upturn in husband killings.

Third, and perhaps most important, Chicago women became less submissive, less willing to endure abuse, and more inclined to defend themselves, with lethal force if necessary, because domestic violence was incompatible with companionate ideals.[111] Wife battering was not new in this era, though Chicago women, especially those in their thirties and from lower-middle-class households, increasingly resisted such violence and searched for viable solutions. Some left their abusive marriages or died trying to do so. Others looked to the police and the courts, strategies that often proved unsuccessful and sometimes generated greater violence from estranged, desperate husbands. A growing number of Chicago women, however, insisted that as respectable wives they had the right to defend themselves against their brutish husbands; they secured guns, hid the weapons in accessible places, reached for them when the abuse began anew, fired round after round into the heads of their attackers, and then offered unapologetic, reasoned justifications for killing their husbands.

These women simultaneously reinforced and challenged early twentieth-century gender norms.[112] On the one hand, they embraced conservative images of gender roles (or they played to the chivalrous impulses of judges and jurors), portraying themselves as dutiful wives and—not inaccurately—as victims of male brutality. On the other hand, however, husband killers explicitly claimed the "right" to use lethal violence while resisting their husbands. In an era when assertive, violent women were considered deviant and particularly dangerous, these Chicago wives refused to remain passive, endure additional mistreatment, or look to men for protection.[113] Instead, they behaved aggressively and resolved the crisis, actions typically reserved for men in turn-of-the-century America.[114] Moreover, the husband killers persuaded local men—journalists, judges, and jurors, in particular—that such traditionally masculine behavior was appropriate. Although the new unwritten law extended this right only to wives who were white, respectable, and battered and thus remained grounded in traditionally gendered and race-specific social relations, the increase in husband killing reflected changing assumptions about both the proper "use" of a wife and the justifiable response to the ill use of a wife. Thus, Emma Nolan not only shot her abusive husband in 1905, she also explained to the police that he "got what he deserved."

"If Ever That Black Dog Crosses the Threshold of My House, I Will Kill Him"

S hortly after 8:00 AM on March 10, 1908, Andrew Williams fired three bullets into the body of his estranged wife, Ophelia, fatally wounding her and causing her to drop their seventeen-month-old child. Startled by the sound of the gun, John Hardy, Ophelia's father and a thirteen-year veteran of the Chicago Police Department, reached for his revolver, rushed toward his daughter, and opened fire at her attacker. The two men, both of whom were African American, exchanged a volley of shots, with Hardy perched at the top of a stairway and Williams returning the fire from a doorway and then from the street in front of Hardy's West Fifty-Ninth Street home. Williams emptied the chambers of his thirty-eight-caliber pistol, reloaded the weapon, and continued shooting at his father-in-law, who also emptied the chambers of his revolver. Each man suffered a gunshot wound in the left arm during the battle. At his trial for his wife's murder, and in petitions filed after his conviction, Andrew Williams insisted that he had not intended to kill Ophelia. The twenty-three-year-old day laborer explained that he carried a gun that day only for self-defense—because his father-in-law detested him and had repeatedly threatened to shoot him. "If ever that black dog crosses the threshold of my house," John Hardy had warned, "I will kill him."[1] Williams argued that he was frightened of his father-in-law, that he had talked with his wife from the doorway (without actually crossing the threshold of Hardy's house), and that he had accidentally shot his twenty-one-year-old wife in the confusion of the moment.[2] According to his attorney, Williams was not a hardened criminal; he was merely a terrified, skittish youngster whose behavior had been "impulsive and emotional."[3] Jurors, however, disagreed, as did Judge George Kersten, the Illinois Board of Pardons, and Governor Charles S. Deneen. On October 22, 1909, the State of Illinois hanged Andrew Williams for the murder of Ophelia Williams. Ophelia was Chicago's thirty-ninth homicide victim of 1908.[4]

In the eyes of many residents, Andrew Williams was typical of the killers who prowled the streets of early twentieth-century Chicago and who made the Illinois metropolis the "worst city on Earth."[5] Some observers blamed Chicago's "epidemic of lawlessness" on immigrants or hoboes.[6] Other commentators, such as Municipal Court Judge John R. Newcomer, emphasized the baneful effects of "liquor, lust, bad associates," and "cigarette smoking."[7] But even as they quibbled over the impact of tramps, toughs, trollops, and tobacco, most Chicagoans agreed that the recent influx of African-American ruffians generated much of the city's violence.

The "Great Migration" from the South profoundly changed Chicago during this period. Between 1890 and 1920 the city's African-American population increased from 14,271 to 109,458. According to many observers, the waves of newcomers flooded Chicago with "rowdies, gun-carrying bullies and other worthless characters."[8] In *The Jungle,* Upton Sinclair described "big buck negroes with daggers in their boots" who "were free—free to gratify every passion."[9]

White Chicagoans, but also many long-established African-American residents, feared this invasion of young African-American migrants, among them Andrew Williams, who moved to Chicago at the age of nineteen.[10] In 1907, a writer for *McClure's Magazine* reported that the "vicious negro from the countryside of the South . . . furnish[es] an alarming volume of savage crime." Even the *Chicago Defender*, an African-American newspaper, expressed concern about the newcomers. Exposing class divisions within Chicago's African-American community, the newspaper lamented that the "influx of contraband idlers and outlaws from the South has brought death and injury to a number of men, women, and children recently and thrown Chicago and nearby cities into the wildest excitement and caused law-abiding citizens to go about with fear and trembling for their lives." Many Chicagoans maintained that "Negroes possess a constitutional character weakness, and a consequent predisposition to sexual crimes, petty stealing, and crimes of violence."[11]

Such beliefs, and their apparent confirmation in the Williams homicide and similar acts of violence, influenced public policy in Chicago and other northern cities for decades. Intense, fierce racism created the African-American ghetto of the early twentieth century, as white city dwellers confined the newcomers to particular neighborhoods. The process proved to be self-perpetuating; the concentration of people in cramped, dilapidated housing exaggerated social problems, such as crime, disease, and poverty, thus reinforcing the discrimination that forged the ghetto and bolstering the resolve of white city dwellers to isolate African-American residents.

White Chicagoans became desperate to insulate themselves from contact with men such as Andrew Williams. They used zoning ordinances and restrictive covenants to exclude African Americans from white, ethnic neighborhoods and to concentrate the newcomers in the city's South Side "Black Belt." By the end of the 1920s, three-quarters of all residential property deeds in Chicago included restrictive covenants that precluded sale to African Americans.[12] Even Al Capone's house, with its concrete-reinforced walls and steel-encased windows, had a restrictive covenant to keep the property out of African-American hands.[13] When administrative and contractual efforts failed to maintain the racial purity of neighborhoods, some white Chicagoans turned to more coercive tactics, forming home-owners' associations to intimidate realtors who sold property to African Americans. Other frantic white residents relied on still more aggressive defenses of their turf.[14] Between July 1917 and March 1921 whites firebombed an African-American residence an average of once every twenty days.[15] Jesse Binga, an African-American real estate agent, had his property bombed seven times.[16]

At the same time, policy makers, acting in concert with law enforcers, forced houses of prostitution and gambling into African-American sections of the city, leading many white Chicagoans to conclude that "Negroes willingly tolerate vice and vicious conditions."[17] This process was self-perpetuating as well. Because white Chicagoans typically associated African-American residents with crime, disease, and licentiousness, efforts to concentrate vice industries within African-American areas enjoyed widespread, if tacit, support. As a consequence of this cycle, white Chicagoans expected to see moral decay in the African-American community, undertook policies that forced vice activities into African-American neighborhoods, and then saw the prostitutes, numbers runners, and petty criminals there, which confirmed their belief in the moral shortcomings of African Americans.[18] Racism infused public policy, which, in turn, reinforced racism, seemingly providing irrefutable evidence that the "tendency toward crime is greater among Negroes" and that the Great Migration produced "a tremendous increase in the problems of crime and vice."[19]

Popular and even scholarly assessments of life on the South Side of Chicago cemented these caricatured images. Journalists, particularly crime-beat writers, seized on the language of the rural South to describe the behavior of African Americans, much as they evoked images of stiletto-toting Sicilian peasants when they discussed Italian immigrants. Local newspaper reporters, for example, often described fights between African Americans as "duels," a term seldom used when white Chicagoans brawled.[20] Sociologists from the University of Chicago unwittingly bolstered such imagery as well, suggesting that the isolation of the newcomers, in combination with the overwhelming, discordant pressures of the big city, undermined "traditional ideas of right and wrong" in the "Negro peasant."[21] "Above all, in considering the negro criminal," a local judge wrote, "one is required to remember his history. A hundred generations of civilization lie behind the white man. Five generations ago the ancestors of the colored doctors, lawyers, teachers, waiters, servants, and bankers we meet every day were hunting one another in the jungles."[22]

In short, most white Chicagoans believed that African Americans were violent and deviant. Again and again, antilynching crusader Ida B. Wells encountered this view in early twentieth-century Chicago. "Have you forgotten," a high-born, well-bred resident lectured Wells, "that 10 percent of all crimes that were committed in Chicago last year were by colored men"—at a time when African Americans comprised approximately 2 percent of the city's population.[23] Newspapers repeatedly carried headlines reading "Negroes Far Ahead in Crime."[24] During 1916 and 1917, nearly 40 percent of the articles on "racial matters" that appeared in Chicago's leading newspapers focused squarely on crime or vice.[25]

Violence ravaged Chicago's African-American community. In 1910, African Americans comprised one fiftieth of Chicago's population and one eighth of its homicide victims. A decade later, African Americans comprised one twenty-fourth of Chicago's population and made up one fifth of the city's killers and homicide victims.

The patterns of African-American violence, however, and particularly shifts in these patterns, suggest that African-American residents were remarkably similar to other Chicagoans. To be sure, levels of homicide were significantly higher among these newcomers, though African-American residents killed and died in ways comparable to white city dwellers. Moreover, changes in the nature of lethal violence in Chicago's Black Belt echoed the shifts that occurred elsewhere in the city. Even Andrew Williams's deadly encounter with his wife revealed tensions similar to those destroying white families. Andrew and Ophelia Williams had lived together "in comparative contentment" until he lost his job and thus "failed to properly provide for her."[26] Like many women in early twentieth-century Chicago, Ophelia left her husband when he could not support her "properly," and she returned to her parents' home. Desperate to find work and frantic to reconcile with his wife, Andrew Williams pleaded with Ophelia to come back to him. On her deathbed, Ophelia Williams recounted the events leading to the shooting on March 10, 1908. She described a conversation identical to those that preceded dozens of uxoricides in early twentieth-century Chicago, with her estranged husband "asking her if she would go back and live with him, and then saying, as he shot, 'well, if I can't have you, nobody else can.'"[27]

African-American homicide reflected the same pressures that triggered lethal violence in white Chicago, though poverty and racism interacted in ways that exaggerated the level of bloodshed in the city's Black Belt.[28] White Chicagoans were certain that African-American residents were "constitutionally" different from white residents, particularly in their tendency to engage in violent behavior. A hundred generations behind whites, savage by their very nature, and uniquely vulnerable to the pernicious effects of lust and alcohol, African Americans, according to early twentieth-century observers, killed because they were controlled by their base emotions and driven "to gratify every passion." "Because crimes of deliberation and plan-ning require more brains than Negroes possess," they tended to com-mit "quick, uncalculated crimes of violence." "As you know," the pres-ident of the Illinois Federation of Women's Clubs explained, "a white woman has to fear a colored man."[29] In fact, the sources or triggers for homicide among African-American Chicagoans were compara-ble to those for whites. Racism, however, affected the level of Afri-can-American violence, making it a caricature of white homicide in early twentieth-century Chicago.

No group of Chicagoans endured more lethal violence than African-American residents. From 1875 to 1920, African-American Chicago-ans killed and died from criminal violence at more than seven times the rate of white Chicagoans—and by the standards of the era, white Chicagoans were extremely violent.[30] In three years during this era the African-American homicide rate exceeded the white rate by a factor of more than fifteen, and it was always at least quadruple the white level.[31] During the 1910s, when the African-American homi-cide rate dipped and the white rate continued to rise, the gap nar-rowed, but it remained wide. The homicide rate for African-Ameri-can Chicagoans was so much greater than the white rate that the latter, as Figure 6 indicates, appears nearly flat in comparison, al-though it in fact quadrupled between 1875 and 1920 and exceeded the comparable rates of almost every large northern city in the United States.[32]

The character of African-American homicide changed as dramat-ically as the rate of African-American homicide during this period. Three factors collided to shape this violence. First, African-Ameri-can Chicagoans were buffeted by the same social and cultural pres-sures that other residents of the city suffered. Second, the Great Mi-gration redefined African-American life in the city, transforming lethal violence in the process. And third, the unstable, volatile, and

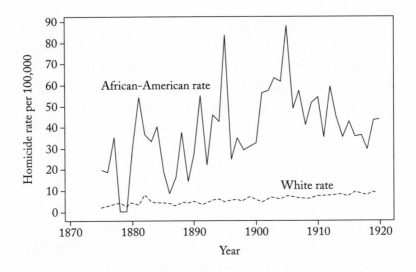

FIGURE 6   *Homicide rates by race (source: see Appendix)*

acrimonious racial climate of Chicago influenced every aspect of African-American life, including lethal violence.

African-American Chicagoans in the late nineteenth century lived, worked, fought, and died at the edges of plebeian society. At least by comparison with their twentieth-century counterparts, the city's African-American population was diverse and widely dispersed. Although discrimination was commonplace, until the end of the nineteenth century Chicago was largely free of the kinds of institutional racism that infected social life for most of the twentieth century. African-American Chicagoans voted, lived in mixed-race neighborhoods, patronized mixed-race stores, and attended nonsegregated schools, and a small business and professional class commanded respect and influence within the larger community.[33] Comprising just over 1 percent of the city's population during the final quarter of the century, African Americans garnered little attention and generated scant concern from their white neighbors, whose anxieties typically focused on the class tensions and labor violence that rumbled beneath the surface of Gilded Age Chicago—and that exploded in 1877, 1886, and 1894.[34] But despite the heterogeneity of the community and the relative absence of overt, institutional racism, African Americans tended to be poor and to live in working-class sections of the city.[35]

Like white violence, African-American violence during the late nineteenth century most often occurred between young toughs and typically erupted in Chicago's low dives and raucous saloons. Between 1875 and 1890, African-American killers, like their victims, were young, poor, and aggressive, and they usually committed homicide while swaggering to impress their peers. Fifty-eight percent of African-American killers during this period were in their twenties, and the average age was twenty-six, making them slightly younger than white killers. Moreover, four-fifths of African-American killers held unskilled positions, and, as with white killers in this era, drunken brawls provided the leading spark for African-American homicides, accounting for 35 percent of deaths from criminal violence. These men also tended to kill their peers, with 42 percent of African-American homicides occurring between acquaintances.[36] Again like their white counterparts, African Americans killed in public settings, on Saturdays, and late in the evening. In short, plebeian culture transcended racial lines and generated the lion's share of both African-American and white homicide during the late 1870s and the 1880s.

Regardless of race, Gilded Age killers tended to congregate in Chicago's roughest bars, gambling halls, and houses of ill repute, where they tested their masculinity and shot, pummeled, and stabbed their victims in displays of recreational ferocity. On October 4, 1884, for example, Joe Williams fatally stabbed two people in a local brothel during a dispute about payment for a round of drinks. According to witnesses, the twenty-five-year-old Williams "has always borne a bad reputation, and was known as a 'levee nigger.' He always carried a knife and when provoked did not hesitate about using it." Similarly, "Big" Stephen Alexander, known as the "Emperor of Craps," died in a gambling-house brawl when he bullied twenty-three-year-old John Johnson on January 22, 1884. Feared for his "pugilistic propensities," the twenty-eight-year-old Alexander, who "had been dowsing," became enraged and embarrassed when he lost $11 at faro and announced "he would 'do up'" Johnson. Others at the faro table, including John Morris (alias "Coyote Tobe"), Gus Green (alias "Bamboo Chief"), and "Baltimore" George Tubman, knew Alexander's reputation and quickly backed away to safety. True to his word and faithful to his reputation, Alexander attacked Johnson, who shot and killed his assailant. Alexander "was a friend of mine," John Whiting remarked after the shooting, "but he thought himself the cock of the walk, and that's how he came to die."[37]

Other than the race of the participants, these homicides differed little from those in which white toughs killed and died. African-American and white homicides, in short, were products of the same culturally encoded activities. Why then was the rate of African-American homicide more than six times greater than the white homicide rate between 1875 and 1890?

The rituals of plebeian culture interacted with demographic factors and racial conflict to exaggerate the potential for violence among Gilded Age African-American Chicagoans. First, the modest size of the city's African-American population made the everyday encounters of working-class life especially unstable and bloody. Comprising just over 1 percent of the city's population during this era, the African-American community could not support its own saloons or other leisure-time institutions. Thus, these residents were conspicuous outsiders in working-class haunts and, as a result, obvious targets for ruffians seeking attention.

Second, and closely related, African-American men, also by virtue of their relatively small number, typically found themselves without a network or a group of loyal friends who could discourage attacks or intercede in brawls and thereby transform public disagreements into ritualized contests in which each man strutted and roared but no violence erupted. Groups of white, frequently Irish, toughs often "bull-dosed" African-American residents during the 1870s and 1880s, crowding them off sidewalks and into alleys or streets.[38] While this game was intended to cow and to humiliate isolated African-American pedestrians and hence to affirm the manliness of the aggressors as well as the racial hierarchy of working-class society, the ritual occasionally deviated from the script. Many African-American Chicagoans, adopting a strategy of conflict aversion, resisted the temptation to respond to the ruffians, but a few challenged their attackers.[39] One such victim who turned killer in 1881 explained, in the words of the crime-beat reporter for the *Chicago Times*, that "dey all come at me like dey was going to knock me clean out a sight, an' I drew my gun an' shot one of 'em." The reporter added that "the negro whipped out a great navy revolver, and blasted away at the three men."[40] Chicagoans who belonged to large groups or who roved in packs seldom faced such threats.

Third, when an African-American tough fought and bested a white brawler, the racism festering below the surface of working-class society often exploded into open view, and white Chicagoans suddenly felt racial solidarity. In such circumstances, white residents sometimes invoked the language and embraced the rituals of their southern counterparts, revealing the national scope of racial ideologies. For example, after Joe Bales, a thirty-two-year-old "burly negro whose evil eye and distorted countenance mark him as a desperate man," stabbed a fellow dockworker named Cornelius Sullivan (alias "Boston Kelly") during a "general fight" in 1891, five hundred white dockworkers pursued the killer, chanting "Lynch him," "String him up," and "Hang the nigger."[41] Men such as Joe Bales knew there were no fair fights or codes of honor governing interracial skirmishes. They could either avoid the battle or strike decisively and then flee immediately. Bales's "evil eye and distorted countenance" may have been a deliberate strategy to discourage white bullies from targeting him, though his demeanor also served to inflame the enmity of his white enemies, increasing the potential for serious violence if a fight erupted.

Other demographic factors contributed to African-American violence as well. If uneven sex ratios nourished a rough-hewn bachelor subculture among white Chicagoans, such conditions were more pronounced among African-American Chicagoans, for whom the surfeit of men was greater. In 1890, for example, the local population included 125 African-American men for every 100 African-American women. White Chicago had 107 men for every 100 women. Likewise, the proportion of young men and the proportion of bachelors were significantly greater among African-American residents. Of Chicago's African-American men in 1890, 17 percent were in their late twenties, compared with 12 percent of white men. In addition, 51 percent of African-American men between the ages of twenty-five and thirty-four in 1890 were unmarried; the figure for white men in the city was 41 percent.[42] Thus, the demographic imbalances that encouraged drinking and brawling in white Chicago existed in a more extreme form in African-American Chicago.

These forces distorted social life and influenced the character of African-American homicide. Competition for status was violent within white bachelor society, but it was even more violent within African-American circles, reflecting an exaggerated form of plebeian culture, a greater surplus of young, single men, and powerful taboos that discouraged interracial sexual unions. If white bachelors sauntered and scuffled to intimidate other men and to capture the attention of young women, African-American men experienced even more pressure to do so. Jealousy, for instance, sparked 23 percent of African-American homicides between 1875 and 1890, compared with 8 percent of white homicides.

Racism also clustered African-American residents in the most combustible settings in late nineteenth-century Chicago, enhancing the prospects for violent disputes. Local bordellos and gambling dens typically employed African-American men as porters, waiters, and janitors and African-American women as maids and prostitutes, where they routinely encountered drunken, boisterous young men eager to demonstrate their manliness.[43] When young white men became disorderly in the city's houses of assignation, African-American brothel employees found themselves having to restrain the patrons.[44] Thus, African-American men attempted to control wild bachelors at their wildest, and African-American men and women became convenient targets for local toughs who failed at faro and lost at lust. Nearly 20 percent of the homicides committed by African-American Chicagoans and 15 percent of the homicides committed against African-American Chicagoans between 1875 and 1890 occurred in brothels, compared with 4 percent of the homicides involving white residents.

The cumulative weight of racism, proximity to dangerous activities, and plebeian ferocity generated violence. Most homicides occurred within racial lines. Between 1875 and 1890, five-eighths of the victims of African-American killers were African American. Similarly, nearly three-fourths of African-American homicide victims died in intraracial killings. Nonetheless, the potential for interracial violence—at the hands of rowdy "bull dosers," raucous brothel patrons, and disgruntled gamblers—increased African-American homicide. While some African-American Chicagoans avoided conflict with white toughs, others, particularly young bachelors, armed themselves to resist such aggression and to buoy their own sense of manliness in the process, a response that produced deadly violence both across and within racial lines. In sum, African-American city dwellers inhabited a social world in which demographic pressures, cultural forces, and racial attitudes magnified the most unstable and violent aspects of plebeian Chicago. As a result, during the late 1870s and the 1880s African-American homicide resembled white homicide—but at more than six times the level.

The Great Migration remade Chicago's African-American community.[45] The Illinois metropolis was one of the major beneficiaries of the African-American exodus to the industrial North in the age of Jim Crow and the boll weevil. Reports of high wages and relative racial equality, often trumpeted in the pages of Robert S. Abbott's newspaper, the *Chicago Defender*, made the city a lodestone for migrants fleeing southern poverty and racial oppression.[46] Between 1890 and 1920, Chicago's African-American population increased nearly eightfold. During the decade of the 1910s alone it grew by 148 percent, a rate of increase more than seven times that of Chicago's booming white population.[47] Migrants accounted for 94 percent of the African-American population growth during the 1910s; in 1920, 15 percent of African-American Chicagoans had been born in Illinois, compared with 53 percent of white residents.[48]

Young adults made up a disproportionate share of the newcomers. During the late 1910s, when fifty thousand migrants settled in Chicago, the newcomers tended to be concentrated in their late twenties.[49] Fully 80 percent of African-American Chicagoans between the ages of twenty and thirty-four in 1920 had arrived in the city during the previous decade; and 26 percent of Chicago's African-American residents were in their twenties, compared with 20 percent of the city's white residents.[50] The enormous influx of young people facilitated family formation and institutional development. But it also struck fear in the hearts of many white Chicagoans, who felt besieged by the "swarm" of "darkies from Dixie."[51] Furthermore, early twentieth-century commentators, including criminologists, were quick to note that the migrants were clustered in the "violent ages." As one expert observed in 1922, "An overbalance exists in the Negro population." Moreover, "a greater proportion of these adults were men without families, another factor known to overweight crime figures."[52]

As African-American migrants poured into Chicago, and as white residents became increasingly alarmed, policy makers, realtors, and landowners forced the newcomers into an already crowded, small section of the city.[53] The process was rapid and pernicious. In 1910, Chicago had no census tracts in which African Americans made up more than 61 percent of the population. A decade later, twenty-four tracts were more than three-quarters African American.[54] Similarly, in 1910, 34,335 African Americans—or 78 percent of Chicago's African-American residents—were squeezed into the densely packed "Black Belt" on the city's South Side, which ran from Twelfth Street to Thirty-First Street and from Wentworth Avenue to Wabash Avenue. By 1920 the area held 92,501 African-American residents—85 percent of Chicago's African-American population.[55] "The 'black belt,'" a University of Chicago sociologist observed during the 1920s, "has become quite as rigidly a designated area for Negroes as if it had been provided by law."[56]

Living conditions for African-American Chicagoans deteriorated, and the South Side ghetto soon stood apart from the rest of the city. "In no other part of Chicago," reformer Sophonisba P. Breckinridge reported, "was there found a whole neighborhood so conspicuously dilapidated."[57] By the 1920s, the overall death rate was double the white level, and the death rate from tuberculosis was almost six times as great. According to one expert, Chicago was an unusually healthy city, though the death rate for African-American residents was comparable to that of Bombay.[58]

As migrants poured into the city and found themselves largely confined to the Black Belt, politicians and policemen conspired to concentrate the local vice industry in the city's South Side.[59] Brothels and gambling halls competed with the newcomers for space, even though city officials crowed that they had closed the local red-light district in 1912. "The resorts are forced on the colored people," the *Chicago Daily News* reported in 1916. "Many white owners of real estate who speak in horrified whispers of vice dangers view such dangers with complacency when these are thrust among colored families."[60] Also in 1916, a police captain sounded a familiar refrain when he bemoaned the "unspeakable conditions of immorality" in the Black Belt, eliding the presence of vice with the collective character of Chicago's African-American residents.[61] For white Chicagoans, the South Side ghetto was the city's "plague spot" where young, uncontrollable African-American "bucks" skulked, where vice abounded, and where African Americans assaulted and corrupted whites who wandered in.[62]

Racial tensions simmered and then exploded during the opening decades of the twentieth century. With white Chicagoans feeling threatened, mundane social encounters and trivial disagreements easily and frequently erupted into violence. News of the 1908 race riot in Springfield, Illinois, for example, nearly produced a lynching in Chicago, when local whites mistakenly believed that an African-American resident had murdered a local white woman.[63]

The increasingly charged atmosphere left white Chicagoans primed to view routine jostles and disagreements as challenges to a beleaguered racial hierarchy. One such incident occurred on a crowded trolley on March 11, 1908. John H. Mapp, a twenty-year-old African-American coachman, accidentally brushed against twenty-four-year-old James McDonald when the car lurched. When Mapp tried to explain that he had "not been to blame" for the mishap, McDonald bellowed, "Don't give me any of your lip," adding, "I'll fix you in a minute." He then produced a revolver, placed it directly against Mapp's chest, and pulled the trigger, killing the young coachman.[64] A similar incident occurred on July 2, 1917, when Fred Hohing and his wife boarded an elevated train and moved toward the rear of the car. In the process, Hohing stumbled on the foot of Clarence Kelly, a thirty-three-year-old African American. Hohing insisted that Kelly "whipped out" a knife and "leaped" at Mrs. Hohing, thus invoking white fears of African-American beasts attacking white women. Other passengers rushed to Hohing's aid, particularly after Hohing flashed the secret Shriner's "distress sign." The rapidly growing mob chased Kelly off the train and onto the platform, where Hohing and the other passengers caught Kelly and mauled him. Finally, a Chicago policeman arrived and fatally shot Kelly, after which Hohing boasted that they had "beaten a d—— nigger to death." The city's festering racial tensions also transformed Thomas J. Cantrell's disagreement with Walter Ashmore into a homicide on May 23, 1917. Both men worked on the elevated train platform at Sixty-First Street, Cantrell as a lamp trimmer and Ashmore as a painter. When Cantrell refused to share his lantern, Ashmore reacted with outrage, drew a gun, and shot the forty-five-year-old worker. Justifying his quick resort to violence, Ashmore told a coroner's jury that he was unaccustomed to "back talk from a Negro." The coroner's jury accepted the explanation and exonerated Ashmore.[65]

Early twentieth-century labor turmoil also contributed to the deterioration of race relations in the city. Relatively high wages in Chicago's burgeoning industrial sector had long attracted migrants. But local employers especially relied on African-American workers during strikes, often neglecting to tell the newcomers that they would be strikebreakers. White workers learned to view African Americans as "scabs" or potential scabs, and racial solidarity trumped ethnic conflict in such circumstances.[66] In May 1905 the volatile mixture of class tensions and racial enmity ignited when the Teamsters' Union, supporting local garment workers, went on strike against Marshall Field and Company, Chicago's premier retailer. The job action quickly spread, affecting every major department store in the city. The Employer's Teaming Company responded by recruiting and bringing in railroad car after railroad car of African-American workers to replace the striking teamsters. "Negro hating concerns such as Marshall Field and Company, Mandel Brothers, and Montgomery Ward and Company," the *Chicago Broad Ax* reported, "have no use for Negroes in general except to use them as brutish clubs to beat their white help over the head."[67] The strategy succeeded: the African-American newcomers simultaneously kept the freight moving and became the principal targets for angry strikers. Union teamsters and their supporters attacked the strikebreakers—or those perceived to be scabs—on street corners, by lunch wagons, and in alleys and bars throughout the city. The teamsters' strike lasted for more than three months, and twenty-two Chicagoans died from the labor violence during this period, one-third of whom were African American.

More important than the precise death toll from the Teamsters' Strike, such labor conflict added to the brittleness of race relations in early twentieth-century Chicago, inciting white residents to attack African Americans and conditioning African-American residents to anticipate violence when they encountered whites. According to the *Chicago Tribune,* the 1905 strike created "race war conditions" in the city.[68] When a streetcar conductor, for example, discovered that an African-American rider, Walter Jones, possessed an incorrect streetcar transfer, the conductor waited until he saw a group of white workers at the street corner before ordering Jones off the car. When Jones hesitated, the obliging workers "dragged" him to the street and "pummeled" him.[69]

More often than not, public tensions produced private violence, and the weapons procured for self-defense were used against friends and loved ones.[70] Only about one-quarter of homicides involving African-American Chicagoans—either as killers or as victims—crossed racial lines in 1905.[71] The African-American homicide rate, however, rose by 43 percent, and the African-American domestic homicide rate spiked by 237 percent during 1905.[72]

In a series of skirmishes that eerily presaged the bloody 1919 race riot, Chicagoans beginning in the 1890s battled over turf. With increasing frequency and brutality, whites established "dead lines" beyond which African Americans ventured at their own peril. Following an interracial confrontation in the summer of 1896, for example, white residents posted a sign on Forty-Seventh Street, announcing that "there's to be no coons allowed on this street after this."[73] During the Teamsters' Strike, union "sympathizers and race rioters" posted a large sign at Twenty-Seventh Street and Wentworth Avenue, stating "Negroes not allowed to cross this Dead Line." According to the *Broad Ax*, an African-American newspaper, violators "were assaulted, spat upon, dragged from street cars, and beat into insensibility."[74] Similar warnings and violence erupted repeatedly, typically following rumors of African-American attacks on white residents.

If white Chicagoans felt besieged, African-American Chicagoans were besieged. They faced mounting discrimination at the workplace, increasing violence on the streets, and rising institutional racism as local clubs and service organizations, including hospitals, the YMCA and YWCA, and athletic facilities, closed their doors to African-American residents.[75] The new size of Chicago's African-American community, however, resulted in complex responses to the surging levels of racism and the growing threats of violence, simultaneously exposing and blunting class divisions. Middle-class and elite African Americans, many of whom were longtime residents of the city, launched programs of social uplift and self-help in the hopes of improving life in the Black Belt, reducing friction with white residents, and preserving their own status atop Chicago's African-American community.[76] Many local ministers, for example, urged newcomers to resist "strong drink and ways of vice."[77] The Reverend H. E. Stewart, the president of the Lincoln Law and Order League, suggested that "a systematic effort should be made by the better class of negroes as well as of the other race to rid the community as far as possible of that disturbing element which tends to incite crime and vice." Likewise, Robert S. Abbott's influential *Chicago Defender* encouraged readers to cooperate with local law enforcers. "Detect and turn over to justice offenders of our race," the newspaper advised, and undertake a "general house-cleaning."[78]

Other voices in the community suggested more strident responses to racial discrimination—and particularly to white aggression. As Chicago's African-American population grew, and as residents felt less isolated, a new kind of racial consciousness and confidence emerged, which often muted class tensions.[79] Some community leaders hinted that African-American Chicagoans should react more forcefully to racial violence. During the Teamsters' Strike, for example, the *Chicago Broad Ax* reported that "in many instances the police have stood idly by and permitted the so-called better element of the whites to assault colored people—to drag them from the street cars— to beat them up and otherwise mistreat them, simply to furnish them with amusement." The newspaper also wryly observed that "the only wonder is that more Negroes do not commit acts of violence and arm themselves to protect their wives, their children, and their lives."[80] A few community leaders offered less subtle prescriptions. In the wake of a 1917 race riot in East St. Louis, a local attorney urged African-American Chicagoans to "get enough guns to protect yourselves."[81]

White residents began to encounter a "New Negro" on the streets of Chicago.[82] African-American residents increasingly responded to familiar slights and insults. Eugene Tucker, for example, died in a fight that began when he objected to being called a "nigger."[83] In a similar incident, on September 21, 1917, Arthur Eugene, a twenty-seven-year-old chauffeur, shot and killed Russell Dale, a thirty-five-year-old white businessmen. "Say, nigger, do you want to drive me home?" Dale had asked Eugene in a local parking garage. Eugene recoiled at the term, and the two men quarreled, with an astonished Dale protesting, "I meant no insult. I have had a colored boy for twenty-five years and I often called him nigger." Rejecting the explanation and, according to the *Chicago Tribune,* in "sulky humor," Eugene produced a gun and fired from close range.[84] In an editorial entitled "That Nigger Word," the *Chicago Defender* reminded white Chicagoans that the "type of a man who felt he could not exist without enduring the humiliation and insults of his white employer is now extinct."[85]

White ruffians, many of whom prowled in small gangs or "athletic clubs," sometimes learned the same lesson. Twenty-five-year-old Frank Hurley was known as a brawler and as someone who "frequently insulted the colored man." Standing on a street corner with a group of friends on May 12, 1901, Hurley saw Frank Wilson approaching and announced, "Here comes that nigger again." Wilson replied, "I'm as good as you are, you good-for-nothing white man," prompting Hurley to grab a whip and to instruct Wilson to "dance." The twenty-three-year-old Wilson drew his gun and fired a single shot into Hurley's face. Similarly, during the 1905 Teamsters' Strike, three men, whose self-stated goal was "driving the blacks off the face of the earth," descended on "Black Jack" Taylor, a driver for a local coal company, and ordered him to "get down on his knees." Taylor, however, proposed a different option. According to a bemused local journalist, Taylor "whipped out a revolver and told the men to 'duck.'"[86] Most homicides occurred within racial lines, though an increasing proportion of African-American killers targeted whites. During the opening decade of the century, whites comprised 22 percent of the victims of African-American killers, but by 1920 the figure had risen to nearly 30 percent. At the same time, more white killers targeted African Americans, with the proportion of African-American victims jumping from 4 percent to 8 percent. Race relations deteriorated over time, and this process revealed itself in homicides as well as in segregated neighborhoods, restrictive covenants, and fire-bombings.

Nor could African-American Chicagoans expect help from the local police. Again and again, community leaders complained that municipal law enforcers watched passively as white residents attacked local African Americans, a charge that would be repeated during both the Teamsters' Strike of 1905 and the Race Riot of 1919.[87] In May 1905 the *Chicago Broad Ax* fumed that "the majority of the policemen in what is called the 'Black District,' for some cause or other, think they have no other mission to perform than to arrest all colored men with fire-arms and to permit white men to go heavily armed, so they can beat up and shoot the colored people down like Jack Rabbits."[88] A similar sequence of events fueled the 1919 riot.[89] Chicago policemen often responded to interracial confrontations by launching mass arrests of African-American residents.[90] Journalists also pointed out that Chicago law enforcers often participated in racial violence. On February 27, 1911, Frank W. Knack, a city policeman, was riding on a streetcar when he saw Robert Nelson's wagon obstructing traffic on Elston Avenue. As he left the streetcar, Knack remarked that he "would show how 'niggers' were done in the 'South.'" With his baton, Knack bludgeoned to death the thirty-four-year-old Nelson—and was later exonerated for the attack.[91] The number and the proportion of African-American residents killed by Chicago policemen soared during the early twentieth century, more than doubling between its first and second decades. In 1920, African Americans made up 4.1 percent of Chicago's population and 23 percent of the residents killed by Chicago policeman. Expecting either indifference from the police or abuse from municipal authorities, African-American Chicagoans handled conflict themselves.[92] At its best, this strategy contributed to the steadying influence of local ministers and other community leaders. But at its worst, it produced violence in the Black Belt and reinforced the antagonistic stance of white Chicagoans, including white policeman.

In other, less direct ways as well, racism transformed minor disagreements into deadly fights. Institutional discrimination insured that African-American Chicagoans received inadequate medical attention, increasing the likelihood that they would bleed to death from treatable injuries or that they would succumb to infections from nonlethal wounds. Only two of the ten hospitals located near the Black Belt in the early 1920s admitted African Americans "without restriction," and these two facilities, with a combined 110 beds, served an African-American population of over 100,000.[93] Two-thirds of all Chicago hospitals placed restrictions on the admission and treatment of African-American residents.[94] African-American Chicagoans were more likely to be shot or stabbed than white Chicagoans, and they were more likely to die as a consequence of inadequate medical care, adding to the lethality of criminal violence in the city's Black Belt.

Tensions over jobs, space, and institutions overlapped on Sunday, July 27, 1919, on the shores of Lake Michigan, precipitating what became known as the Chicago Race Riot. For four days white and African-American residents engaged in open warfare, which extended deep into the Black Belt. White gangs inflicted much of the carnage, though the police and African-American rioters contributed as well. By the time the violence subsided, thirty-eight Chicagoans were dead, including twenty-three African Americans, and over five hundred people were injured, two-thirds of whom were African American. Over the course of 1919, seventy African-American Chicagoans were killed, and nearly two-thirds died at the hands of the city's white residents.[95]

In most ways, however, 1919 was an aberration.[96] Despite the death toll from the riot, the lion's share of lethal violence between 1890 and

1920 occurred within racial lines. Moreover, rioting claimed only a few percent of all African-American homicide victims during this period. But the kinds of pressures that exploded in the summer of 1919 significantly affected African-American life and African-American violence throughout the era. Racism contributed to African-American homicide in powerful, if subtle, ways, exacerbating more mundane stresses and conflicts. Just as racial conflict exaggerated the violent facets of plebeian culture during the late 1870s and the 1880s, it also distorted the social and cultural wellsprings of interpersonal violence in the decades after 1890.

Like white homicide, African-American homicide moved out of local saloons, away from plebeian rituals, and into the home and family life after 1890. For white Chicagoans, such a shift reflected closely related demographic and cultural changes, particularly the balancing of sex ratios, the waning of the bachelor subculture, and the increasing embrace of domestic masculinity. For African-American Chicagoans, a similar, though intensified, process occurred. The Great Migration launched a period of rapid family formation, for the huge influx of newcomers quickly reduced the surplus of men in Chicago's African-American community. In 1890, the city had 125 African-American men for every 100 African-American women. A decade later the surfeit of men dropped by nearly 50 percent, and by 1910 Chicago's African-American population included 106 men for every 100 women, a sex ratio that made the city's African-American population slightly better balanced than the city's white population. With nearly equal numbers of men and women, and with migrants eager to restart their lives in the industrial North, Chicago's African-American residents established families. In 1900, 53 percent of African-American men between the ages of twenty-five and thirty-four were unmarried. A decade later the figure dipped below 42 percent, which was comparable to the white population. By 1920, just 34 percent of

African-American men in this age group remained unmarried, a figure below that of the city's white men.[97]

These shifts produced a sea change in African-American social
life and in African-American lethal violence. Homicides in saloons
fell, and lethal violence in the home rose, reflecting the new patterns
of social interaction. Between 1875 and 1890, 6 percent of the homicides committed by African-American Chicagoans occurred in the
home. From 1890 to 1910, 38 percent took place in private residences,
a sixfold increase. The motives for violence changed in correspond-
ing ways. In the earlier period, drunken brawls triggered 35 percent of
deaths from African-American criminal violence, compared with less
than 17 percent during the later era. Despite the blaring newspaper
headlines and omnipresent reports that alcohol inflamed the savage passions of African Americans, white Chicagoans committed a
higher proportion of homicides as a result of drunken brawls after
1890. Similarly, the relationship between killers and their victims
shifted. The proportion of African-American homicides occurring
between acquaintances fell by nearly one-third between 1875–1890
and 1890–1910.

As with white Chicagoans, African-American family violence
soared after 1890. The proportion of homicides involving relatives
rose by 37 percent between 1890 and 1910. Nearly all of the increase,
however, occurred in spousal homicide. During the late 1870s and the
1880s, spousal violence accounted for 6 percent of African-American
homicides. Between 1890 and 1910, the figure rose to over 14 percent, an increase of 119 percent. In part, this pattern reflected the
unusual demographic composition of Chicago's African-American
community. The Black Belt had relatively few children and very few
young homicide victims. In 1910, children under the age of five made
up 5.6 percent of the city's African-American population, compared
with 10.2 percent of Chicago's white population.[98] Children were
even more underrepresented in African-American homicides; Afri-

can-American parents who killed their children made up less than one-half of 1 percent of African-American homicides between 1890 and 1910—one-seventh the figure for white residents. Nor did other relatives comprise a significant share of African-American homicide victims. Homicides involving family members other than children or spouses accounted for only 3 percent of African-American deaths from lethal violence during this period, compared with 7 percent for white residents.

African-American Chicagoans killed their spouses and their lovers at extremely high levels. The African-American spousal homicide rate was nearly seven times the white spousal rate, and during the first decade of the twentieth century, it averaged more than eleven times the white level.[99] Fatal lovers' quarrels followed a similar pattern, increasing sharply among African Americans after 1890 and far outpacing the comparable white rate. Between 1875 and 1890, lovers' quarrels accounted for 3 percent of African-American homicides. During the next two decades, as sex ratios balanced and marriage rates soared, lovers' quarrels made up nearly 9 percent of African-American homicides, more than double the figure for white Chicagoans. These changes also increased the proportion of African-American women who died from criminal violence. Between 1875 and 1890, women made up 9 percent of African-American homicide victims. Over the next two decades the percentage tripled.

Except in its frequency, African-American spousal homicide was similar to white spousal homicide, for the tensions and battles that triggered such violence transcended racial lines. As in white uxoricides, separation was a leading catalyst for African-American wife killing. Between 1890 and 1910, 36 percent of white couples and 46 percent of African-American couples were separated at the time of the spousal homicide. And in both instances, the final battle of a faltering marriage usually occurred when a frantic husband begged his determined wife to reconcile. On July 17, 1904, for example, Charles

Rollins, an African-American tailor, followed his estranged wife to her sister's apartment and "pleaded" with her to return to him. "When she refused," according to a local reporter, "Rollins drew a revolver and fired a shot at the woman," killing her. Daniel Francis shot his wife in 1905, and John Ewing murdered his spouse, Gertrude, in 1907 under similar circumstances, comparable to dozens of white wife killers.[100]

African-American women also left their husbands for the same reasons as did white women. Occasionally drunkenness or infidelity triggered the separation, but more often turn-of-the-century wives—regardless of race—left their marriages when their husbands failed to support them appropriately and failed to meet the women's expectations for the unions. Ophelia Williams left her husband in 1908 because Andrew Williams "failed to provide properly for her," just as Anna Bernard left her husband, also in 1908, "because he failed to provide for the family."[101]

The conversations—and even the specific language—that preceded African-American uxoricides during this era were nearly indistinguishable from those that unfolded immediately before white wife murders. Husbands typically insisted that they loved their wives, that they were doing their best but would try harder, and that they desperately wanted to reconcile. When the women, many of whom had separated and reconciled before, refused to return, their husbands, like Andrew Williams, would announce, "If I can't have you, nobody else can," and reached for their knives or guns. "You know I love you," Thomas Bishop sobbed as he begged his estranged wife, Virginia, to come home. Seconds after she rejected his plea, he fatally stabbed her.[102]

For both African-American and white men, crumbling marriages threatened core notions of manliness. No less than their white counterparts, African-American men in turn-of-the-century Chicago embraced an ideal of domestic masculinity, and thus an inability to support their families and to satisfy their wives cut to the essence of their self-image as men. Such a challenge to gender identity accounted both for the shift from peer homicide to wife killing and for the extraordinarily high rates of African-American uxoricide.

Racial discrimination and poverty compounded the pressures facing African-American men. Husbands in every Chicago neighborhood struggled to support their families and to meet their own and their wives' expectations for family life. But these challenges were particularly imposing for African-American men, who migrated to the industrial North with lofty hopes and ambitious plans for the future only to find themselves trapped in the most menial, low-paying, and insecure jobs, having to endure harassment and bullying on the streets and at work. As Chicago's racial climate deteriorated, employers and unions excluded African-American workers, further miring these men and their families in poverty. Not surprisingly, 83 percent of African-American killers and 86 percent of African-American wife killers between 1890 and 1910 were unskilled workers.[103]

In his background, in the problems that he encountered, and in the pressures that contributed to his crime, Andrew Williams was a typical African-American wife killer. But because he was arrested, indicted, tried, convicted, sentenced to death, and executed for the 1908 murder of his wife, Ophelia, the sequence of events leading to this homicide was recounted in unusual detail—in newspaper accounts, police records, court documents, and petitions and appeals to the State Board of Pardons and to the governor of Illinois. Like many African-American men, and like the majority of African-American wife killers, Williams had tried to establish a household, support his family, and deal with the ignominy and humiliation of failure. Literate but unskilled, he migrated from Kansas to Chicago in 1904. Once in the city, Williams worked at "different occupations," mainly as a day laborer, and he endured frequent bouts of unemployment.[104] At the age of twenty-two, he married Ophelia Hardy, an eighteen-year-old woman from a respectable Chicago family.

Unable to secure "steady employment," Williams could not support his wife. In the first month of their marriage, the couple resided with Andrew's sister. For the next few months, they lived on their own, but Williams lost his job and was unable to pay for their apartment. The Williamses then moved in with Ophelia's parents, with Andrew "paying for their room and food when he had work."[105] Often, however, he was unemployed, which enraged his father-in-law, John W. Hardy, who questioned his son-in-law's "inclination to work."[106] When Andrew once again lost his job, Ophelia left him. Andrew returned to his sister's apartment, still hoping to reconcile with his wife as soon as he could find work. At the insistence of her father, Ophelia swore out a complaint against her husband and charged him with "abandonment"—because the couple no longer lived together and because Andrew failed to support his family, which now included a baby. A Chicago policeman and a resident of the city for nearly a quarter of a century, John Hardy arrested his son-in-law and vowed that he would "not rest until I have separated that worthless hound from my daughter."[107] Hardy also threatened "to kill Andrew Williams the first opportunity he got." But the Williamses reconciled, and Ophelia refused to testify against Andrew, compelling a judge to dismiss the abandonment charge—and infuriating Hardy.[108] For the next few months, the couple lived on their own and happily, though once again Andrew suffered "misfortunes in the matter of losing his employment" and was unable to provide for his wife and child.[109] In December 1907 Ophelia left her husband and returned—again—to her parents' house, prompting John Hardy to comment that "he ought to have taken him [Andrew Williams] out on the prairie the day he arrested him and killed him then, the same as a dog, and no one would have known it."[110] Desperate to reconcile with his wife, but terrified of his father-in-law, Andrew Williams began carrying a gun when he visited his wife and child, being careful to avoid setting foot in Hardy's home. "Every [sic] since I have been married," Williams wrote shortly before he was executed, "I all ways [*sic*] worked and try to make my wife and baby happy."[111] On the morning of March 10, 1908, Andrew Williams went to see his wife and begged her to reconcile. She refused, and in a swirl of confusion, despondence, anger, and fear, Andrew Williams shot his wife and became involved in a gun battle with his father-in-law.[112]

For men such as Andrew Williams, poverty undercut their self-esteem as they struggled to establish themselves as heads of households. Racism heightened the potential for domestic violence for several reasons: because it contributed to poverty and unemployment in the African-American community of early twentieth-century Chicago; because it threatened men's status as breadwinners; and because it subjected African-American men to abuse and humiliation at the hands of employers, coworkers, law enforcers, and ruffians. Unable to control their public activities, men such as Andrew Williams were desperate to exert control over their private lives. The urban setting also magnified the cultural impact of poverty for young men who had grown up experiencing the patriarchal authority commanded by heads of southern farm families.

Routine responses to dearth compounded the emasculating effects of poverty and racism and thus the sources of domestic conflict. Housing was especially expensive for African-American residents, who already endured unemployment and underemployment. Property owners, for example, typically gouged their South Side tenants, charging African-American renters as much as 50 percent more than white Chicagoans for comparable units.[113] "The combination of these high rents and low wages," one observer explained, "necessitated the taking in of lodgers in order to meet expenses."[114] According to a contemporary survey, two-thirds of African-American households included such a boarder, many of whom were young, single men.[115] These boarders enabled heads of households to pay the rent. But the presence of lodgers often intensified marital strife, as husbands struggling—and failing—to support their families grew suspicious of the relationship between their wives and their lodg-ers. Twenty-five-year-old Lester Gardner, for example, became con-vinced that his estranged wife, Letitia, was romantically involved with her boarder, Charles Washington. After failing to convince Letitia to reconcile, Lester Gardner shot and killed his wife, Wash-ington, and Gardner's mother-in-law, whom he believed—cor-rectly—had encouraged Letitia to reject his overture.[116] Although African-American and white uxoricides were sparked by similar cir-cumstances, the one area of difference involved jealousy-inspired vio-lence: between 1890 and 1920 African-American men were twice as likely to kill their wives during fights sparked by jealousy, and many of these fights were prompted by the presence of lodgers.[117] Contem-porary sociologists and social workers recognized this danger and warned of the "enduring evil of lodgers."[118]

Other strategies for weathering hard times were also fraught with problems. Income pooling, a common strategy for financially strapped families during this era, generated considerable friction among Afri-can-American Chicagoans. Many urban families, particularly those headed by immigrants, depended on the resources contributed by young children, who were either sent into the workforce or encour-aged to scavenge for coal, wood, or other household necessities. But African-American parents had fewer sons and daughters and so had to look elsewhere for extra sources of money.[119] More than any major group of Chicagoans, African-American wives and mothers worked outside of the home.[120] In 1920 over one-third of married African-American women held jobs, compared with one-eighth of native-born white women and one-twelfth of foreign-born white women.[121] These African-American women were probably more independent and less willing to submit to patriarchal authority, for they often in-sisted on controlling the wages that they earned. To men, such be-havior represented an assault on patriarchal authority and triggered many violent episodes, as insecure husbands tried to maintain their household and assert their dominance.

Both the diminished authority of African-American husbands and the enhanced autonomy of African-American wives created still more pressure on gender roles, which ignited still more domestic violence. Accustomed to greater independence than white women, African-American women were particularly willing to leave unhappy marriages, especially if relatives lived close by and could take in the women. It was not coincidental that African-American Chicagoans had unusually high rates of separation, divorce, and uxoricide.[122]

Targeted by saloon toughs, white workers, and local policemen, trapped in low-paying jobs, compelled to rely on the money provided by young, single lodgers, and dependent on the earnings of their independent wives, African-American men felt attacked on all sides in turn-of-the-century Chicago. The indignities suffered in the workplace and on the streets of the city combined with a devastating loss of control and authority in private settings to fuel violence, particularly uxoricide.[123] African-American men experienced many of the same pressures as white men, but poverty and racism exaggerated these pressures and therefore produced extraordinarily high levels of domestic homicide.

The African-American homicide rate leveled off and fell during the 1910s, even as the white lethal violence rate continued to increase. Between the 1900s and the 1910s, for example, the African-American homicide rate dropped by 28 percent, while the white homicide rate rose by the same proportion. For the period between 1875 and 1920, the African-American homicide rate peaked in 1905, at 88 per 100,000 residents—twelve times the rate for white Chicagoans. The African-American spousal homicide rate reached its zenith two years later, in 1907, when it spiked to thirty-six times the white spousal homicide rate.[124] The gap between African-American homicide and white homicide narrowed, though it remained substantial.[125] During the late 1910s the African-American homicide rate dropped, though it was more than quadruple the white rate, and the African-American spousal homicide rate hovered at nearly eight times the white level.

Although racism and poverty remained intertwined and continued to rack African-American residents during the 1910s, the increasing maturity of the city's South Side community may have provided informal mechanisms for resolving disputes and reducing violence, particularly as churches and other local institutions became firmly established.[126] Moreover, despite the increasing flow of newcomers to the segregated Black Belt, the most frenetic and unstable days of dating and family formation may have passed by the 1910s.[127] The drop in African-American uxoricide reflected broader changes as well, for white uxoricide rates also rose in the middle years of the opening decade of the new century and then fell over time.

In one other respect, African-American homicide tracked white homicide, though at elevated levels. Just as white women became more murderous during the 1910s, so too did African-American women. But once again, the pattern was more pronounced for African-American Chicagoans. Women made up 6 percent of white killers and 15 percent of African-American killers between 1910 and 1920. In addition, the rate at which African-American women committed homicide rose by 27 percent between the first and the second decades of the new century.[128] During the 1910s, African-American women committed homicide at eleven times the rate of white women, further convincing white Chicagoans that their South Side neighbors were deviant, depraved, and dangerous.[129]

Homicide by African-American women differed in some ways from that committed by white women. When white women killed during the 1910s, 35 percent of their victims were children.[130] African-American women, however, did not kill their sons and daughters.[131] Chicago police files contained no cases of African-American women killing children between 1910 and 1920. Nor did local law enforcers link any African-American women to infanticides during this period.[132] These women typically had fewer children than their white counterparts, though such a demographic factor would not account for the complete absence of child victims.[133]

When African-American women killed, 84 percent of their victims were men, two-thirds of whom were lovers or husbands.[134] Compared with white Chicagoans, African-American men fared badly in domestic disputes between 1910 and 1920. In fatal lovers' quarrels involving white residents, women committed one-fifth of the homicides. Among African-American Chicagoans, women committed three-fifths of these homicides. Jilted and betrayed African-American women were significantly more violent than their white counterparts. Similarly, white women committed 16 percent of spousal homicides, while African-American women committed 37 percent.

Conflict over gender roles, in combination with the brutalizing effects of racism and poverty, fueled much of this bloodshed and accounted for the unusual rate and character of African-American women's homicide during the 1910s. More accustomed to working outside of the home and supporting themselves than white women, and especially more than immigrant women, African-American women were quicker to resist abusive partners and to employ aggressive self-help in doing so.[135] Just as white women typically killed their husbands in self-defense during the early twentieth century, the pattern was exaggerated in African-American households. During the 1910s, half of white husband killers acted in self-defense, while 57 percent of African-American husband killers struck, stabbed, or shot their spouses to protect themselves. Explaining why she killed her thirty-six-year-old husband, Belle Benson stated, "He started to beat me again and I shot him."[136]

African-American women were more likely than white Chicagoans to kill abusive husbands.[137] At least in part, this was because African-American women had fewer options than white Chicagoans other than self-help.[138] The police, for example, offered scant protection to African-American women, preferring to ignore problems on the city's South Side and believing that such difficulties merely reflected the natural tendencies of the residents. Nor did the courts provide adequate protection. Judges expressed little concern about domestic violence in the Black Belt and often dismissed complaints filed by African-American women. As in white households, husbands who had been arrested but not convicted on wife-beating, desertion, or abandonment charges were often enraged that their wives had challenged their authority and threatened to punish them. Thus, when legal solutions failed, these women were simultaneously at increased risk for battering and left to protect themselves. "Young colored women," the Chicago City Council's Committee on Crime reported in 1915, "find themselves in a peculiarly defenceless [sic] and unprotected position."[139]

These African-American women may have been unprotected, but they were not defenseless. A few hours after a judge dismissed her assault complaint against her husband, Minnie Smith shot Walter Smith four times. "He had always said if I ever had him arrested he would kill me, and I knew he would do it," she said. "I knew he meant to kill me," Minnie Smith repeated, "so I shot him—and then I shot him some more." Minnie had desperately tried to escape from her husband during their "stormy" two-year marriage. The twenty-three-year-old woman left her abusive spouse five times; finally she turned to the legal system for protection. When Walter Smith walked out of the Harrison Street Court, Minnie Smith believed that she would be killed unless she acted first—so she acted first. African-American women, in short, were accustomed to relying on their own initiatives, and their actions after committing their violent acts attested to such survival skills. Police officers investigating African-American husband killings often remarked that the women seemed "cool and deliberate." Minnie Smith, who was one of those called "cool and deliberate," had stood over her husband's bullet-ravaged body and said, "I didn't get you this morning [in court], but I got you now." When Edward Franklin, a neighbor, saw Smith poised over her husband's body, Minnie turned to him and shouted, "If you don't go back [inside the house], I'll shoot you, too."[140] While white husband killers aroused sympathy from Chicago jurors, African-American husband killers were seen as vicious and were convicted at nearly four times the rate of white husband killers; during the span in which jurors exonerated or acquitted every white husband killer, half of African-American husband killers were convicted and sentenced to prison.[141] The combination of embattled men and strong women— or, as early twentieth-century sociologists St. Clair Drake and Horace P. Cayton noted, "dependent men and forceful women"—proved to be deadly, especially for abusive husbands and unfaithful lovers.[142] The collision of class-based, race-based, and gender-based pressures fueled soaring levels of homicide by Chicago's African-American women and contributed to the city's rising homicide rate.

The Great Migration transformed Chicago, enriching the city's cultural environment and accelerating its industrial development. But reactions to the migrants exposed political tensions, intensified group rivalries, spawned tenacious forms of institutional discrimination, and added to Chicago's unenviable record for lethal violence. Already the most violent major urban center outside of the South, Chicago became significantly more murderous during this era. Its homicide rate nearly doubled from 1890 to 1920, and the newcomers were overrepresented in the number of shootings, beatings, and stabbings. African Americans comprised 2.3 percent of the city's residents between 1890 and 1920, and they made up 14 percent of killers and 15 percent of homicide victims.[143]

White Chicagoans associated African Americans with deviant behavior, illicit activities, and violent crime, a combination that galvanized efforts to isolate and segregate the newcomers. According to

white observers from across ethnic, political, and economic spec-
trums, African Americans were by nature different from other residents; the migrants from the South were savage peasants who were
prone to impulsive acts, particularly when primed with alcohol or
driven by lust.[144] Some Chicagoans launched uplift programs to curb
these wild, dangerous tendencies, though other residents responded
to their fears with firebombs and firearms. If Chicago was "the worst
city on Earth," African Americans played a central role in its descent
into barbarism, according to many commentators.[145]

Contrary to the impressions of most observers, however, African-
American violence was similar to white violence. It resembled white
homicide in the form it took; and African-American violence paralleled white violence in how that form changed. White Chicagoans
became more orderly in public but more violent at home, and so did
African-American Chicagoans. For both white and African-American killers, shifting demographic and cultural forces eroded the raucous bachelor subculture of the late nineteenth century and hence reduced barroom scuffles and brothel fights.

Shifts in the nature of lethal violence, unlike shifts in Chicago's
social geography, crossed racial lines at the start of the twentieth century. Like its white counterpart, African-American homicide moved
from public space to private settings and became less impulsive, but
the violence increased in frequency. Killers, regardless of their race,
shot, stabbed, and slugged their victims in frantic attempts to regain
control of their households and to reestablish masculine authority in
the home. Uxoricides, white and African-American alike, occurred
in households where men struggled to support their families and
where women threatened to usurp patriarchal authority. The sources
of discord were similar; the sparks leading to lethal explosions tended
to be comparable; and the cycle of escalation, even the specific words
uttered before the homicides, was often identical. Finally, in both
African-American and white households, wife killing spiked during

the first decade of the new century, while husband killing surged during the second decade.

Across the city, the interaction of demographic shifts, class ideologies, and gender identities redefined the nature of social conflict—and generated rising levels of homicide. The same cluster of factors contributed to African-American violence, but racism compounded the volatility of these conflicting and colliding forces. The intersection of population factors, class tensions, gender tensions, and racial tensions triggered astronomically high levels of violence on Chicago's South Side.[146] The pressure points in masculine identity, for example, proved to be more raw for African-American men than for white men in turn-of-the-century Chicago. African-American men had a harder time providing for their families than white husbands and fathers did. In addition, African-American men were more likely to be challenged, humiliated, and belittled in public, making them more desperate to find stability and to maintain control at home. Finally, African-American husbands were more apt than white husbands to clash with independent wives who refused to submit to patriarchal authority and for whom separation or divorce seemed an increasingly viable response to marital dissatisfaction. Discrimination on the city's streets and in its workplaces simultaneously undermined the authority of African-American men and enhanced the autonomy of African-American women, adding to the potential for marital discord and violence.[147]

Andrew Williams thus shared a great deal with other men in Chicago and particularly with other early twentieth-century killers. He longed for a secure family life, struggled to preserve his household and to make his wife and child happy, and measured his status in these terms.[148] Having failed to meet these expectations, with his wife having seized control of their crumbling marriage and left him, with his father-in-law deriding him, calling him a "worthless hound" and threatening to kill him "if ever that black dog crosses the threshold of my house," Andrew Williams begged his wife to return and murdered her when she refused. In his aspirations and in his violence, Andrew Williams differed little from other early twentieth-century killers in the city. In the Black Belt, in Packingtown, along the Lake Front, and throughout Chicago, life became more orderly and less violent in public but more freighted with inner turmoil and more violent in private.

Chapter 5

"The Dead Man's Hand"

On the evening of Friday, February 17, 1911, Vincenzo Lubio, a forty-nine-year-old saloonkeeper, stood behind his bar playing cards with a stranger. Fifteen or twenty customers, all Italian immigrants, filled the saloon, drinking, relaxing, and enjoying the evening. Suddenly, without explanation, the stranger laid four cards on the bar: two black jacks and two black eights. This was the dreaded "dead man's hand," and Lubio knew that he was about to die.[1] Just as the stranger placed the fourth card in front of Lubio, a second stranger entered the saloon. "Making a mysterious signal which parted the crowd of Italians drinking at the bar," the newcomer walked directly to the saloonkeeper, produced a revolver, and "fired point blank." Despite the shooter's proximity to his victim, the first bullet missed its mark, but the second struck Lubio squarely in the face, between his mouth and the left side of his nose, and penetrated his brain. Police sergeant John Tierney arrived moments later, as the patrons, "gesticulating wildly," spilled out of the saloon and onto Oak Street in Chicago's "Little Sicily" neighborhood. The crowd initially buzzed about the shooting and especially about the cards arrayed on the bar, though the witnesses quickly became quiet and uncooperative. Only Lubio's daughter, Maria, and son-in-law, Joe Dizedero, remained in the saloon. As Tierney rushed toward Lubio, he heard Joe Dizedero "muttering 'Mafia, Mafia.'" According to a reporter for the *Chicago Inter Ocean,* the sergeant immediately concluded that Dizedero was "referring to the Italian secret organization of that name." Joe Dizedero, however, "absolutely refused to talk" to Tierney. Eager to reveal what she knew, Maria Dizedero turned to the police sergeant, but her husband, who "seemed paralyzed with fear," "immediately silenced" the woman. The Lubio family lived above the saloon, and the victim's wife soon appeared. She, too, provided no information, assuring police investigators that "her husband had received no threatening letters and had no enemies." None of the bar patrons would identify or even describe the killer and his card-playing accomplice. Pronounced dead at the saloon, Lubio's body was loaded into an ambulance and sent to the morgue. On the way, M. B. Wallen, the "Ambulance Surgeon," noticed that the dead man continued to breathe. Wallen frantically alerted the driver and instructed him to hurry to Passavant Hospital. There Lubio died as the attendants lifted him onto an operating table.[2] Vincenzo Lubio was the twenty-second homicide victim of 1911.[3] He was also the second victim of Mafia assassins in the new year and the fifth since the beginning of 1910.

The Lubio murder was not a typical homicide. Few Chicago killers announced their intentions with an assortment of playing cards, and rarely did they offer cues to their victims or to witnesses. But neither was Vincenzo Lubio's 1911 murder particularly unusual. During the opening decades of the twentieth century Chicagoans grew increasingly accustomed to new forms of lethal violence, such as Mafia assassinations. Vendettas and feuds exploded on the streets of the city; relatives of victims rebuffed police investigators, vowed vengeance, and exacted revenge in grisly reprisals; and peasant rituals seemed to replace old-fashioned barrooms brawls and labor violence as the local population changed.

Early twentieth-century Chicago was a city of immigrants, and most residents recognized that the increasing waves of newcomers affected their community in complex ways. The transplantation of Europeans spurred Chicago's legendary growth and contributed to its energy and dynamism, but it also crammed "parasites," "defectives," and "criminals" into the city's most densely packed, poverty-ridden, and culturally isolated slums.[4] Old-stock Americans—the native-born children of Americans—comprised only one-fifth of Chicago's population in 1910. A decade later the figure was only slightly higher. By 1920, Chicago had more than fifty thousand German-, Irish-, Polish-, Bohemian-, Russian-, Swedish-, and Italian-born residents.[5] Among American urban centers, only New York City had more immigrants than did Chicago. But more unsettling than the volume of newcomers was the fact that the immigrants who peopled Chicago's ethnic neighborhoods seemed increasingly alien. Hailing principally from southern and eastern Europe, they often possessed darker complexions, spoke foreign languages, practiced strange customs, and were typically Roman Catholic, Eastern Orthodox, or Jewish.

Even if the newcomers made positive contributions to local society, many Chicagoans feared that the tide of immigrants included a dangerous, even vicious, element. On the one hand, contemporary observers boasted that "Chicago is the lodestone that attracts the enterprise and commercial talent of two hemispheres." But on the other hand, these writers also believed that "our whole unskilled, manual laboring population is composed almost entirely of the classes which have not yet advanced beyond the stage of impulse and unreflective action." "Chicago is the dumping ground for the different nations of

Europe," Chief of Police John M. Collins warned in 1906. "It is a kind of rallying point for the scum of the earth."[6]

Between 1900 and 1920, Chicago's homicide rate climbed by nearly 50 percent and the city's foreign-born population bulged by almost 40 percent.[7] At least in part because of the colorful, almost lurid, attention directed to immigrant violence, such as the murder of Vincenzo Lubio, Chicagoans often linked the increase in homicide to the arrival of southern and eastern European immigrants. Contemporary observers, even those sympathetic toward the newcomers, frequently concluded that "the increase in crimes of violence in Chicago is due to the presence of a large foreign-born element of an inferior economic and social status." With the settlement of the "Italian ex-bandit, and the blood-thirsty Spaniard, the bad man from Sicily, the Hungarian, the Croatian and the Pole," local crime expert James Edgar Brown explained in 1906, "is it any wonder that altercations occur and blood is shed? The farmer does not turn the vicious, sharp horned bull into the pasture with his horses, or permit small chickens to mingle with his hogs."[8]

As Chicago grew, as the city became more heterogeneous, as immigrants created small "colonies" throughout the community, as local sociologists panicked about the effects of such isolation, and as employers, municipal officials, and reformers struggled to teach the newcomers industrial discipline, self-control, survival skills, and "American ways," the nature of lethal violence changed. The "strange," "savage" customs of immigrants introduced new—and, in some instances, revived old—forms of conflict, discord, and bloodshed.[9] Sicilians, who seemed to live apart from the larger society, brought distinctive kinds of domestic homicide, altering citywide trends in family violence. Likewise, Greek immigrants killed and were killed in different ways than native-born Chicagoans or oldstock Americans. "Illiterate, turbulent Poles and Czechs" also preferred familiar methods of settling disputes.[10] Though the newcomers rapidly adjusted to daily life in the big city and quickly adopted local conventions of lethal violence, the shifting composition of Chicago's population transformed the character of homicide during the early twentieth century.

Immigrant violence, however, represented only one of the sources of increasing homicide in Chicago. The spike in spousal violence by established residents also contributed significantly to the city's rising homicide rate. Moreover, violence by and against African-American residents produced a greater death toll than Italian or Polish or Greek or Bohemian or Russian killers did, a trend that anxious Chicagoans recognized, except during xenophobic panics. In short, violence ravaged some ethnic neighborhoods and some groups of immigrants endured high levels of homicide, though the newcomers from Europe did not cause the increase in Chicago violence as much as they added to an already rising tide. Even without Mafia assassins or Polish brawlers, the Cook County coroner faced a ballooning workload during the opening decades of the twentieth century. But with the arrival of huge waves of European immigrants in the city during the 1900s and the 1910s, many of them poor and badly treated by both longtime residents and other newcomers, Chicago's homicide rate surged.

Immigrants poured into Chicago during this period. In 1890 the city's foreign-born population approached half a million. Ten years later it was 100,000 more, and by 1910 Chicago had almost 800,000 foreign-born residents. Chicago's booming population increased two-and-a-half-fold in the thirty years between 1890 and 1920. During the same period, the city's Polish-born population grew nearly six-fold; the Italian-born population rose more than tenfold; and the Greek-born population jumped forty-seven-fold.[11] These figures, however, understate the demographic transformation in two important ways. First, they exclude the hundreds of thousands of southern and eastern European newcomers who passed through the city between the decennial tabulations and thus failed to appear in Chicago's census population figures. Second, many American-born children of immigrants remained a part of ethnic communities, even though they were in legal terms natives and citizens. Nearly two-thirds of native-born Chicagoans in 1920 were the children of immigrant or of "mixed" parents.[12] A turn-of-the-century visitor termed Chicago the "most American of American cities, and yet the most mongrel; the second American city of the globe, the fifth German city, the third Swedish, the second Polish, the first and only veritable Babel of the age."[13]

Settlement patterns exaggerated the impact of immigration. "These foreigners," an early twentieth-century scholar explained, "settle in whole districts."[14] By the outbreak of the Great War, nearly two dozen distinct "Little Italies" or "Little Sicilies" dotted the river wards and the north side of Chicago.[15] Larger Swedish "colonies" and Polish enclaves took root as well. But the ethnic landscape of the city proved to be even more complicated and more internally divided than many early twentieth-century writers understood. Chicago's Little Sicilies, for example, were not comprised entirely of Sicilians, and neither were they entirely Italian, as no group of immigrants completely controlled any section of the city. Instead, clusters of residents and anchor institutions, such as churches, meeting halls, shops, and saloons, cleaved the city into a confusing tangle of neighborhoods where village and regional attachments initially clashed, gradually blurred, and eventually melded into new forms. Contemporary observers, especially middle-class and native-born Chicagoans, elided these small, heterogeneous sections of the city into unified "Italian" or "Polish" or "Greek" districts, even though cultural and linguistic divisions parsed the newcomers into smaller units.[16] Local law enforcers were especially inclined to see larger, more clearly defined areas.

Journalists and other popular writers explained local violence in blunt terms. Discussing why "Chicago leads America in homicides," police chief John Collins pointed to the "foreign population" of the city. "A large proportion of Chicago homicides," he reported, "are committed by foreigners." Mrs. Willard P. Thorpe, the wife of a prominent pastor, concurred, stating that "crime in Chicago is due largely to the influx of European immigrants." She added that "such a heterogeneous mass of ignorance is a menace to our country, and is, in a measure, largely responsible for the lawlessness of this city." Some Chicago observers offered more precise explanations. "Our really vicious foreign element," an analyst of local crime argued in 1906, "comes from Russian Poland, Sicily, and the Calabrian portion of Italy." According to a 1907 reporter, Chicago murders "were [the] hasty, savage acts of a crude population"—mainly "the European peasant, suddenly freed from the restraints of poverty and of rigid police authority."[17]

Eugenicists, alienists, and criminologists employed scientific methods to reach comparable conclusions. Many violent offenders were "born criminals." The Bertillon system of measurement, for example, confirmed the innate criminality of Lazarus Averbuch, a twenty-five-year-old Russian Jew who in 1908 tried to kill George Shippy, Chicago's police chief, and died in the attempt.[18] Dr. J. M. Lavin termed Averbuch "a pronounced degenerate. . . . The general features, the low forehead, receding chin, the pronounced simian ears, high cheek bones, and large mouth, all indicate the degenerate." Similarly, Dr. W. T. Belfield warned a joint meeting of Chicago's Physician's Club and Law Club about "race suicide." "Society carefully rears all its defectives—criminals, imbeciles, idiots, etc.—to breed more of their kind, and robs its own worthy citizens to do so. The cattle breeder," he quipped, "is wiser."[19] According to these observers, immigration had deposited the weakest, most defective, and most dangerous members of the human race, in enormous numbers, in the ethnic neighborhoods of early twentieth-century Chicago, and this fact accounted for the sharp increase in violent crime in the city.

Even dissenters from the harshest scientific racism of the era often contributed to these stereotypes and to the resulting xenophobia. For example, the Senate Commission on Immigration, better known as the Dillingham Commission, challenged popular attitudes in its 1911 report. The commission's forty-one-volume report painted a generally bleak picture of the "new" immigrants, although the volume *Immigration and Crime* rejected the conventional wisdom of the day. Based on surveys of prison populations as well as arrest data from Massachusetts, New York City, and Chicago, the Dillingham Commission asserted that "no satisfactory evidence has yet been produced to show that immigration has resulted in an increase in crime disproportionate to the increase in adult population."[20] Still, some groups did not escape unscathed. On the second page of the same volume, the commission stated that "the increase in offenses of personal violence in this country is largely traceable to immigration from southern Europe, and especially from Italy. This is the most marked in connection with the crime of homicide." Confirming popular images, the Dillingham Commission's analysis of Chicago arrest data for 1905 through 1908 revealed that "the Italians, Lithuanians, Slavonians, Austrians, Greeks, and Poles all exceed in relative frequency of homicide the peoples of northern and western Europe and the peoples of North America with the exception of the American negroes."[21]

Progressive reformers and social workers, including Jane Addams, offered similarly double-edged assessments of immigrants and crime in Chicago. Although her celebrations of quaint, colorful peasant customs were sometimes laced with condescension, Addams found richness and intrinsic value in the ethnic traditions she encountered in the Near West Side Italian neighborhoods around Hull-House. But even while defending immigrants from xenophobic screeds and focusing on the environmental roots of social problems, she endorsed less sanguine notions about newcomers and crime. "They come to us with their petty lawsuits, sad relics of the vendetta, with their incorrigible boys," Addams wrote in 1892.[22]

Scholars, journalists, and others who embraced the ecological perspectives of the Chicago School of urban sociology also simultaneously rejected popular arguments about the innate criminality of immigrants and contributed to contemporary fears about the newcomers. William Thomas, Florian Znaniecki, Robert Park, and their University of Chicago colleagues found aggressive, vicious, impulsive residents concentrated in Chicago's ethnic neighborhoods. These observers, however, eschewed the biological determinism of eugenicists and nativists. Instead, the sociologists of the Chicago School argued that newcomers lost their moral bearings on the alienating, atomizing streets of the big city. Cut off from their "traditional" social moorings and cast adrift by the scale and anonymity of Chicago, overwhelmed peasants too often succumbed to the emotional bombardment of urban life and engaged in violent behavior.[23] Embracing this ecological perspective, a 1908 writer for *Popular Science Monthly* explained, "The fact should be borne in mind that the greater frequency of crimes of violence [in Chicago] among certain elements of the foreign-born population does not imply an inherent and eradicable viciousness or criminality among these unfortunate immigrants, but merely a lawlessness due to unfavorable environment and inadequate education, mental and manual."[24] Thus, even Chicago's most progressive, pluralistic observers linked foreign-born residents to violent crime.

But not all immigrants were alike, and some groups of newcomers appeared more menacing than others. As both the Dillingham Commission and local law enforcers recognized, patterns of crime were as diverse as Chicago's ethnic neighborhoods. At one end of this spectrum were Scandinavian immigrants. Nearly 25,000 Norwegian-born residents lived in Chicago in 1910, and they committed homicide at less than half the rate for the entire city. A still larger population of Swedish immigrants, numbering 63,035 in 1910, formed Chicago's "Swede town" and a few smaller ethnic enclaves in the city. These foreign-born residents, whose appearance and customs elicited scant concern from old-stock Americans, engaged in little violent behavior. During the early 1910s, Swedish immigrants committed homicide at less than one-quarter the overall rate of the city—and at less than one-twentieth the rate of African-American Chicagoans.[25] Newcomers from northern and western Europe settled into established communities and seldom committed violent offenses, which underscored differences between blond-haired, fair-skinned, well-behaved, civilized immigrants and their dark-haired, swarthy, violent, Mediterranean-born counterparts.

If Swedes occupied one end of this spectrum, Italians anchored the opposite end, seemingly more alien, more dangerous, and more violent than even Greeks, Turks, or other naturally "hot-tempered" southern European immigrants. From the middle decades of the nineteenth century, Chicago had had a small population of transplanted Italians. In 1880, the city's Italian community numbered fewer than 1,500, most having come from the northern portion of Italy, immigrating in family units. As in the rest of the United States, Chicago's Italian population changed during the 1880s. The number of Italian immigrants rose, and their backgrounds shifted. Increasingly, the newcomers came from southern Italy and Sicily. By World War I young men from the *Mezzogiorno* (southern Italy) predominated. In 1890 Chicago's Italian-born population approached 6,000. It nearly tripled during the final decade of the nineteenth century and almost tripled again by 1910. World War I, however, choked off the flow of immigrants; relatively few Italians arrived in Chicago after 1914. Nevertheless, by 1920 close to 60,000 Italian-born residents, three-fourths of whom were from the south, lived in the city. In Chicago's Near West Side colony, according to Jane Addams, newcomers from particular villages seemed to fill entire tenement houses.[26] Despite this clustering, most contemporary observers continued to use the generic term "Italian" to describe all these newcomers, and as the number and the proportion of immigrants from the south rose, especially in the context of discussions of crime, "Sicilian" and "Italian" became interchangeable labels. A large neighborhood, Little Sicily, formed on the Near North Side of the city. Notorious for its violence, this area became known as "Little Hell."[27]

Lethal violence seared daily life in Chicago's "Little Hell." During the first decade of the twentieth century, Italian immigrants made up between 1 percent and 2 percent of the city's residents, yet they committed 7.5 percent of Chicago's homicides. The Italian-immigrant homicide rate for the decade was nearly five times the rate for the entire city (see Figure 7, page 170). Similarly, during the 1910s, when these newcomers made up 2 percent of the local population, Italian-born Chicagoans accounted for almost 13 percent of local killers. This group's homicide rate peaked during the early 1910s, when it was seven times the overall rate for the city and almost thirty times the Swedish homicide rate. One out of every fifty Chicagoans during this period was born in Italy, but one out of every seven killers came from there. Only African-American Chicagoans suffered from or committed homicide at a higher level, and for much of the 1910s the Italian rate topped the African-American rate.

Between 1875 and 1920, Italian immigrants committed over 400 homicides, far more than any group of Chicagoans other than native-born and African-American residents. In 1910, 1911, 1912, and 1913, according to the Cook County coroner, the Italian death toll from homicide exceeded the combined total of Bohemian, Greek, Hungarian, Polish, and Russian homicides.[28] Similarly, the coroner reported that Italian homicide remained greater than the combined to-

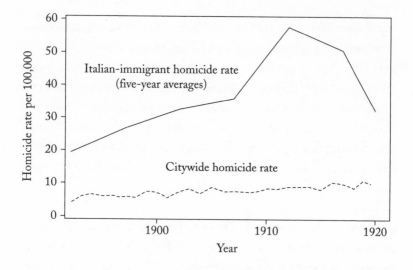

FIGURE 7   *Italian-immigrant homicide rate (source: see Appendix)*

tal for these groups at the end of the decade, even though Bohemian, Greek, Hungarian, Polish, and Russian residents outnumbered local Italians by a factor of nearly six.[29]

Local observers grew accustomed to Italian violence. Newspaper accounts of violent crime blended scientific and social scientific perspectives to exoticize Sicilian Chicagoans, simultaneously treating Italian homicide with wide-eyed, almost voyeuristic fascination and with calm acceptance.[30] In a 1914 article entitled "Revenge Rules Little Sicily," a writer for the *Chicago Tribune* explained that "three thousand years of violence and continuous revolt are not to be balanced by half a century of freedom. If ever the savage customs and the bloody code of a people were the product of heredity and environment the history of Sicily proves the case." The article went on to inform its readers that "revenge" was an "inborn trait" of Chicago's Sicilian residents. Crime-beat reporters expected Italian immigrants to be violent and expected their violence to be excessive. The headline "Just Another Shooting in Little Italy," for example, announced the murder of Peter Parino on December 29, 1916. Reporting on the murders of Pasquale and Salvatore Marello, one newspaper noted that the victims' faces were "disfigured beyond recognition by cuts inflicted with a hatchet and an ice pick." Casting Sicilian violence as brutal yet routine, the newspaper account added that the "walls and floor of the room were spattered with blood, but otherwise there was no sign of a struggle." Between 1904 and 1912 more than three-fourths of the news stories about Italians that appeared in the *Chicago Record-Herald* focused on crime and violence.[31]

Italian violence was as distinctive as it was legion. For one thing, it rarely extended outside of the ethnic community. More than any other group of Chicagoans, Italian killers targeted their compatriots. Over 81 percent of Italian homicide victims were killed by other Italian immigrants, a proportion of intragroup violence higher than that of any other residents, including African Americans.[32] In part, this reflected settlement patterns. Although Chicago had no "pure" ethnic ghettos, Italian immigrants were more concentrated in particular enclaves than any group of immigrants. Until the 1910s, they were even more segregated or isolated from other groups, particularly from native-born whites, than African-American Chicagoans.[33] Reinforced by occupational clustering, such concentration reduced Italian Chicagoans' daily contact with non-Italians and hence increased the likelihood that any conflict would be "confined to their own."[34] But contemporary observers also pointed to this group's secret "codes" and "customs" for settling disputes.[35] "Racial isolation," an assistant police chief explained in 1910, "leads them to build a barrier about [sic] what they regard as strictly their own affairs."[36] The inward, mysterious, primitive focus of Italian homicide fueled public fascination.

Another distinctive feature, and one giving these killers a special raw and exotic quality, Italian killers disproportionately used knives, particularly the infamous stiletto. Between 1890 and 1910, nearly one-fourth of Italian killers relied on knives, compared with one-seventh of all Chicago killers. Although the overwhelming majority of Italian killers employed other weapons, this group became identified with the stiletto. Police pronouncements and newspaper accounts of violence linked knife killings to Italian immigrants, terming the stab to the heart, for example, a "characteristic Italian murder." "A revolver is not an Italian's weapon," a Chicago police investigator asserted in 1910. "Their weapon is a knife." Crime-beat writers referred to "the murderous certainty of an Italian knife-thrust" and described a fatal knife fight between Italians as an "Italian carving bee." Such battles probably reflected the remnants of Old World notions of honor, in which gun violence and one-sided fights seemed unmanly. Recoiling at the popular image of the wild, volatile Sicilian with "anger in his heart and a knife in his belt," leaders of the city's Italian community feebly challenged the stereotype. In an impassioned defense of his countrymen, Dr. C. Volini, a prominent Italian physician, unwittingly reinforced the stylized portrait of the Sicilian immigrant in 1899 when he insisted that "the use of the knife by our race is to be lamented, but we do not use a knife any oftener than others use a revolver."[37] Italian knife killing fell sharply during the 1910s, dropping by more than 52 percent. After 1910, Italian killers used knives at a lower rate than the overall figure for the city, though the image of the stiletto-toting Sicilian endured long after the weapon fell out of favor.

Third, Italian killers targeted only men, and only Italian men were killers. Across the city, in every block and every neighborhood and ethnic group, homicide was a man's activity. Men made up 92 percent of Chicago's killers and 79 percent of its victims. But Italian homicide was even more of a masculine activity. Close to 97 percent of Italian killers and over 90 percent of Italian victims were men. Simply put, Italian women and children did not kill and were rarely killed. Only Greek immigrants, who shared the Mediterranean cultural ideals of

Italian immigrants, had fewer women killers, and no group of Chicagoans had fewer women victims or a higher proportion of male-on-male homicides than Italians did.

Italian homicide changed markedly over time. In some ways, the shifts in the nature of Italian lethal violence paralleled larger changes in Chicago homicide, though at higher rates. Before 1910, when Chicago's Italian population consisted primarily of single, young men, violence reflected the character of the ethnic neighborhoods; these immigrants had a high proportion of homicides committed in saloons and resulting from drunken brawls.[38] During the 1890s, 54 percent of the homicides committed by Italian immigrants in the city were the result of drunken fights, compared with 23 percent of all Chicago homicides. Moreover, the Italian drunken-brawl homicide rate did not fall until the opening years of the twentieth century, a decade after the citywide brawl homicide rate began to plunge. Both Italian killers and their victims were typically single, young, and poor, and resided in boarding houses in one of Chicago's Little Sicilies. But at least from the perspective of the police and local journalists, these brawlers seemed different from the street toughs who drank, tussled, and killed in earlier decades, in part because Italian brawlers continued to drink and kill in saloons at a time when deadly barroom scuffles were becoming unusual. Thus, longer-established residents felt that the immigrants murdered their drinking pals and neighbors in particularly "backward," "uncivilized" ways.[39]

During the opening decade of the twentieth century, Italian drunken-brawl homicide plummeted, dropping from 54 percent of Italian homicides in the 1890s to 22 percent. Between 1910 and 1920, the figure plunged to 9 percent, below the proportion for the city generally.[40] As with other Chicago newcomers, Italian immigrants gradually settled into local society. Sex ratios evened, and the newcomers established families, accelerating the erosion of the plebeian, bachelor world that had flourished in earlier decades. Between the late 1890s and the late 1910s, the Italian brawl homicide rate fell by 64 percent.

Despite the drop in drunken-brawl violence, however, the Italian homicide rate rose steeply during this period. From the 1890s through the first decade of the twentieth century it swelled by 44 percent, and from the 1900s through the 1910s it jumped by another 34 percent. As with other groups of Chicagoans, Italian violence moved into family life, and the surge in domestic homicide more than offset the drop in saloon carnage.

Italian family homicide assumed unique forms. Among other groups of Chicagoans, husband killing rose, wife killing climbed, and child murder soared. But this did not occur in Chicago's Little Sicilies. Between 1900 and 1920, one-eighth of the city's homicide victims died at the hands of their spouses. By contrast, just one Italian homicide victim in eighteen was killed by a spouse. Similarly, spouses comprised nearly half of all victims of domestic homicide in Chicago but less than one-third of Italian domestic homicide victims. Although spousal homicide increased among Italian immigrants during the early twentieth century, this form of violence occurred at modest levels, particularly in view of the high rate of homicide in Chicago's Little Italy neighborhoods. During the 1910s Italian immigrants were the single most homicidal group of Chicagoans, though they rarely murdered their spouses. Italian women were particularly unlikely to engage in spousal homicide. Citywide, wives committed 22 percent of spouse killings between 1900 and 1920. Italian women, however, accounted for only 10.5 percent of Italian spouse killers. Nor did these immigrants kill their children. Italian Chicagoans murdered their sons and daughters at one-sixth the proportion of all city dwellers.

Yet Italian Chicagoans were not immune from the pressures that tore apart families and fueled domestic violence in other neighborhoods. Family formation was as stressful and laced with conflict for

Italian immigrants as it was for other Chicagoans; men felt inadequate when they failed to meet their own or their wives' expectations, and they endured poverty, struggled to support their households, and responded defensively and angrily to interference from relatives, neighbors, law enforcers, and social workers. If anything, the strong patriarchal tradition of Italian family life heightened these pressures, as economic conditions and the anonymity of urban life weakened long-established forms of social control and masculine dominance.[41] Violent responses, however, were displaced more than they were suppressed, for although they seldom murdered their spouses or children, Italian Chicagoans engaged in domestic homicide at four to eight times the rate for the entire population of the city.

While other desperate, overwhelmed Chicago men murdered their wives and children, Italian men killed their brothers, brothers-in-law, fathers, and cousins. These relatives made up half of Italian intimate-homicide victims, compared with less than one-fifth of all family-homicide victims in the city—and one-seventeenth the proportion of German family killers. Powerful familial bonds in Chicago's Little Italies discouraged immigrant husbands from killing their wives.[42] Rather, Italian domestic homicide nearly always involved men, both as killers and as victims.

Italian men killed in the defense of family honor, striking down sons-in-law who mistreated daughters, brothers-in-law who deserted sisters, fathers who abused mothers, or other relatives whose behavior toward women violated cultural norms and impugned the respectability of the family. Bernard Barasa, a prominent Italian-American attorney and later a municipal court judge, reported that the murders in Chicago's Italian neighborhoods "in nearly every instance grow out of some violation of the sanctity of the home."[43] Even Italian residents eager to downplay the scale of bloodshed in Chicago's Little Italies acknowledged such actions. The newspaper *L'Italia* compared the violence of 1911 with that of earlier eras and argued that older forms of behavior were beginning to wane. "Today," the newspaper explained, "not [as] many crimes are committed to avenge the honor of wives, sisters or children as in the past."[44]

Acting as heads of the family, Italian men committed homicide to protect their sisters' or daughters' reputation—and thus to protect the family's reputation. These were honor killings in which patriarchs demanded personal vengeance, believing that legal remedies could not restore a family's reputation. A divorce decree, a court order mandating financial support, or an assault conviction could not repair the damage inflicted on a dishonored woman. Nor could policemen, judges, and social workers restore the reputation of the victim's male relatives. Traditions of honor and manly responsibility had infused family life in the southern Italian villages that sent immigrants to Chicago, and these traditions enjoyed a rebirth in the city's Italian neighborhoods.[45] Writing in the 1920s, a University of Chicago sociologist observed that "the head of the [Sicilian] family takes the responsibility of protecting the women and girls very seriously." Another local commentator explained, "A Sicilian never forgets nor forgives, and an injury done to the father is handed down as a legacy of vengeance to the son."[46]

Such a code of honor and personal vengeance compelled Emilio Filippi to shoot and kill James Palermo, his brother-in-law, on January 17, 1912. A thirty-year-old day laborer, Palermo left his wife—Filippi's sister—in Italy and settled in Chicago. When the woman had another child while the couple was living apart, Palermo concluded that she had been unfaithful and refused to support her. Defending his family's honor, Filippi tracked his brother-in-law to a Chicago boardinghouse and, as Filippi put it, "told him I would make trouble for him if he didn't support my sister." Palermo, for his part, believed that his manly honor had been besmirched and "said he would never support" the woman who had betrayed him. Filippi left Palermo's boardinghouse but "returned in the morning and waited for him to come out the back gate on his way to work. I shot him as soon as he walked into the alley."[47] Immigration patterns, in which young newcomers predominated, forced men like Filippi to assume patriarchal roles, as their fathers either remained in the old country or assumed truncated roles in their new setting. As a result, Italian family killers were younger than other Chicagoans who murdered their loved ones.[48]

Far from evading law enforcers or denying their violent deeds, Italian family killers such as Emilio Filippi frequently claimed responsibility for the deaths, announcing that the bloodshed had been necessary, appropriate, and honorable. The defense of family honor simultaneously required a decisive response to affronts, afforded the right of personal vengeance, and constituted a dire warning about the consequences of mistreating women in the city's Italian enclaves.[49] Such strident justifications represented the public face of honor-based violence and provided an opportunity for a man to defend and reclaim his family's honor—and to dishonor the transgressor. Italian family violence, in other words, had both a private and a public function, which enhanced its visibility and magnified its impact on popular perceptions of this ethnic group.

Italian family killers sometimes invoked the "unwritten law" to justify their actions, though they defined this code very differently than did abused wives in early twentieth-century Chicago. Young Italian men in the city argued that an unwritten law required them to defend the honor of their sisters and to exact revenge against anyone who sullied the family name. Inquests and trials offered these killers a forum, a public arena in which to swagger and crow that they had fulfilled their patriarchal responsibilities. Because the killers publicly defended their behavior, and because such performances conformed to popular stereotypes about savage, honor-driven Sicilian immigrants, the trials of Italian family killers attracted a wide audience, generating a great deal of information about the motives of at least a handful of Italian family killers.

Local newspapers, for example, eagerly reported the details of

Michael Pacellano's 1909 murder trial. Twenty-three-year-old Frank Serino persuaded Pacellano's sister, Josie, to leave her husband and elope with him. Serino and Josie traveled to New York City, where, according to Pacellano, Serino "detained her in a disorderly house" (that is, a brothel). Josie's nineteen-year-old brother "took the law into his own hands and acted as executioner in avenging the wrongs done to his sister." He followed the couple to New York, hunted down Serino, and "induced" him—at gunpoint—to return to Chicago. "I have a perfect right to kill you," Pacellano told Serino as they began their trip to the Midwest. After they arrived in Chicago, Pacellano shot and killed Serino. "When he said he would not live with her or support her I knew it would make her a thoroughly bad woman," Pacellano explained. "So I shot him. He deserved to die." After his arrest, Pacellano announced that Serino "had ruined my sister's life and I killed him. I would do it again if I had the chance." As the trial approached, Pacellano remained unrepentant, maintaining that the "unwritten law" compelled him to kill Serino. True to his word, Pacellano relied on the unwritten law as his defense, and a Cook County jury acquitted him.[50]

Similarly, Gregorio Tamprullo and Caleroga Piro confidently invoked the unwritten law to justify their brutal killing of forty-six-year-old Pasquale Piro. The men explained that they shot and stabbed Caleroga's cousin Pasquale on August 17, 1918, "because he talked about our wives." "We decided Piro must die," Tamprullo added. "It is not wrong to kill a man who speaks ill of one's wife. We will defend ourselves under the unwritten law. We do not repent."[51] Cook County jurors agreed, acquitting the men on May 9, 1919. A jury also acquitted Emilio Filippi, the young immigrant who "ambushed" his brother-in-law as he left his boardinghouse.[52] All these killers insisted that their violent behavior was both necessary and justified.

Like other Chicagoans, Italian immigrants killed family members in response to threats or challenges to gender roles, though these newcomers defined the threats in ways that reflected their own southern European cultural traditions. More than any other group of family killers, Italian men committed homicide on behalf of their relatives, using violence to fulfill their role as the protectors of women and as the defenders of the family's reputation. Speaking of Italians, an early twentieth-century Chicago sociologist, asserted, "Seduction is an almost unheard-of thing among these people, and in the few instances where a girl has been wronged it has meant certain death to her betrayer."[53] Nor was divorce or desertion commonplace in Chicago's Little Italies, where deeply ingrained religious beliefs and cultural ideals bolstered patriarchal authority and where fathers and brothers protected family honor and punished ill-behaving husbands and lovers.[54] Italian women were less likely than other local wives to leave their partners, less likely to divorce their husbands, less likely to threaten to do either, and less likely to die at the hands of their spouses. These wives had a different range of options for addressing family conflict than had other Chicago wives. Grounded in resilient familial bonds, these options protected Italian women, but they did not necessarily discourage family violence.[55] Instead, the battles were fought between the male "heads" of the families. As a result, levels of domestic homicide were high among Italian Chicagoans, though the final, lethal confrontations rarely involved women either as killers or as victims.

This code of honor and personal vengeance extended beyond domestic relations to other forms of social conflict, as men avenged the wrongs committed against their kin. Thus, the defense of family honor triggered violence against non-relatives. For example, after three men fatally stabbed Michael Laporta, the victim's brother, Antonio, "swore vengeance," promising "to kill the three men, if it took him a lifetime." A Chicago police sergeant predicted that "if Antonio Laporta knows or even suspects the identity of his brother's slayers, we will have another murder on our hands in a short time." Likewise, Stephano Montalvano vowed to avenge the death of his brother. On March 17, 1914, as thirty-five-year-old Anton Montalvano walked down Milton Avenue, in Chicago's biggest Little Sicily, two men shot and killed him. When the police arrived on the scene, they found Stephano Montalvano crouched over his brother's body, drinking the "blood which flowed from the wounds." Two befuddled detectives from the city's Chicago Avenue police station then watched as Stephano Montalvano "stood erect beneath the arc light on the corner, bared his head and raising his right hand aloft swore to avenge the death." Similarly, policemen drawn to the saloon where fifty-six-year-old Salvatore DiAgnostino had just been murdered found Antonio DiAgnostino dipping his fingers into his brother's blood and roaring, "I swear by my saints and by my life never to rest until the man who killed you, Salvatore, has paid for your life with his." Thus, local law enforcers lamented, one Sicilian murder led to the next and the next. "Ideas of private vengeance and of contempt for the law," a 1916 observer concluded, "are the birthright of the lower class Sicilian."[56]

During the 1910s Italian codes of personal vengeance and revenge leached beyond the confines of family violence, igniting an explosion of homicide that ripped through the immigrant community. The rate of lethal violence among Italian immigrants increased by two-thirds during the early 1910s, soaring above the African-American homicide rate and making Italian immigrants the most violent Chicagoans. In some respects, the nature of homicide remained unchanged even as the level of lethal violence surged. Few women, for example, killed or were killed, and children rarely died. But despite such continuity, a monumental shift in violence occurred after 1910.

The Black Hand, or the Mafia, arrived in Chicago during this period and transformed Italian violence. Before 1910 the police believed that the Sicilian secret society had committed few murders in Chicago. But between 1910 and 1920, local law enforcers linked nearly one hundred homicides, all committed by and against Italian residents, to the Black Hand or the Mafia, accounting for almost one-third of the killings committed by Italian Chicagoans.[57] The rate of Mafia murders between 1910 and 1920 was more than three times the Italian domestic homicide rate.

Chicagoans, like other Americans, became acquainted with the term "Mafia" in October 1890, when New Orleans law enforcers announced that members of a Sicilian secret society had murdered their city's police chief, David C. Hennessy. Across the United States, newspapers described a secret network of Italian killers and issued warnings about Sicilian assassins lurking in the nation's major urban centers.[58] After a New Orleans jury failed to convict the alleged murderers, enraged Louisianans, convinced that Mafia bribes and threats had corrupted the judicial process and subverted justice, stormed the parish prison and lynched eleven Italian immigrants, four of whom had no connection with the Hennessy case.[59] In the wake of the Hennessy assassination and the subsequent lynchings, Chicagoans were introduced to the "Mafia."[60] Within days of the mob violence in New Orleans, a Chicago piano player reported to the police that "he had been attacked by three Italians—members of the Chicago Mafia." His claim, however, was "laughed at" by city officials."[61]

By 1892, only eighteen months after the Louisiana lynchings, law enforcers asked, "Has the Mafia gained a foothold in Chicago?"[62] Police Lieutenant John Wheeler broached the issue directly on October 6, 1892, sparking a firestorm of prurient interest and anxious speculation. Four days earlier Antonio Mersineo had shot Antonio Martino and John Charchiro, both Italian immigrants, during a saloon row. A forty-seven-year-old peddler, Martino died in the brawl. When the men in the crowded barroom insisted that they heard the shots ring out but saw nothing, and when relatives of the victim became uncooperative, police investigators focused their attention on an "Italian murder society." Lieutenant Wheeler divulged that "several Italians, men of prominence, too, have called upon me and stated that the Mafia exists here and that Martino is a victim of it." Other police officials, however, expressed doubt and even dismissed Wheeler's assertion. One inspector announced that he found "not the slightest" evidence that the Mafia was responsible for the Martino murder or that such an organization even existed in Chicago. The Italian-language press erupted in anger at Wheeler's declaration and flatly rejected his theory of the Martino murder. "This is all sheer nonsense, stupidity, imbecility," roared Oscar Durante, the editor of *L'Italia*, Chicago's leading Italian newspaper. "Every time a drunken row among Italians occurs the people and the press cry 'Mafia.'" Underscoring the point, Durante wrote, "I repeat there is not now and never was such an organization as the Mafia either here or in Italy."[63]

The Mafia and the Black Hand commanded increasing attention during the opening decade of the new century. In Chicago, as well as in other urban centers, law enforcers speculated that Italian, particularly Sicilian, immigrants operated blackmail and extortion rings. Exposés with titles such as "The Problem of the Black Hand" and "Amputating the Black Hand" appeared in newspapers and leading periodicals throughout the nation during the early 1900s, feeding off the frenzy that followed the Hennessy murder and the lynching of his alleged killers.[64]

The phrase "Black Hand" referred to the signature on extortion letters that were sent to Italian immigrants.[65] These notes demanded money and threatened violence if the recipients failed to comply or if they contacted the police. George Bour, an Italian real estate dealer in Chicago, received a typical "Black Hand" letter. "You got some cash. I need $1,000.00," the note declared. "You place the $100.00 bills in an envelope and place it under a board at the northeast corner of Sixty-ninth Street and Euclid Avenue at eleven o'clock to-night.

If you place the money there you will live. If you don't, you die. If you report this to the police, I'll kill you when I get out. They may save you the money but they won't save you your life.—Black Hand."[66]

According to John Landesco, an early twentieth-century sociologist who studied organized crime in Chicago, the "'Black Hand' is extortion, using the anonymous threatening letter. It existed and exists in Sicily. The victims, in fear of death, refuse to talk or aid the police in prosecution. The law-abiding Italians are convinced, through experience, of the futility and danger of giving the police information."[67]

Chicago police officials, as well as other observers, found it difficult to identify Black Hand crimes. On rare occasions, victims violated the infamous "code of silence" and reported the extortion notes to the authorities.[68] But even in these instances, law enforcers seldom knew if such blackmail schemes represented the coordinated efforts of an organized criminal network that reached from halfway across the European continent, across the Atlantic Ocean, halfway across the North American continent, into tiny ethnic enclaves in Chicago. Some believed that local pranksters or small groups of neighborhood toughs sent the letters, exploiting the mystique of the Mafia to extract money from their skittish neighbors.[69] Simply invoking the "high-sounding and terror-inspiring" words "Black Hand" or "Mafia" often sufficed to separate an immigrant from his money, according to turn-of-the-century commentators.[70]

During the first decade of the twentieth century, the "Black Hand society" frightened and bluffed its victims into compliance. City officials admitted and local journalists revealed that the "members of a supposed Black Hand society" also assaulted immigrants and bombed their property in order "to show that they mean business."[71] In 1907 local toughs, in an attempt to blackmail local gamblers, bombed six homes and businesses.[72] In addition, Chicago law enforcers suspected that the secret organization was responsible for at least a handful of homicides between 1900 and 1910.[73] The police, however, explicitly attributed only one murder to an Italian secret society during the decade, and even in this case, municipal law enforcers had no direct evidence of Mafia involvement. Rather, it was the absence of any evidence that led the police to suspect a connection to organized crime.[74]

Early in the morning of January 6, 1910, however, Chicagoans learned that Mafia assassins were indeed at work in their city. Shortly after 6:00 AM, sixty-five-year-old Rose Sinene opened the West Oak Street clothing store she operated with her sixty-year-old husband, Benedetto. Moments later, three young men entered the store, and one of the group asked to see a pair of gloves. When Rose Sinene moved around the counter, the young man grabbed her around the neck, held a gun to her head, and threatened "to blow out her brains if she did not keep quiet."[75] The other two men quickly moved to the back of the store and into an adjoining apartment, where the Sinenes lived. There they found Benedetto asleep, and they fired between three and five bullets into his body, killing him.

Sinene had repeatedly tangled with Chicago's Black Hand. Two years before he was murdered, the shopkeeper had received a letter signed "Black Hand," "commanding him to place $5,000 where it could be found by the writers. He was told that death would be the penalty of his refusal." Not only did the stubborn merchant refuse to pay the "tribute," he also reported the letter to the police. Three additional letters arrived, and the blackmailers punctuated their demand by tossing a bomb through the window of the Sinenes' clothing shop. Five months before he was killed, Sinene once again violated the code of silence that ruled Little Sicily, helping the police recover a child who had been kidnaped by Sicilian blackmailers. As a consequence of his cooperation with the authorities, Benedetto Sinene knew that the "hand of death was constantly hanging over him," and he always slept with his "old Italian army rifle" at the head of his bed and with "a keen bladed stiletto" on his nightstand. Because Sinene never revealed the source of the information he conveyed to the police about the kidnaping, local law enforcers suspected that the merchant himself had once been a member of the Black Hand society.[76]

This time the police were certain: the "Black Hand Society" had "assassinated" a local resident. Chicago law enforcers immediately "declare[d] war" on the secret organization. Herman Schuettler, an ambitious assistant police chief who would later become the chief of police in the city, announced, "I intend to clean out the Italian quarter and from now on members of the secret society will find Chicago a poor place to live in." A hundred policemen stormed the city's two largest Sicilian neighborhoods, and Schuettler ordered "raids on the Italian dives where members of the 'Black Hand' society are believed to meet." Within a day, the police had arrested and detained nearly two hundred immigrants, all of whom "professed ignorance." "When the name of the feared band was mentioned they grew sullen and seemed to have been struck dumb," a local journalist reported.[77] "All the reply I could get," complained one police sergeant, "was 'me don't know.'"[78] The Sinene murder, the fiercely public, well-choreographed police response, and the highly stylized newspaper coverage that followed made Chicagoans believe that the Mafia and the Black Hand (the terms were often used interchangeably) had taken up residence in their city.

The homicides attributed to the Mafia or the Black Hand typically followed a common pattern. They occurred in public settings and involved two or three killers who were usually armed with sawed-off shotguns. The assassins discharged their weapons from close range, dropped the guns at the scene of the shooting, and disappeared into the fabric of Little Sicily. Witnesses would first instinctively turn toward the sound of the shotgun blasts and then, recognizing what had just transpired, immediately look away, close their windows, shut their doors, and go about their business, purposefully oblivious to the shooting of their neighbor. According to the *Chicago Evening Post*, for example, immediately after the December 29, 1915 "assassination" of forty-one-year-old Vincenzo Monco, "lips became silenced as they do in all Black Hand tragedies and the police could learn nothing of the possessor of the sawed-off shotgun, the crime itself, or the motive."[79]

The murders became routine and were brazenly public. Observers described the relentlessly repetitious sequence of Black Hand assassinations. "The circumstances are nearly always the same," sociologists from the University of Chicago noted. "The victim is shot from ambush, his body riddled with slugs and nails from a sawed-off shotgun or with the entire charge from a revolver; the weapon is found near the body; there are no witnesses and the murderer is never found."[80] "The same thing over again," another commentator lamented in 1914.[81] The murders often occurred near the corner of Milton Avenue and Oak Street in the heart of the North Side Sicilian neighborhood, an intersection dubbed "Death Corner."[82]

Journalists, politicians, and police officials counted the killings, frequently announcing the latest tally of Black Hand murders committed around Death Corner in Little Hell. On April 2, 1911, for example, an "undiscovered assassin" at Death Corner fired five shots into the body of twenty-three-year-old Frank Fernerno, making him the "forty-ninth victim in fourteen months of the Black Hand in Chicago," according to the *Chicago Tribune*.[83] The newspaper counted twenty-five such murders in 1910, forty in 1911, thirty-three in 1912, thirty-one in 1913, forty in 1914, and thirty-five in 1915.[84] The *Chicago Record-Herald* arrived at a similar yearly total of Black Hand assassinations.[85] Carter H. Harrison, a former mayor of the city, offered a slightly lower estimate for the early 1910s. "At Milton ave. and Oak st.," Harrison observed, "prior to 1915 100 or more killings of the sawed-off shotgun had taken place. All were ascribed to the Mafia and the victims were all Italians."[86] In 1916 the *Chicago Tribune* calculated that "murder by organized Black Hand *camorras* has produced more deaths in Chicago in the last five years to the credit of the bomb and the sawed-off shotgun than the total of all murders in the British isles and Canada for the same period." The police offered more modest figures, but they, too, contributed to the frenzy by speculating about future death tolls. Following the 1916 shooting of thirty-four-year-old Gennaro Scrimmento, a jeweler reputed to have had ties to the Black Hand, Chicago Detective Sergeant Gabriel Longobardi predicted that "there will be from fifteen to twenty murders in the [Sicilian] quarter during the next six months."[87]

The Black Hand ritual shaped Italian homicide, giving it a distinctive form. Nearly 80 percent of Black Hand killings occurred on the streets of the city, and as a result Italian homicides were uniquely public events. Whereas 37 percent of all Chicago homicides took place on the streets during this period, 54 percent of Italian killings occurred there.

The ritualized violence attracted widespread attention to Italian immigrants and to the Chicago police, and both groups paradoxically affirmed the looming threat and denied that the Mafia existed. At least until the Sinene murder, local law enforcers had usually maintained that the Mafia or the Black Hand did not exist. "Black Hand? Pish!" Police Chief George Shippy said disdainfully in 1907 after Mariano Scardina was murdered in a saloon brawl. "The task for the police department in putting down crime among the Italians," Shippy explained, "is not the stamping out of any big organization, but the arrest and punishment of scattered lawbreakers as they appear, just as with the people of other nationalities. The only difference is that the peculiar traits of the Italians—their superstitious fears and clannishness—make the work all the harder." Herman Schuettler concurred, stating that "many of the killings among the Italians are purely because of their clannishness and excitability, and not because of extortion plots."[88]

After the Sinene murder, city officials acknowledged the menace of organized crime. The police chief and the mayor organized "an Italian detective squad." According to Schuettler, "It takes an Italian to catch an Italian."[89] The Italian detective squad specialized in Black Hand murders.[90] Creating this new police unit, and defining Sicilian behavior as unique, enabled Chicago law enforcers to separate Italian homicide from the rest of the city's lethal violence. In view of the customs and legendary "clannishness" of Italian residents, Black Hand murders were simply unstoppable, according to the police, though this violence posed scant threat to other Chicagoans. "They never bother anyone but each other," a police chief explained.[91] Gabriel Longobardi, the police department's most visible Black Hand specialist, conceded that "the police are helpless." "I'd build a high brick wall around the Italian district," he suggested, "and let these people fight out their differences until one faction kills the other or all of them are dead. Then I'd try to hang the survivor, if there was one. It's about the only way to end this situation."[92] Such statements, along with police announcements of the annual Black Hand murder tally, helped to sustain the legend of Italian organized crime.

Journalists, sociologists, and other commentators bolstered these images, cementing the reputation of Italian Chicagoans in the process and adding to the mystery surrounding violence in the city's Little Sicilies. Newspapers reported Italian crime with a tone of what might be called casual hysteria, highlighting the unabashed brutality, the numbing regularity, and the Black Hand's involvement in local murders. On February 11, 1911, for example, the *Chicago Inter Ocean* termed Black Hand activities "an epidemic of murder and destruction which is rapidly growing more widespread." Less than two months later the front-page headline of the *Chicago Tribune* calmly reported a shooting on the city's North Side, announcing "Another Italian Murdered at 'Death Corner.'" The article began with the latest "Death Corner's Toll" and then described the victim's body, "riddled with five bullets." Similarly, in January 1914 the newspaper's front-page headline proclaimed "Three Murders within One Hour," two of which occurred in the "Black Hand belt." "'Little Italy' holds the dark secret of a hundred murders in the night," the newspaper noted in 1918.[93] Local sociologists concluded that "when a murder is committed it is either reported as a minor occurrence in a single paragraph, or absurdly elaborated in highly romantic style."[94]

Prominent members of Chicago's Italian community responded in complex and contradictory ways. Initially, Italian-language newspapers and influential residents denounced the Black Hand as a "hoax." "The so-called Black Hand exists in the imagination of reporters in search of sensationalism and of police officials incapable or unwilling to solve a crime," one Italian Chicagoan charged. "There is no such thing as a 'black hand' organization," insisted Guido Sabetta, the Italian Consul in Chicago. "The Black Hand is a myth," agreed Bernard Barasa. "No such organization has ever existed." Perhaps undermining his crusade to counter negative images of Italian immigrants, Barasa added that "an investigation of crimes among Italians will show that they are either assaults or murders. The Italian is not often a thief. He is hot-tempered and that accounts for the assaults."[95]

Gradually, a group of affluent Italian residents acknowledged the existence of the Mafia and the Black Hand in Chicago. They established the "White Hand Society" in an attempt to "exterminate the Italian blackmailers" and to cooperate with local law enforcers.[96] But the formation of the White Hand confirmed newspaper and police accounts of Death Corner, Little Hell, and the Chicago Mafia.[97]

During the 1910s the Black Hand became a method, or modus operandi, rather than a specific organization undertaking particular actions, especially as local observers used the labels "Black Hand" and "Mafia" loosely.[98] If a murder occurred on the street or in some other public setting, with a shotgun, in one of Chicago's Little Sicilies, and the witnesses refused to cooperate with investigators, the police and local journalists assumed Black Hand involvement.[99] Many times the mere form of the homicide was enough to indicate the work of the secret Italian society. In other cases, investigators suspected that the victim had received extortion letters, and therefore the police concluded that the Black Hand had targeted a noncompliant resident. In other fatal shootings, it was the absence of evidence, the silence of the witnesses, the terror of the relatives of the victim, or the rapid disappearance of the suspects that suggested the role of the Black Hand. And finally, in some murders the connection to organized crime was obvious and well known, such as the May 11, 1920, execution of "Big Jim" Colosimo, the "vice lord" of Chicago's South Side.[100] "The police call every mystery murder in the Italian community a 'black hand' murder," a contemporary sociologist noted. "The fact is that 'black hand' is only a method."[101]

The Black Hand "method" conveniently masked other forms of violence and other motives for murder in Italian districts. The police suspected that some Italian residents falsely reported receiving extortion letters in order to be granted gun permits. Not only would this allow these purported victims to carry weapons, it also provided them with a justification for using their weapons—against blackmailers, coworkers, or anyone else.[102] Likewise, some killers relied on the Black Hand trope to disguise neighborhood rows or even family fights. Local journalists and police investigators, for example, assumed that the Black Hand murdered Mariano Zacone, a forty-eight-year-old cigar maker who was shot to death on Gault Street in the Near North Side Italian neighborhood. Relatives of the victim told Chicago law enforcers "that Zagone [*sic*] on three occasions narrowly escaped death through his refusal to comply with the demands for money from members of a supposed Black Hand Society." When Zacone's wife, Biagio, acknowledged the previous shootings but denied that her husband had received extortion letters, the police assumed that the distraught, frightened woman was lying about the letters in order to avoid becoming the next victim of the secret society of Sicilian assassins—in other words, because she denied that her husband had received extortion letters, the police concluded that he had in fact received them. The headline in the *Chicago Tribune* announced "'Black Hand' Victim Shot." Police investigators, however, were forced to abandon this explanation when they discovered blood on the floor of a nearby saloon owned by Joseph Nicolasi, Mariano Zacone's son-in-law and the person who found the body.[103] By dragging Zacone's body to the street, reporting previous murder attempts, and refusing to provide any other information, Nicolasi cloaked a domestic homicide in the mystery of the Black Hand.

The tenacious Sicilian "wall of silence" and the code of personal vengeance abetted this strategy of misdirection, confounding the police and encouraging them to view Italian homicides as both unsolvable and unstoppable.[104] "Not once in a thousand times," Chicago police officials complained in 1911, "does the true Mediterranean-born Italian place revenge in the hands of the law."[105] The *Chicago Record-Herald* attributed Italian violence specifically to "the barbaric code of the Sicilians, which demands a life for a life." According to the newspaper, "they know no law save that of the stiletto and the revolver."[106] In 1920 Assistant State's Attorney E. J. Raber testified at a clemency hearing, "My experience is if any Italians violate the code [of silence] it means instant death to them. Two or three years ago [we] had an Italian give us some information. The next day he was found dead. These fellows want to take the law into their own hands."[107] Jane Addams offered a similar assessment: "A certain type of Sicilian for centuries had a training in taking care of his own affairs outside of the law."[108]

By providing only "shoulder shrugs" when law enforcers investigated crimes, Italian immigrants rebuffed outsiders and maintained control over social life in Chicago's Little Italies. The murders committed in the Black Hand mode sometimes reflected struggles over identity and influence in ethnic neighborhoods rather than the work of extortioners and blackmailers.[109] On October 26, 1915, for example, the Black Hand was said to have murdered Agostina Giovenco, a Sicilian barber and saloon keeper who "became Americanized." Crime-beat reporters explained that the twenty-four-year-old Sicilian had "succeeded among Americans, but failed among his own people."[110]

The overlapping codes of silence and personal vengeance also preserved masculine agency in a setting where the authority of recent immigrants seemed to be slipping away. At least in part, these traditions enabled men to reassert control—to restrict the autonomy of their wives and daughters, to avenge slights, to preserve honor, and to avoid becoming passive, feminized victims.[111] If male relatives failed to respond to a slur, a threat, an attack, or a murder, family honor was sullied, just as allowing the police and the courts to punish offenders was cowardly, unmanly, and dishonorable. In 1911, the president of the White Hand Society admitted that "many Italians [in Chicago] still believe that the right of vengeance lies with the injured man's relatives." The police discovered this as well. Again and again, local policemen encountered "Black Hand victims" who refused to divulge the names of their attackers but vowed revenge—often from their deathbeds. For example, on March 13, 1911, an assassin armed with a shotgun fatally wounded Pasquale Marcadnano, a Sicilian laborer who had failed to respond to an extortion note—allegedly sent two years earlier. At the county hospital, a doctor told Marcadnano that he "could not live." The police detective at the hospital immediately chimed in, imploring the injured man to "tell us who you had trouble with." "I tell you nothing," the dying immigrant responded. "I get well. I find out then, and I fix the man." Similarly, as he lay dying from gunshot wounds, twenty-six-year-old Annunzio Delgila told a policeman, "Sure I know him [his attacker], but I'm going to get him myself." These men believed that, if they died, their brothers or cousins would avenge their deaths and restore family honor. In one instance, police tracked a murderer to the relatives of his victim, who planned to "nurse" the injured killer back to health so that the victim's brother could then kill him. "Man after man has been shot down there at 'death corner,'" a local journalist reported, "but every one of them lived and died by the code—never a victim ever would tell the name of the man who 'bumped him off.'"[112] Although the code of personal vengeance generated violence, it also shored the lines of authority within the family and the community.

The codes of silence and personal vengeance protected the relatives of victims even as they forced other family members into violent exchanges. "Death is the penalty for all who violate the *omerta*—the Sicilian 'law of silence,'" a newspaper reporter explained in 1916.[113] Many victims led the police to believe that they remained silent to safeguard loved ones.[114] Nicholas Viana, a nineteen-year-old armed robber who was charged with six counts of murder, convicted, and eventually executed, barely participated in his own defense and refused to identify his accomplices after "his mother and two sisters received letters from the Blackhand [*sic*] Society of Chicago telling them that if this boy confessed [to being part of a robbery gang] they would be put to death."[115]

The behavior identified with the Black Hand, in short, obscured the motives of many Italian murderers and stymied police investigations, fueling the Black Hand mystique and encouraging killers to hide behind its shroud. This strategy succeeded. Between 1910 and 1920 Chicago policemen and prosecutors secured convictions for 21 percent of the city's homicides.[116] Among homicides labeled Black Hand killings, only 4 percent of killers were convicted—providing another incentive for non-gangsters to kill in public (ideally near Death Corner), use sawed-off shotguns, and whisper about extortion letters, *omerta*, and the code of personal vengeance. Similarly, the police made arrests in only 21 percent of Black Hand killings, compared with 71 percent for all of the city's homicides.[117] During the trial in one of the few cases in which law enforcers made an arrest and secured an indictment, a stranger walked into the courtroom and waved a red handkerchief. Seeing this, the Italian immigrant on the witness stand instantly fell silent and "refused to answer any questions by the prosecutor."[118] During the early 1910s, thirty-four consecutive Black Hand "assassinations" went unsolved, according to an Italian-language newspaper.[119] From 1915 through 1920 another forty-seven consecutive Black Hand murders went unsolved.[120]

Neither law enforcers nor newspaper reporters were able to distinguish Black Hand murders from murders merely committed in the Black Hand style. Thus, the Black Hand provided a kind of default explanation for Italian homicides. Italian killers eager to disguise their motives invoked the name and the imagery of the secret society of assassins, but so, too, did law enforcers unable to solve Italian crimes and journalists itching to write about shotgun-packing Sicilians.

This swirl of custom, myth, popular perception, social pressures, and violence proved to be self-perpetuating. Italian immigrants arrived with cultural traditions that valorized honor and personal vengeance.[121] Stylized descriptions of crime in the city's Italian enclaves, particularly in combination with police reactions to Italian violence, bolstered these traditions. Because local law enforcers believed that murder in Italian neighborhoods was unstoppable, they largely left Italian Chicagoans to resolve their own disputes, which encouraged aggressive self-help and exaggerated the public nature of contests over authority, honor, and reputation.[122] The code of personal vengeance therefore flourished in early twentieth-century Chicago, and the resulting explosions of bloodshed enhanced the Mafia legend and spawned Black Hand imitations.

The intertwined effects of popular stereotypes and police resignation also triggered cycles of reciprocal violence.[123] Killers were rarely punished—or even arrested—by the police. Instead, the relatives of victims, who felt honor-bound to retaliate, sought redress and meted out punishment. Such retaliation reinvigorated the code of personal vengeance, contributing to the terror identified with the Black Hand, reinforcing the inclination of the police to watch the violence from a safe distance, and thus sustaining the cycle of conflict that made Little Italies the most murderous neighborhoods in Chicago.

Regardless of the sources of Italian violence or the porous, indistinct boundary between Black Hand murders and those mimicking the Black Hand, the death toll was enormous. The Italian Black Hand homicide rate was twice the overall homicide rate of Chicago during the 1910s. Italian residents were more than twice as likely to die from Black Hand or Mafia violence as the average Chicagoan was likely to die from all forms of homicide combined.

By the late 1910s, the spiral of custom, myth, police inaction, and violence began to slow. Between the early 1910s and 1920, the Italian homicide rate fell by 45 percent. The Black Hand homicide rate peaked during the early 1910s and then dropped sharply, plunging by 51 percent and accounting for much of the dip in the Italian homicide rate. The interaction among demographic, cultural, and institutional forces reduced the level of violence, although Chicago's Italian immigrants continued to suffer from homicide at more than three times the rate of the overall population of the city. Because World War I slowed the rate of immigration, by the late 1910s the city's Italian community included few newcomers. Italian-born residents were older, better established, increasingly occupied with family life, and less wedded to the old ways. Improving language skills and occupational contacts translated into greater stability, gradual upward mobility, and expanding opportunities outside of Chicago's densely packed Italian neighborhoods.[124] Citywide leisure activities and consumption further chipped away at traditional mores. When Italian immigrants moved out of Little Italies and into the larger currents of urban life, they became better able to use legal forms of redress, less dependent on aggressive self-help, and less invested in older notions of honor and personal vengeance. This process worked hand in glove with festering racial divisions. As white Chicagoans became increasingly concerned about African Americans invading the city, Italian residents seemed less alien, less swarthy, and less "dangerous." These changing perceptions, in turn, reduced popular fascination with the Black Hand and the Mafia and thus weakened the grip of myth and custom—at least until the 1920s, when Prohibition generated new sources of violence in the city and produced an explosion of gangland killings.[125]

Even if "sensation mongers" exaggerated the newcomers' impact on local crime, immigrants murdered and were murdered at high rates and contributed significantly to the rising level of lethal violence in early twentieth-century Chicago.[126] During the early 1910s immigrants comprised slightly over one-third of the city's population but one-half of its homicide victims.[127] For old-stock Chicagoans, however, the link between immigrants and violent crime was stronger and more visceral than such statistical evidence would suggest. The patchwork of ethnic neighborhoods that defined Chicago's landscape, in combination with fashionable ideas about eugenics and nativism, insured that anxious observers would view individual explosions of lethal violence as evidence of the alien, inborn, savage traits of the immigrants.

The relationship between image and reality was interactive. Local conditions, including poverty, the stress of the migration process, and natives' reaction to the newcomers, strained social relations and contributed to violence. For Italian immigrants, as it was for African-American Chicagoans, police indifference or reluctance to wade into "internal disputes" encouraged aggressive self-help, thus reinforcing police inaction and leaving aggrieved residents to handle their disputes in their own ways. Such pressures fueled the Black Hand hysteria and hence Italian violence.

In the short run, the resilience of cultural traditions and neighborhood bonds increased the potential for lethal violence in Chicago's ethnic enclaves, as newcomers struggled to adjust to local conditions and tried to resolve disputes using familiar, traditional means of redress.[128] The pressures of family formation also frayed lines of authority and hierarchy for many newcomers, and young immigrant men, anxious to establish their manliness and bolster their patriarchal control, avenged slights to their own and to their family's reputation and committed honor killings. Attempting to stave off threats to their status, Italian men killed their relatives at high rates, though the violence nearly always occurred between men. Greek immigrants, who embraced similar notions of patriarchal authority and personal honor, engaged in comparable forms of homicide; and they too invoked the unwritten law to justify violence committed in the name of family honor. After he murdered George Barbaresso and "dismembered his body," Achilles Pentarakis, for instance, explained that "the killing was a justifiable execution of the unwritten law. . . . If they hang me the American law is queer. In Greece we protect our women."[129] In sum, for many newcomers, the combination of Old World customs, poverty, discrimination in their new location, and the jarring transition to urban, industrial society encountered by most residents produced a short-term spike in domestic homicide and added to the citywide surge in family violence.

In its form and its magnitude, Italian homicide was unique, though other European newcomers also committed homicide at high rates. During the early 1910s, Italian immigrants made up 6 percent of Chicago's immigrant population, but they were 28 percent of local foreign-born homicide victims.[130] Greek immigrants had the second-highest homicide rate among white Chicagoans. In 1913, these immigrants committed homicide at nearly triple the rate of "Americans" and at four-fifths the rate of Italian residents, according to the Cook County coroner.[131] Chicago's Greek community, however, was tiny, numbering only 6,601 in 1913, and just two homicides produced this high rate. Because of the group's small size, Greek violence did not attract enough attention to produce the kind of alchemy that spurred Italian homicide. Hungarian immigrants, too, killed at more than double the rate of native-born residents, though their population and their death toll was small as well. Also in modest numbers, Poles, Russians, and Bohemians contributed to the increase in lethal violence and to concerns about law and order in the city.[132] During the late 1910s, the Polish, Russian, and Bohemian homicide rates exceeded the overall rate for the city, but only Italian and Greek immigrants committed homicide at levels significantly above the city-wide rate.[133]

For municipal officials, local politicians, settlement house workers, and other reformers, the battle against the savage ways and alien customs of the newcomers seemed unabating. Every day more immigrants arrived, and the mission of these officials—to inculcate order, to ingrain industrial work habits, to break the hold of primitive traditions, and to encourage the new residents to rely on the police and the courts—began anew. While most immigrants endured only a short-term increase in interpersonal violence, the impact of the immigrants on Chicago violence was cumulative, and the city's homicide rate swelled.

Immigrant violence affected Chicago homicide in other ways as well. The newcomers contributed to rising levels of domestic violence, though immigrants, particularly those from Italy and Greece, committed family homicide in distinctive ways. These new Chicagoans also killed in public settings more often than their native-born or old-stock counterparts, exaggerating popular perceptions of the Black Hand, the code of personal vengeance, and the vicious tendencies of local immigrants. Vincenzo Lubio's well-publicized murder, and the "dead man's hand" that announced it, increased the resolve of city officials, reformers, and other anxious residents to tame the immigrants, to teach them self-control and "American ways," and to reduce violence in the city. Such efforts, however, would have unexpected effects on homicide in early twentieth-century Chicago.

Chapter 6

"A Good Place
to Drown Babies"

argaret Furganich drowned her infant son, Rudolph, on June 18, 1913. For several months before the murder, friends and neighbors had feared that Maggie Furganich teetered "on the verge of insanity." Someone even notified the county physician, who sent an agent to the Furganich home. Maggie Furganich, however, refused to allow the investigator to enter the dwelling, and county officials, having been rebuffed, failed to pursue the matter. On June 18, Furganich left the home she shared with her husband, John, who was a steel worker, and her two children, and she walked four miles to Lake Calumet, near the southern edge of the city. She carried young Rudolph, while her three-year-old daughter, Elizabeth, "trudged" alongside. When they finally reached their destination, Maggie left Elizabeth at the shore, waded into the lake, and hurled Rudolph into the deeper water. She then returned to the shoreline, "seized" Elizabeth, and threw the terrified older child into the lake. Bigger and heavier than her brother, Elizabeth Furganich landed closer to the shore, where the water was shallow. She "floundered to her feet and started for shore, crying." Vincenzo Oswich, a local steel worker, heard Elizabeth's screams, dashed into the water, grabbed both the weeping child and the determined mother, and pulled them to the shore, as Maggie clawed and bit him. But Oswich lost sight of Rudolph and was unable to locate the young boy, whose body was never recovered. Later examined by the police, Maggie offered no explanation for her behavior, except to report that Lake Calumet was "a good place to drown babies."[1] Nine-month-old Rudolph Furganich was Chicago's one hundred third homicide victim of 1913.[2]

Until the early twentieth century, Chicagoans had seldom imagined that young children such as Rudolph Furganich could be homicide victims. Deadly violence was supposed to involve saloon toughs, levee-district rowdies, savage young "bucks" from the south, or Black Hand assassins and their victims, all of whom were to varying degrees participants in debauched and dangerous activities. To be sure, an increasing number of wives died at the hands of their husbands, though even these homicide victims seemed to exercise some control over their lives—and their deaths. Rudolph Furganich was different; he was entirely innocent. But he was not alone. The number of homicide victims like Rudolph increased sharply during this period. In 1913, police had to cope with six other infant murders in the city.[3] Local law enforcers investigated as many infanticide cases in 1913 as they had during the final twenty-five years of the nineteenth century. Lethal violence appeared to be changing—and in particularly horrifying, nearly unspeakable ways.

Infants were not the only seemingly new group of homicide victims. Chicago policemen and Cook County coroners investigated a rapidly growing number of homicides in which innocent residents died at the hands of parents, neighbors, or other city dwellers. If nineteenth-century Chicagoans could avoid violence by staying away from rough saloons, labor rallies, or particular sections of the city, twentieth-century residents felt more vulnerable, as deadly violence appeared to bleed across social lines. The discovery of murdered infants and the soaring number of other innocent victims of violent crime underscored the increasing dangers of urban life in the age of industry.

At the same time that more Chicagoans died, middle-class residents became better informed about the daily carnage around them. Flash photography, muckraking journalism, and social-scientific research and investigative techniques exposed suffering that had occurred beyond the gaze of polite society. But the sheer numbers were upsetting enough. Between 1900 and 1910, the number of accidental deaths in Chicago jumped by 67 percent, and the number of homicides ballooned by 97 percent.[4] This rising death toll shocked local law enforcers, social workers, moral reformers, and professionals, who bemoaned the wholesale "slaughter of the innocents" in the city and vowed to protect the weak and the vulnerable.[5]

New ideas about urban society and new assumptions about the role of government galvanized the crusade to care for the innocent. Protecting infants—and other residents—from harm overlapped with two powerful legal currents. First, early twentieth-century reformers believed that the state possessed a responsibility to promote order and to safeguard its citizens. While law enforcers and social workers sought to protect the most vulnerable Chicagoans from violence, other reformers, both locally and nationally, launched movements to restrict child labor, improve sanitation, regulate food and drugs, establish health and safety codes, and provide support for orphans, waifs, injured workers, and widows. In short, during the Progressive era, a growing concern about infants and infanticide emerged from a broad-based understanding of the vulnerability of the weak, the dangers of industrial life, and the responsibility of government to address social problems.[6]

Second, Chicago Progressives, like their counterparts across the nation, embraced new ideas about personal responsibility and individual liability. Into the early years of the twentieth century, Americans had held fatalistic attitudes toward life and death, typically attributing most forms of accidental death and even some kinds of seemingly criminal violence to simple misfortune. Coroners' jurors, for example, had been reluctant to indict killers and had searched for any sort of mitigating circumstance, frequently returning verdicts of "death by misadventure" or relying on expansive, loose definitions of self-defense. Unless brawlers intentionally and explicitly sought to kill their opponents, jurors were usually content to dismiss deadly affrays as the unfortunate and unintentional outcomes of "fair fights."[7] At the start of the twentieth century, Cook County coroners' jurors were loathe to convict Chicagoans who killed without clear, unmistakable criminal motivation. A jury, for instance, exonerated William E. Doherty for the 1904 death of Elmer Hunt. While inebriated, Doherty had boasted to fellow drinkers in a local bar that he was the "best shot ever" and forced Hunt, an African-African porter in the saloon, to place a cuspidor on his head. The drunken sharpshooter fired his pistol at the cuspidor and struck Hunt "squarely between the eyes, killing him instantly."[8] Similarly, jurors and jurists typically held victims responsible for the industrial and transportation accidents that injured or killed them. In a society that celebrated rugged individualism and personal liberty, citizens worked, crossed streets, rode on streetcars and trains, visited doctors, consumed food and drugs, brawled in saloons, and even became the unwilling victims of drunken marksmen at their own risk.

Early twentieth-century Americans, however, increasingly believed that individuals had a social and legal obligation to avoid needlessly hurting their fellow citizens. In civil proceedings, jurors held those who injured others to higher standards of liability and penalized individuals who maimed and killed through reckless behavior. Transportation-suit awards, for example, rose sharply during this era, as did awards in a variety of other personal-injury lawsuits.[9] Lawmakers did their part as well, attempting to regulate a wide range of dangerous public activities.

These new cultural and legal sensibilities also affected law enforcers, who devoted increasing attention to those who inflicted harm on others and endangered the public. Reducing the legal significance of criminal motivation, law enforcers and reformers criminalized the unintentional but reckless infliction of harm.[10] Likewise, the police began investigating familiar but long-ignored forms of violent behavior, such as infanticide. Although the definition of homicide changed little, the range of cases falling within the scope of criminal violence grew during the opening decades of the twentieth century, as coroners and police officials sought homicide indictments against automobile drivers who killed pedestrians, midwives whose patients died as a result of abortions, drug dealers whose customers died from the effects of illegal narcotics, and others whose negligent or careless conduct caused the death of local residents. The Cook County coroner even rejected the jury's exoneration of William E. Doherty, the unskilled William Tell with a gun, and bound him for trial on a homicide charge.[11] If deaths were preventable, then those who killed through reckless behavior could be charged with homicide, and local government had a responsibility to pursue such cases.[12] Law enforcers also intruded into social relationships long considered sacrosanct, even attempting to regulate the relationship between mother and child. In incidents of infanticide, medical malpractice, and other violent deaths with innocent victims, the police and the courts prosecuted cases that would have been ignored in earlier eras.

Such efforts to discourage dangerous behavior and to reduce violence and death were destined to fail, at least in the short term. Each time law enforcers used the criminal law to protect the innocent and make the city safer, they created a new category of homicide and unintentionally inflated Chicago's homicide rate. Moreover, the increasing use of statistical evidence to understand social problems confirmed the worst fears of anxious residents, revealing that the city's homicide rate far exceeded that of other industrial centers.[13] Again and again, "scientific" data repeated the familiar chorus: daily life in Chicago was dangerous. A volatile, festering racial climate contributed to Chicago's unenviable stature as a city of violence, as did mounting pressures on family life and difficulties encountered by immigrants. But the expanding use of homicide charges also produced a sudden increase in the city's rate of violent death—and fed on itself. When Chicagoans counted homicide victims and panicked at the comparisons with other places, they redoubled their efforts to protect the innocent and the vulnerable.[14] These efforts, however, resulted in a further broadening of the definition of criminal violence and increased the body count, causing citizens' fears to be heightened, reinforcing the expanding use of homicide indictments to enhance public safety, and again elevating the city's homicide rate in the process. In short, the more Progressive reformers tried to make Chicago safer, the higher the city's homicide rate climbed. Perception became reality, and fears of soaring homicide rates became self-fulfilling.

The streets of the city, the Cook County coroner announced in 1914, were becoming "more perilous than a battle field."[15] Even as Chicagoans became more sober and less impulsive, a new, colossal threat to life and limb appeared: "auto slaughter."[16] Powerful and dangerous, the automobile burst onto the scene in turn-of-the-century America.

Automobiles transformed daily life in Chicago, beginning in 1892, when an Iowa entrepreneur showcased his prototype electric vehicle in the city.[17] Like their counterparts elsewhere in the nation, Chicagoans quickly discovered "automobiling" and became infatuated with the flashy new machines. At the start of the twentieth century, approximately 400 cars operated in the city. Eight years later the figure topped 5,000; and by 1920 it was close to 90,000; and in 1924 the city had more than 250,000 registered automobiles.[18] These machines rapidly dominated public space, forcing children onto sidewalks and into alleys, sending pedestrians scurrying for safety, and displacing horse-drawn vehicles. In 1912, more than twice as many horse-drawn wagons as automobiles operated on Chicago streets. By 1916, automobiles outnumbered wagons, and by the end of the decade Chicago had more than four automobiles for every horse-drawn vehicle.[19]

The great power of the automobile, in combination with its wild popularity, posed special problems for policy makers. Early twentieth-century driving was largely unregulated. Just as it had not occurred to municipal officials to license horse riding or carriage and wagon driving, local officials did not initially license automobile operators. Anyone could purchase and drive such a vehicle during the opening decades of the century.[20] Neither youthfulness, nor impaired vision, nor lack of familiarity with the new machines barred an individual from taking to the roads. The earliest municipal efforts to license drivers focused exclusively on professional operators, such as chauffeurs, and the state of Illinois did not begin issuing drivers' licenses until the 1920s.[21] Furthermore, proposed restrictions on automobiles faced considerable opposition from an increasingly powerful set of lobbying groups tied to the new pastime and to the industries that sustained it, as well as from wealthy residents who insisted that poorer city dwellers were simply jealous of and vindictive toward "automobilers." In addition, the opponents of regulation successfully argued that requiring special permits for automobiles but not for horses would be unfair.[22]

Automobiles presented unique challenges for both drivers and pedestrians. Untrained drivers often did not know how to operate brakes, horns, or lights—or even whether their machines were equipped with such features. And unlike horses, the automobile was incapable of exercising independent judgment. Accidents with horse-drawn vehicles were commonplace on the crowded streets of the early twentieth-century city, though the horses themselves tried to avoid collisions even when the drivers remained inattentive. Automobiles, however, forged ahead, slamming into any obstacle in their path. The speed of automobiles also distinguished these vehicles from other forms of transportation. Early twentieth-century automobiles could travel thirty-five or forty miles per hour, faster than any horse. Similarly, the congestion that discouraged horses from galloping through crowded downtown streets failed to deter automobiles from traveling at top speed. Local government, in short, was unprepared to cope with the automobile; early drivers were unprepared to operate their machines; and pedestrians were unprepared to share public space with these vehicles.[23]

The automobile also proved to be extraordinarily dangerous. Streetcar and railroad accidents claimed thousands of lives in Chicago during this era, though pedestrians knew to exercise caution around train tracks and streetcar lines. Automobiles, however, strayed beyond such boundaries and killed and maimed careful people who exercised caution and thought themselves safe. The automobile could injure anyone on or near a street. Furthermore, automobile accidents, more than industrial accidents or most other forms of violent death in early twentieth-century America, were public events.

The first fatal automobile accident in Chicago occurred in 1899, and the death toll mounted thereafter (see Figure 8, page 208).[24] Until 1905, city and county officials folded automobile fatalities into broader categories, such as "run over by other than railroads or street cars" and accidents with "vehicles and horses."[25] But the automobile soon claimed a category of its own and, with growing horror, local officials began tallying and announcing the annual "slaughter" from automobile accidents.[26] From 1905 to 1906, the number of fatal automobile accidents in Chicago more than doubled, and the "automobile death toll" nearly doubled again by 1909.[27] In 1910, accidents

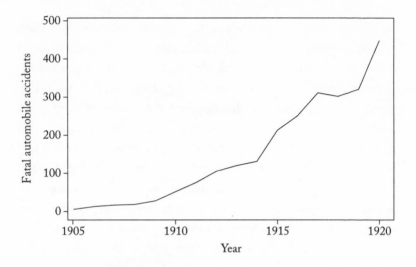

FIGURE 8   *Automobile fatalities (source: Report of the Department of Health of the city of Chicago [1931], 1136)*

involving horses claimed more lives than those involving automobiles. The numbers were equal the following year, but in 1912 twice as many Chicagoans died from accidents involving the new machines.[28] By 1920, as automobiles displaced horses from local streets, motor vehicles claimed nearly seventeen lives for every one lost from a collision with a horse or a horse-drawn vehicle. In addition, that same year automobiles killed three times as many Chicagoans as railroads and four and one-half times as many as streetcars.[29] Between 1905 and 1920, the number of automobile fatalities in Chicago rose from 5 to 450. Transportation accidents had long been legion in American cities, but automobile accidents quickly stood apart.

Law enforcers responded quickly and aggressively to this public safety crisis. Most horse-driven wagons were work vehicles, and trains and streetcars also played central roles in the economic life of the city. Early automobiles, by contrast, were toys, and the lion's share of their carnage came from frivolous, reckless use. "This will stop,"

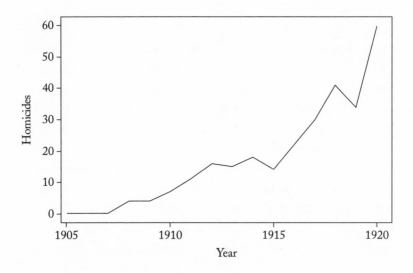

FIGURE 9   *Automobile homicides (source: see Appendix)*

Cook County's coroner roared. "This wholesale destruction of life will stop almost immediately. It cannot go on."[30] Beginning in 1908, the coroner, the state's attorney, and policemen joined forces and charged automobile drivers held responsible for deaths due to recklessness with homicide, a charge seldom preferred against the drivers of horse-drawn carriages or wagons. Municipal authorities pursued homicide indictments for four automobile deaths in 1908, and the number rose rapidly over time (see Figure 9). In 1920, policemen and the coroner labeled sixty automobile fatalities as homicides. Police records listed the cause of death in these cases as "criminal carelessness," and coroners and state's attorneys typically charged the drivers with manslaughter. In automobile homicides, the offender killed as a consequence of his carelessness or recklessness, with no intention to inflict harm.[31]

Local officials used the criminal justice system to reduce the death toll from automobile accidents, to protect innocent pedestrians, and to punish reckless drivers. Cook County Coroner Peter M. Hoffman spearheaded this public-safety campaign. Again and again, he announced that "something's got to be done"—because, he asserted, "human life is too valuable to be sacrificed to reckless drivers and drunks." In 1912, he pledged, "We are holding automobilists over to the grand jury wherever there is a chance [of conviction]."[32] "Speeders" and "drunken drivers," Police Chief John McWeeny added, "are playing with dynamite." Assistant State's Attorney Roy Fairbank joined the chorus in 1912, when he announced that "a grand jury [which could return a homicide indictment] can do much toward stopping this reckless driving of machines."[33] By 1920, Hoffman had assigned two deputy coroners and the state's attorney had assigned a special assistant state's attorney "exclusively" to the "war" against reckless drivers.[34] One local judge, Sheridan E. Fry, proposed legislation that would "send any man who kills with an automobile to the penitentiary for manslaughter." He explained, "If the driver of an automobile knew that the taking of a human life meant imprisonment for him in the penitentiary for manslaughter regardless of the elements of intent, you may be sure that this terrible slaughter would end."[35]

To make such an argument, law enforcers defined automobiles as "deadly weapons." As Coroner Hoffman put it, "In the hands of incompetent, careless or inebriated persons, the automobile is one of the most dangerous devices that human ingenuity has contrived."[36] Municipal Judge Hugh R. Stewart explicitly termed the vehicles deadly weapons in 1912, and prosecutors began charging drivers with "assault with a deadly weapon."[37] In 1916, the Illinois Supreme Court concurred, whereupon the *Chicago Tribune* quipped, "Though it is not customary to carry one in the hip pocket, the automobile is none the less a deadly weapon, the Illinois Supreme Court decided today."[38] Four years later this interpretation survived an appeal, with the court holding that "a deadly weapon within the meaning of the Statute on Assault is any instrument so used as to be likely to produce death or great bodily harm, and an automobile may be such a deadly weapon within the meaning of the statute, when so used."[39]

In 1910 Chicago law enforcers experimented with charging drivers who killed pedestrians with murder, and in 1913 Assistant State's Attorney Stephen Malato secured the first such murder conviction in the nation, when a Cook County jury found Laurence Lindbloom guilty in the 1910 traffic death of Joseph Weiss.[40] A twenty-two-year-old chauffeur and garage mechanic, Lindbloom had a questionable reputation: he smoked, used profanity, and had "mixed associates."[41] Witnesses to the fatal accident estimated that Lindbloom's automobile was traveling at thirty-five miles per hour—more than triple the speed limit—when it struck Weiss. To make matters worse for Lindbloom, he attempted to flee the scene of the accident. Joseph Weiss's body, however, foiled the escape, becoming "entangled in the machine" and forcing Lindbloom's vehicle to a stop a few blocks from the location of the accident. Fatally injured by the combination of the collision and being dragged for two blocks, Weiss, a forty-nine-year-old cigar manufacturer with a wife and a seven-year-old daughter, lingered for three days before dying. His daughter died shortly after the accident, presumably from "grief" over the horrific death of her father. Assistant State's Attorney Malato argued that "if Lindbloom had stopped his car after striking the man there would have been a chance for the victim to have survived." Malato emphasized the "cold-blooded brutality" of this "slaying."[42] In his instructions to the jury, Judge William Fennimore Cooper stretched the definition of murder. Unlike manslaughter, Cooper said, murder typically required the intent to kill or "malice aforethought," but he suggested that wanton recklessness implied a kind of intent or malice.[43] The Lindbloom case, according to Cooper, hinged on the issue of the killer's recklessness and not on his motivation: "If the jurors were satisfied beyond a reasonable doubt that at the time of the accident Lindbloom was driving his machine in such a manner as to endanger human life they should find him guilty regardless of whether the killing was accidental or intentional."[44] After deliberating for one hour, the jurors returned a guilty verdict, and Cooper sentenced the chauffeur to fourteen years in Joliet Penitentiary. "The conviction is a good thing for the community," State's Attorney Maclay Hoyne asserted. "It will serve as a warning to reckless and careless automobile drivers and drunken chauffeurs."[45]

More often, however, jurors balked at such aggressive law enforcement tactics. Even if they endorsed the impulse to protect society from "speed fiends," jurors were reluctant to use homicide charges against drivers who killed as a consequence of traffic accidents.[46] Prosecutors secured few murder convictions, and Governor Edward F. Dunne commuted Lindbloom's sentence after the chauffeur had served twenty months of his sentence.[47] Coroners and state's attorneys usually failed to secure manslaughter convictions as well. In more than half of automobile homicide cases, the juries exonerated or "no billed" the driver, and over two-thirds of the cases that advanced to trial ended with an acquittal.[48] Between 1908 and 1920 the state's attorney won convictions in only 4 percent of automobile homicide cases.[49] But state's attorneys and Cook County coroners, particularly the loquacious Peter M. Hoffman, insisted that prosecuting such homicide cases conveyed an important message to "speed maniacs" and "death-dealing 'joy riders.'"[50]

Frustrated by their lack of success before juries, coroners and prosecutors grappled with the core legal issue in such cases, as they redefined "criminal recklessness" and thus expanded the scope of homicide charges. Coroners and prosecutors usually charged drivers with manslaughter or involuntary manslaughter rather than with murder. Illinois law during this period defined manslaughter as "the unlawful killing of a human being without malice, express or implied, and without any mixture of deliberation whatever" and defined involuntary manslaughter as "the killing of a human being without any intent to do so, in the commission of an unlawful act, or a lawful act, which might produce such a consequence, in an unlawful manner."[51] Coroners and state's attorneys argued that driving recklessly on a crowded city street amounted to criminal negligence, criminal carelessness, or criminal recklessness and thus met the legal standard for either manslaughter or involuntary manslaughter. A 1914 coroner's jury, for example, found that Charles S. Harris, whose "Cadelac" struck a surrey and killed Louise Nay, "ran" his automobile "at an exceedingly high and dangerous speed" and therefore "was guilty of gross and criminal negligence amounting to manslaughter."[52]

According to aggressive coroners and prosecutors, a person driving a powerful machine in Chicago possessed "a legal duty" to exercise "reasonable care to prevent injury to others." Samuel Adams, who killed Helen O'Connell on December 2, 1917, was guilty of "culpable negligence in failing to keep a proper lookout for people."[53] Similarly, after his vehicle struck and killed Agnes Sauter, John Kuchta "was guilty not merely of a negligent omission of duty but of a criminal disregard of consequences and the rights of others."[54] In the hundreds of cases in which law enforcers charged drivers with homicide, the need to safeguard innocent residents supplanted older notions of rugged individualism; no longer did pedestrians assume all of the risk when they crossed Chicago streets. Instead, prosecutors shifted the burden of responsibility, arguing again and again that in automobile fatalities "an utter disregard of the safety of others under circumstances likely to cause injury" was manslaughter.[55] Fifteen years after a local jury exonerated William E. Doherty for his deadly impersonation of William Tell, Samuel Adams was convicted because his driving indicated "a reckless heedlessness of consequences."[56] State's attorneys even secured convictions in cases in which drivers unfamiliar with their new automobiles lost control of their vehicles and struck pedestrians.[57] Gradually, prosecutors and judges forged a new category of homicide—negligent homicide—in which "wanton recklessness" was the proximate cause for an accidental death.[58] Homicide charges, in short, provided a new tool for law enforcers determined to protect the public.[59]

Prosecutors framed their legal arguments in cautious terms, emphasizing that their actions were an effort to safeguard the innocent rather than a crusade to expand the reach of the law or extend the authority of the state. During inquests and trials, coroners and state's attorneys highlighted the need to protect the weak, the young, and the defenseless. In his landmark courtroom victory, Stephen Malato urged jurors to imagine "if Lindbloom had run into your automobile, knocked it over, thrown out your wife or one of your children and dragged her a distance and killed her." Identifying the victims in his hypothetical example as a wife or daughter, Malato exhorted jurors to protect the innocent, as a husband or a father would protect his wife and children.[60]

Policemen and coroners sought manslaughter or murder indictments in 12 percent of automobile fatalities between 1908 and 1920. Two elements distinguished these homicide cases from the traffic deaths judged to be unfortunate accidents.[61] First, the drivers were "joy riders," a label that underscored their frivolity and "disregard of the safety of others."[62] According to the local prosecutor, for example, Arthur Watts was "joy riding" when his vehicle struck forty-five-year-old Rosa Behr on May 9, 1910, entangling her in the "running gear" of the automobile until the spinning wheel ripped her head from her body. The twenty-one-year-old Watts and his companions had visited Chicago's "'red light' district" as well as a number of local saloons just prior to the accident, and they immediately fled from the scene of the collision.[63] Chicago Police Chief McWeeny attributed most automobile fatalities to "joy riding by intoxicated persons." Although drunken driving was not by itself illegal during this period, McWeeny and Hoffman explicitly linked joy riding and "intoxication," thus emphasizing the drivers' frivolity, recklessness, and disregard for public safety. Hoffman repeatedly warned of the threat posed by "drunks, speed maniacs and joy riders."[64]

Joy riders tended to be irresponsible as well as reckless. Often they were unfamiliar with their vehicles. An ideal candidate for a homicide prosecution, Alex W. Fotzke was both inebriated and driving on the wrong side of Michigan Avenue when his "big seven-passenger automobile" struck and killed Anna Shadaris. Similarly, Christ Camberis's behavior convinced law enforcers to pursue homicide charges. A Greek immigrant, Camberis had driven his new automobile only once before he struck and killed Andrew Bock on April 10, 1919. At the moment of the accident, Camberis could not remember which foot operated the brake petal or whether his vehicle was equipped with a horn.[65]

Consistent with the emphasis on joy riding and frivolity, the incidents in which drivers were charged with homicide disproportionately occurred on Sundays, and in nearly half of the cases the accident occurred between 9:00 PM and 6:00 AM.[66] These accidents did not involve work vehicles or respectable citizens. The drivers charged with homicide were also young: the average driver charged with homicide was twenty-two years old, and 86 percent were under thirty.

The second factor separating automobile homicides from accidental deaths related to the victims, who tended to be innocent and vulnerable, in terms of both their conduct and their social position. Typically, the cases treated as homicides featured both wild, irresponsible killers and innocent, vulnerable victims. Nearly half of the victims were women or children.[67] Furthermore, 40 percent of the adults were over fifty, and 60 percent of the children were under ten. Not surprisingly, a coroner's jury returned a murder indictment against a driver who was traveling fifty miles an hour when he struck a sixty-eight-year-old pedestrian hobbling—with a cane—to church.[68] Public officials believed that respectable women, the elderly, and young children, all considered less agile than the "ordinary man," were particularly in need of, and entitled to, protection.[69] In the civil courts of the early twentieth-century city, lawyers and jurors reached similar conclusions and held transportation companies increasingly liable for accidents in which women, elderly residents, and children were injured or killed.[70] Coroner Peter M. Hoffman zealously stretched the definition of homicide as "a means of halting the slaughter of the innocents."[71]

Law enforcers also stretched the definition of innocence, arguing that the careless behavior of women, the elderly, and children did not free reckless drivers from criminal responsibility for automobile fatalities. Although government officials launched "Safety First" educational campaigns to teach pedestrians "restraint" and to train children to "stop, think, look, and listen," they also prosecuted automobilists whose conduct contributed to accidents.[72] Even if residents thoughtlessly strayed into the street, speeders and reckless operators could still be charged and convicted. In Abe Schwartz's manslaughter trial for the death of twenty-year-old Cecilia Grabinski, the judge instructed the jury that "the fact that the deceased herself at the time of the killing, if such was the fact, was herself guilty of negligence, or want of care for her own safety, would not of itself exculpate the defendant in this case, if he himself was guilty of criminal negligence."[73] The legal system, according to policemen, coroners, prosecutors, and judges, assumed responsibility for protecting pedestrians, and drivers possessed a "legal duty" to "keep a proper lookout for people."[74]

Regardless of the legal reasoning or the number of convictions, the criminalization of reckless driving significantly increased Chicago's homicide rate during the early twentieth century.[75] A form of behavior that had not existed until the 1890s and a form of homicide that had not existed until 1908 added 276 homicides to the coroner's and to the police department's workload in the next twelve years. Between 1908 and 1920 automobile accidents accounted for over 8 percent of all homicides in Chicago, claiming more victims than drunken brawls and nearly three times as many victims as were attributed to the dreaded Black Hand.[76] From 1915 to 1920 automobile homicides produced a 14 percent surge in Chicago's homicide rate. In 1908, 5,475 passenger vehicles were registered in the city; the local police issued 68 traffic citations; automobiles killed 18 residents; and automobile accidents increased the city's homicide rate by less than 3 percent. In 1920, 89,973 passenger vehicles were registered in the city; the police issued 18,366 traffic citations; motor vehicles killed 450 residents; and automobile accidents increased Chicago's homicide rate by 23 percent.[77]

Shifting sensibilities about the obligations of the individual, about the use of the legal system to achieve social goals, and about the need to protect the innocent from violence resulted in the criminalization of other kinds of behavior in addition to the reckless operation of a motor vehicle.[78] Abortion-related deaths commanded particular attention from law enforcers during the opening decades of the twentieth century. Despite his pronouncements about "auto slaughter," Coroner Hoffman dubbed abortion the "greatest of all civic evils," and in 1907 Police Chief George Shippy assigned two city policemen to work with the coroner and local physicians to "aid in the collection of evidence" in criminal abortion cases.[79] Abortion had long been a crime in Illinois, punishable by up to ten years in prison, and those who killed women while performing "illegal operations" had been subject to prosecution for murder since 1867.[80] Such cases, however, were rare during the late nineteenth century, accounting for less than 1 percent of homicides between 1875 and 1899.

If law enforcers attributed few women's deaths to the effects of criminal abortion, this was not because abortions or abortion-related deaths were uncommon. In 1888 the *Chicago Times* published an exposé on abortion in the city.[81] The newspaper reported that women encountered scant difficulty finding midwives or physicians willing to perform the procedure. The article identified fifteen midwives who performed abortions and ten physicians who would either perform the operation or assist a woman in finding someone willing to do so. Thinly veiled advertisements for "abortionists" filled the pages of Chicago newspapers during this period, promising "guaranteed success" in treating "female diseases," "female complaints," and "all women's problems."[82] Abortion providers made arrangements with drugstore clerks in the towns around Chicago and with local porters to direct young women seeking the procedure to their "private hospitals" in the city.[83] The paucity of abortion-related homicide cases reflected the decisions of law enforcers during the late nineteenth century, not the absence of deaths from botched abortions.

Early twentieth-century policemen and coroners, however, "discovered" abortion-related deaths.[84] Law enforcers and anti-abortion crusaders conceded that most such deaths escaped their notice, estimating that "not one case in 100 is ever heard of, except by physicians who are called in after the harm has been done."[85] Nonetheless, between 1900 and 1920 policemen investigated 231 deaths as abortion-related homicides, compared to 11 cases in the previous quarter-century (see Figure 10).

Unlike those who sought to criminalize reckless driving, the law enforcers and reformers dedicated to eliminating the "abortion horror" faced few legal obstacles. "Abortion [causing the mother's death] is murder under the law," Assistant State's Attorney James O'Brien reminded jurors during the trial of Margaret Wiedemann in 1915.[86] Further simplifying the legal terrain, Illinois courts ruled that the mere fact of performing an "illegal operation" constituted murder if the woman died. "The criminal intent necessary to be established to convict a defendant charged with committing an abortion is the intent to commit a criminal operation,—that is, an abortion for a purpose other than to preserve the life of the mother."[87]

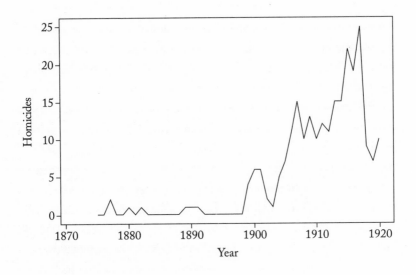

FIGURE 10 *Abortion-related homicides (source: see Appendix)*

Identifying the victims of botched abortions, however, proved to be difficult. Every year dozens—probably hundreds—of women died from such illegal operations or from other pregnancy-related problems. Until the late 1890s, few such deaths were investigated. Midwives, physicians, and undertakers did not report the cases; the police did not investigate them; and coroners' juries routinely judged such deaths to be accidents or the result of illness. Even when abortion-related deaths captured the attention of law enforcers, the police and the coroner struggled to separate self-induced abortions and "spontaneous abortions" (or miscarriages) from "illegal operations." Early twentieth-century coroners estimated that between one-quarter and one-third of the cases they considered were the result of self-induced abortions, and in many other abortion-related deaths, coroners ruled the cause of death to be "undetermined."[88]

Furthermore, the midwives and physicians who performed abortions worked hard to cover their tracks. They urged women to deny that such a procedure had been performed.[89] Concealing this information, they insisted, protected the reputation of the victim—and, of course, served the needs of those who performed the procedure. In many instances, women dying from the effects of botched abortions returned to the midwives or physicians who performed the operations, desperate for help. Recognizing the medical emergency at hand, some abortion providers encouraged these women to go to a local hospital or to another physician for care but reminded the victim of her pledge to conceal the truth. Physicians and nurses treating dying women occasionally notified the police, who recorded "dying declarations" that could be used in subsequent criminal investigations. "Believing I am about to die," twenty-five-year-old Marie Hecht made her "dying statement," in which she recounted a conversation with the physician who performed the abortion. In intense pain and expecting to die, Hecht confronted Dr. Louise Hagenow, exclaiming, "What did you do to me? I have got to die." Hagenow retorted, "What did you do to me? See in what trouble you bring me; you promised me not to say anything to anybody."[90] Abortion providers also developed support networks to help them evade law enforcers. When their patients succumbed from blood poisoning or bled to death from perforations of the uterus or even perforations of the urethra, midwives and physicians called in other physicians whom they trusted to conceal the cause of death. The relatives of the victims, anxious to preserve the reputations of their wives, daughters, or sisters, were also sent to specific undertakers who could be trusted to ask no questions, ignore evidence of botched abortions, and begin the embalming process immediately.[91]

Led by Peter M. Hoffman, early twentieth-century coroners and coroner's physicians assumed a central role in the inquests in which botched abortions were identified as homicides. Whereas earlier officials had been content to overlook falsified death certificates, Hoffman and his physicians increasingly questioned the "cause of death," launching investigations, requesting autopsies, and in some cases disinterring remains in order to confirm their suspicion that an illegal operation had caused the death. Hoffman, for example, instructed county officials to exhume the body of twenty-six-year-old Annie Horvatich. The subsequent autopsy revealed that, although the death certificate indicated that she had died from pneumonia and bronchitis, Horvatich had, in fact, "died from the effect of peritonitis, caused by the rupture and laceration of the uterus."[92] Never reluctant to take his campaigns to wider audiences, Hoffman also publicly demanded an explanation from a physician who "issued a certificate giving heart disease as the cause of death" in an abortion case. The coroner's physician, Hoffman announced to local reporters, determined that "death was caused by blood poisoning following an illegal operation."[93] In case after case, coroner's physicians discovered that attending doctors had misidentified the causes of death, confusing septicemia (blood poisoning) or a perforated uterus with pneumonia. Coroner's physicians typically "found no evidence of pneumonia" in such cases.[94]

Some attempts at subterfuge backfired and sparked intense scrutiny. When Julia Lawlynowicz died as a result of a botched abortion on September 10, 1915, Drs. A. W. McLaughlin and Stanislaw T. Boguszewski attributed her death to "foot and mouth disease," triggering a brief panic in the city and threatening to cripple Chicago's livestock trade and meatpacking industry. "Before the coroner could arrive" and begin his work, a local undertaker embalmed the body, no doubt hoping to conceal evidence of the abortion. Only a last-minute court order prevented the immediate slaughter of the herd of cattle from which Lawlynowicz was thought to have contracted the "plague." Within three weeks, Dr. Henry G. W. Reinhardt, the coroner's physician, and Dr. William D. McNally, the coroner's chemist, corrected the diagnosis and linked Lawlynowicz's death to an illegal operation performed by Boguszewski, allaying the fears of consumers and local cattlemen as well as saving "Mrs. Scott Durand's prize herd of sixty-one Guernsey cattle."[95]

The deception of doctors who completed death certificates was not new. What was new was the greater inclination of the police and the coroner to investigate abortion-related deaths compared to the nineteenth century. "We are pushing our investigations in these cases and intend to make a campaign against those responsible for this butchery," Chief Deputy Coroner David R. Jones explained in 1915. "Charges ranging from malpractice to manslaughter and murder will be preferred in all cases where we can get the right kind of evidence." The county coroner also vowed to "suppress" this "nefarious practice of trafficking [sic] in immorality and criminality."[96]

The public responses of law enforcers and reformers to early twentieth-century abortion-related homicides mirrored their responses to deaths from automobile accidents. In both instances, reckless, negligent, or careless individuals murdered the vulnerable and the weak. Local officials even emphasized that abortionists, like joy riders, preyed on the innocent, although such an argument required law enforcers to focus their public pronouncements on particular kinds of illegal operation cases.

In some respects, the women who died from botched abortions represented a less sympathetic group of victims than Chicagoans killed in traffic accidents, many of whom were young children and most of whom could not possibly have been blamed for the fatal incident. Three-fourths of the abortion-related homicide victims in the city, however, were married women, and most of the victims were foreign-born. Moreover, these women were not necessarily young. Their average age was twenty-seven, and one-third of the victims were over thirty.[97] Particularly for relatively older and immigrant women, poverty contributed to the decision to seek an abortion. James and Marie Borglum, for example, could barely provide for themselves, and the "thought of a family brought up in such poverty as they were obliged to suffer was repugnant to both." Thus, when Marie became pregnant, the Borglums secured the services of Mary Kempfer, a midwife. Marie Borglum, however, died from the procedure.[98]

Although the police and the coroner pursued the Borglum case, they focused their public comments on cases involving young country girls who had been "assaulted" (i.e., raped) or seduced and "thrown down" (i.e., abandoned) by their lovers.[99] Betrayed, alone, pregnant, and "dishonored," these naive women drifted into the city, where they were victimized again, this time by incompetent midwives and irresponsible physicians. The carefully scripted morality tales side-stepped questions about the sexual activity of the young women. In-stead, they cast young rakes and especially "illegal practitioners" as the villains. Desperate country girls, according to Hoffman and other crusaders, became "victims of the abortionist's scalpel." Before travel-ing from her home in Etna Green, Indiana, to Chicago for an abor-tion, Marie Rockhill, a nineteen-year-old Sunday school secretary, told her mother—who later testified before a coroner's jury—that "her life would be nothing there at home, and she would rather risk it than have the disgrace" of having an illegitimate child. Although Mrs. Rockhill initially opposed her daughter's plan to seek an illegal operation, Marie explained that "she would take poison and kill her-self if she did not come here" (that is, to Chicago) for an abortion. Twenty-three-year-old Marie Woodruff, "another out-of-town girl," also traveled from Indiana to Chicago for an abortion after a "young man promised to marry her and then failed to keep his word." Police officials, coroners, and their allies insisted that the goal was to protect the public, especially vulnerable country girls, from such a "hideous practice."[100]

The crusade to punish this "butchery" and thus to save the lives of disgraced and abandoned country girls not only dovetailed with the campaign against reckless driving, but it also resonated with other reform movements dedicated to saving the weak, the innocent, and the vulnerable. Antivice activists and crusaders against white slavery, many of whom believed that access to illegal operations "tends to undermine the moral sense of girls or young women," enthusiastically supported the effort to convict midwives and physicians who performed abortions. Likewise, reformers committed to moral purity and to controlling women's sexual behavior endorsed law enforcement crackdowns on abortionists, as did those concerned about "race suicide," particularly since the botched-abortion cases that were highly publicized featured old-stock, corn-fed country girls as the victims.[101]

More important, physicians and medical organizations donated their professional authority, cultural prestige, and investigative muscle to the campaign to bring homicide charges against illegal practitioners. In 1904 the Chicago Medical Society established a "Committee on Criminal Abortion," which worked closely with the coroner and the police department to detect illegal operations and investigate abortionists. The goal was "to check this evil" and to educate the innocent about the dangers posed by incompetent, reckless abortionists. Prosecuting practitioners and instructing young women to avoid them represented overlapping strategies, for such illegal operations, according to local physicians, constituted a "menace to the maintenance of a wholesome citizenship."[102]

The efforts of the Chicago Medical Society united physicians seeking to professionalize health care with moral crusaders hoping to safeguard innocent young women from the dangers of sexual activity and with law enforcers trying to improve public safety. The battle was particularly compelling to physicians, who sought to criminalize abortion and prosecute abortionists in order to drive midwives out of business.[103] During the early twentieth century, midwives attended to half of the childbirths in Chicago and performed about an equal proportion of abortions. Midwives especially appealed to immigrants, who preferred to be treated by women and particularly by women who were themselves foreign born, as were the majority of Chicago's midwives during this era. Midwives also charged half as much as physicians who performed abortions.[104] Appalled by the lack of training of many midwives and perplexed by the loyalty of their patients, local physicians teamed with local law enforcers in a campaign to control the delivery of medical care in the city. Thus, Chicago's leading medical organizations and many of the city's most influential physicians threw their weight behind the effort to expand the definition of homicide to include abortion-related deaths.[105]

Physicians' support for the enforcement of anti-abortion laws also reflected an effort to transform medicine into a masculine profession. Because they were women and because they successfully competed with physicians for patients, midwives undermined the authority and stature of the medical field, at least in the eyes of many prominent doctors. Portraying midwives as incompetent and poorly trained thus served the needs of local medical organizations, as did enlisting the aid of an ambitious coroner and a police department under pressure to restore order in the city. But the crusade against abortionists sometimes crossed professional and gender lines. Over 40 percent of those charged with homicide for abortion-related deaths were physicians, and 84 percent of them were men.

The most notorious physician performing criminal operations in early twentieth-century Chicago, however, was a woman. Louise Hagenow, who was fifty-one years old in 1900, was born in Germany and practiced medicine in Chicago for more than three decades, "specializing" in "all women's troubles." She advertised her services in local newspapers, accumulated "a large fortune," and had many "influential friends." Hagenow also killed at least seven of her patients, was indicted nearly a dozen times, was convicted on manslaughter or murder charges at least three times in Chicago and once in California, and was sentenced to prison terms of as long as twenty years. During one seven-year period, she was indicted for homicide four times. Autopsies on Hagenow's patients revealed a recurring pattern: their vaginas, vulvas, and uteruses had been "mutilated." In one case Hagenow called in another physician for assistance with a dying patient; as Dr. A. M. Morrow later testified, he found that Annie Horvatich's "intestines were protruding from the vagina through a large rent from the abdominal peritoneal cavity." The *Chicago Evening Post* dubbed Hagenow, who also advertised under the name Ida Von Schultz, "one of the most notorious woman doctors in the West." During one of her trials, the state's attorney described Hagenow as someone who "publicly and notoriously engaged in the business of murder." Hagenow, however, used her "money freely in defending herself," and her powerful friends repeatedly rallied to her aid, helping her with her legal battles and successfully lobbying for her parole and discharge from prison. Though she spent nearly nine years in Joliet Penitentiary, Hagenow served only a fraction of her sentences and immediately resumed her medical practice each time she left prison.[106] A woman, an immigrant, and a killer of "young girls," Louise Hagenow personified the threat posed by abortionists, cemented the alliance between law enforcers and local medical organizations, and symbolized the urgent need to use murder charges to protect the weak and vulnerable.[107]

This newly discovered form of homicide accounted for 5 percent of all homicides in Chicago between 1900 and 1920, an increase of 444 percent over the late nineteenth-century proportion.[108] Abortion-related deaths produced a 6 percent increase in the city's homicide rate during the opening decades of the century and a 10 percent increase in 1917, when the anti-abortion campaign reached its peak.[109] Even where the behavior of Chicagoans did not necessarily change, cultural, institutional, and legal pressures resulted in an increase in the city's homicide rate.

Early twentieth-century assumptions about the innocent and about the role of the state also sparked a new concern with infanticide, though law enforcers demonstrated less concern for the welfare of infants than they did for the victims of automobilists or abortionists. Despite the other crusades on behalf of the innocent and the vulnerable, and despite new ideas about the mission of government, Chicago officials only reluctantly investigated infanticide cases, perhaps because protecting young children required the police, the coroner, and prosecutors to challenge the sanctity of the home and the relationship between mothers and their babies.

Young children died in enormous numbers during this era. During the late nineteenth century, infants accounted for approximately one-third of all deaths in the city, and the figure hovered around one-fifth during the early twentieth century, even with stiff competition from accidents involving automobiles, trains, and industrial machinery. In 1900 over five thousand children under the age of one died in Chicago; one child in eight died before the age of one, and one in four died before the age of five.[110] Some survived only briefly, often succumbing from breathing difficulties, or atelectasis.[111] Others died under more mysterious and inexplicable, yet not unusual, circumstances, succumbing from what modern experts call "sudden infant death syndrome." Infants typically slept in the same beds as their parents and frequently suffocated when an adult rolled on top of them in the middle of the night. Young children stumbled into fires, crawled off balconies and roofs, drowned in water basins, choked to death, consumed poisonous substances, or succumbed from malnutrition or any number of the diseases that ravaged the tenements of turn-of-the-century Chicago.

Law enforcers lacked the technical skills to investigate these deaths, but more important, they felt little need to launch investigations, particularly since early twentieth-century Americans were accustomed to young children's dying from natural causes or from accidents. Furthermore, interrogating grieving parents intruded into a private and religious realm long considered sacrosanct. In short, the harsh realities of childhood in the late nineteenth and early twentieth centuries conditioned law enforcers to ask few, if any, questions, when infants died.

Chicagoans, like city residents elsewhere, often came upon the dead bodies of young children. Although urban dwellers typically arranged for funerals and the formal burial of older children, they felt differently about infants, with whom the bonding process was at best incomplete.[112] Newborns, in life or in death, were not necessarily treated as members of the family or even as human beings. It was not uncommon for Chicagoans to find dead infants in alleys and gutters, in trash heaps and privies, along desolate roads, and in any body of water. Throughout this period, sewer workers, street cleaners, and policemen routinely found dead babies. Beginning in 1906, the annual reports of the police department listed the "number of foetuses" found, and each year between 1906 and 1920 the police came across at least fifty such bodies. Most probably died from natural causes.

Also reflecting the sensibilities of the day, "baby farms" persisted through the early decades of the new century, offering desperate or callous parents an institutional mechanism for infanticide and child murder. For a small maintenance fee, parents left their very young children with families who specialized in taking in infants and sick babies. Most of the children died shortly thereafter. Their parents must have known this fact and probably left their infants at baby farms expecting such an outcome.[113] Occasional newspaper exposés told gruesome tales of mass graves and sick infants starving to death, though baby farms generated little interest from law enforcers. Nor were other city dwellers particularly interested in eliminating these infamous institutions. When an especially stubborn policeman or coroner demanded that a baby-farm operator be held for a coroner's inquest, jurors preferred to look away and to exonerate the caretaker, attributing such frequent deaths to "starvation due to illness."[114] Baby farms were open secrets, and their continued existence illustrated the disposability of infants in late nineteenth-century and early twentieth-century America.

Nonetheless, early twentieth-century law enforcers slowly and haltingly became less tolerant of infanticide. During the final quarter of

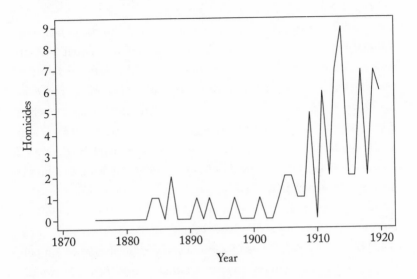

FIGURE II   *Infanticide cases (source: see Appendix)*

the nineteenth century, the police identified seven infanticide cases in the city, and the number rose to thirteen for the ten-year period 1900–1910.[115] During the next decade, the police and the coroner identified fifty infanticide cases (see Figure 11). Some law enforcers pursued such cases energetically. In 1914, for example, Captain John H. Alcock assigned six detectives to investigate the death of an infant found in a sugar bag in the basement of an apartment building.[116] Moreover, Coroner Hoffman instructed his physicians to try, in the "cases of new born infants or very young children," to "determine whether death was from natural causes, from willful neglect or by the hand of parents."[117]

Although law enforcers devoted greater attention to the murder of infants, they continued to investigate such cases reluctantly and selectively, often choosing to overlook grotesque, unmistakable signs of lethal violence. On August 9, 1902, for example, a watchman found the body of a baby boy, thought to be "a few days old," at the edge of the Ninety-Third Street pier. "Around the neck" of the infant was "a deep gash." The watchman reported his discovery to the police, who did not treat the case as a homicide. Nor was this an unusual decision or an isolated case. In April 1906, a one-day-old infant was found at the edge of the Chicago River with a rope around its neck. The *Chicago Record-Herald* captured popular—and law enforcement—sentiment about such cases, writing that "the body was wrapped in a cloth and bore no marks of violence beyond the bruises made by the rope." Again the police were notified but did not treat the death as a homicide. Five months later a sales clerk in a local store found a valise containing the body of a one-day-old boy. The coroner's physician reported that he detected "traces of finger marks on the child's neck, [and] that the skull had been fractured and the face bruised." Yet neither Coroner Hoffman nor the police concluded that this was a murder. Sewer workers, watchmen, and pedestrians found infants whose "head and stomach [had been] crushed," who bore signs of "knife wounds," and who had "a deep wound in the skull." None of these cases was ruled a homicide. On November 17, 1917, Abram Poole, a local laborer, stumbled upon the body of a newborn girl. The account in the *Chicago Tribune* revealed the depth of local indifference toward infanticide. "A string was about the baby's neck," the newspaper reported, "but it was impossible to determine without further investigation whether the child had been strangled."[118] The police and the coroner opted not to undertake further investigation and did not treat the case as a murder.

Thus Margaret Furganich's arrest, indictment, and prosecution for the drowning of her son, Rudolph, reflected a departure from the past and a new attitude toward criminal violence and toward the protection of the innocent, despite the uneven enforcement. Such cases had been routinely overlooked, but law enforcers investigated infanticides and prosecuted the killers more frequently than before. By the late 1910s the police and the coroner preferred homicide charges even against some parents who abandoned their infants and left them to die in the cold.[119]

The slightly increased effort to investigate infanticides produced a 1.6 percent rise in Chicago's homicide rate during the early twentieth century. Although the broad-based crusade to protect the vulnerable encouraged Chicago law enforcers to pursue infanticide cases, legal and moral reformers invested little energy in this cause. Unlike automobile homicide, infanticide did not pose a threat to all Chicagoans. Furthermore, unlike abortion-related homicides, infanticide enforcement was not championed by a powerful professional organization. Nonetheless, more cases were investigated. As a consequence, the number of homicides in early twentieth-century Chicago increased, even without an increase in homicidal behavior.

A few dozen other homicide cases also revealed the growing inclination of city and county officials to use the criminal law to protect the innocent and to expand the definition of unlawful violence. The number of such cases was modest, too small to affect the city's overall homicide rate. But as a result of these prosecutions, additional deaths were added to the official homicide rate as law enforcers resolved to discourage and punish reckless, dangerous, and deadly behavior.

Early twentieth-century policemen and coroners used homicide charges against physicians suspected of medical malpractice. In early June 1902, for example, the police arrested E. Wesley Johnson, a "facial massage physician," for causing the death of twenty-seven-year-old May Thompson, a stenographer from Wisconsin. In preparation for her upcoming wedding, Thompson had received a "special" treatment from Johnson to "beautify her complexion." He covered the face of the woman with an enamel over which he placed a rubber and plaster-of-Paris mask. When the mask hardened, Thompson began to suffocate and experience convulsions. Panicking neighbors urged Johnson to summon a physician, but he dismissed their pleas, snapping that he "knew what he was doing and [calling] another physician would be superfluous." May Thompson died a short time later. One of the physicians conducting the postmortem examination established that Thompson had been "a young woman of good character," and with this news the coroner held Johnson for a jury.[120] The police and the coroner, with the prodding of local physicians, investigated an additional handful of quackery and medical malpractice cases during the 1910s.[121] Before the Thompson case, however, no deaths from such malpractice had been treated as homicides in Chicago.

In other instances as well, early twentieth-century law enforcers labeled as homicides deaths that would have been dismissed as accidents only a few years earlier. In December 1911 law enforcers arrested Charles J. Errant, a contractor, and William M. Lidke, his carpenter, for criminal negligence in causing the death of three people, two of them young children, who were crushed in the collapse of a building Errant was constructing. In 1919, the police arrested thirteen people and charged them with homicide in the cases of eight Chicagoans who died after consuming wood alcohol. Joseph Weikus, a saloon owner, and Tony Keriz, his bartender, were arrested and charged for serving seven "coroner's cocktails" to bar patrons on November 24, 1919. The coroner, the state's attorney, and the police homicide squad launched a joint effort in 1919 to "hold to the grand jury on charges of homicide every one [sic] found guilty of serving or selling a drink or concoction containing the poison." Borrowing language from the crusade against reckless drivers, the city's health commissioner announced that "wood alcohol is no less dangerous than a lethal weapon." A few "dope handlers" faced homicide charges during the mid-1910s for deaths from "cocaine poisoning" as well.[122]

The city's health commissioner proposed an even more expansive use of homicide charges in 1920, when he threatened to bring murder charges against irresponsible landlords. "In cases where death results from lack of heat for babies or sick persons [who are tenants] I will compile the evidence and personally present it to the state's attorney for indictment on the charge of murder," Dr. John Robertson announced. State's Attorney Maclay Hoyne "agrees with me," Robertson added, "that to take life through failure to supply heat is as amenable to the criminal code as to take life by the use of poison or pistol. The commandment 'Thou halt not kill' covers the situation."[123] No such arrests were made, though Robertson's approach was consistent with the ongoing efforts of Chicago law enforcers during the early twentieth century. The "babies or sick persons" who died in unheated buildings were seen as innocent victims of negligent behavior, similar to the victims of speed fiends, illegal medical practitioners, murdering mothers, and "facial massage physicians."

To the horror of local residents, Chicago's homicide rate surged during the opening decades of the twentieth century, despite the best efforts of city officials, moral reformers, and law enforcers. At the turn of the century, the crude homicide rate was slightly above 7 per 100,000 residents.[124] In 1920, it approached 13, an increase of 74 percent. A prominent local scholar revealed that the city's 1920 murder rate was nearly twenty-five times that for London.[125] The sources of this rising tide of homicide, however, were complex, as diverse social and demographic processes affected the city in ways that reduced some forms of violence but increased others.

Demographic shifts affected criminal violence in conflicting ways. On the one hand, the aging of the local population, in combination with changing cultural values, undercut plebeian violence, the great wellspring of nineteenth-century homicide. But on the other hand, the same demographic and cultural shifts contributed to a sharp increase in domestic violence during the early twentieth century. Migration patterns, operating hand in glove with social and cultural forces, produced new or exaggerated forms of homicidal conduct as well, particularly in African-American and Sicilian sections of the city.

Progressive crusades to make Chicago safer also worked in complicated ways. In most respects, the campaign to discourage impulsive, reckless, and dangerous behavior succeeded. Chicagoans were more cautious during the early twentieth century than they had been during the late nineteenth century. Residents were less likely to drink themselves to death or to drown, engaged in fewer drunken brawls, and learned to be careful around dangerous machines. In 1885, the average age at death in the city was twenty. Three decades later, the average age was thirty-six. The accidental death rate also fell, dropping from 82 per 100,000 residents during the 1890s to 75 during the 1910s.[126] Although the contrivances of industrial society—the assembly line, the automobile, the streetcar, the elevator, electricity—posed colossal threats to life and limb, Chicagoans, like other Americans, adjusted to the new dangers. In part, they learned through experience. They further benefited from safety campaigns, improvements in public health, and government regulation of the workplace and public life.[127]

The campaigns to inculcate self-control and protect the public, however, also contributed to Chicago's swelling crime rate. As one historian noted, over half of the criminal arrests in Chicago during 1912, for example, "were for violations which had not existed twenty-five years before."[128] Likewise, increasingly zealous efforts to discourage dangerous behavior created new categories of homicide—or, in some instances, newly enforced categories of homicide. "Criminal carelessness," "negligent homicide," and "involuntary manslaughter," for example, expanded assumptions of culpability, responsibility, and reasonable care, broadening the definition of homicide in the process. Such changes produced a 15 percent increase in Chicago's crude homicide rate during the first two decades of the century (see Figure 12).[129] Put another way, more than 22 percent of homicides in 1920 were either for activities that had not existed in 1890, such as the reckless operation of an automobile, or for behavior that would have been overlooked three decades earlier, such as Margaret Furganich's

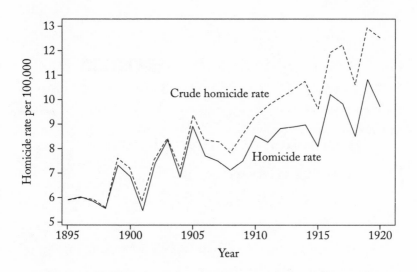

FIGURE 12 *Homicide rate and crude homicide rate (source: see Appendix)*

1913 murder of her son, Rudolph. Even where the behavior of Chicagoans remained unchanged, the death rate from criminal violence rose.

In short, efforts to make the city more orderly simultaneously succeeded and failed. Early twentieth-century Chicago was healthier and safer than it had been during the late nineteenth century. But at the same time it was more homicidal. If Chicago became more violent as it became more orderly, it also had a higher homicide rate because law enforcers tried to make the city safer.

Chapter 7

"A Butcher at the Stockyard Killing Sheep"

At 1:15 AM on January 19, 1918, Earl Dear shot and fatally wounded Rudolph Wolfe, a twenty-four-year-old chauffeur. Earlier in the evening, Wolfe had driven his employer to the theater. Having finished his day's work, he joined friends at a local "chop suey" restaurant, where they held a farewell party for another chauffeur, Harold Tucker, who had just enlisted in the British army and would soon be fighting in the Great War. Peering out the window of the restaurant, Wolfe saw two men entering his employer's automobile and raced to the street. He confronted the automobile thieves, both of whom carried revolvers. One of the men, Earl Dear, drew his weapon and fired at Wolfe. Witnesses to the shooting heard the unarmed chauffeur exclaim, "Oh my god, I am shot." Two bullets entered Wolfe's abdomen, slicing through his left lung, pericardium, liver, and right parietal artery and causing massive internal bleeding. Only a block away at the time, two Chicago police officers heard the gunshots, rushed to the scene of the shooting, and chased the would-be auto thieves as they ran off. A recent snowstorm had blanketed the city and hampered the escape of Dear and Eugene Hartnett, his accomplice. Harnett slipped on a patch of ice, fell into the snow, and was quickly apprehended. Detective John Quinn tackled Dear in a snowbank on North Avenue, pummeled him, and then escorted the badly beaten robber to Henrotin Hospital in the hope that the dying chauffeur could identify his assailant. Though barely clinging to life, Wolfe instantly recognized the shooter, saying, "Yes, that is the son of a bitch that shot me." Three hours later, Wolfe, a husband and the father of two small children, died from his injuries. During Earl Dear's trial for murder, the assistant state's attorney, James C. O'Brien, argued that the twenty-five-year-old defendant, who had a long arrest record for larceny, automobile theft, bank robbery, and related crimes and had been released from custody the day before the Wolfe shooting, was a "beast of prey." According to O'Brien, on the night of the crime, Dear had acted like "a butcher at the stockyard killing sheep."[1] Rudolph Wolfe was Chicago's fifteenth homicide victim of 1918.[2]

Earl Dear belonged to a new breed of local killers: he was younger, better armed, and more "fish-blooded" than his predecessors.[3] Late nineteenth-century Chicago had had more than its share of tough characters. But at least in the eyes of early twentieth-century Chicagoans, these men had killed according to a well-established, if barbaric, code of behavior and, more important, they had typically targeted one another. Though savage, they were not "beasts of prey."

Local commentators recognized the change in the character of Chicago killers, although they usually limited their observations to public violence, overlooking the rise in domestic homicide. Replacing fists, knives, and brawls in crowded barrooms were revolvers and holdups; and homicide somehow appeared more deadly and more menacing when it was accomplished with firearms, against strangers, on the street, and by very young men. Horrified by the epidemic of bloodletting, the city's irrepressible expert on death, Coroner Peter M. Hoffman, reported that in 1914 alone, twenty more people died from gunshot wounds in Chicago than were killed during the entire Spanish-American war.[4]

Even as informed observers tracked, measured, and bemoaned this terrifying trend in violent crime, industrialism, both as an economic arrangement and as a set of cultural values, seemed to be triumphing in the city. Volatile, impulsive behavior decreased in early twentieth-century Chicago, reflecting the erosion of older notions of plebeian masculinity. The culture of honor waned among Chicagoans, as did the veneration of toughness, the rough-and-tumble brawl, the bare-knuckle boxing contest, and the fair fight. The gratuitous infliction of pain gradually lost its cachet as well. Saloon patrons were less interested in watching drunken toughs throttling one another, and local reformers assaulted other manly rituals during this period, such the city's annual cattle-slaughtering contest, which anticruelty protesters termed a "brutal exhibition."[5] The criminalization of reckless behavior represented yet another attack on the risk-taking, aggressive hypermasculinity that had fueled much of the violence of the late nineteenth century.[6]

Early twentieth-century Chicagoans internalized the culture of the marketplace and the factory. Not only did prominent residents denounce wild, impulsive conduct, but also local residents were less likely to engage in such behavior. They demonstrated greater caution at the workplace, in the home, and in the streets. Recreation, long the haven for raucous activities, became more restrained as well. Arrest rates for drunken and disorderly behavior plunged, even though law enforcers were more numerous and less tolerant of boisterous conduct.[7] Drunkenness and brawling became less common, and between the late 1890s and the late 1910s the rate of drowning in the city fell by nearly 50 percent, as Chicagoans refrained from drinking while swimming and increasingly bathed at public beaches.[8] Furthermore, spectator sports, moving pictures, and other passive forms of entertainment supplanted the active, aggressive, oppositional pastimes of the late nineteenth century.[9] Demographic factors also contributed to this transformation: early twentieth-century Chicagoans were older, more likely to be married, and more experienced with the challenges of city life than their late nineteenth-century counterparts. The regimen of the workplace reinforced the process, and local wage earners, more than ever before, toiled in large factories or other supervised work settings, where foremen demanded self-control and imposed discipline. Chicago's public schools, which experienced a 50 percent increase in enrollment during this period, conveyed similar messages to hundreds of thousands of local children.[10]

These social and cultural pressures affected homicide in complex ways. If the nickelodeon, the factory, and the classroom taught Chicagoans self-control and personal restraint, such lessons changed the character of criminal violence more than they reduced the level of bloodshed. Between the early 1890s, when plebeian masculinity flourished, and the late 1910s, when levels of disorderly behavior and accidental death fell, the city's homicide rate jumped by 87 percent.[11] Residents, in short, did not become less homicidal as they became less impulsive. Instead, in their murderous behavior, as well as in their patterns of material consumption and their working lives, they demonstrated greater discipline. Always a city of paradoxes, Chicago became significantly more violent during the early twentieth century, and its killers, such as the "beast of prey" Earl Dear, became more purposeful and more predatory as the city grew and modernized.

Early twentieth-century Chicago was an industrial giant. In 1920 the local population topped 2.7 million, and Chicago had more residents than the combined populations of Detroit, Cleveland, and St. Louis, the nation's fourth, fifth, and sixth largest cities. The explosive economic growth of the late nineteenth century continued into the new century. Between 1890 and 1920, the average number of wage earners per factory nearly doubled, as gargantuan employers, such as Armour, Swift, and International Harvester, dominated the marketplace, both locally and nationally.[12]

The scale of local industry helped to transform the habits of Chicagoans. Industrialists organized their factories using principles of Taylorism and scientific management in order to maximize productivity. And Chicago was a city of enormous factories. By the late 1910s, almost three-fourths of local industrial wage earners toiled in factories with more than one hundred workers, and 44 percent worked in factories employing more than five hundred wage earners.[13] The city's forty-six packinghouses alone employed 45,695 workers.[14] In such settings, managers and supervisors required workers to be punctual, sober, and orderly, while time clocks dictated the pace of the day and the week, eviscerating long-established work traditions, such as Blue Monday and beer-fortified lunch breaks.[15] This socialization process, with its emphasis on self-control, discipline, and efficiency, tamped down rebellious behavior and choked off surviving remnants of the raucous plebeian culture of the previous century.

Likewise, Chicago's population in 1920 was older and more stable than it had been for decades. Because World War I sharply reduced immigration to the United States, the proportion of foreign-born residents in the city dropped, falling from 35 percent at the turn of the century to 30 percent in 1920. As the number of newcomers fell, the local population increasingly consisted of residents familiar with the rhythms, demands, and dangers of urban, industrial life. Also contributing to social stability, the percentage of young men in Chicago's population dipped during this period, and the marriage rate rose by 60 percent between 1900 and 1920.[16] Simply put, Chicago had relatively fewer young, single men, the residents most likely to engage in violent behavior.

Industrialization altered virtually every facet of society. With remarkable speed, technology revolutionized daily life in the city. Between 1890 and 1920, automobiles seized control of Chicago streets,
crowding out all other forms of transportation. Methods of com-
munication changed nearly as quickly. The number of telephones
increased from 6,518 to 575,840.[17] Chicagoans also discovered new
sources of power—the consumption of electricity, for example, surged
twentyfold between 1890 and 1920.[18] Industrialization, in short, redefined social life.

The culture of the factory and marketplace also transformed homicide during the opening decades of the twentieth century. "Crime in
Chicago," according to the operating director of the Chicago Crime
Commission, "assumed an entirely new aspect."[19] Like the city's economy, homicide became more efficient during the opening decades of
the twentieth century, and killing became better organized and more
purposeful. Moreover, the increasing scale, structure, and rationality
of local society created new opportunities for Chicago criminals, who
quickly adjusted to the changing conditions and discovered the virtues of order and efficiency.

By the 1910s, robberies accounted for more homicides than any
other single source. Chicago's robbery-homicide rate rose by 744 percent between 1875 and 1920. In 1920, robbers claimed almost one-fifth
of all homicide victims and 36 percent of all murder victims in the
city.[20] Chicago's robbery-homicide rate was nearly double the city's
spousal homicide rate and nearly triple its drunken-brawl homicide
rate.

Robberies, and particularly robbery homicides, had been rare in
nineteenth-century America. During the late 1870s, for example,
fewer than one Chicagoan per year died at the hands of robbers in a
city with more than 400,000 residents. Such homicides were so unusual that they commanded front-page coverage from local news-

papers. Under the headline "Weltering in Blood," for example, the *Chicago Tribune* described the 1875 robbery murder of Julius Wilcke, a fifty-year-old German saloonkeeper. A stunned, incredulous reporter observed that "there had been nothing to provoke the attack; it was a deliberate cold-blooded slaughter for robbery, and in this light stood distinct from most of the Chicago murders which have generally been the result of brawls in which murderer and murdered had been participants."[21] The decade of the 1880s, during which Chicago's population passed the one million mark, brought just thirteen robbery homicides, compared with seventy-one brawl homicides. Robbers accounted for approximately 4 percent of homicides during this period.[22] Nor was Chicago unique in this regard. Murderous hold-ups in New York, Philadelphia, and other major urban centers were so exceptional that these killings received national newspaper coverage.[23] Nineteenth-century city dwellers, especially saloon toughs, killed at the drop of a hat, literally and figuratively, though they seldom engaged in predatory violence, which seemed at odds with notions of the fair fight and manly honor.

Late nineteenth-century robbery homicides were distinctive in other ways as well. Unlike their twentieth-century counterparts, these murders occurred in private residences more often than in streets, alleys, or stores. Between 1875 and 1890, 47 percent of Chicago's robbery homicides were botched home invasions. The victims awoke to find burglars in their residences, fought with the intruders, and died in the ensuing scuffle.[24] "With gun and bludgeon in hand, he stole upon his sleeping victims at midnight, bent upon robbery but prepared for murder," Municipal Court Judge William N. Gemmill reported, describing the typical robber of the 1880s.[25] Nearly a third of these killers knew their victims; often they were acquaintances tempted by rumors of a hidden stash of money or jewelry.

Such murders posed problems for law enforcers, who were accustomed to finding killers standing over their victims and boasting of

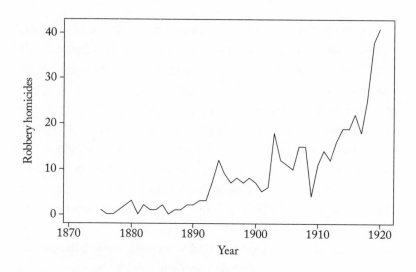

FIGURE 13 *Robbery homicides (source: see Appendix)*

their manliness. Homicide in late nineteenth-century America was rarely a crime of stealth. "Most of them [homicides]," a crime-beat reporter explained in 1875, "have occurred among parties engaged in drunken quarrels and surrounded by witnesses whose testimony made the apprehension of the murderer easy." Robbery homicides, noted the journalist, were "remarkable and hideous criminal mysteries" in an era when murder was seldom shrouded in mystery.[26]

Beginning in the early 1890s, the number of robbery homicides in Chicago surged (see Figure 13). During the late 1870s and the 1880s, Chicago robbers committed 17 murders, compared with 66 during the 1890s, 103 during the first decade of the twentieth century, and 194 during the 1910s. In 1920 alone, robbers killed 41 Chicagoans. Put differently, from 1875 through 1889 robberies accounted for one of every twenty-one homicides in Chicago, while between 1915 and 1920 one of every seven homicide victims was killed by a robber.[27]

Overlapping shifts in the structure of the local economy, the operation of the marketplace, and the values of Chicagoans created new opportunities for criminals. In fact, many of the social, cultural, and economic forces that reduced drunken brawls simultaneously contributed to Chicago's soaring robbery-homicide rate. As the city grew and industrialized, wealth multiplied, resulting in more goods to be stolen. The expansion and increasing anonymity of commerce provided fertile fields for potential burglars, safecrackers, pickpockets, and especially robbers. Perhaps most important, large-scale industrialization imposed structure on the local economy in ways that promised rich rewards to those willing to prey on fellow Chicagoans. Huge factories established regular pay schedules, for example; these proved to be a boon for local criminals. Thousands of workers poured out of factories on Tuesday or Friday or particularly Saturday afternoons with cash or paychecks in hand. With the regularity of the time clock, they then streamed into bars, pool halls, and restaurants, where they spent their newly acquired money, cashed their paychecks, or both. Saloonkeepers and shopkeepers prepared for this weekly ritual, keeping great reserves of money on hand in order to cash paychecks and stocking up on goods in order to serve their tired-but-flush customers. These workers, and both the merchants waiting for the weekly flood of consumers and the shopkeepers carrying their receipts to the bank, presented inviting targets for holdup men. More aggressive and daring robbers focused on still earlier stages in this cycle, attacking the couriers who transported cash from local banks to the counting rooms of Chicago businesses or raiding payroll offices before the cash was distributed to wage earners. In short, the increasing structure and predictability of the marketplace produced concentrations of cash.

Ongoing shifts in mass culture added to the flow of cash and goods that local criminals could intercept, as consumption played an expanding role in the lives and values of Chicagoans. A growing variety of manufactured items fell within the reach of working-class residents, who came to covet these possessions as signs of status. Chicago's great monuments to this new culture of consumption, such as Marshall Field's palatial department store on State Street, displayed these symbols of success for residents, which were also objects to be stolen by local criminals, who also craved both the finer things in life and the cash to secure them.[28] The world of consumerism generated extraordinary prosperity for the city's robbers.

The technological innovations of the era provided new and better tools for Chicago's aspiring holdup men and made it easier for criminals to separate local residents from their cash and their material possessions. Firearms were increasingly available and inexpensive, enabling robbers to use the threat of lethal force to cow their victims into compliance. Automatic weapons and silencers also proved to be attractive to the well-outfitted Chicago holdup man during the early twentieth century. The "master thug" who murdered Franklin Voorhees on October 23, 1915, for example, was "equipped with the cleverest instruments of the calling," according to the *Chicago Daily News*. John Burke employed a "Maxim silencer, shot the broker down, swiftly sniped the $600 diamond from his stickpin and fled without leaving a trace."[29]

The most important new tool for local criminals, however, was the automobile. Many robbers arranged to have a motor vehicle and driver waiting to whisk them away from the scene of the holdup.[30] Such a means of escape was especially crucial for robbers undertaking big heists. "To do day jobs and payroll jobs," an assistant state's attorney explained, robbers "have to have a machine." This practice became so common that crime-beat reporters termed such holdup men "auto bandits." On April 23, 1917, according to a local newspaper reporter, three "automobile bandits" robbed and murdered a local saloonkeeper, "while a fourth sat in a chugging automobile outside." Perhaps overstating the role of these escape vehicles, one local expert asserted that "90 per cent of Chicago's robberies are preceded by the theft of motor cars, most of which are abandoned after they have been used in the commission of crime." Judge Marcus Kavanagh also detected a significant change in the nature of local crime, writing that "the automobile encourages daring robberies." Sociologist John Landesco concurred. "The great increase in robbery," he observed, "is to be assigned to the emergence of a new factor in our civilization, the automobile, greatly facilitating the chances of escape from apprehension."[31]

These conditions were not unique to Chicago, though burglars, holdup men, and especially murderous robbers hit the city particularly hard. A 1915 crime commission concluded that Chicago led the nation in robberies, far outpacing even New York City. Both local and national commentators invoked the customary comparison when documenting high levels of violence: Great Britain. In 1917, one contemporary author noted that Chicago suffered "sixty times as many robberies" as London. According to one of the nation's foremost authorities on crime, in 1918 the Illinois city had fourteen times as many robberies as all of England and Wales.[32]

Chicago achieved national infamy for its robberies. "The great specialty of Chicago crime is, of course, the holdup: that is, the robbery on the open street," crime and vice writer George Kibbe Turner reported in *McClure's Magazine*. "It is this particular thing—the murderous street robbery—which more than all others has given Chicago its reputation for crime." Insurance companies also recognized the trend in crime during the 1910s, for Chicago's burglary and robbery insurance rates were among the highest in the nation. Furthermore, Chicago's burglars, and especially its robbers, were notoriously brazen, which attracted still more unfavorable attention to the city and inspired fear among the city's residents. A 1917 payroll robbery and the murder of two Brinks guards, a crime committed at the height of the day by five men in a "big maroon automobile," sparked panic from the Chicago Association of Commerce, which issued a desperate plea "for taking steps to curb crimes of violence." In such crimes, Alderman John N. Kimball sardonically announced in 1918, "we lead, others follow."[33]

As robbery homicide surpassed all other forms of lethal violence, the holdup transformed the overall character of homicide in early twentieth-century Chicago. The rituals of plebeian masculinity and the barroom brawl had shaped late nineteenth-century violence in the city, concentrating killing in saloons and around guzzling ruffians. But by the 1910s, the practices and the preferences of holdup men had reconfigured homicide. The setting for lethal violence, for example, shifted. Robbers increasingly struck on the streets of Chicago. Largely as a consequence of this, local streets became the most violent location in the city, supplanting bars and private residences.[34] By the early decades of the twentieth century, Chicagoans associated violence with street life and public space rather than with the seamy netherworld of the working-class saloon.

The surge in robbery homicide triggered changes in other settings as well. Even barroom violence was affected. Between 1875 and 1890, one saloon homicide in thirty-six occurred during a holdup. The figure rose to one in seven for the decade 1910–1920, as local robbers targeted the bars that cashed paychecks and served recently paid working men. The proportion of homicides occurring in stores also ballooned, tripling between 1875 and 1920. From 1910 to 1920 nearly one-fourth of robbery homicides occurred in stores, and almost half of the homicides taking place in retail establishments occurred during a robbery. Local shops were not particularly dangerous settings, at least by comparison with streets, alleys, and private residences, though the sharp rise in store-robbery homicides added to the increasingly public, predatory aura of Chicago violence.

Reflecting the shift from brawls to robberies, the relationship between killers and victims changed. Fewer robbery homicides occurred between acquaintances, with the proportion dropping from 31 percent between 1875 and 1890 to 6 percent between 1910 and 1920. The proportion of robbery victims killed by strangers rose from 69 percent to 83 percent.[35] But at the same time, the number and rate of robbery homicides shot upward, and consequently the proportion of all homicide victims killed by strangers increased significantly. During the late 1880s, one-third of Chicago homicide victims died at the hands of friends or acquaintances, compared with 13 percent who died at the hands of strangers. By 1920, strangers were the most common homicide victims, accounting for nearly one-quarter of homicide deaths and exceeding friends, acquaintances, spouses, neighbors, or coworkers.[36] In the process, lethal violence left the scripted world of plebeian sociability and entered the settings where all Chicagoans, rich and poor, rough and respectable, gathered. While late nineteenth-century homicides had tended to emerge from leisure-time activities, early twentieth-century killers more often followed the money and targeted merchants, storekeepers, saloonkeepers, couriers, and guards.

Homicide became increasingly impersonal, instrumental, and calculated. "Crime is an organized business in Chicago," the Chicago Crime Commission's Henry Barrett Chamberlin contended in 1920, as he urged the governor to reject a clemency request from the members of a murderous holdup gang. "Modern crime, like modern business, is tending towards centralization, organization and commercialization," Chamberlin explained. "Ours is a business nation. Our criminals apply business methods."[37]

Early twentieth-century holdup men often worked in gangs and carefully planned their heists. Half of robbery homicides, for instance, involved at least three holdup men. Chicago robbers frequently "cased" or "scouted" their targets before striking. On some occasions, a member of the gang even arranged to be one of the victims—to help establish a compliant, submissive tone for the other victims and to provide misleading clues to crime-scene investigators.[38] Early twentieth-century Chicagoans, according to Chamberlin, "contended with the activities of well-organized, heavily armed, highly disciplined bandit gangs who feared neither the light of day nor the presence of the police during their operations." Chamberlin reported that "there were payroll robberies, banks were held up and jewelry stores and other places where merchandise of small bulk and large value could be obtained were looted, and anyone who interfered or a victim who hesitated was wantonly murdered."[39]

Many Chicago robbers learned the payroll schedules of local businesses in planning their crime. Having determined the pay cycles of garter manufacturer A. Stein and Company, for example, a gang of five holdup men on early Saturday morning, May 19, 1917, intercepted two special policemen who were returning from a bank loaded with satchels of cash to pay the firm's employees. One of the special policemen—and one of the robbers—died during the holdup, which netted $7,000 for the gang. Robbers often struck saloons, pool halls, and restaurants shortly after the workers in local factories received their pay. Because the Henneberry Printing Company paid its employees on Tuesday afternoons and Andrew Bowman, a neighborhood saloonkeeper, typically cashed the workers' paychecks, Sam Cardinelli's holdup gang robbed Bowman's saloon on a Tuesday night, making off with over $2,600. In November 1919, Thomas Errico identified a local pool hall where International Harvester employees congregated after getting paid. Errico visited the pool hall "several times to spy out the land [and] arrange the job" and then he "went ahead as a decoy."[40] Early twentieth-century robberies required this kind of planning and discipline, and the homicides that resulted thus differed considerably from the spontaneous, impulsive violence that characterized late nineteenth-century homicides.

No single crime symbolized the "new aspect" of Chicago violence more than the August 30, 1903, robbery of the Sixty-First Street car barn of the Chicago City Railway, in which three masked holdup men disabled an alarm system, murdered two workers, injured two others, and escaped with $2,250 in neatly rolled bills. Because Saturday was the busiest day of the week on local streetcars, the gang struck the car barn late on a Saturday night. The holdup men expected the cashier's office to have at least $2,000 cash on hand, and their planning had been exhaustive. Over a period of ten days, Harvey Van Dine, Pete Niedermeier, and Gustave Marx had visited local car barns repeatedly, tracking the flow of money and personnel. They anticipated every aspect of the robbery and executed the holdup with machinelike precision. According to the *Chicago Tribune,* the "calculations of the robbers was [*sic*] so close that the last man to pay in [with his receipts] hardly had left the barn when he heard the shots fired." Similarly, William B. Edmond, the receiving cashier at the Sixty-First Street facility, had just "finished sorting the silver and paper money and had wrapped the last roll of bills and laid them on the counter" when the gang struck. Fifteen minutes earlier or later and the haul would have been considerably smaller. Even the police noted the "amazing knowledge of the robbers, who made their attack at exactly the right moment." Dubbing themselves the "Automatic Trio," the robbers had also familiarized themselves with the car barn's security system and identified the best escape routes. For example, according to crime-beat reporters, the gang members "knew the location of the wires connecting the burglar alarm with the large gongs" and "knew where a window was open in the washroom and how to escape from this window across a vacant lot and through rear alleys to less frequented streets."[41]

Still more frightening were the murders that occurred during the car-barn robbery. According to witnesses, the holdup men slaughtered their victims with the same cold-blooded efficiency that they demonstrated in other elements of the heist. Louis Martin, a car washer who watched the robbery and the murders from across the car barn, reported that the "man who did the shooting knelt and fired as deliberately as though he were in a shooting gallery." A journalist described the robbers in identical terms: "Nothing more absolutely fish-blooded and inhuman has been produced by modern civilization than the type of the 'car-barn bandits,' who shot down human beings with exactly the same dispassionate accuracy that they employed against the rocking images in the State Street shooting galleries."[42]

But why did well-planned robberies so often become robbery homicides? Having gathered the loot and terrified the car-barn employees, why did the Automatic Trio—or other robbers—kill their victims? The growth and maturation of the local marketplace attracted the attention of local criminals, though such golden opportunities for theft and robbery did not necessarily encourage robbery homicides. Holdup men typically carried weapons for intimidation, in order to render their victims passive and compliant—not to murder them.[43] But Chicago's early twentieth-century robbers were quick to use their guns. "There has been a marked and significant change in these crimes during recent years," the *Chicago Daily News* lamented in 1903. "Formerly the footpad rarely resorted to violence save as a means of avoiding arrest. To day [*sic*] the robber's weapon is used to injure, maim, and kill. Having robbed, he is likely to beat his unresisting victim into insensibility. In short, he is a murderer as well as a robber."[44] Between 1900 and 1920 Chicago's robbery rate increased, yet the city's robbery-homicide rate rose nearly ten times faster.

The holdup business became increasingly dangerous during this period, for victims but also for local robbers. By the mid-1890s, the surge in robberies in general and robbery homicides in particular had generated panic in the city, and this panic triggered a self-perpetuating cycle of violence. Residents of the city, local law enforcers, and the robbers themselves each responded in ways that exaggerated the reactions and anxieties of the others. As a result, the death toll from robberies soared.

Some shifts in the level and the nature of homicide were imperceptible to late nineteenth- and early twentieth-century Chicagoans, but such was not the case for the rise in robbery homicides. Virtually every facet of these crimes commanded public notice. They occurred in public, struck at the core of the industrial economy, and crossed social lines in uniquely frightening ways. Unlike other killers, robbers targeted residents different from themselves. While the brawlers of the Gilded Age had focused their bloodletting on other brawlers, and turn-of-the-century wife beaters and their victims were usually drawn from the same social background, the robbers of the early twentieth century set their sights on those who were older and wealthier. Between 1875 and 1890, the average age of the victims of brawl homicides was twenty-eight. By comparison, the average victim of a robbery homicide between 1910 and 1920 was forty-three. Similarly, holdup men preyed on merchants, saloonkeepers, and payroll clerks rather than day laborers or barroom loafers. But even more important than demographic or social differences was the cultural gulf that robbers traversed. At least in the eyes of their victims or potential victims, holdup men crossed the imaginary barrier that separated good from evil, order from chaos, respectable from disreputable. "These birds of prey who slink out into the night with guns in their pockets and potential murder in their hearts" victimized solid, middle-class Chicagoans, who reacted to this "epidemic of crime" with alarm.[45]

The panic began at the same time as the explosion in robbery homicides, during the mid-1890s. In 1895, the *Chicago Times-Herald* reported that "fear of the footpad's gun and the sandbagger's weapon is worrying a great many people in this big city." The following year the *Chicago Tribune* noted that "highway robbery and holdups of the most daring character, robbery in broad daylight, even petty thievery and pick-pocketing—all this dread menace to life and property and public health flourishes as never before."[46]

Local law enforcers came under particular criticism. An 1897 observer, for example, voiced a common complaint, writing that "the police force is so weak that men and women are held up and robbed almost nightly within the city limits." Turn-of-the-century law enforcers vowed to begin "cleaning up Chicago." In 1899 Inspector John D. Shea announced, "It is about time for the policemen of Chicago to be instructed to shoot to kill when they have a gang of holdup men pointed out to them." Shea added that local law enforcers should "kill these fellows wherever and whenever they find them committing crimes." In 1907 Police Chief George Shippy promised, "We will strike awe to the cheap murderous thugs who think nothing of killing a man to get his money. I have told my men to shoot to kill." Thirteen years later Alderman Joseph O. Kostner argued that "some incentive is needed to quicken the trigger finger of the police." He proposed an immediate "promotion for police patrolmen and sergeants who kill hold up men."[47]

Nor was this empty rhetoric, for the police responded with both barrels blazing, literally. Between 1875 and 1890, local law enforcers killed four robbers. During the 1890s, the body count jumped to eleven, and from 1900 through 1920 an additional seventy-six robbers were struck down by Chicago policemen. Law enforcers sometimes killed robbers during gun fights, but more often policemen felled fleeing holdup men. Patrolman Henry Baumgartner, for example, shot and killed nineteen-year-old Frances Aloysius Boddy on the morning of April 18, 1915. Walking his beat, Baumgartner saw Boddy and three others "scuttle from the doorway" of a West Grand Avenue confectionery store they had just robbed. The patrolman chased the men, commanded them to stop, and then fired at Boddy. According to the *Chicago Tribune,* the "bullet jumped from the darkness in the interest of the law and crumbled the boy as he fled." Similarly, just after midnight on April 10, 1915, Detective Sergeant John J. Sullivan and his partner chased, shot, and killed L. C. Rapp, a thirty-two-year-old, unemployed steelworker who had just tried to rob a West Madison Street restaurant. "It was me or him," said Sullivan. Cook

County juries endorsed such aggressive tactics; no law enforcer was tried and convicted of homicide in these cases, though the increasingly forceful policies of the Chicago police clearly contributed to the death toll from local robberies.[48]

Anxious to safeguard their money, protect their property, and lower their insurance rates, local businessmen added watchmen and guards to their payrolls, and these private security officers became aggressive as well. From 1875 to 1889, before the panic set in, Chicago guards, private detectives, and watchmen killed three holdup men. During the late 1890s, they killed twice that number, and between 1900 and 1920 an additional forty-two robbers died during holdups. As local businesses hired more private policemen and encouraged them to resist holdup men, the violence surrounding Chicago robberies mounted.

Private citizens responded still more ferociously, killing eighty-seven holdup men during the first two decades of the century, compared with eight between from 1875 to 1889 and sixteen during the 1890s. Uncooperative robbery victims were nearly as deadly as Black Hand assassins during the opening decades of the twentieth century. As the robbery panic grew, ordinary citizens, feeling vulnerable, prepared to do battle with holdup gangs. "Men who never thought of firearms except as part of a duck hunting outfit are becoming regular patrons of gun stores and absorbing information on the relative adaptability and merits of 'thirty-twos,' 'thirty-eights,' 'bulldogs,' hammerless, self-acting and short range tools of war," a local journalist observed in 1895. He added that "the man who has something in his pocket he knows will kill if properly handled feels safer than the man without it. And that is the way fully 75 per cent of Chicago men are feeling just now." Hardware merchants reported "booming" guns sales. The *Chicago Record* noted, "Good citizens are taking lessons in how to remain self-possessed, fish the weapon from a deep hip-pocket and get it leveled at the footpad before the latter has time to think of shooting." The American Bulldogs and Maxims purchased to repel robbers, however, often found their first and only use during family squabbles, and thus the turn-of-the-century robbery panic generated collateral violence.[49]

Saloonkeepers, pool hall operators, and store owners were particularly vulnerable to holdup men and were especially ready to resist. Bartenders and saloonkeepers tended to be tough customers and frequently kept firearms readily available. During the late nineteenth century, they typically used these weapons to control drunken, belligerent patrons. But during the early twentieth century many saloonkeepers also armed themselves to fend off holdup men. Because they kept long hours and often maintained sizable cash reserves, bars presented obvious targets for robbers. Some saloonkeepers both carried a handgun and kept a second revolver behind the bar.[50]

Accustomed to dealing with the roughest element in the city, local bartenders proved to be especially irascible, noncompliant victims. Thomas Morgan tended bar at Ben Brace's State Street saloon when two strangers entered the establishment. "They came toward me," Morgan explained, "and one of them told me to throw up my hands. He kept the gun leveled at my head and told the other man to get the money." An "ex-pugilist," Morgan "was not to be coerced so easily." "My gun was lying on the bar alongside of the whiskey glasses," Morgan reported, "and watching his eye I picked it up and fired three shots in quick succession." One of Morgan's shots struck twenty-six-year-old Thomas A. Cantwell behind the right ear. Eddie Harrity and three accomplices encountered another, similarly combative saloonkeeper on December 30, 1894. In just twenty minutes, the four men, all in their early twenties, held up two Chicago saloons. First, they struck N. J. Melin's bar on Kinzie Street, where they cleaned out the cash register and murdered the bartender, Nelson Beck. A few minutes later and half a mile away, the gang entered Austin McGrail's Huron Street saloon. The strangers ordered beers, and then, reported the *Chicago Tribune,* "when McGrail turned around from having drawn the refreshment he looked into the muzzle of a revolver and was astonished to hear the command: 'throw up your hands.'" The "wiry and ready" McGrail, however, "had seen troublous time before," noted the crime-beat reporter for the *Chicago Record;* "and besides, he carries a medal for good shooting." Rather than complying with the robbers' demand, McGrail said coolly, "No you don't. Come, be good fellows and have another round of drinks with me." Having distracted the holdup men, McGrail "reached beneath his bar and seized his own weapon, which was lying there, leveled it at the foremost of the men" and shot him in the chest, killing Harrity. Startled by the sudden turn of events, the other robbers ran for the door. "I only wish that I had had a better revolver," the saloonkeeper later added, "and I would have caught another of them."[51] Twenty-four robbers died during botched saloon holdups between 1890 and 1920.[52]

Chicagoans, including policemen, watchmen, saloonkeepers, and store owners, killed 238 robbers between 1890 and 1920. By comparison, only 15 holdup men had died from 1875 through 1889 during commission of their crimes. Although local juries exonerated or acquitted nearly all of the men who killed robbers, typically ruling the deaths "justifiable homicides," these shootings were considered homicides and thus added to the city's homicide rate.[53] More important, such killings received enormous publicity, emboldening potential victims and unnerving the city's criminals. If holdup men contributed to Chicago's reputation as a tough town, so did their victims.

Men such as Thomas Morgan and Austin McGrail made local robbers skittish and, as a consequence, quicker to kill their victims. When bartenders, shopkeepers, or other victims moved haltingly or did not immediately raise their hands and turn over their valuables, local highwaymen feared resistance. For example, after Albert Kubalanza tried to "secret his money in his clothes when ordered to put up his hands" during a pool hall heist, Frank Campione concluded that his victim "was reaching in his back pocket for a weapon" and "shot him through the heart."[54] Simply put, robbers recognized that they confronted growing resistance from their victims and responded by employing greater force. The proportion of murderous robbers who relied on firearms rose by 49 percent between 1875 and 1920. As the financial opportunities for robbers increased, they faced greater risks in the form of resistance from victims, making Chicago holdup men quicker to carry guns and more inclined to kill their victims. At the same time, because robbers became more violent, potential victims more frequently carried weapons and resisted their attackers, increasing the risks encountered by the robbers and creating a mutually reinforcing interaction between victims' resistance and holdup men's use of violence.[55]

The murders of William Kniering and Paul J. Loberg combined many of the characteristic elements of early twentieth-century Chicago robbery homicides, including this cycle of escalating violence. A sixty-one-year-old saloonkeeper, Kniering had been robbed and beaten, and he pledged that he would never again be victimized. He began carrying a revolver and kept a second weapon tucked behind his bar, telling friends that if he were to be held up again, "One or the other of us will go to the morgue." According to one report, "He was waiting for the chance to kill some of those hold-up fellows," and on October 23, 1904, Kniering got his chance. During the previous days, two young men had "scouted" his saloon, repeatedly visiting Kniering's establishment and wandering around the neighborhood. Then, on the afternoon of October 23, Kniering's imposing Great Dane disappeared. A few hours later four robbers entered the saloon and ordered Kniering to raise his hands. True to his word, the saloonkeeper drew his weapon, whereupon the edgy robbers immediately shot and killed Kniering. Paul J. Loberg, a thirty-nine-year-old jeweler, died under similar circumstances on December 22, 1920.

"Fearing a holiday robbery," the jewelry store owner "prepared himself for such an emergency by wearing a holster slung from his shoulder under his coat." When two strangers entered his store and snarled, "Hands up," Loberg fumbled for his gun. One of the robbers quickly cracked him on the top of his skull while the other shot him; Loberg died four hours later.[56] In these murders, and dozens of others, local robbers employed lethal force in response to the armed resistance of their victims. Although some of the holdup men might have resorted to violence even if their victims had been compliant, the aggressive self-defense of bartenders and shopkeepers accelerated the cycle of bloodshed.

The character of the city's holdup men also contributed to their volatility—and to the rising robbery-homicide rate. The men who planned their capers, cased their victims, disabled alarm systems, mapped their escape routes, filed off the registration numbers on their weapons, stole getaway vehicles, hit hard, and then disappeared into the night appeared to have little in common with the impulsive, swaggering young killers of earlier generations.[57] At first glance, early twentieth-century highwaymen and payroll robbers seemed cool, deliberate, disciplined, and calculating, and their crimes were instrumental and purposeful. On closer inspection, however, a more complex picture emerges.

The new breed of killers tended to be very young. In fact, these men were, on average, five years younger than the homicidal brawlers of the late nineteenth century. The mean age for early twentieth-century holdup killers was under twenty-four. Perhaps the city's most notorious gang of the era, the Cardinelli gang, which committed six murders and forty-two robberies in 1919, consisted of an eighteen-year-old and two nineteen-year-olds. Similarly, the holdup men who pulled off the 1903 car-barn robbery and committed eight murders and eight robberies ranged in age from twenty-one to twenty-three. "It is the young fellows from 17 to 22 that does [sic] the gun work" in robbery homicides, a spokesman for the Chicago Crime Commission reported in 1920. Local writers labeled the new killers "boy bandits" or "baby bandits." Teenagers James Formby, William Formby, David Kelly, and Peter Dulfer, who killed two men during robberies in 1904, were dubbed the "baby bandit quartet."[58]

Contemporaries found this trend unsettling. Early twentieth-century experts contrasted these "baby bandits" with the seasoned, professional holdup men of "former years," who only reluctantly killed their victims. "The average age of robbers and thieves has been steadily decreasing," Police Chief John Healey remarked in 1916. "Formerly holdup men as a rule were in the neighborhood of 45 years of age, sometimes older." Such "professional" robbers, a crime writer noted, would not "deliberately engage in murder or the graver crimes." A police lieutenant investigating a 1905 robbery and murder agreed, saying that "no veteran criminal takes a life with as little provocation as did these boys." Not only were Chicago holdup men who killed their victims younger than late nineteenth-century robbers (or, for that matter, brawlers), they were also younger than the holdup men who refrained from committing murder. On average, robbers who killed were more than two years younger than the nonmurderous robbers sent to Joliet Penitentiary during the late 1910s. "Inexperienced thieves," a local journalist agreed, "are the first to shoot."[59]

Homicidal holdup men were also poor, even by comparison with other Chicago killers. Industrialization transformed the structure of Chicago's labor force during this period, producing an increase in semiskilled jobs, such as machine tenders and factory operatives, and a relative decrease in unskilled jobs. As a result of this shift, the proportion of day laborers and other unskilled workers contracted, producing a comparable contraction in the proportion of unskilled killers in the city. Unskilled men, for example, had comprised 46 percent of male killers during the late nineteenth century but 39 percent of male killers during the early twentieth century. The percentage of unskilled robber-killers, however, increased between 1875 and 1920. During the late nineteenth century, 49 percent of robber-killers were unskilled, while 59 percent were unskilled during the opening decades of the twentieth century. As the structure of the local economy changed, those who wound up as robber-killers became more disadvantaged.

Although few killers discussed the social pressures that launched their criminal careers, Harvey Van Dine, one of the infamous car-barn robbery gang, delved into such issues as he argued for the commutation of his death sentence. His brief, but busy, criminal career, which spanned only a few months, began after a visit from two friends who "had on good clothes." Van Dine continued, "I asked than [sic] what they were doing for a living." In reply, "they laughed and said they did not have to work." A short time later, the friends visited again and offered to include Van Dine in their next robbery. "I was out of money, as I had given mother all my pay," Van Dine recalled, adding that he was exhausted from working long hours with a bad back for meager pay, and he was angry about his inability to get ahead. That night, he said, he committed his first holdup, and two nights later the teenager was involved in his first robbery homicide.[60] At least for Harvey Van Dine, who was executed on April 22, 1904, grinding poverty, bleak prospects for the future, and the lure of easy money and "good clothes" made crime attractive. Van Dine's accomplices came from similar backgrounds. Unable to secure stable jobs and believing that they had fallen behind their peers, these young men joined holdup gangs.

Chicago's early twentieth-century robbers were also less capable and less disciplined than contemporaries believed or than successful heists implied. Like other sensational holdups, the Sixty-First Street car-barn robbery went off like clockwork. But Van Dine later gave a more complicated description of the heist. He and his friends had initially planned to rob an express train on the Wisconsin Central

Line, but, he said, "we did not do it for some reason." Then the young men decided to hit the Seventy-Ninth Street car barn of the Chicago City Railway; this was postponed because two members of the gang quarreled. Three of the holdup team assembled for a second try "but did not carry it out." Three days later, the gang returned to the Seventy-Ninth Street car barn, but they "got there too late." Finally, said Van Dine, "We came back to the 61st Street barns at three o'clock." At that point, "We saw that all was clear and went." In his first robbery homicide, Van Dine and his Automatic Trio gang netted $2.35, and in a subsequent holdup, they murdered two people and reaped $8.00 for their efforts. "We killed two men—four dollars apiece," Van Dine lamented.[61] The Automatic Trio was simultaneously meticulous and sloppy, and their jobs were both precisely planned and haphazard. Other seemingly well-organized gangs murdered for similarly meager hauls and also bungled their heists. For smaller gangs of holdup men or lone-wolf robbers, the financial returns were typically modest, though the death toll was frequently high.[62]

Despite the forethought involved in Chicago holdups, robbery homicides often bore the unmistakable imprint of volatile, immature young men. The organizational structure of holdup gangs fueled this volatility and the accompanying violence. Many robbery gangs, particularly those that pulled off major heists, were headed by older men, or "Fagins"—a reference to the character in Charles Dickens's *Oliver Twist* who taught children to steal. These experienced, seasoned criminals coordinated the robberies—they identified the targets, planned the crimes, supplied the guns and automobiles, and assembled the teams of robbers and drivers. Ordinarily operating out of pool halls, Fagins, such as forty-year-old Sam Cardinelli, offered young, poor men the sense of belonging, status, and control that eluded them in the home and the workplace. Robbery gangs also provided members with comrades, cash, flashy new weapons, and adventure, many of the same elements that other frustrated working-class residents found in athletic clubs or youth gangs. According to law enforcers, men such as Cardinelli conducted "crime schools."[63]

But the holdups themselves were undertaken entirely by the young men. Fagins remained in their pool halls during the robberies, far from the crime scene and thus out of the reach of law enforcers. Unleashed in a tension-filled activity, heavily armed, eager to prove themselves, and beyond the gaze of their mentors, baby bandits were often wild and unpredictable. As a result, the most carefully planned robberies could become needlessly violent. Chicago Police Chief George Shippy believed that young robbers "love to shoot at the slightest provocation." Detecting a "vicious" streak that exceeded anything he had encountered in his "thirty-four years of experience," Judge Kickham Scanlan concluded that young holdup men "killed when they didn't have to kill, just recklessly and wantonly." The killers themselves often agreed with this assessment. "Shooting came cheap," Harvey Van Dine conceded. In 1917, Frank Zager murdered his victim, Paul Pelipo, because "he was a mutt—wouldn't stick up his hands quick enough . . . so I just bumped him off." Asked why he shot and killed a second, more compliant victim, Zager shrugged, "O [sic], I just thought I might as well kill him, I guess." Urging Governor Frank O. Lowden to deny the clemency appeal of Nicholas Viana, an eighteen-year-old member of the Cardinelli gang who was convicted of two murders, was under indictment for six other murders, two counts of assault with intent to commit murder, four counts of robbery, two counts of burglary, and who was believed to have participated in two hundred robberies, Assistant State's Attorney E. J. Raber noted how Viana's case contrasted with the usual homicide case. Viana, Raber explained, "is entirely different from some person who has some great passions in him who kills someone or something he has been brooding over. Here is a man that is a persistent outlaw and as ruthless as any outlaw I ever met."[64]

Although young men such as Van Dine, Zager, and Viana were explosive and vicious, their violent outbursts were neither random nor indiscriminate. These murderous holdup men resorted to lethal violence when they felt challenged. Reminiscent of the bluster of late nineteenth-century brawlers, they often believed that their victims were demonstrating disrespect, and the young robbers reacted accordingly. Already anxious because they were in the process of committing armed robbery, holdup men easily misread cues and murdered submissive victims. On November 17, 1918, for example, two highwaymen commanded Simon J. Levi to hold up his hands. A newcomer from Russia with scant command of English, Levi obediently "extended his arms horizontally." Believing the immigrant was mocking his assailants, one of the robbers snapped, "Shoot him," and his accomplice did so, killing Levi. A 1919 holdup man killed his victim for similar reasons, explaining, "I shot him because he thought he was a smart guy." Nicholas Viana boasted to his friends and fellow gang members that "if anybody makes a crooked move" he would kill them, asking rhetorically, "What do you think I have a gun for?" Facing token resistance from his victim, sixteen-year-old Elmer Fanter shot and killed August Jantzen during a 1915 store robbery. Giggling as he testified at his trial, Fanter averred that "he [Jantzen] swatted me on the cooo [i.e., head]. Well, I ain't takin' that sort of stuff off'n no one, so I ups with my rod and lets him have it right through the heart."[65] Both teenagers, Viana and Fanter murdered their victims in order to get money but also in order to convey or feel power.

Early twentieth-century robbery homicides were complex crimes, blending economic and cultural motives. The robberies themselves were typically calculated acts, planned and executed to secure money and goods. Although some holdup men killed their victims in order to complete the robberies, the violence employed by murderous holdup gangs also served the cultural needs of the baby bandits.[66]

The demographic, social, and cultural shifts of the early twentieth century undercut the older bases of plebeian masculinity, where working-class men had demonstrated their mettle in brawls, surrounded by their peers. By the opening decades of the new century, Chicago had an older population, a smaller proportion of bachelors, fewer neighborhood saloons, and a wide assortment of alternative activities. The proliferation of firearms also transformed the rules of working-class manliness. In early twentieth-century Chicago, where guns abounded, local ruffians were less inclined to swagger into crowded barrooms and announce that they would abide no disrespect or that they would take on all comers.

Instead, for young men unable to secure status in the home, the workplace, or even in the local saloon, reputations could be forged in the course of robberies, especially if the perpetrators murdered their victims. Early twentieth-century expressions of plebeian authority and masculinity increasingly involved guns and displays of dominance over unarmed strangers. Shorn of the rituals of challenge and response, these new assertions of power were not bound by established rules or by the collective judgment of large audiences. Members of holdup gangs gained the respect of their immediate peers through bold actions, bald brutality, and overt violence, much as the members of youth gangs earned their stripes by attacking unsuspecting pedestrians or by fighting rival gangs.[67] When the police arrested James Formby for killing John Lane during a 1904 saloon holdup, the seventeen-year-old requested that law enforcers charge him with murder, boasting, "I'm a killer, not a robber." Poor young men, such as Formby and Fanter, reveled in scaring, dominating, and humiliating others, particularly older, wealthier strangers. Violence, or even the potential for violence, not only impressed their peers, it was also intoxicating—or, as a 1920 crime commission report explained, it provided "a spicy risk flavoring the carrying out of their criminal enterprises."[68]

For some holdup men, the thrill that came from dominating others outweighed the financial rewards of robbery. And since the members of holdup gangs rejected older notions of the fair fight, they often targeted those who were merely vulnerable, regardless of the potential loot that the crime would yield. The line separating robbery gangs from youth gangs thus often disappeared entirely. On October 20, 1911, six young Polish men (three of whom were under eighteen), armed with "two revolvers, a bread knife, a pocketknife and a large club," resolved to commit a robbery. The first potential victims they encountered seemed too formidable, and so the young men waited for a less imposing victim. Finally, they held up Fred Guelzow, a farmer transporting a wagonload of vegetables to Chicago. Although Guelzow complied with the instructions of the robbers and surrendered his silver watch and chain, the young men were "not satisfied with the mere hold-up," a contemporary sociologist wrote. "They were nonplussed to find that it was all over and there had been no killing. It was not complete and did not correspond to a hold-up as they had come to understand it."[69] Thus, the six young men brutalized their victim. They crushed Guelzow's skull, ripped out his tongue, "mutilated him horribly with bullets and knives, and cut off a piece of his leg and put it in his mouth."[70] For their efforts, the robbers escaped with $8.00, a team of horses, and Guelzow's boots, which one of the killers triumphantly wore until he was arrested.[71] Vicious, gratuitously violent, and predatory, such robbers were far more frightening to respectable Chicagoans than late nineteenth-century saloon toughs or turn-of-the-century wife beaters.

Other young men robbed mainly for sport and chose the most risk-free victims they could find. Robbing and occasionally killing inebriated men—"variously known as 'jack rolling,' 'rollin' de bums,' 'rollin' de dinors,'"—became "a universal practice among gangs" in Chicago during this period.[72] Small groups of young men often decided on the spur of the moment to follow drunken men out of bars and into dark alleys, where the attackers beat and robbed their largely defenseless victims.[73] These holdups, occurring on streets and in alleys, reinforced the predatory and public nature of early twentieth-century robbery homicide.

A highly visible series of robberies committed by African-American residents contributed to the surge in holdup murders and magnified the robbery panic of the era. Between 1910 and 1920, African-American Chicagoans robbed and murdered forty-two people, seven times the total of the previous decade. Comprising 3 percent of the city's population between 1910 and 1920, African Americans committed 18 percent of robbery homicides—and 29 percent in 1920. The impact of these holdup murders, however, transcended the numbers.

The form and the character of the homicides exaggerated some of the most frightening aspects of city life during the early twentieth century, at least for white, middle-class Chicagoans. African Americans rarely belonged to well-organized holdup gangs and did not pull off payroll heists or other high-profile robberies. "Their weak minds conceive the idea of obtaining easy money by means of robbery. With a dollar in sight they take desperate chances to obtain it," an early twentieth-century expert noted. "They do not tackle big jobs. They do not feel competent to undertake, for instance, large payroll robberies. As a rule, they hold up taxi-cab drivers, store-keepers, and pedestrians."[74] One-third of African-American robbery homicides occurred in local stores, double the citywide figure.

Two additional aspects of these robberies added to their terror. First, the victims were nearly always white.[75] Holdup men usually chose victims likely to have money, and thus African-American robberies and robbery homicides crossed racial lines. Although three-fourths of African-American killers targeted African-American victims, 86 percent of African-American robbery homicides had white victims. While white Chicagoans, like other white Americans, heard rumors about African-American rapists, it was African-American robbers who generated particular fear.

Second, and closely related, African-American robbery homicides tended to be especially gruesome crimes, even relative to other homicides. Across the city, two-thirds of murderous holdup men relied on guns. But fewer than half of African-American robbers employed firearms. Many used clubs or other blunt instruments and beat to death older, white, neighborhood shopkeepers and pedestrians. Two "negro thugs," for example, bludgeoned Morris Lipschultz just before noon on October 14, 1910. Sam Huston and Victor Butler heard the fifty-three-year-old Jewish junk dealer calling out to customers, yelling "Rags, old iron," and they lured him into a barn. There the two robbers, one of whom was nineteen and the other twenty-two, took $7.00 from their victim, crushed his skull with a club, and choked him so forcefully that the police were able to take wax impressions of the finger marks on the peddler's corpse. Joseph W. Springer, the coroner's physician, said that "never before in his experience did he see a body so badly mutilated." Springer concluded that "the negroes not only throttled the old man after knocking him unconscious but kicked him and jumped up and down on his prostrate body as it lay in the alley." Similarly, on the afternoon of August 28, 1918, a tall, powerfully built, "light-skinned negro" attacked seventy-three-year-old Ferdinand Theiner from behind, "striking one terrific blow with a bludgeon." The robber then stole $48.00 and left the tea shop manager crumbled in a heap and bleeding to death in his store. A "kindly, gentle, patriarchal man," Theiner, according to his neighbors, was "feeble" and "could not have offered any resistance." Joseph Calber both beat and shot his victim in a 1916 street robbery that a police captain termed "the most cold blooded" he had encountered in his law-enforcement career. Calber approached Charles Brown, a fifty-two-year-old tinner, on Thirty-Fifth Street and told him to "throw up his hands." Brown complied and offered no resistance. "When I went through his clothes," the twenty-three-year-old robber later explained to the police, "he didn't have a cent, and I got sore and shot him three times. After I shot him, I struck him on the head with the revolver," Calber added.[76] In Chicago's Black Belt and at the southern fringes of the city's Loop, African-American robbers stalked, preyed on, and brutally murdered older, vulnerable, white storekeepers, peddlers, and pedestrians, providing a new and enduring rationale for white racial antipathy and concern about street crime. More than ever before, Chicagoans feared the streets and young strangers, who were at once purposeful, acquisitive, coldhearted, volatile, and vicious.

Finally, this elision of expressive and instrumental violence probably contributed to the gangland crime of the 1920s. During the 1910s, local observers worried that the American-born children of immigrants, particularly the children of Sicilian immigrants, were becoming murderous holdup men, blending the older traditions of violent behavior with the instrumental, cold-blooded calculation of robbers. "The younger generation," a 1916 writer warned, "have seen their elders kill their enemies with impunity inside the boundaries of Little Sicily in the pursuit of private feuds. From that it is only a step to outside violence and murder as holdup men and robbers."[77] When Prohibition transformed small-scale criminal networks into unstable, immensely profitable crime syndicates, second-generation immigrants, such as Al Capone, seized their opportunity and expanded the scope of their violence.[78] They were volatile and gratuitously vicious, but they also used violence in calculated ways and for clear purposes—to control markets and to eliminate competition. According to a contemporary sociologist, gangsters committed over two hundred murders during the "Beer Wars" of the mid-1920s. The Illinois Crime Commission reported that in 1926 alone organized crime gangs committed forty-five murders in Chicago. This carnage peaked on February 14, 1929, when four members of Capone's gang murdered seven rivals in a North Side garage, an assassination known as the St. Valentine's Day Massacre.[79]

*   *   *

By the late 1910s robbery was the leading, as well as the fastest-grow-
ing, motive for homicide in Chicago. Between 1890 and 1920, the
city's population rose by 146 percent. But the number of homicides
increased by 376 percent, despite the fall in drunkenness and disorderly behavior. During the same period, the number of robbery
homicides jumped by 1,950 percent. More than domestic violence,
Black Hand murders, or any other source, robberies were responsible
for the sharp increase in Chicago's homicide rate.[80]

Social, cultural, and economic changes in turn-of-the-century Chicago produced this pattern. Such forces simultaneously transformed
plebeian culture, reducing brawling violence, and created growing
opportunities for local robbers, thus contributing to the surge in robbery homicide. Holdup men were not as disciplined as contemporaries sometimes believed, and their violent behavior retained elements
of the swaggering hypermasculinity of earlier drunken brawlers. At
the same time, the new Chicago killers were distinct from their predecessors. They were younger; they planned their actions; they killed
with purpose and premeditation in unprovoked attacks; and they targeted older, wealthier residents. Murderous behavior did not disappear under the pressure of industrial culture. Instead, violence became more calculated and instrumental.

The surge in robbery homicide in early twentieth-century Chicago redefined broader patterns of violence and profoundly influenced perceptions of crime and public order, as well as race relations.
It also generated an ancillary development, with hundreds of Chicagoans arming themselves and then killing the men who attempted to
rob them. Together, robbery murders and deaths in which the holdup
men were killed accounted for almost one-quarter of all Chicago homicides during the late 1910s.

In less than half a century, homicide changed from a closed, relatively infrequent activity largely confined to bachelors and concentrated in working-class saloons to a far more common, predatory

form of behavior in which the "lower sort" hunted down and slaughtered their social betters. This shift both reflected and caused important cultural shifts in early twentieth-century Chicago. First, as a result of cultural, economic, demographic, legal, and institutional developments, robbery (and particularly robbery homicide) emerged as a marker or badge of status for a small segment of urban society, producing a new variant of plebeian violence, one that crossed into respectable Chicago. Second, as local holdup men targeted merchants, shopkeepers, and pedestrians, middle-class residents began to see the city, the streets, poor young men, strangers, and especially African-American Chicagoans in different ways.

For respectable city dwellers, robbery homicide was particularly alarming. In brawl homicides, middle-class Chicagoans were not victims. Proper, hardworking, solid citizens could be victims of domestic violence, but early twentieth-century residents typically viewed wife beating as improper but private behavior. Outsiders and innocents, therefore, typically remained safe. Mafia assassins were more intriguing than frightening, since their violence, replete with its colorful rituals, rarely left Little Sicily and seldom involved non-Italians. Automobile homicides were disturbing because good people could become innocent victims. But robbery homicides were far more terrifying, for respectable Chicagoans were targeted because they were respectable. Most robbery victims, however, though they were older and wealthier than their killers, occupied the lowest rungs of middle-class society. Guards and clerks, not merchants and industrialists, died in payroll robberies; and neighborhood shopkeepers, not prominent retailers, died in store holdups. Nonetheless, the threat to proper society seemed tangible, and the city gained a reputation for violence throughout the nation. The *Pittsburgh Dispatch*, for example, reported that robbery homicides were so frequent in Chicago "that any man who has to walk three blocks from a car line to his home hasn't even a chance of reaching his fireside."[81] And according to the *Literary Digest*, Chicagoans were too frightened to attend local theaters at night.

Murderous robbers took advantage of the order, regimen, and discipline of industrial society, using the efficiency of the marketplace to prey on it and transforming the cultural indicators of progress and prosperity into sources of vulnerability. These killers destroyed the comforting notion that respectable people, as a result of the behavior and lifestyle that made them respectable, were safe from violent crime. In short, discipline, order, and wealth no longer protected respectable Chicagoans. To the contrary, these qualities put them at risk, making them easy prey for men such as Earl Dear, who slaughtered respectable residents like "a butcher at the stockyard killing sheep."

Conclusion

etween 1903, when Lincoln Steffens pronounced the city "first
in violence," and 1920, Chicago's homicide rate continued to
climb. Despite the campaigns of moral crusaders, the successes of
Progressive reformers, the ongoing efforts of law enforcers, and the
expanding influence of middle-class values, lethal violence surged in
Chicago during the early twentieth century. In homicide, Chicago
stood far above comparable urban centers, though its homicide rate
remained below most southern cities and some smaller western cities.
Even if Lincoln Steffens overstated the case, Chicago was a very
violent city—and an increasingly violent one. By the early 1920s, its
homicide rate was nearly double that of New York City, Philadelphia, and San Francisco and more than triple that of Boston and
Hartford.[1]

According to Norbert Elias's "civilizing process" theory, Chicago's
homicide rate should have fallen during the late nineteenth and early
twentieth centuries. Core elements of Elias's theory of the civiliz-

ing process seem to fit the Chicago experience. Elite and middle-class reformers condemned impulsive, undisciplined behavior, defining such conduct as deviant and dangerous. Law enforcers, factory managers, schoolteachers, and other city dwellers conveyed overlapping messages as they cajoled, manipulated, and coerced Chicagoans into exercising self-control, remaining orderly, delaying gratification, working diligently, and sitting quietly—in school, at the factory, and during leisure-time activities. With the criminalization of reckless driving, local policy makers and law enforcers explicitly attacked impulsive behavior.

By some measures, these efforts succeeded. Early twentieth-century Chicagoans drank less, brawled less, drowned less, fell off roofs less, and stumbled into dangerous machinery less often than their late nineteenth-century counterparts.[2] They also became more cautious, learning to be careful around flammable materials, power lines, streetcars, and automobiles. Both reflecting and reinforcing these values, Chicagoans became increasingly intolerant of drunken brawling, wife beating, child abuse, infanticide, and reckless driving.

Yet contrary to Elias's theory, Chicago's homicide rate rose during the late nineteenth century and continued to increase during the early twentieth century. In 1875, the city's homicide rate was 2.25 per 100,000 residents, whereas the 1920 figure was 9.7 per 100,000, an increase of 331 percent (see Figure 14, page 274).[3] During this time the number of residents in the city swelled by a factor of seven, while the number of homicides committed by Chicagoans ballooned by a factor of twenty-nine.

Broad-based efforts to inculcate order did indeed influence violence in the city. Residents became more restrained but also more homicidal. Between 1875 and 1920 Chicagoans became more disciplined and more purposeful in their violent behavior—and, as a consequence, more deadly. Even while "civilizing missions" attacked expressions of plebeian hypermasculinity, poor young men continued

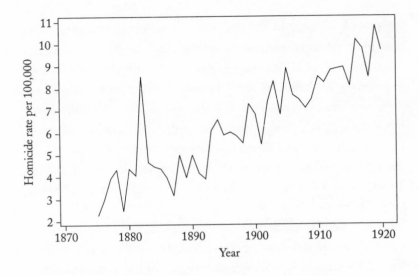

FIGURE 14 *Chicago homicide rate, 1875–1920 (source: see Appendix)*

to use violence to affirm their status. But robbery homicide supplanted drunken brawls, with the former requiring greater discipline and calculation. A similar process occurred within Chicago households. Husbands continued to slaughter their wives in explosions of rage, though such eruptions became relatively less common over time. Instead, Chicago men increasingly killed their spouses in acts of premeditated violence—and often accompanied the murder with suicide. The city's most violent groups experienced this change as well. Italian homicide, for example, left the neighborhood barrooms of Chicago's Little Sicilies and became more instrumental, as murder became a tool for extorting money or became an act so well planned that its causes were intentionally shrouded in dissembling rituals. African-American violence also moved away from the volatile world of the local saloon and became concentrated in premeditated domestic violence and in robbery homicide. In short, self-discipline and violence were not mutually exclusive in Chicago, and this fact may help to account for the tripling of the city's homicide rate over the course of the twentieth century.

Both the level of homicide and the form of homicide changed dramatically between 1875 and 1920. Moreover, the forces that influenced the rate of Chicago violence also altered its form, though this did not take place in a straightforward or linear fashion. A collision of social, cultural, demographic, and institutional pressures reshaped urban life in ways that redefined notions of status, power, and masculinity. Those caught in the shifting cultural ideals of manliness, for instance, often used violence to control others or to fend off their falling status. As the nature of identity and authority changed, cultural fault lines multiplied, and many Chicagoans believed that the emerging value systems undermined their social status. For example, an unusually large cohort of late nineteenth-century bachelors felt most secure in the social world of working-class saloons and plebeian rituals, both of which were withering by the 1890s. Fearing that their status as men was slipping away, they sometimes brawled to affirm their standing among peers. Likewise, changing material conditions and cultural ideals threatened the status of many Chicago husbands, particularly those who coveted a middle-class lifestyle but lacked the social standing or occupational stability to achieve it. When they failed to live up to their own or their wives' expectations, many of these men turned to violence in a desperate attempt to stave off implicit challenges to their masculinity, often murdering the women whose perceived independence mocked and threatened their patriarchal authority.

Far from eliminating conflict, the era's industrialization, urbanization, and cultural changes produced many new cultural fault lines for Chicagoans—circumstances in which residents felt themselves to be losing either status or control over their world. Pressures for conformity also increased over time, which at once discouraged impulsive behavior and increased frustration.[4] The police, the courts, local schools, and a host of other formal and informal forces celebrated middle-class values, domestic masculinity, and consumerism. Homicidal behavior was often a desperate reaction to perceived failure.

This blend of conflicting, overlapping, and dovetailing social and cultural forces reduced some forms of violence as it fueled other kinds of conflict. Demographic and cultural changes undermined the bachelor subculture of the late nineteenth century. As a result, saloon fights became less common, and drunken-brawl homicide plummeted. But the same process, with its veneration of middle-class domesticity and companionate marriage, exerted increasing pressure on working-class men to redefine themselves as husbands and breadwinners. Thus, the drop in brawl violence and the surge in domestic violence were related effects of the same process, as a cohort of Chicagoans left bachelorhood, became heads of households, and struggled to reestablish a sense of manliness.

With these broad shifts in the character of lethal violence, homicide began to assume its modern form. Violence left the industrializing, rough-hewn world of the nineteenth century and catapulted into the modern, industrial world of the twentieth century. Homicide largely moved out of bars, erupted less often between friends and acquaintances, and was no longer largely confined to men in their late twenties and early thirties. Instead, many of the characteristic features of late twentieth- and early twentieth-first-century violence emerged during the opening decades of the twentieth century. The level of gun use, for example, surged. During the late 1870s just over half of Chicago homicides were committed with firearms. By 1920, more than three-quarters of killers relied on guns. Similarly, homicide migrated from the roughest bars to the streets and homes of the city. Lethal violence also increasingly erupted between either strangers or loved ones. The sharp upturn in robbery homicide created a new sense of vulnerability, especially among "respectable" Chicagoans. The segmented, relatively closed world of nineteenth-century violence gave way to a more diffuse and unsettling social geography of risk and vulnerability, in which armed robbers prowled the streets in search of prey.

Early twentieth-century killers also began to differ from their victims. The former became younger and the latter older, particularly as baby bandits targeted strangers with cash and other valuables. Similarly, Chicagoans became increasingly concerned about African-American killers attacking older, white residents, planting fears that would fester and infuse public policy for the remainder of the twentieth century.

When homicide traveled from the "low dives" of the levee district and into the streets, violence became more predatory, more calculated, more disciplined, more instrumental, and more deadly. If Albert Burke, the volatile, knife-wielding Chicagoan who killed John Rathgeber in an 1897 barroom dispute over a drinking ritual, was the archetypal late nineteenth-century killer, Earl Dear, the young, gun-toting "beast of prey" who murdered Rudolph Wolfe while stealing an automobile in 1918, was more characteristic of twentieth-century killers.

To many Americans, Chicago was the city of progress, renowned for its phoenixlike rebirth after the Great Fire and its pioneering roles in architecture, literature, sociology, juvenile justice, and municipal reform. But Chicago was also the city of the Haymarket bombing of 1886, the Race Riot of 1919, Al Capone, and the St. Valentine's Day Massacre. Ironically, as Chicago became more modern and more orderly, its violence changed accordingly. With little of the bluster or swagger of their predecessors, twentieth-century killers proved to be far more deadly, and the metropolis that Steffens labeled the "'tough' among cities" became tougher and more violent in the new century.[5]

Appendix: Methodology

The quantitative evidence presented in this book, unless otherwise noted, was drawn from a data set of 5,645 homicide cases—every homicide reported to the Chicago police from 1875 through 1920. I constructed the data set, layer by layer, with overlapping and dovetailing source material. An extraordinary collection of ledger books, which were compiled by the Chicago Police Department between 1870 and 1920, formed the foundation of the data set. Titled "Homicides and Important Events," these records contained handwritten entries on every homicide reported to the police.[1] Individual entries, however, were brief, consisting of the name of the victim, the location of the crime, a few phrases or a sentence describing the homicide, and often a summary of the legal disposition of the case. Some killers were identified, and occasionally the entries provided the age and ethnic or racial backgrounds of those involved. Using with this source, I established a case file on every homicide. The ledger entries were erratic during the first few years, and thus I began the data set with the entries for 1875 and include every homicide through 1920.

The police records are remarkably complete. Because they were maintained by the lowest layer of the criminal justice system, the ledgers listed cases in which no arrest, indictment, or conviction was secured, and therefore the files provide a record of homicide that was not filtered by coroners, prosecutors, judges, or other gatekeepers in the legal system. Nor did the files hinge on the effectiveness of the police, since it was the discovery of a body, rather than an arrest or an indictment, that initiated each entry in the ledger books. Comparisons with aggregate data compiled by health department officials, coroners, and newspapers demonstrate that the police log is an extremely reliable source; between 1875 and 1920, for example, it included 5,645 cases, a figure within 3 percent of the total of annual tallies from health department reports.[2] The police files, in fact, recorded the greater number. Comparisons with various municipal investigations and other tallies and lists of victims yielded comparably close matches, as did "test borings" I made, using a capture-recapture technique for estimating missing data.[3]

When I compared my list of every case included in the police files to a list of every homicide reported in Chicago newspapers, however, discrepancies emerged.[4] Eager to beat their competitors and plagued by tight deadlines, local newspapers often rushed to press and to judgment, transforming nonlethal assaults into homicides and pronouncing Chicagoans dead before their time. The death and rebirth of John St. John in October 1890 illustrates the dangers of relying only on newspaper accounts—and helps to explain the divergence between police, coroner's, and health department records on the one hand and newspaper accounts on the other. At 1:00 AM on October 7, 1890, St. John, a thirty-three-year-old shoemaker, became embroiled in a barroom brawl with Marshall De Mars, a local saloonkeeper. In its October 7 edition, the *Chicago Tribune* reported that the saloon-keeper "shot and killed" St. John. The *Chicago Herald* concurred; its headline read "Murder in a Saloon Row." Slightly more cautious in its account, the *Chicago Times* reported that St. John "was shot twice in the head and mortally wounded" and "can not [sic] recover."[5] On the following day, both the *Herald* and the *Tribune* reported that the already-dead victim was "dying" and "his death is expected at any time."[6] Three days later—that is, four days after it announced his death—the *Chicago Tribune* wrote that St. John "now has a good chance of recovery"; and on October 13, six days after he had been declared dead by the newspaper, the *Tribune* reported that the shoemaker's condition "is growing more favorable daily for recovery." According to the doctor who treated him, "St. John lost a great deal of genuine brain substance in the operation, but he had some to spare and the loss did not materially affect his case."[7] Newspapers are valuable sources, but not by themselves. The police records, which are consistent with a host of other sources, provide a more reliable record of homicide cases.

For all of the strengths of the police files, however, they also possess shortcomings, such that they too should not be used in isolation from other sources. Although the ledgers included every reported homicide, the list of victims was more complete than were the descriptions of the events. Information about the crimes was often incorrect, and entries typically failed to provide data on the background of the killer and the victim, the age of the assailant, or the events that sparked the homicide. Some entries failed to identify the victim. Misspellings and confusion over names also resulted in many duplicate entries. In short, the police records provide a starting point, but for a more accurate portrait of homicide, other sources need to be consulted—and the information cross-checked.

Subsequent layers of the data set were the product of record linkage—the information culled from the police ledgers being supplemented, corroborated, and corrected with data from other sources. John St. John's miraculous recovery notwithstanding, newspapers provided a gold mine of information on Chicago homicides, even if their "facts" needed corroboration from other sources. I traced every case into at least five Chicago newspapers, which represented a broad spectrum of the daily press. The newspapers reported on approximately 80 percent of the homicides, and in most cases at least two newspapers provided an account of each incident. The 20 percent of homicides not found in the newspapers were largely automobile accidents, infanticides, abortion-related deaths, and other crimes that were not seen as newsworthy or appropriate for local readers.

I drew from the newspaper accounts in two ways. First, I used them to fill out and corroborate the quantitative information in the data set. Newspaper accounts often included the ages and occupations of killers and victims, as well as more detailed and complete explanations of the causes of lethal fights. Culling such information from all of the newspapers, I corrected and expanded the quantitative case files.

Second, I gathered qualitative evidence on the homicides, which added human flesh to the statistical bones. The newspaper accounts were typically detailed, gossip filled, and occasionally salacious, containing interviews with witnesses, killers, and policemen. Some reporters managed to interview dying victims or report deathbed utterances to police investigators, doctors, nurses, or family members. News stories often included excerpts from suicide notes and sometimes ran them in their entirety. Follow-up articles frequently included testimony from witnesses at trials and quotations from defendants, defense attorneys, prosecutors, and judges. I assembled this material into a second, qualitative, set of case files.

I consulted a broad range of other sources, which I also used to corroborate and complete the quantitative data on each homicide and to reconstruct the events leading to the violence. Particularly useful were court records, clemency applications, coroners' inquest files, and prison records. The customary range of primary sources about Chicago during this era provided additional detail about individual homicides and about the perceptions and actions of the residents of the city. Travel accounts, magazine articles, novels, political and moral tracts, muckraking exposés, and personal memoirs proved revealing and useful. Finally, the pioneering sociologists of the Chicago School produced valuable studies about the city during the early twentieth century.

The data set that emerged from this record-linkage process is extremely detailed, with twenty-six columns of data on every homicide.[8] Although the resulting files are very complete, it would naive to believe that the data set is flawless. No doubt some lethal violence fell through the institutional cracks, though it is unlikely that many deaths went unnoticed. Moreover, the data set suffers from some unevenness. It includes nearly complete information on the weapons used in the homicides, for example, but data on other variables, such as killers' and victims' places of birth, are more fragmentary. Even when sources provided information on the ethnic backgrounds of killers or victims, such data was difficult to interpret. Was a killer who was identified as "German," for example, born in Germany or the American-born child of immigrant parents? As a result of these problems, I was unable to explore some issues in as much detail as I would have liked. Two groups of Chicagoans, however—African Americans and Italians—were described in the sources with greater precision.[9]

My coding protocol was very cautious. To minimize errors, I checked every source and every entry against multiple sources. Still, quantitative evidence needs to be interpreted with caution and with a good dose of common sense, particularly when the data are disaggregated and the number of cases in particular statistical analyses is small.[10]

I analyzed the quantitative data using both standard descriptive statistics, especially two-, three-, and four-way correlations, and inferential statistics, such as regression analysis. To a considerable extent, the rationale of including every case and assembling a large data set is that it minimizes potential errors. In a data set with nearly six thousand cases, each containing more than two dozen pieces of information, it is unlikely that inaccurate or missing information on particular cases, or even a few homicides that went unreported, would distort the larger quantitative patterns.

The qualitative evidence, consisting of thousands of quotations and other pieces of descriptive information, also posed methodological challenges. Often the most colorful, tantalizing quotations came from atypical cases. To avoid mistaking the "barnacles for the boat," I used the quantitative and statistical evidence as a guide to the qualitative evidence.[11] First, I undertook the quantitative analysis; then I focused attention on the qualitative evidence that shed light on the trends identified with the statistical techniques. In short, the layering of sources, the cross-checking of evidence, and the meshing of quantitative and qualitative approaches undergirded my analysis.

Notes

Introduction

1. Lincoln Steffens, "Chicago: Half Free and Fighting On," *McClure's Magazine* 21 (October 1903): 563.

2. *Chicago Record-Herald,* July 31, 1906; Frederic M. Thrasher, *The Gang* (1927; abridged, with an introduction by James F. Short, Jr., Chicago, 1963), 311. For similar assessments, typically based on the number of homicides occurring in the city, see *Chicago Tribune,* November 6, 1913; Maynard Shipley, "Crimes of Violence in Chicago and in Greater New York," *Popular Science Monthly* 73 (August 1908): 127; "Murderous America," *Literary Digest* 47 (November 22, 1913): 994.

3. *Report of the General Superintendent of Police of the City of Chicago to the City Council for the Fiscal Year Ending December 31, 1912* (Chicago, 1913), 8.

4. See, for example, "Explaining Our Homicide Record," *Literary Digest* 45 (October 19, 1912): 656.

5. Robert A. Silverman and Leslie W. Kennedy, "Relational Distance and Homicide: The Role of the Stranger," *Journal of Criminal Law and Criminology* 78 (Summer 1987): 273.

6. Scholars associated with the "Chicago School" of urban sociology expressed this concern. For example, see Robert E. Park, "Human Migration and the Marginal Man," *American Journal of Sociology* 33 (May 1928): 881–893; William I. Thomas, with Robert A. Park and Herbert A. Miller, *Old World Traits Transplanted* (1921; reprint, with an introduction by Donald R. Young, Montclair, NJ, 1971), 10–11.

7. Norbert Elias, *The Civilizing Process: The History of Manners* (1939; reprint, New York, 1978); Elias, *The Civilizing Process: Power and Civility* (1939; reprint, New York, 1982).

8. Peter N. Stearns, *Battleground of Desire* (New York, 1999), 31–39.

9. See, for example, Eric A. Johnson and Eric H. Monkkonen, eds., *The Civilization of Crime* (Urbana, IL, 1996); Heikki Ylikangas, "What Happened to Violence?" in *Five Centuries of Violence,* ed. Heikki Ylikangas, Petri Karonen, and Martti Lehti (Columbus, OH, 2001), 1–83; Martin J. Wiener, *Men of Blood* (Cambridge, UK, 2004), 11–13.

10. See, for example, Roger Lane, *Violent Death in the City* (Cambridge, MA, 1979); Eric H. Monkkonen, *Murder in New York City* (Berkeley, CA, 2001), 152–157; Jeffrey S. Adler, "'My Mother-in-Law Is to Blame, But I'll Walk on Her Neck Yet': Homicide in Late Nineteenth-Century Chicago," *Journal of Social History* 31 (Winter 1997): 253–276; Adler, "'Halting the Slaughter of the Innocents': The Civilizing Process and the Surge in Violence in Turn-of-the-Century Chicago," *Social Science History* 25 (Spring 2001): 29–52.

11. These scholars have recognized both the limitations and the explanatory power of Elias's ideas. None would argue, however, that long-term rates of lethal violence have moved in a linear fashion. For a sample of scholarly assessments of the "civilizing process" model, see Jonathan Fletcher, *Violence and Civilization* (Cambridge, UK, 1997); Manuel Eisner, "Modernization, Self-Control and Lethal Violence," *British Journal of Criminology* 41 (Autumn 2001): 618–638; Robert van Krieken, "Violence, Self-Discipline, and Modernity: Beyond the Civilizing Process," *Sociological Review* 37 (May 1989): 193–218; Eric Dunning, "A Response to R. J. Robinson's 'The Civilizing Process': Some Remarks on Elias's Social History," *Sociology* 23 (May 1989): 299–307; George Mosse, review of *The Civilizing Process* by Norbert Elias, *New German Critique* 5 (Fall 1978): 178–183; Eric A. Johnson and Eric H. Monkkonen, "Introduction," in *The Civilization of Crime*, 1–13; Monkkonen, "The Power of 'Excuse Me,'" in Monkonnen, *Crime, Justice, History* (Columbus, OH, 2002), 203–206.

12. For New York, Boston, and Philadelphia, see Monkkonen, *Murder in New York City;* Theodore N. Ferdinand, "The Criminal Patterns of Boston since 1849," *American Journal of Sociology* 73 (July 1967): 84–99; Lane, *Violent Death in the City;* Ted Robert Gurr, "Historical Trends in Violent Crime: Europe and the United States," in *Violence in America,* ed. Ted Robert Gurr (Newbury Park, CA, 1989), 21–54.

13. Wesley G. Skogan, "Chicago since 1840" (typescript; Urbana, IL, 1976), 18–19, 90–91, 95–96.

14. Homer Hoyt, *One Hundred Years of Land Values in Chicago* (Chicago, 1933), 481–482.

15. For a sample of the enormous scholarly literature on these developments, see Mina Carson, *Settlement Folk* (Chicago, 1990); Maureen A. Flanagan, *Seeing with Their Hearts* (Princeton, NJ, 2002); Victoria Gettis, *The Juvenile Court and the Progressives* (Chicago, 2000); David S. Tanenhaus, *Juvenile Justice in the Making* (New York, 2004); Michael Willrich, *City of Courts* (New York, 2003).

1. "So You Refuse to Drink with Me, Do You?"

1. *Chicago Record,* June 11, 1897.

2. *Chicago Times-Herald,* June 11, 1897; *Chicago Tribune,* June 11, 1897.

3. *Chicago Record,* June 11, 1897.

4. *Chicago Times-Herald,* June 11, 1897.
5. Ibid.
6. Chicago Police Department, "Homicides and Important Events, 1870–1920," Illinois State Archives, Springfield.
7. *Chicago Record,* June 11, 1897.
8. *Chicago Tribune,* April 24, 1882; *Chicago Times,* April 24, 1882.
9. *Chicago Times,* April 24, 1882.
10. Ibid.; *Chicago Daily News,* April 24, 1882.
11. Lincoln Steffens, *Shame of the Cities* (1904; reprint, with an introduction by Louis Joughin, New York, 1957), 163; *Chicago Tribune,* June 14, 1896. The Steffens quotation originally appeared as "Chicago . . . the 'tough' among cities, a spectacle for the nations." See Steffens, "Chicago: Half Free and Fighting On," *McClure's Magazine* 21 (October 1903): 563. For Henson, see *Chicago Tribune,* June 14, 1896. L. O. Curon, *Chicago, Satan's Sanctum* (Chicago, 1899), 18. Rudyard Kipling, *American Notes* (1899; reprint, New York, 1974), 91. James Maitland, *Chicago Sensations; or, Leaves from the Note Book of a Chicago Reporter and Detective* (Chicago, 1886), 6. George Kibbe Turner, "The City of Chicago: A Study of the Great Immoralities," *McClure's Magazine* 28 (April 1907): 575. Upton Sinclair, *The Jungle* (1906; reprint, with an introduction by Jane Jacobs, New York, 2002), 20.
12. Kipling, *American Notes,* 102.
13. Eric L. Hirsch, *Urban Revolt* (Berkeley, CA, 1990), 1; Bruce C. Nelson, *Beyond the Martyrs* (New Brunswick, NJ, 1988), 26; Homer Hoyt, *One Hundred Years of Land Values in Chicago* (Chicago, 1933), 129; Wesley G. Skogan, "Chicago since 1840" (typescript; Urbana, IL, 1976), 24; Rick Halpern, *Down on the Killing Floor* (Urbana, IL, 1997), 16.
14. Louise Carroll Wade, *Chicago's Pride* (Urbana, IL, 1987), 200.
15. Frederic Cople Jaher, *The Urban Establishment* (Urbana, IL, 1982), 473.
16. Skogan, "Chicago since 1840," 90, 95.
17. Karen Sawislak, *Smoldering City* (Chicago, 1995); Herbert Asbury, *Gem of the Prairie* (1940; reprint, with an introduction by Perry R. Duis, DeKalb, IL, 1986), 82–85.
18. See Carl Smith, *Urban Disorder and the Shape of Belief* (Chicago, 1995), 106–111; Hirsch, *Urban Revolt,* 30; Richard Schneirov, "Chicago's Great Upheaval of 1877," *Chicago History* 9 (Spring 1980): 3–17. The city health department recorded seven deaths during the strike. See *Report of the Department of Health for the City of Chicago, for 1876 and 1877* (Chicago, 1878), 58.
19. Smith, *Urban Disorder,* 101–174.
20. Ibid., 2.
21. Steffens, "Chicago: Half Free," 563.
22. Sawislak, *Smoldering City,* 49–67.
23. Thomas Lee Philpott, *The Slum and the Ghetto* (New York, 1978), 44–45; Robert M. Fogelson, *America's Armories* (Cambridge, MA, 1989), 28.

24. Fogelson, *America's Armories*, 28; Philpott, *Slum and Ghetto*, 44.

25. Smith, *Urban Disorder*, 221.

26. Sawislak, *Smoldering City*, 220–227; Thomas R. Pegram, *Partisans and Progressives* (Urbana, IL, 1992), 21, 61.

27. The Sunday closing law was enacted in 1845 and had fallen into abeyance long before the 1870s. Sawislak, *Smoldering City*, 221–229; Perry R. Duis, *The Saloon* (Urbana, IL, 1983), 98, 178.

28. *Chicago Tribune*, April 17, 1886.

29. Skogan, "Chicago since 1840," 90.

30. Duis, *The Saloon*, 49, 231, 234.

31. See, for example, Jane Addams, *Twenty Years at Hull-House* (New York, 1910); Louise de Koven Bowen, *Growing Up with a City* (New York, 1926); Pegram, *Partisans and Progressives*, 61, 106; Victoria Gettis, *The Juvenile Court and the Progressives* (Chicago, 2000); Mina Carson, *Settlement Folk* (Chicago, 1990); Maureen A. Flanagan, *Seeing with Their Hearts* (Princeton, NJ, 2002).

32. See Anthony M. Platt, *The Child Savers* (Chicago, 1969); Gettis, *Juvenile Court and the Progressives;* David S. Tanenhaus, *Juvenile Justice in the Making* (New York, 2004).

33. For an insightful analysis of the impact of this process on violence, see Roger Lane, *Violent Death in the City* (Cambridge, MA, 1979).

34. Halpern, *Down on the Killing Floor*, 8, 19. James R. Barrett, *Work and Community in the Jungle* (Urbana, IL, 1987), 25. Sinclair, *The Jungle*, 40.

35. Pegram, *Partisans and Progressives*, 89.

36. These figures were calculated from health department data. See *Report of the Department of Health of the City of Chicago for the Years 1926 to 1930 Inclusive* (Chicago, 1931), 1138. Police files contain slightly lower figures, though the rate of growth is equally impressive and within the same range as the health department data.

37. For a discussion of local saloons, see William T. Stead, *If Christ Came to Chicago* (Chicago, 1894), 140.

38. *Chicago Tribune*, March 5, 1883. *Chicago Times*, October 27, 1875.

39. For a discussion of the role of the saloon in working-class life in Chicago, see E. C. Moore, "The Social Value of the Saloon," *American Journal of Sociology* 3 (July 1897): 1–12. For brief discussions of the free lunch offered by saloonkeepers, see Royal L. Melendy, "The Saloon in Chicago, Part II," *American Journal of Sociology* 6 (January 1901): 457; Stead, *If Christ Came to Chicago*, 139–140.

40. I define a drunken-brawl homicide as one in which the primary sources indicated that the combatants were drunk and that no other specific spark, such as a fight over money or a jealousy-inspired melee, generated the violence. Thus, drunken-brawl homicide overlapped with saloon homicide, but the two categories were not identical. Not every homicide occurring in

a saloon involved drunken men, and not every drunken brawl occurred in a saloon. For the use of the "general fight" phrase, see *Chicago Herald*, August 31, 1893; for the use of the "free fight" phrase, see Curon, *Chicago, Satan's Sanctum*, 57.

41. *Chicago Tribune*, January 2, 1893.

42. Ibid., October 28, 1875.

43. *Chicago Herald*, July 7, 1891.

44. *Chicago Tribune*, September 6, 1884.

45. Flynn v. Illinois, 78 N.E. 617 (Illinois 1906).

46. During this period, 57 percent of drunken-brawl homicides occurred in saloons. For an analysis of this issue in a modern context, see Kenneth Polk, *When Men Kill* (Cambridge, UK, 1994), 63–68.

47. Kenneth Polk finds a similar pattern in modern violent confrontations. Ibid., 64.

48. *Chicago Record*, August 31, 1893.

49. *Chicago Times*, January 23, 1889. For similar homicides, see *Chicago Tribune*, November 10, 1880, and August 31, 1906.

50. Perry R. Duis argues that saloons represented not so much public space as semipublic space. See Duis, *The Saloon*, 3–5.

51. To be more precise, 45.12 percent occurred between 9:00 PM and 1:00 AM, and 18.3 took place between 6:00 PM and 9:00 PM.

52. *Chicago Times*, July 19, 1880.

53. Among drunken-brawl assailants, the figure was 64.9 percent. Among all Chicago killers during this period, 51.4 percent were unskilled workers. Among Chicago killers other than drunken-brawl killers, 46.2 percent were unskilled between 1875 and 1890.

54. Data on the ethnic backgrounds of late nineteenth-century drunken brawlers are too fragmentary to permit reliable quantitative analysis. Between 1875 and 1890, surviving sources fail to identify the place of birth of 30.7 percent of drunken-brawl victims and 38.6 percent of drunken-brawl killers. Although Irish immigrants and native-born men formed the largest groups, many of the latter were the children of the former, furthering blurring the lines.

55. *Chicago Tribune*, January 23, 1878. *Chicago Daily News*, October 5, 1891. *Chicago Times*, September 21, 1890. Turner, "City of Chicago," 590.

56. *Chicago Tribune*, February 11, 1899.

57. *Chicago Times-Herald*, January 2, 1898.

58. Describing similar behavior in late nineteenth-century Ireland, Carolyn A. Conley terms such fights "recreational violence." See Conley, *Melancholy Accidents* (Lanham, MD, 1999), 17.

59. *Chicago Tribune*, April 30, 1878; *Chicago Times*, May 19, 1880. Turner, "City of Chicago," 591. For the "plague spots of rottenness" description, see *Chicago Tribune*, January 22, 1906. Turner, "City of Chicago," 580, 591.

60. See Polk, *When Men Kill*, 90.

61. By 1920 the sex ratio had changed significantly; the city had 97 men for every 100 women in their late twenties.

62. The 6 percent figure is for 1890, while the 33 percent figure covers the 1875–1890 period; during the late 1880s, 37.5 percent of drunken-brawl killers were in their late twenties.

63. In 1890, men in their late twenties comprised 6.1 percent of the city's population, a figure that would fall by 15 percent during the next three decades. For a broader discussion of sex ratios and violence, see David T. Courtwright, *Violent Land* (Cambridge, MA, 1996).

64. Howard P. Chudacoff, *The Age of the Bachelor* (Princeton, NJ, 1999), 48.

65. This comparison expands on the idea presented in Chudacoff's book, where he compares Chicago's bachelor population in 1890 with Louisville's total population. See ibid., 51. See also *The Thirteenth Census of the United States (1910), Vol. 1 (Population)* (Washington, DC, 1913), 643; *Report of the Population of the United States at the Eleventh Census: 1890, Part 1* (Washington, DC, 1895), clxii.

66. Specifically, 51 percent of Chicago men in their late twenties were single in 1890.

67. Chudacoff, *Age of the Bachelor*, 3–4. For a discussion of related themes set in an earlier era, see Patricia Cline Cohen, "Unregulated Youth: Masculinity and Murder in the 1830s City," *Radical History Review* 52 (Winter 1992): 33–52.

68. Frederick Howard Wines, *Report of the Defective, Dependent, and Delinquent Class of the Population of the United States, as Returned at the Tenth Census* (Washington, DC, 1888), 566. The figure for adult men is based on the male population over the age of fifteen. The figure for the entire population was one licensed saloon for every 160 residents.

69. Duis, *The Saloon*, 8. Also see Pegram, *Partisans and Progressives*, 89.

70. *Chicago Times-Herald*, September 1, 1895; Royal L. Melendy, "The Saloon in Chicago [Part I]," *American Journal of Sociology* 6 (November 1900): 289–306; Melendy, "Saloon in Chicago [Part II]," 433–464; *Chicago Inter Ocean*, December 29, 1904; Samuel Painter Wilson, *Chicago and Its Cesspools of Infamy* (Chicago, 1909), 142; Vice Commission of Chicago, *The Social Evil in Chicago* (Chicago, 1911), 108. For the regional figure, see Duis, *The Saloon*, 28.

71. Nelson, *Beyond the Martyrs*, 12; Barrett, *Work and Community in the Jungle*, 18–19; Wade, *Chicago's Pride*, 220.

72. Halpern, *Down on the Killing Floor*, 16–17; Nelson, *Beyond the Martyrs*, 18.

73. Barrett, *Work and Community in the Jungle*, 29, 41; Halpern, *Down on the Killing Floor*, 18.

74. *Special Reports: Occupations at the Twelfth Census* (Washington, DC, 1904), 518.

75. As many historians, such as Stephen J. Ross and Susan E. Hirsch, have demonstrated, the control exerted by skilled workers waned unevenly over the course of the century. See Ross, *Workers On the Edge* (New York, 1985); Hirsch, *Roots of the American Working Class* (Philadelphia, 1978). Butchers, however, maintained significant control over the production process until the closing decades of the nineteenth century.

76. See Alexander Keyssar, *Out of Work* (New York, 1986).

77. See Madelon Powers, *Faces along the Bar* (Chicago, 1998), 29–30. For discussions of honor and violence, see Elliott J. Gorn, "'Good-Bye Boys, I Die a True American,'" *Journal of American History* 74 (September 1987): 388–410; Bertram Wyatt-Brown, *Southern Honor* (New York, 1982); Thomas W. Gallant, "Honor, Masculinity, and Ritual Knife Fighting in Nineteenth-Century Greece," *American Historical Review* 105 (April 2000): 359–382; Pieter Spierenburg, "Masculinity, Violence, and Honor," in *Men and Violence*, ed. Pieter Spierenburg (Columbus, OH, 1998), 1–29; Chudacoff, *Age of the Bachelor*, 227–228.

78. Chudacoff, *Age of the Bachelor*, 244. For the construction of middle-class identity, see John F. Kasson, *Rudeness and Civility* (New York, 1990); Stuart M. Blumin, *The Emergence of the Middle Class* (New York, 1989); Peter N. Stearns, *Battleground of Desire* (New York, 1999). For the process through which such values were inverted, see Elliott J. Gorn, *The Manly Art* (Ithaca, NY, 1986); Marvin E. Wolfgang and Franco Ferracutti, *The Subculture of Violence* (London, 1967).

79. For a related discussion, see Michael Kaplan, "New York City Tavern Violence and the Creation of a Working-Class Male Identity," *Journal of the Early Republic* 15 (Winter 1995): 591–618.

80. See Chudacoff, *Age of the Bachelor*, 224–231; Gail Bederman, *Manliness and Civilization* (Chicago, 1995), 5–20; E. Anthony Rotundo, *American Manhood* (New York, 1993), 223–227, 244–246; Gorn, *Manly Art*, 185–196; Shani D'Cruze, "Unguarded Passions: Violence, History, and the Everyday," in *Everyday Violence in Britain, 1850–1950*, ed. Shani D'Cruze (Harlow, UK, 2000), 14–16; Conley, *Melancholy Accidents*, 18.

81. See Margo Wilson and Martin Daly, "Competitiveness, Risk Taking, and Violence: The Young Male Syndrome," *Ethology and Sociobiology* 6 (1985): 59–73; Courtwright, *Violent Land*, 9–21.

82. See Elijah Anderson, *Code of the Street* (New York, 1999), 66. For an analysis of this behavior based on the theories of evolutionary psychology, see Martin Daly and Margo Wilson, *Homicide* (New York, 1988), 128.

83. For a discussion of the psychological forces contributing to such behavior, see Hans Toch, *Violent Men* (Washington, DC, 1969), 135, 141–142. See also Anderson, *Code of the Street*, 73.

84. For discussions of this cycling process, see Wolfgang and Ferracutti, *Subculture of Violence*; Kenneth Levi, "Homicide as Conflict Resolution," *Deviant*

Behavior 1 (April–September 1980): 281–307; Anderson, *Code of the Street*, 73; David P. Barash and Judith Eve Lipton, *Making Sense of Sex* (Washington, DC, 1997), 89.

85. Sociologists and criminologists have sometimes argued that such behavior reflects a "subculture of violence." Discussions of this idea have been heated, in part because scholars have struggled to identify the sources or origins of the value system as well as its boundaries. My analysis suggests that the intersection of particular demographic, economic, social, and ecological forces during the nineteenth century forged the value system that venerated aggression and violence. For studies that explore this issue, see Wolfgang and Ferracutti, *Subculture of Violence*; Sandra J. Ball-Rokeach, "Values and Violence: A Test of the Subculture of Violence Thesis," *American Sociological Review* 38 (December 1973): 736–749; Robert Nash Parker, "Poverty, Subculture of Violence, and Type of Homicide," *Social Forces* 67 (June 1989): 983–1007.

86. For the phrase "without any provocation," see *Chicago Tribune*, November 5, 1886. For the phrase "slightest provocation," see *Chicago Record-Herald*, January 4, 1908 (quoting the police chief); *Chicago Record-Herald*, December 7, 1903 (quoting the coroner); *Chicago Broad Ax*, May 6, 1905; *Chicago Defender*, May 9, 1914. For the phrase "slender provocation," see *Chicago Times*, October 28, 1890. For the phrase "it would not be well to encounter in a fight," see *Chicago Tribune*, June 11, 1897.

87. For a related discussion, see Anderson, *Code of the Street*, 66.

88. Wolfgang observed that challenges appeared "trivial" to observers who did not understand the unspoken clues and norms of working-class society. See Marvin E. Wolfgang, *Patterns in Criminal Homicide* (New York, 1958), 189. Also see Polk, *When Men Kill*, 81, 89; Anderson, *Code of the Street*, 68. Describing the same kind of volatility among early twentieth-century Polish immigrants in Chicago, William I. Thomas and Florian Znaniecki concluded that "it is not the objective side of the act which is important but the meaning given to it by the man who answers by a murderous attempt." See Thomas and Znaniecki, *The Polish Peasant in Europe and America* (1927; reprint, New York, 1958), 2:1772.

89. For Peterson and Watson, see *Chicago Tribune*, October 19, 1883. For Whittemore and Fox, see *Chicago Times*, January 15, 1881. For Dillitsch and Mingel, see *Chicago Times*, June 19, 1887.

90. *Chicago Times*, July 27, 1879; *Chicago Inter Ocean*, April 21, 1902; *Chicago Tribune*, January 3, 1909, and August 30, 1887. In many instances, the taunts employed coded terms. The fatal fight between Christopher Malone and James Keegan, for example, began when Malone said "Kegan [*sic*], you're all mud." According to the *Chicago Tribune*'s crime-beat reporter, "you're all mud" was "a contemptuous expression in use by the men who board at Boone House." See *Chicago Tribune*, January 24, 1875. Similarly, Lieutenant

J. A. Manley shot Captain Albert Hedberg at Fort Sheridan after an argument in which the combatants used "names that in army circles are considered fairly good cause for a shooting." See *Chicago Tribune*, October 31, 1893.
91. *Chicago Daily News*, August 25, 1916. To the dismay of judges and prosecutors, killers typically insisted that they had acted in self-defense and thus should be exonerated or acquitted in legal proceedings, because their protagonists, after all, attacked a man's most cherished possession: his honor. See Instructions to the Jury, People v. Patrick Furling, February 1899 term, Criminal Court of Cook County, Cook County Circuit Court Archives, Chicago, Illinois.
92. For Anderson, see *Chicago Tribune*, September 19, 1880; *Chicago Times*, September 19, 1880; *Chicago Daily News*, September 18, 1880. For McCaffrey, see *Chicago Tribune*, July 14, 1880; for a similar chain of events leading to a homicide, see *Chicago Tribune*, January 25, 1880. For other examples regarding hats, see *Chicago Daily News*, January 26, 1880; *Chicago Daily News*, November 11, 1880; *Chicago Broad Ax*, May 6, 1905. Hats were particularly freighted with symbolic meaning in working-class bars. Many lethal brawls began with one man knocking another man's hat off his head. Moreover, open challenges in saloons frequently started with a man tossing his hat onto the floor and then announcing he could "whip" anyone in the place on the drop of his hat. For Shrosbree, see *Chicago Times-Herald*, April 26, 1898. For Ljiljak, see Illinois v. Popovich, 121 N.E. 729 (Illinois, 1918). For McMullen, see *Chicago Inter Ocean*, July 29, 1886; *Chicago Times*, July 29, 1886. Sullivan quoted in Chudacoff, *Age of the Bachelor*, 242. Carter H. Harrison, who would later serve as Chicago's mayor, recalled Sullivan fighting an exhibition in the city in 1881. The "Boston Strong Boy" offered "$50 to any pug able to withstand his berserker rushes through 4 rounds of boxing." Harrison, *Growing Up with Chicago* (Chicago, 1944), 59.
93. See Conley, *Melancholy Accidents*, 1, 3.
94. For a discussion of treating, see Powers, *Faces along the Bar*, 93–105. For Rathgeber and Burke, see *Chicago Tribune*, June 11, 1897. For examples of similar brawls, see *Chicago Daily News*, February 22, 1883; *Chicago Tribune*, July 16, 1888, December 25, 1893, and November 21, 1909. For an example of refusing to offer a treat, see *Chicago Daily News*, February 22, 1883.
95. For Blum, see *Chicago Tribune*, November 13, 1898. For examples of armed bartenders, see *Chicago Inter Ocean*, November 27, 1882; *Chicago Tribune*, October 25, 1890; *Chicago News Record*, January 2, 1893; *Chicago Times-Herald*, December 22, 1895; *Chicago Record*, March 2, 1898. For a related discussion, see Clare V. McKanna, Jr., "Alcohol, Handguns, and Homicide in the American West: A Tale of Three Counties, 1880–1920," *Western Historical Quarterly* 26 (Winter 1995): 471.
96. For Galena and Martin, see *Chicago Times*, October 27 and 29, 1875. For other cases in which jostles or competition over space initiated a cycle of

confrontation and violence, see *Chicago Tribune,* January 27, 1880, and March 5, 1883; *Chicago Daily News,* April 16, 1891; *Chicago Herald,* April 16, 1891. For Thielen and Sullivan, see *Chicago Inter Ocean,* June 29, 1900; *Chicago Tribune,* March 26, 1900. For similar cases, see *Chicago Tribune,* March 21, 1896; *Chicago Record,* July 16, 1900. In a related discussion, Elijah Anderson argues that men gain status by taking the possessions of others, thus claiming "trophies" that symbolize dominance. See Anderson, *Code of the Street,* 75. In late nineteenth-century Chicago, taking another man's particular place at the bar, favorite chair, or spot on the sidewalk was an act freighted with similar symbolic value. For an interesting discussion of this issue, see Courtwright, *Violent Land,* 42.

97. For handgun sales, see *Chicago Inter Ocean,* September 20, 1881; *Chicago Times,* August 11, 1882; *Chicago Tribune,* April 30, 1884; Clifton R. Wooldridge, *Twenty Years a Detective in the Wickedest City in the World* (Chicago, 1908), 509. Only workplace fights had a higher proportion of knives than did drunken brawls, probably reflecting the fact that virtually every job site had sharp tools. Fourteen percent of drunken brawlers killed with their fists, compared with 11 percent of all killers between 1875 and 1890. Similarly, 15 percent of drunken brawlers relied on blunt instruments, compared with 12 percent of all killers.

98. See Gallant, "Honor, Masculinity, and Ritual Knife Fighting," 375. For the Arado incident, see *Chicago Record,* February 1, 1894; *Chicago Tribune,* February 1, 1894; *Chicago Herald,* February 1, 1894.

99. See Richard B. Felson, *Violence and Gender Reexamined* (Washington, DC, 2002), 24, 73.

100. Raggio v. Illinois, 26 N.E. 377, 379 (Illinois, 1891). For Kinney and Waldron, see *Chicago Daily News,* November 9, 1880; *Chicago Tribune,* November 10, 1880; *Chicago Times,* November 10, 1880. For similar cases, see *Chicago Times-Herald,* March 12, 1896; *Chicago Tribune,* May 24, 1901. For Pflaum and Markey, see *Chicago Times-Herald,* March 12, 1896. On the role of the crowd generally, see Erving Goffman, *Interaction Ritual* (New York, 1967), 167; Polk, *When Men Kill,* 60; Powers, *Faces along the Bar,* 46–47.

101. Illinois v. Barrett, 103 N.E. 969 (Illinois, 1913). For another example of a fight in which a bystander was supposed to guarantee "fair play," see *Chicago Inter Ocean,* August 6, 1886.

102. *Chicago Times,* June 9, 1877; *Chicago Tribune,* June 9, 1877. Though the homicide unfolded under very different circumstances, James B. Duncan offered a similar interpretation after fatally shooting Thomas Lowerre in 1881. "When a big man tackles a small one," Duncan explained, "Providence will direct things so that the little fellow has an even chance." *Chicago Tribune,* September 1, 1881.

103. See, for example, *Chicago Times,* October 10, 1885. Sociologist Jack Katz has argued that some violent individuals derive a sense of euphoria, or thrill,

from their wild, brutal behavior. See Katz, *Seductions of Crime* (New York, 1988).

104. *Chicago Tribune,* September 25, 1896.

105. Ibid., October 13, 1918, and February 16, 1904. Sociologist Elijah Anderson terms such public settings "staging areas" where "campaigns for respect are most often waged." Anderson, *Code of the Street,* 77.

106. *Chicago Daily News,* January 26, 1880; *Chicago Tribune,* January 27, 1880; *Chicago Inter Ocean,* January 26, 1880.

107. For a related discussion, see Polk, *When Men Kill,* 63

108. Such violence was both expressive and instrumental. The killers intended to inflict pain on particular individuals, but they did so in order to achieve a larger goal. For discussions of these categories of violent behavior, see C. Gabrielle Salfati, "The Nature of Expressiveness and Instrumentality in Homicide," *Homicide Studies* 4 (August 2000): 268–288; Felson, *Gender and Violence Reconsidered,* 28.

109. *Chicago Daily News,* August 2, 1881.

110. For the concentration of saloons, see Duis, *The Saloon,* 28. During the early 1880s, drunken brawls accounted for 29 percent of Chicago homicides. By the early 1910s, the figure had dropped to 14 percent, and by 1920 7 percent of the city's homicides were from drunken brawls. In terms of the rate (as opposed to the proportion), brawl homicides also peaked in the early 1880s. For the late 1870s, the number of cases is modest, and thus the proportion fluctuates wildly, peaking at 67 percent for 1876. The three-year and five-year figures, therefore, are more reliable. Similar social and cultural forces were at work in other industrial centers of the era, though the rapid pace of growth in Chicago and the particular combination of pressures in the Illinois city probably produced an exaggerated level of plebeian violence.

111. The proportion of homicides occurring in saloons peaked for the 1875–1920 period during the early 1890s, closely followed by the late 1870s and the early 1880s.

112. Between the late 1870s and 1920, the spousal homicide rate nearly quadrupled and the robbery-homicide rate increased more than eightfold. The rate of killings by Chicago policemen rose more than sevenfold between the late 1870s and 1920.

113. The figures are crude homicide rates for the period from 1875 through 1895. If the rates are adjusted to eliminate socially constructed categories of homicide, such as infanticides and abortion-related deaths, the figures fluctuate between 3.1 and 5.6 per 100,000 residents. Age-standardized rates for the period are slightly higher, moving between 4.8 and 7.5 for the 1880–1900 period. (Thanks to Eric H. Monkkonen for help in calculating the age-standardized figures.) For other cities during this era, see Monkkonen, "Homicide in New York, Los Angeles, and Chicago," *Journal of Criminal Law and Criminology* 92 (Spring–Summer 2002): 820–822; Monkkonen,

Murder in New York City (Berkeley, CA, 2001), 21; Clare V. McKanna, Jr., *Homicide, Race, and Justice in the American West* (Tucson, AZ, 1997), 41; Lane, *Violent Death in the City,* 60. For data on Chicago's homicide rates during the twentieth century, see Lyle Benedict and Ellen O'Brien, "Deaths, Disturbances, Disasters, and Disorder in Chicago: A Selective Bibliography of Materials in the Municipal Reference Collection of the Chicago Public Library" (pamphlet; Chicago, 1996), 14.

114. In 1906 city officials established higher licensing fees, which drove many saloons out of business. See Duis, *The Saloon,* 259; Pegram, *Partisans and Progressives,* 105–113; Maureen A. Flanagan, *Charter Reform in Chicago* (Carbondale, IL, 1987), 33–34. For an example of neighborhood efforts to regulate saloons, see *Chicago Record-Herald,* December 9, 1903.

115. For 1880 figures, see Wines, *Report on the Defective, Dependent, and Delinquent Classes of the Population of the United States,* 566. In 1882 the ratio fell to one saloon for every 149 residents. See Perry Duis, "The Saloon in a Changing Chicago," in *A Wild Kind of Boldness,* ed. Rosemary K. Adams (Grand Rapids, MI, 1998), 316. For 1895, see Chudacoff, *Age of the Bachelor,* 108. The turn-of-the-century figure was one saloon for every 262 residents. See Robert Hunter, *Tenement Conditions in Chicago: Report by the Investigating Committee of the City Homes Association* (Chicago, 1901), 188. For 1910 figures, see Vice Commission of Chicago, *The Social Evil in Chicago* (Chicago, 1911), 108; Wilson, *Chicago and Its Cesspools of Infamy,* 142. A 1906 ordinance stipulated that no new licenses for saloons would be "granted or issued until the number of licenses in force at the time shall be less than one for every five hundred of the population." See Vice Commission of Chicago, *The Social Evil in Chicago,* 320.

116. See Duis, *The Saloon,* 234; Asbury, *Gem of the Prairie,* 158–160; Mark Haller, "Police Reform in Chicago, 1905–1935," *American Behavioral Scientist* 13 (May–August 1970): 653–654; Morton Keller, *Regulating a New Society* (Cambridge, MA, 1994), 110–125. By 1917, according to Duis, "the free lunch was widely viewed as an anachronism." Duis, *The Saloon,* 297.

117. Duis, *The Saloon,* 291–292.

118. Ibid., 151, 292–293. On nickelodeons and dance halls, see Perry R. Duis, *Challenging Chicago* (Urbana, IL, 1998), 230–232; Joanne J. Meyerowitz, *Women Adrift* (Chicago, 1988), 102. On spectator sports, see Duis, *Challenging Chicago,* 169–203; Chudacoff, *Age of the Bachelor,* 154; and Rotundo, *American Manhood,* 282–283. On amusement parks, see Duis, *Challenging Chicago,* 231; on cycling and automobiles, see ibid., 178–193. Although these activities were especially popular among wealthier residents, poorer Chicagoans also participated. The chauffeurs who ferried elite residents around the city, for example, were drawn from the working class. Over 80 percent of those who committed homicide with an automobile (as a result of fatal accidents) were semiskilled workers.

119. For a compelling explanation of this process, see Lane, *Violent Death in the City.*

120. The ratio of male residents to female residents fell by 57 percent (from 107 : 100 in 1890 to 103 : 100 in 1900), and the ratio of male residents over the age of fifteen to female residents over the age of fifteen dropped by 50 percent (from 110 : 100 in 1890 to 105 : 100 in 1900). During the first decade of the twentieth century, this trend reversed, though the new residents, drawn in huge numbers from southern and eastern Europe, introduced a different social and cultural dynamic. For these figures, see *Thirteenth Census of the United States (1910), Vol. 1 (Population),* 278, 643. For discussions of the relationship between demographic forces and violence, see Eric H. Monkkonen, "New York Homicide Offender Ages: How Variable? A Research Note," *Homicide Studies* 3 (August 1999): 256–271; Rosemary Gartner, "Age and Homicide in Different National Contexts," in *The Crime Conundrum,* ed. Lawrence M. Friedman and George Fisher (Boulder, CO, 1997), 61–74.

121. In 1890, 44 percent of men over the age of fifteen were single, compared with 41.9 percent in 1900 and 41.6 percent in 1910.

122. Figure 1 presents the drunken-brawl homicide rate in three-year periods. The 85 percent figure is based on a comparison of the individual year 1880 and the individual year 1920. Although Prohibition contributed to the decline at the end of the era, the rate had been falling sharply since the turn of the century.

123. The rate of accidental death for the 1875–1920 period peaked in 1893, while the rate of death from alcoholism for this era hit its high point in 1882. See *Report of the Department of Health . . . for the Years 1926 to 1930 Inclusive,* 1136, 1140.

124. See Thomas and Znaniecki, *Polish Peasant,* 2:1772.

125. These figures, gathered by Frederick L. Hoffman, cover the period 1902–1911. See *Chicago Tribune,* November 6, 1913; Maynard Shipley, "Crimes of Violence in Chicago and in Greater New York," *Popular Science Monthly* 73 (August 1908): 127; "Explaining Our Homicide Record," *Literary Digest* 45 (October 19, 1912): 656; "Murderous America," *Literary Digest* 47 (November 22, 1913): 994. Chicago led the nation's cities in the number—not the rate—of homicides and suffered from a homicide rate higher than that of other large urban centers.

2. "I Loved My Wife So I Killed Her"

1. *Chicago Evening Post,* December 15, 1913; *Chicago Inter Ocean,* December 15, 1913; *Chicago Tribune,* December 15, 1913.

2. Chicago Police Department, "Homicides and Important Events, 1870–1920," Illinois State Archives, Springfield. This figure is based on the total number of homicides for the year, including infanticides, abortion-related

deaths, automobile accidents, and other kinds of newly "discovered" (that is, newly enforced or newly criminalized) forms of homicide.

3. Specifically, spouses comprised 58 percent of domestic violence victims, and wives made up 79 percent of spousal homicide victims. Husbands killed 53 percent of the women who were homicide victims in Chicago between 1875 and 1920, while wives killed 3.6 percent of the men who were homicide victims in the city.

4. *Chicago Times,* July 1, 1878, March 30, 1888; *Chicago Tribune,* June 14, 1896.

5. Theodore Dreiser, *Newspaper Days* (1931; reprint, New York, 1974), 20. George W. Steevens, *The Land of the Dollar* (1897; reprint, Freeport, NY, 1971), 144. Lincoln Steffens described the curious blend of corruption and innovation in local government. See Steffens, "Chicago: Half Free and Fight On," *McClure's Magazine* 21 (October 1903): 563–577. For another discussion of corruption, see George Kibbe Turner, "The City of Chicago," *McClure's Magazine* 28 (April 1907): 575–592. The "most beautiful and the most squalid" description comes form Steevens, *Land of the Dollar,* 144.

6. Homer Hoyt, *One Hundred Years of Land Values in Chicago* (Chicago, 1933), 481.

7. Wesley G. Skogan, "Chicago since 1840" (typescript; Urbana, IL, 1976), 24.

8. For life expectancy data, which is based on average ages at death, see *Report of the Department of Health of the City of Chicago for the Years 1926 to 1930 Inclusive* (Chicago, 1931), 683. For a critique of the Health Department's figures on life expectancy, see "Death-Rate and Health," *The Nation* 90 (February 3, 1910): 107. In 1890 the average age at death was approximately twenty-two; by 1910 it exceeded thirty-four. A drop in infant mortality produced much of the increase in the age at death, though improvements in public health contributed significantly as well. For death-rate data, see Skogan, "Chicago since 1840," 31. According to data for 1925, Chicago had a death rate lower than Berlin, New York, Vienna, Philadelphia, and Paris. See H. L. Harris, Jr., "Negro Mortality Rates in Chicago," *Social Service Review* 1 (March 1927): 59.

9. The Teamsters' Strike of 1905, which blended labor conflict and racial tensions, produced some violence, but nothing comparable to the earlier riots.

10. The adjusted homicide rate rose from 3.12 per 100,000 residents during the late 1870s to 8.75 per 100,000 residents during the early 1910s. Between 1875 and 1915, the rate of arrest for disorderly conduct fell by 34 percent, even though law enforcers were increasingly intolerant of public drunkenness and disorder. For arrest figures, see the *Annual Report* of the Chicago police from 1875 to 1920 and Skogan, "Chicago since 1840," 90–91.

11. Maynard Shipley, "Crimes of Violence in Chicago and in Greater New York," *Popular Science Monthly* 73 (August 1908): 127; Turner, "City of Chicago," 591; "Race Suicide for Social Parasites," *Journal of the American Medical Association* 50 (January 4, 1908): 55.

12. Shipley, "Crimes of Violence in Chicago and in Greater New York," 127.

13. In theory, these categories could overlap, though my coding protocol treated violence between relatives, regardless of the role of alcohol, as domestic violence rather than drunken-brawl violence. The categories were socially constructed in different ways, typically reflecting very different forms of conflict and different notions of status and power. Spousal homicide, for instance, was not triggered by drinking rituals, contests over space, or the like.

14. For studies that examine the ways in which wife beating is linked to a defense of patriarchal authority, see Noel A. Cazenave and Margaret A. Zahn, "Women, Murder, and Male Domination," in *Intimate Violence*, ed. Emilio C. Viano (Bristol, PA, 1992), 83–97; Shani D'Cruze, "Unguarded Passions: Violence, History, and the Everyday," in *Everyday Violence in Britain, 1850–1950*, ed. Shani D'Cruze (Harlow, UK, 2000), 16; Jeffrey Fagan and Angela Browne, "Violence between Spouses," in *Understanding and Preventing Violence: Social Influences* (Washington, DC, 1994), 115–292; DeAnn K. Gauthier and William B. Bankston, "Gender Equality and the Sex Ratio of Intimate Killing," *Criminology* 35 (November 1997): 577–600. For studies that explore this theme in historical context, see Pamela Haag, "The 'Ill-Use of a Wife': Patterns of Working-Class Violence in Domestic and Public New York City, 1860–1880," *Journal of Social History* 25 (Spring 1992): 447–477; Linda Gordon, *Heroes of Their Own Lives* (New York, 1988); David Peterson del Mar, *What Trouble I Have Seen* (Cambridge, MA, 1996); Cynthia Grant Bowman and Ben Altman, "Wife Murder in Chicago: 1910–1930," *Journal of Criminal Law and Criminology* 92 (Spring–Summer 2002): 739–790; Reva B. Siegel, "'The Rule of Love': Wife Beating as Prerogative and Privacy," *Yale Law Journal* 105 (June 1996): 2117–2207.

15. For Walsh, see *Chicago Tribune*, February 20, 1883; for Nolan, *Chicago News Record*, August 29, 1892; for Pollner, *Chicago Times*, August 11, 1882; for Slaby, *Chicago Record-Herald*, November 7, 1912. Between 1875 and 1890, 44 percent of wife killers were described as being overcome with "rage."

16. The data on the ethnicity of wife killers are fragmentary and thus are more suggestive than definitive. Between 1875 and 1890, Irish immigrants comprised 12.5 percent of all wife killers but 21.4 percent of wife killers who acted in rage.

17. For Becker, see *Chicago Record*, March 15, 1899; for Gates, *Chicago Record-Herald*, September 29, 1906. Between 1875 and 1890, rage killers used their fists at five times the rate nonenraged killers did; 43 percent of rage wife killers used firearms compared with 61 percent of nonenraged wife killers.

18. For the shooter's quotation, see *Chicago Times*, July 2, 1878; for Page, *Chicago Tribune*, March 1, 1903; for Schultz, *Chicago Evening Post*, August 6, 1901. For the Koehler case, see *Chicago Evening Post*, August 6, 1901, and *Chicago Record-Herald*, October 29, 1901; Springer quote in *Chicago Tribune*, Octo-

ber 29, 1901. Koehler's attorney argued that Effie "went to bed intoxicated and sustained the fatal bruises by rolling and tossing upon the sharp points of two flatirons that had been left on the bed." After deliberating for thirty minutes, a jury acquitted Edward Koehler. See *Chicago Record Herald,* March 26, 1902; *Chicago Record Herald,* March 27, 1902. Buskin quotation in *Chicago Daily News,* December 1, 1917.

19. Jealousy triggered 49 percent of rage uxoricides.

20. For Zimmerman, see *Chicago Tribune,* August 24, 1880; for Ford, *Chicago Tribune,* May 12, 1889, and *Chicago Times,* May 12, 1889.

21. Evolutionary psychologists argue that jealousy often sparks this kind of violent outburst because a man fears "losing control of his wife's reproductive capacity." See Martin Daly and Margo Wilson, *Homicide* (New York, 1988), 197; Margo Wilson and Martin Daly, "An Evolutionary Psychological Perspective on Male Sexual Proprietariness and Violence against Wives," *Violence and Victims* 8 (Fall 1993): 271–294.

22. For a related analysis, see Thomas W. Gallant, "Turning the Horns: Cultural Metaphors, Material Conditions, and the Peasant Language of Resistance," in Gallant, *Experiencing Dominion* (Notre Dame, IN, 2002), 95–115.

23. *Chicago Tribune,* December 27, 1885. For similar homicides, see *Chicago Tribune,* August 11, 1882; *Chicago Tribune,* February 20, 1883; *Chicago Times-Herald,* May 29, 1895; *Chicago Record-Herald,* November 7, 1912.

24. For a thoughtful discussion of this issue, see Nancy Tomes, "'A Torrent of Abuse': Crimes of Violence between Working-Class Men and Women in London, 1840–1875," *Journal of Social History* 11 (Spring 1978): 334.

25. For the shooter, see *Chicago Daily News,* August 10, 1882; for Pflugradt, *Chicago Tribune,* December 21, 1903.

26. For the exchange between brother and sister, see *Chicago Tribune,* December 27, 1885; for Nolan, *Chicago News Record,* August 29, 1892, and *Chicago Tribune,* August 29, 1892; for Walsh, *Chicago Times,* February 20, 1883. These men believed that, as men and husbands, they possessed what Reva B. Siegel has called a "chastisement prerogative." See Siegal, "Rule of Love," 2151.

27. In 53 percent of rage uxoricides, police records and newspaper accounts revealed a history of domestic violence, compared with 31 percent of uxoricides not prompted by rage. This is a conservative figure, since investigators often did know about or did not feel inclined to mention previous episodes of wife beating.

28. In some instances, neighborhood women tried to intervene but arrived too late. See *Chicago Evening Post,* December 21, 1908; *Chicago Tribune,* January 30, 1909.

29. For Walsh, see *Chicago Tribune,* February 20, 1883; for the 1885 case, *Chicago Tribune,* December 27, 1885; for the Clancy quote, *Chicago Daily News,* July 5, 1881, and for the husband, *Chicago Times,* July 5, 1881. For Thomas, *Chicago*

Tribune, June 21, 1888, and *Chicago Times,* June 21, 1888. For Painter, *Chicago Daily News,* February 2, 1892, and *Chicago Herald,* May 19, 1891. For Merry, *Chicago Times-Herald,* November 24, 1897, and *Chicago Record,* November 24, 1897.

30. For Pollner, see *Chicago Daily News,* August 10, 1882; for Nitz, *Chicago Record,* October 8, 1896; for Schultz, *Chicago Record-Herald,* August 6, 1901; for Johnson, *Chicago Times,* September 6, 1889.

31. The average age of the men who focused their assaults on their wives' breasts was nearly forty-two.

32. *Report on the Population of the United States at the Eleventh Census: 1890, Part 1* (Washington, DC, 1895), 884.

33. In 1890, the uxoricide rate was .546 per 100,000 residents, while the drunken-brawl homicide rate was 1.455 per 100,000 residents.

34. For example, see *Chicago Tribune,* February 24, 1877.

35. For a discussion of a related theme, see Gordon, *Heroes of Their Own Lives,* 260.

36. *Chicago Daily News,* February 2, 1892; *Chicago Tribune,* December 27, 1885.

37. The stakes for violating this rule were high. One woman, for example, explained that "when my husband spoke to Culbertson [a wife beater who would later kill his wife] he pointed the revolvers at him and said he would kill him also [in addition to Culbertson's wife] if he interfered with his affairs." See *Chicago Times-Herald,* April 23, 1896.

38. According to social psychologist Richard B. Felson, "survey research shows that the presence of an audience inhibited violence in mixed-gender disputes but encouraged violence in conflicts between men." Felson, *Violence and Gender Reexamined* (Washington, DC, 2002), 73.

39. For a provocative discussion of this issue, see Daly and Wilson, *Homicide,* 215. Data on divorce in early twentieth-century Chicago indicate that marital tensions simmered before they exploded. On average, Chicago couples had been married for approximately seven years before separating and divorcing. See Ernest R. Mowrer, "The Trend and Ecology of Family Disintegration in Chicago," *American Sociological Review* 3 (June 1938): 345; Mowrer, *Family Disorganization* (Chicago, 1939), 304.

40. During the 1875–1890 period, 50.8 percent of family killers held unskilled positions, compared with 37.6 percent during the 1890–1910 period. For semiskilled killers, the proportion rose from 19.7 percent to 29 percent, while for skilled workers it rose from 18 percent during the 1875–1890 period to 21.8 percent during the 1890–1910 period.

41. Between 1890 and 1910, German immigrants comprised 12.5 percent of the city's population but committed less than 5 percent of the city's homicides. These Chicagoans, however, committed 13 percent of the city's uxoricides and 37 percent of local child murders.

42. Harmut Keil, "Chicago's German Working Class in 1900," in *German*

Workers in Industrial Chicago, 1850–1910, ed. Harmut Keil and John B. Jentz (DeKalb, IL, 1983), 21.

43. Ibid., 27.

44. Scholars from a wide range of disciplines have argued that homicide and suicide are the product of different, even opposite impulses. See Emile Durkheim, *Suicide,* trans. John A. Spaulding and George Simpson (1897; reprint, New York, 1951), 346; Andrew Henry and James Short, *Suicide and Homicide* (New York, 1954), 15; Martin Gold, "Suicide, Homicide, and the Socialization of Aggression," *American Journal of Sociology* 63 (May 1958): 652, 655; Raoul Naroll, "A Tentative Index of Cultural Stress," *International Journal of Social Psychiatry* 5 (1959): 107–116; Roger Lane, *Violent Death in the City* (Cambridge, MA, 1979), chap. 2. Also see Howard I. Kushner, *Suicide* (New Brunswick, NJ, 1989).

45. I combined suicides and attempted suicides into a single category in this analysis.

46. During the 1875–1890 period, 54.6 percent of German wife killers attempted suicide, and during the 1890–1910 period the figure rose to nearly 62 percent. See Jeffrey S. Adler, "'If We Can't Live in Peace, We Might As Well Die': Homicide-Suicide in Chicago, 1875–1910," *Journal of Urban History* 26 (November 1999): 8, 17. Germans, both in Germany and in the United States, had high suicide rates, but they had low homicide rates, making homicide-suicide a particularly intriguing phenomenon. For Germans and suicide, see Durkheim, *Suicide,* 50; Kushner, *American Suicide,* 88, 154–158; Lane, *Violent Death in the City,* 27. For German immigrants in Chicago, see "Crowner's Quest, 1876" in *Three Annual Reports of Emil Dietzsch* [Second Annual Report of the Cook County Coroner] (Chicago, 1878), 27; Ruth Shonle Cavan, *Suicide* (Chicago, 1928), 80.

47. This pattern reflects changes in the causes and in the nature of family violence—not simply the fact that more wife killers committed suicide in the latter period and thus were unable to defend their actions. In fact, many wife killers left detailed suicide notes providing an explanation of their motivations.

48. For important studies of this process, see Elaine Tyler May, *Great Expectations* (Chicago, 1980); Robert L. Griswold, *Family and Divorce in California, 1850–1890* (Albany, NY, 1982); Karen Lystra, *Searching the Heart* (New York, 1989); Norma Basch, *Framing American Divorce* (Berkeley, CA, 1999); Hendrik Hartog, *Man and Wife in America* (Cambridge, MA, 2000); A. James Hammerton, *Cruelty and Companionship: Conflict in Nineteenth-Century Married Life* (London, 1992).

49. For analyses of the crusades to inculcate emotional restraint, see Norbert Elias, *The Civilizing Process: The History of Manners* (1939; reprint, New York, 1978); Elias, *The Civilizing Process: Power and Civility* (1939; reprint, New York, 1982); Peter N. Stearns, *Battleground of Desire* (New York, 1999); John F. Kasson, *Rudeness and Civility* (New York, 1990); Manuel Eisner,

"Modernization, Self-Control, and Lethal Violence," *British Journal of Criminology* 41 (Autumn 2001): 619. For the criminalization of masculine behavior, see Martin J. Wiener, "The Victorian Criminalization of Men," in *Men and Violence*, ed. Pieter Spierenburg (Columbus, OH, 1998), 197–212.

50. *Report on the Population of United States at the Eleventh Census: 1890, Part 1*, 884. *Twelfth Census of the United States, Taken in the Year 1900, Population: Vol. 2* (Washington, DC, 1902), 314.

51. See Hammerton, *Cruelty and Companionship*, 81–82.

52. Rick Halpern, *Down on the Killing Floor* (Urbana, IL, 1997), 17–25.

53. Keil, "Chicago's German Working Class in 1900," 27.

54. *Chicago Tribune*, April 29, 1899; *Chicago Times-Herald*, April 29, 1899.

55. For Andrew, see *Chicago Tribune*, August 27, 1907; for Haugard, *Chicago Record*, January 14, 1896; for Lehman, *Chicago Times-Herald*, April 15, 1896, *Chicago Record*, April 15, 1896, and *Chicago Tribune*, April 15, 1896; for Wasserman, *Chicago Evening Post*, July 14, 1916.

56. *Chicago Inter Ocean*, May 26, 1902; *Chicago Tribune*, April 22, 1902.

57. See *Chicago Times*, August 11, 1882.

58. For the O'Shea case, see *Chicago Evening Post*, October 24, 1904; and *Chicago Tribune*, October 25 and 26, 1904.

59. *Chicago Tribune*, February 5, 1899; *Chicago Times-Herald*, February 5, 1899.

60. Specifically, 54 percent of the uxoricides between estranged couples occurred when a husband reacted to his wife's refusal to reconcile.

61. See Stearns, *Battleground of Desire*, 107; Hartog, *Man and Wife in America*, 101.

62. For a related discussion, see Hartog, *Man and Wife in America*, 224.

63. *Chicago Times-Herald*, September 4, 1899.

64. For analyses of similar conflicting expectations, see Gordon, *Heroes of Their Own Lives*, 260; Peterson del Mar, *What Trouble I Have Seen*, 120, 133–134.

65. For the McCarthy case, see testimony of W. P. Hooker, Coroner's Inquest on Addie McCarthy, May 12, 1896, Cook County Court Archives, Chicago, IL; for Lenz, see *Chicago Inter Ocean*, March 8, 1885. For Montag, see *Chicago Times*, June 10, 1890; and *Chicago Tribune*, June 10, 1890. For Lavelle, see *Chicago Tribune*, December 6, 1916; for Baker, *Chicago Evening Post*, March 19, 1912.

66. Sociologists, criminologists, and psychologists have found a similar pattern in modern wife killing. See Holly Johnson and Tina Hotton, "Losing Control: Homicide Risk in Estranged and Intact Intimate Relationships," *Homicide Studies* 7 (February 2003): 59–62, 70; Kenneth Polk, *When Men Kill* (Cambridge, UK, 1994), 28; Margo Wilson and Martin Daly, "Spousal Homicide Risk and Estrangement," *Violence and Victims* 8 (Spring 1993): 4, 7, 8; Carolyn Rebecca Block and Antigone Christakos, "Intimate Partner Homicide in Chicago over 29 Years," *Crime and Delinquency* 41 (October 1995): 506.

67. For the Lenz case, see *Chicago Inter Ocean*, March 8, 1885, and *Chicago*

Times, March 8, 1885; for Bickering, *Chicago Record-Herald,* May 5, 1908; for Montag, *Chicago Tribune,* June 10, 1890; for Arf, *Chicago Tribune,* October 8, 1908.

68. For "vampires of fiction," see *Chicago Tribune,* September 29, 1915; for "Tartar," *Chicago Record,* October 8, 1896. For Kurtz, see *Chicago Tribune,* March 25, 1894; for Buckley, *Chicago Daily News,* January 19, 1891. For the two unnamed would-be suicides, see *Chicago Daily News,* May 10, 1917, and *Chicago Tribune,* April 21, 1901. For Stepenski, see *Chicago Tribune,* April 3, 1901.

69. For Swager, see *Chicago Evening Post,* December 15, 1913; for the Italian immigrant, *Chicago Daily News,* May 10, 1917; for Bauer, *Chicago Daily News,* September 13, 1916.

70. Of the men who killed their children during these decades, 37 percent were German immigrants. For the 1875–1920 period, the figure is 23 percent.

71. For the German immigrant, see *Chicago Times-Herald,* May 25, 1895; for Johnson, *Chicago Tribune,* November 17, 1900; for Meutsch, *Chicago Tribune,* January 31, 1908; for Stech, *Chicago Tribune,* August 26, 1918; for Rose, *Chicago Inter Ocean,* December 12, 1912.

72. This figure excludes infanticides, which were overwhelmingly committed by mothers—or at least overwhelmingly attributed to mothers.

73. Of all these murdering husbands and fathers, 52 percent attempted or committed suicide.

74. For analyses of late twentieth-century homicide-suicide, see Mary Cooper and Derek Eaves, "Suicide Following Homicide in the Family," *Violence and Victims* 11 (Summer 1996): 99–112; Steven Stack, "Homicide Followed by Suicide: An Analysis of Chicago Data," *Criminology* 35 (August 1997): 435–453. Cooper and Eaves found that "most of those who committed suicide after the killing [of loved ones] felt they simply could not cope without their estranged partner or children." See Cooper and Eaves, "Suicide Following Homicide in the Family," 111.

75. For Nitz, see *Chicago Tribune,* October 8, 1896; for Gillen, *Chicago Tribune,* April 21, 1901, and *Chicago Inter Ocean,* April 21, 1901; for Hewitt, *Chicago Tribune,* January 1, 1920; for Artman, *Chicago Inter Ocean,* October 10, 1904.

76. For a discussion of this theme, see Polk, *When Men Kill,* 43–44.

77. For Eck, see *Chicago News Record,* March 7, 1893; for Keil, *Chicago Times-Herald,* July 18, 1895, and *Chicago Record,* July 18, 1895.

78. For McCarthy, see testimony of W. P. Hooker, May 12, 1896, Coroner's Inquest on Addie McCarthy; Daniel McCarthy's statement to the Chicago Police, May 17, 1896, Petition for Commutation of the Sentence of Daniel McCarthy, Commutation File of Andrew McCarthy, Executive Clemency Files, Illinois State Archives, Springfield. For Grush, see *Chicago Inter Ocean,* November 6, 1911; for Ference, *Chicago Daily News,* January 27, 1915.

79. Benedict J. Short to the Illinois Board of Pardons, October 2, 1908, Petition

for Commutation of the Sentence, Commutation File of Andrew Williams, Executive Clemeny Files, Illinois State Archives, Springfield; *Chicago Tribune,* November 23, 1911. In their analysis of modern uxoricide, Margo Wilson and Martin Daly observed that "declarations like 'If I can't have you, nobody can' are recurring features of such cases." See Wilson and Daly, "Spousal Homicide Risk and Estrangement," 3.

80. For Ehrke, see *Chicago Tribune,* June 20, 1883; for Messori, *Chicago Daily News,* May 10, 1917.

81. *Chicago Times-Herald,* February 5, 1899.

82. Between 1875 and 1890, 50 percent of uxoricides were triggered by such conflict, compared with 40.6 percent between 1890 and 1910.

83. For an analysis of the "abandonment" theme, see Neil S. Jacobson and John M. Gottman, quoted in Bowman and Altman, "Wife Murder in Chicago," 775. Also see Polk, *When Men Kill,* 45–47, 56–57; Hartog, *Man and Wife in America,* 101. For a discussion of spousal homicide as a mechanism of control, see Wilson and Daly, "Spousal Homicide Risk and Estrangement," 3.

84. From 1900 to 1920, 51 percent of wife killers were separated from their spouses.

85. Testimony of W. P. Hooker, May 12, 1896, Coroner's Inquest on Addie McCarthy.

86. It is impossible to measure this with precision. The surviving sources, however, suggest that the proportion of wife killers who had beaten their spouses decreased over time. In view of the increasing efforts by the legal system to protect abused women and to criminalize wife beating, it is likely that police and court records would have been more sensitive to the issue over time. In other words, all things being equal, biases and issues relating to the social and legal construction of domestic violence probably would produce an exaggerated trend of increasing spousal abuse. Although the sources on family violence are not without shortcomings, the sharp drop, therefore, is revealing and likely reflects changes in both attitude and behavior. Also see Peterson del Mar, *What Trouble I Have Seen,* 5–6, 70.

87. Also see ibid., 119, 133; Basch, *Framing American Divorce,* 119–20; Hartog, *Man and Wife in America,* 156; Gordon, *Heroes of Their Own Lives,* 276.

88. I compared the late 1880s with the early 1910s in order to include enough years in this calculation that brief fluctuations would not distort the figures or obscure the broader pattern. For local divorce rates, see Skogan, "Chicago since 1840," 30–31.

89. *Chicago Tribune,* March 20, 1913; Mowrer, *Family Disorganization,* 52. Also see Carroll D. Wright, *Marriage and Divorce in the United States, 1867–1886* (Washington, DC, 1897), 152; Bowman and Altman, "Wife Murder in Chicago," 753.

90. Mowrer, *Family Disorganization,* 58. See also Glenda Riley, *Divorce* (New

York, 1991), 90. For discussions of divorce and companionate marriage, see Mowrer, *Family Disorganization*, 160; Kermit L. Hall, *The Magic Mirror* (New York, 1989), 166; Michael Grossberg, *Governing the Hearth* (Chapel Hill, NC, 1985), 85; Basch, *Framing American Divorce*, 118–119; Robert L. Griswold, "Law, Sex, Cruelty, and Divorce in Victorian America, 1840–1900," *American Quarterly* 38 (Winter 1986): 726.

91. See Elizabeth Pleck, *Domestic Tyranny* (New York, 1987), 138–139; Pleck, "Feminist Responses to 'Crimes against Women,' 1868–1896," *Signs* 8 (Spring 1983): 465–468; Mary E. Odem, *Delinquent Daughters* (Chapel Hill, NC, 1995), 72–73. For an example of a case in which the victim sought such legal protection, see *Chicago Defender*, May 14, 1918. For a discussion of the impact of such legal options on martial harmony, see William I. Thomas and Florian Znaniecki, *The Polish Peasant in Europe and America* (1927; reprint, New York, 1958), 2:1750.

92. For the "domestic forum" quotation, see State of North Carolina v. Rhodes 61 N.C. 453, 455 (January 1868). For the "license to correct" quotation, see Wessels v. Wessels, 28 Ill. App. 253, 257 (Illinois, 1888).

93. Wessels v. Wessels, 28 Ill. App. 253, 257–258.

94. See Pleck, "Feminist Responses to 'Crimes against Women,'" 465–468; Pleck, "Criminal Approaches to Family Violence, 1640–1980," *Crime and Justice* 11 (1989): 43–44; Michael Willrich, *City of Courts* (New York, 2003), 128–171; Maureen A. Flanagan, *Seeing with Their Hearts* (Princeton, NJ, 2002), 34; Gwen Hoerr McNamee, "Social Justice and the Chicago Courts: The Work of the Protective Agency for Women and Children, 1886–1905" (paper presented at the annual meeting of the Social Science History Association, Pittsburgh, October 26, 2000).

95. See Pleck, "Feminist Responses to 'Crimes against Women,'" 468; Pleck, *Domestic Tyranny*, 138–139; Bowman and Altman, "Wife Murder in Chicago," 757–758; Siegel, "Rule of Love," 2142–70; Peterson del Mar, *What Trouble I Have Seen*, 47–71.

96. *Chicago Tribune*, October 2, 1906.

97. *Chicago Tribune*, February 5, 1899; *Chicago Times-Herald*, February 5, 1899.

98. For the psychological norms, see Carol Zisowitz Stearns and Peter N. Stearns, *Anger* (Chicago, 1986), 36–156; Stearns, *Battleground of Desire*, 55–186.

99. For Meyer, see *Chicago Tribune*, August 12, 1910; for McCarthy, *Chicago Times-Herald*, May 13, 1896. For examples of threats, see *Chicago Record*, October 8, 1896, December 3, 1897, and August 15, 1899. For examples of letters, see *Chicago Defender*, December 27, 1919, and *Chicago Evening Post*, November 15, 1920. For Tomachesski, see *Chicago Tribune*, October 10, 1911.

100. By comparison, 63 percent of nonstranged wife killers used guns.

101. For Nelson, see *Chicago Times-Herald*, August 18, 1896; and *Chicago Tribune*, August 18, 1896. For Regnet, see *Chicago Tribune*, September 8, 1904; see also *Chicago Times*, August 1, 1882; *Chicago Daily News*, April 16, 1883; *Chicago Times-Herald*, July 23, 1897; and *Chicago Tribune*, November 20, 1907,

and March 9, 1911. For Harworth, see *Chicago Evening Post,* July 14, 1903; *Chicago Tribune,* July 15, 1903; *Chicago Record-Herald,* November 18, 1903. For Compton, see *Chicago Times-Herald,* July 23, 1897. For the condition of the guns used, see *Chicago Tribune,* September 8, 1904.

102. For example, see *Chicago Times-Herald,* September 5, 1899; *Chicago Tribune,* July 30, 1906.

103. For Roessler, see *Chicago Record,* February 27, 1897; for Wagner, *Chicago Record-Herald,* March 1, 1902; for Johnson, *Chicago Inter Ocean,* November 18, 1900; for Stech, *Chicago Tribune,* August 26, 1918; for Jackson, *Chicago Defender,* May 4, 1918; for Summers, *Chicago Tribune,* April 23, 1909, and *Chicago Record-Herald,* April 23, 1909.

104. For example, see *Chicago Evening Post,* March 26, 1901; *Chicago Tribune,* April 21, 1901, March 21, 1917, and August 26, 1918.

105. *Chicago Daily News,* June 9, 1916.

106. Ibid., May 10, 1917.

107. For discussions of related issues, see Griswold, "Law, Sex, Cruelty, and Divorce," 731; Siegal, "Rule of Love," 2144.

108. For a related discussion, see May, *Great Expectations,* 156–163.

109. For an analysis of the ways in which economic and cultural pressures generated self-doubt and unrealistic expectations, see Stearns, *Battleground of Desire,* 107.

110. Early twentieth-century Chicago sociologists—members of the Chicago School—offered a different explanation for the pressures that were disrupting family life. According to Earle Edward Eubank, the anonymity of city life undermined primary-group attachments and thus eroded familial bonds. See Eubank, "A Study of Family Desertion" (Ph.D. diss., University of Chicago, 1916), 10–11.

111. Angus McLaren notes that much of the scholarship on the shifting ideals of marriage and gender relations is based on a reading of the prescriptive literature rather than an examination of actual behavior. "Did the new middle-class ideals filter down to the working class?" he asks. "And is one talking about real changes in behavior or only in cultural stereotypes?" The actions of turn-of-the-century Chicago wife killers may shed light on this issue. For McLaren's thoughtful discussion, see *Trials of Masculinity* (Chicago, 1997), 130.

112. David Peterson de Mar also describes an increasing acceptance of middle-class values, though he argues that wife beating fell during this era and that an "ethos of self-restraint" contributed significantly to the drop. See Peterson del Mar, *What Trouble I Have Seen,* 170.

113. *Chicago Evening Post,* December 15, 1913.

3. "He Got What He Deserved"

1. For Barney Nolan's "carousing," see *Chicago Inter Ocean,* April 12, 1905. Nolan was also rumored to have become "enamored" with another woman;

see *Chicago Record-Herald,* April 10, 1905. For other quotations and information about the case, see *Chicago Record-Herald,* April 10 and 11, 1905; *Chicago Inter Ocean,* April 9 and 12, 1905; *Chicago Tribune,* April 12, 1905.

2. Chicago Police Department, "Homicides and Important Events, 1870–1920," Illinois State Archives, Springfield. This figure is based on the total number of homicides for the year, including infanticides, abortion-related deaths, automobile accidents, and other kinds of newly "discovered" (that is, newly enforced or newly criminalized) forms of homicide.

3. For turn-of-the-century ideas about women criminals, see Samuel Paynter Wilson, *Chicago by Gaslight* (Chicago, 1910), 105–106; Caesar Lombroso and William Ferrero, *The Female Offender* (1895; reprint, New York, 1958); Frances A. Kellor, "Psychological and Environmental Study of Women Criminals," *American Journal of Sociology* 5 (January 1900): 527–543; L. Mara Dodge, *Whores and Thieves of the Worst Kind* (DeKalb, IL, 2002), 16, 47; Nicole Hahn Rafter, *Creating Born Criminals* (Urbana, IL, 1997), 36–41. Marcus Kavanagh, a local judge, contended that "no man can be so bad as a wicked woman. He hasn't the same genius for evil." Kavanagh, *The Criminal and His Allies* (Indianapolis, IN, 1928), 149.

4. Vice Commission of Chicago, *The Social Evil in Chicago* (Chicago, 1911), 41–42; Robert O. Harland, *The Vice Bondage of a Great City* (Chicago, 1912), 191; George Wharton James, *Chicago's Dark Places* (Chicago, 1891), 80–117; Wilson, *Chicago by Gaslight;* Walter C. Reckless, *Vice in Chicago* (Chicago, 1933), 32–68. Also see Joanne J. Meyerowitz, *Women Adrift* (Chicago, 1988).

5. *Fourteenth Census of the United States Taken in the Year 1920,* vol. 4 (Washington, DC, 1923), 1079–80; Dominic A. Pacyga, *Polish Immigrants and Industrial Chicago* (Columbus, OH, 1991), 54–55; James R. Barrett, *Work and Community in the Jungle* (Urbana, IL, 1987), 51–54.

6. Lisa M. Fine, *The Souls of the Skyscraper* (Philadelphia, 1990), 30; *Report on the Population of the United States at the Eleventh Census: 1890,* Part 2 (Washington, DC, 1897), 650; *Fourteenth Census of the United States Taken in the Year 1920,* vol. 4, 1079–80.

7. *Report on the Population of the United States at the Eleventh Census: 1890,* Part 2, 650; *Fourteenth Census of the United States Taken in the Year 1920,* vol. 4, 1079–80.

8. Fine, *The Souls of the Skyscraper,* 30.

9. Ibid., 77–103; Meyerowitz, *Women Adrift,* 33.

10. See Maureen A. Flanagan, *Seeing with Their Hearts* (Princeton, NJ, 2002); Sharon Z. Alter, "Louise de Koven Bowen," in *Women Building Chicago, 1790–1990,* ed. Rima Lunin Schultz and Adele Hast (Bloomington, IN, 2001), 101–106.

11. See Ellen Fitzpatrick, *Endless Crusade* (New York, 1990).

12. For an analysis of this theme, see Barbara Young Welke, *Recasting American Liberty* (New York, 2001).

13. Elizabeth Pleck, *Domestic Tyranny* (New York, 1987), 138–139; Pleck, "Feminist Responses to 'Crimes against Women,' 1868–1896," *Signs* 8 (Spring 1983): 465–468; Pleck, "Criminal Approaches to Family Violence, 1640–1980," in *Family Violence*, ed. Lloyd Ohlin and Michael Tonry (Chicago, 1989), 43–44; Reva B. Siegel, "'The Rule of Love': Wife Beating as Prerogative and Privacy," *Yale Law Journal* (June 1996): 2129–34; Victoria Gettis, *The Juvenile Court and the Progressives* (Chicago, 2000); Michael Willrich, *City of Courts* (New York, 2003).

14. Homicide rates in this paragraph are based on adjusted rather than crude figures; they do not include infanticides, abortion-related homicides, homicides involving automobiles, or other categories of homicide that were criminalized or newly enforced during this era.

15. *Chicago Defender*, August 7, 1920.

16. If infanticides and abortion-related homicides are included in the total, women committed 509 homicides. Excluding infanticides, abortion-related deaths, and the like, 78 percent of the 326 homicides by women occurred from 1900 to 1920.

17. During the 1875–1879 period, the rate for women was .136 per 100,000 residents. During the late 1910s, the rate for women was .754, and in 1920 it was .666. The spike in women's homicide in the specific year 1882 largely reflected the homicides committed by one woman, Mary Syebolt, who poisoned her four children.

18. During the late twentieth century, the proportion was nearly identical. See Robbin S. Ogle, Daniel Maier-Katkin, and Thomas J. Bernard, "A Theory of Homicidal Behavior among Women," *Criminology* 33 (May 1995): 173; Jeffrey Fagan and Angela Browne, "Violence between Spouses and Intimates," in *Understanding and Preventing Violence*, vol. 3, ed. Albert J. Reiss, Jr., and Jeffrey A. Roth (Washington, DC, 1994), 159.

19. *Chicago Tribune*, April 23, 1920. The legality of their marriage was in question, and thus local newspapers and police records referred to Dimick and Schweig using different surnames. Dimick believed that Schweig had not waited the requisite year between his divorce from his first wife and the new marriage, and therefore their marriage was not a legal union. For a similar case, see *Chicago Tribune*, May 9, 1920.

20. For example, see *Chicago Tribune*, May 31, 1907.

21. Only seventy infanticide cases appear in police records for the 1875–1920 period. See Chicago Police Department, "Homicides and Important Events, 1870–1920." L. Mara Dodge found that few women were incarcerated for this offense in Illinois. See Dodge, *Whores and Thieves*, 98.

22. The average age of fathers who murdered children was forty-one.

23. Evolutionary psychologists argue that infanticide is often a strategy employed to direct scarce resources to older, hardier children, thus increasing the likelihood that some offspring will survive until they are mature, inde-

pendent, and able to reproduce. For an interesting discussion of this interpretation, see Martin Daly and Margo Wilson, *Homicide* (New York, 1988),
61–80. Also see Margo Wilson, "'Take This Child': Why Women Abandon
Their Infants in Bangladesh," *Journal of Comparative Family Studies* 30 (Autumn 1999): 687–702.

24. *Chicago Tribune,* November 20, 1917.

25. Evolutionary psychologists speculate that stepchildren are often killed
    because they compete against birth children for resources. See Daly and
    Wilson, *Homicide,* 85–93; Margo I. Wilson and Martin Daly, "Who Kills
    Whom in Spouse Killings," *Criminology* 30 (May 1992): 198–199.

26. For Bertat, see *Chicago Tribune,* February 12, 1914; for Nicholl, *Chicago Daily
    News,* October 25, 1917.

27. For Engelberg, see *Chicago Tribune,* October 4, 1918; for Peterson, *Chicago
    Evening Post,* February 14, 1917; for Klem, *Chicago Tribune,* January 29, 1917;
    for Sitasz, *Chicago Evening Post,* August 9, 1918; for Fiala, *Chicago Tribune,*
    September 23, 1909.

28. For example, see *Chicago Tribune,* July 6, 1910; *Chicago Inter Ocean,* August
    29, 1911; *Chicago Record-Herald,* November 13, 1912; *Chicago Tribune,* January
    9, 1919.

29. For Conkling, see *Chicago Tribune,* June 27, 1900; for Engelberg, *Chicago
    Tribune,* October 4, 1918. For examples of fathers' responses to infanticide,
    see *Chicago Inter Ocean,* August 29, 1911; and *Chicago Tribune,* January 29,
    1917, and October 4, 1918.

30. In 72 percent of these cases, the women killed themselves. In the remaining
    12 percent the suicide attempt was unsuccessful. Except when the woman
    was German, the sources included little information about ethnicity (or re-
    ligion). Surviving records probably mentioned the ethnic backgrounds of
    German murdering mothers because these immigrants had unusually high
    rates of suicide. Every mother identified as German who killed her child
    committed or attempted suicide. For discussions of homicide-suicide among
    German immigrants, see Ruth Shonle Cavan, *Suicide* (Chicago, 1928), 34.

31. For Heubraum, see *Chicago Evening Post,* November 30, 1915 See also *Chi-
    cago Evening Post,* July 1, 1920. For Florin, see *Chicago Tribune,* October 20,
    1917; *Chicago Evening Post,* October 19, 1917.

32. *Chicago Tribune,* May 10, 1900.

33. For example, see *Chicago Tribune,* August 2, 1909.

34. For example, see *Chicago Record-Herald,* November 13, 1912.

35. *Chicago Tribune,* January 29, 1917.

36. For example, see *Chicago Tribune,* June 27, 1900; *Chicago Record-Herald,* No-
    vember 13, 1912; *Chicago Tribune,* August 23, 1915, November 30, 1915, and
    January 29, 1917.

37. Social scientists studying modern child killing have found similar patterns;
    mothers who kill non-newborn children often suffer from depression and

define their behavior as an expression of maternal love. See Daly and Wilson, *Homicide*, 78–79.

38. *Chicago Record-Herald*, April 19, 1913.

39. Daly and Wilson also find that murdering mothers opt not to include their husbands in their "rescue fantasies." See Daly and Wilson, *Homicide*, 216.

40. The location of the opened gas jets underscores the relative affluence of murdering mothers. Very poor Chicagoans seldom lived in settings with private bathrooms or with enough space to be undetected by their husbands.

41. For every child-killing woman who also murdered her husband, six child-killing men murdered their wives. Daly and Wilson, in their analysis of modern homicide, find similar patterns. See Daly and Wilson, *Homicide*, 82–83.

42. The modest number of such homicides, however, makes it difficult to analyze this trend with precision.

43. *Chicago Evening Post*, November 30, 1915.

44. See Christopher Lasch, *Haven in a Heartless World* (New York, 1977).

45. Such a pattern is consistent with the controversial theories of evolutionary psychologists, who suggest that a maternal instinct drives women to protect children until the offspring are old enough to live on their own and to reproduce. See Daly and Wilson, *Homicide*, 73–77.

46. Surviving sources fail to identify the place of birth of 70 percent of murdering mothers. Of the total (including those for whom the information was unknown), 15 percent were German. Without question, some of the 70 percent whose place of birth was not identified were also from Germany. Thus, the data set understates the concentration of Germans among murdering mothers. Even the 15 percent figure indicates a significant overrepresentation, since German immigrants comprised only 8 percent of Chicago's population in 1910 and 4 percent in 1920. Southern and eastern European immigrants probably committed filicide at low rates; Roman Catholic injunctions against suicide may account for this likely trend.

47. The rate rose by 286 percent from the early 1880s to 1920.

48. Data on the ethnic backgrounds of assailants and victims are fragmentary, though husband killers differed from wife killers in at least one way. German women rarely killed their husbands, though German men were overrepresented among wife killers; extant sources identify 1 percent of husband killers but 13 percent of wife killers as German immigrants.

49. Studies of the late twentieth century found a similar pattern of age clustering. See Coramae Richey Mann, "Female Murderers and Their Motives," in *Intimate Violence*, ed. Emilio C. Viano (Bristol, PA, 1992), 75; Elicka S. L. Peterson, "Murder as Self-Help," *Homicide Studies* 3 (February 1999): 37; Ann Goetting, "Homicidal Wives," *Journal of Family Issues* 8 (September 1987): 334. See also Franklin E. Zimring, Satyanshu K. Mukherjee, and

Barrik Van Winkle, "Intimate Violence: A Study of Intersexual Homicide in Chicago," *University of Chicago Law Review* 50 (Spring 1983): 918.

50. The age structure of the victims of spousal homicide reveals a parallel pattern: the victims of murdering wives were approximately five years older than the victims of murdering husbands.

51. This is consistent with data on early twentieth-century Chicago divorces, which indicate that separation and divorce, on average, occurred after approximately seven years of marriage. See Ernest R. Mowrer, "The Trend and Ecology of Family Disintegration in Chicago," *American Sociological Review* 3 (June 1938): 345; Mowrer, *Family Disorganization* (Chicago, 1939), 304.

52. Data on the causes of husband killings were drawn from police, court, and newspaper descriptions of the events leading to the violence. The women involved in these homicides usually provided clear, unequivocal explanations for their actions.

53. In social-scientific terms, these were "victim-precipitated homicides." Studies of late twentieth-century husband killers reported the same motive. See Marvin E. Wolfgang, *Patterns in Criminal Homicide* (Philadelphia, 1958), 76–77, 217; Wilson and Daly, "Who Kills Whom," 206; Richard B. Felson and Steven Messner, "Disentangling the Effects of Gender and Intimacy on Victim Precipitation in Homicide," *Criminology* 36 (May 1998): 407; Fagan and Browne, "Violence Between Spouses and Intimates," 163; Angela Browne, *When Battered Women Kill* (New York, 1987), 10; Goetting, "Homicidal Wives," 337.

54. For Camilla, see *Chicago News Record*, December 5, 1892; for Doyle, *Chicago Tribune*, July 3, 1899, and *Chicago Record*, July 3, 1899; for Frank, *Chicago Evening Post*, October 10, 1903; for McDonald, *Chicago Times*, September 22, 1889, and *Chicago Tribune*, September 28, 1889. For the 1912 example, see *Chicago Tribune*, September 9, 1912; for other examples, see *Chicago Evening Post*, July 23, 1903; *Chicago Inter Ocean*, October 4, 1903; *Chicago Tribune*, January 2, 1905; *Chicago Record-Herald*, March 18, 1905; *Chicago Tribune*, December 27, 1912.

55. For a discussion of this issue, see Felson and Messner, "Disentangling the Effects of Gender and Intimacy," 413.

56. For Doyle, see *Chicago Tribune*, July 3, 1899; for Olsen, *Chicago Tribune*, February 12, 1904. The specific threat to "boil me into potash" was a reference to a sensational Chicago murder case from 1897 in which a husband killed his wife, chopped her body into small pieces, and boiled away the remains. See Robert Loerzel, *Alchemy of Bones* (Urbana, IL, 2003). In 1899 Albert Becker also killed his wife, dismembered her, and boiled away the remains. For his confession, see *Chicago Tribune*, March 15, 1899; *Chicago Record*, March 15, 1899.

57. *Chicago Inter Ocean*, April 12, 1905.

58. For a discussion of this process, see William I. Thomas and Florian

Znaniecki, *The Polish Peasant in Europe and America* (1927; reprint, New York, 1958), 2: 1750.

59. *Chicago Inter Ocean,* July 20, 1911.

60. Approximately 35 percent of wife killers were separated or divorced, compared to 17.5 percent of husband killers.

61. For a discussion of the ways in which support networks appear to reduce domestic violence against women, see M. P. Baumgartner, "Violent Networks: The Origins and Management of Domestic Conflict," in *Aggression and Violence: Social Interactionist Perspectives,* ed. Richard B. Felson and James T. Tedeschi (Washington, DC, 1993), 227.

62. For a brief discussion of the obstacles confronting women who lived apart from their husbands, see Earle Edward Eubank, "A Study of Family Desertion" (Ph.D. diss., University of Chicago, 1916), 15.

63. *Chicago Evening Post,* April 10, 1905.

64. See Donald Black, "Crime as Social Control," *American Sociological Review* 48 (February 1983): 41; Baumgartner, "Violent Networks," 214; Peterson, "Murder as Self-Help," 33, 43. Zimring and his colleagues describe such violence as "female use of lethal counterforce." See Zimring, Mukherjee, and Van Winkle, "Intimate Violence," 923.

65. These trends, of course, relate only to spousal homicide. It is likely that separation and divorce reduced the risk for subsequent abuse, even if estranged husbands were especially violent. The evidence on spousal homicide indicates that husbands more often killed their separated or divorced wives but were more often killed by wives who eschewed separation or divorce. In both instances, the violence of husbands usually set in motion the sequence of events that ended in a homicide: wife killers murdered their spouses, while husband killers employed deadly force to fend off violent husbands.

66. For Wiley, see Testimony of James Holmes, October 25, 1899, Illinois v. Mary Jane Wiley, Archives of the Criminal Court of Cook County, Chicago, Ilinois; *Chicago Tribune,* August 15, 1899. For Hopkins, see *Chicago Tribune,* January 2, 1905. For Burnham, see *Chicago Inter Ocean,* June 11, 1912; *Chicago Tribune,* September 22, 1889; *Chicago Record-Herald,* November 27, 1907. For Smith, see *Chicago Inter Ocean,* October 4, 1903. The Smith homicide was unusual in that Kate Snowden had recently divorced her husband and remarried. Henry Smith, an ex-policeman, threatened to kill his ex-wife, told friends he planned to shoot her, and was carrying a revolver when Kate Snowden killed him. For Barnes, see *Chicago Evening Post,* September 6, 1916; *Chicago Tribune,* September 7, 1916.

67. In her study of women who killed their abusers in the late twentieth century, Angela Browne also found a high rate of gun use: 80 percent. See Browne, *When Battered Women Kill,* 140.

68. Murdering husbands committed homicide using gas at the same rate as murdering wives.

69. For McDonald, see *Chicago Tribune*, September 28, 1889; for Wiley, *Chicago Tribune*, August 15, 1899.

70. Many men, even city dwellers, had grown up hunting and continued to hunt. Men also became acquainted with firearms during military service. Most important, guns abounded in the working-class saloons where bachelors (and some husbands) spent their leisure hours. Shooting galleries were also popular in Chicago during this period and appealed mainly to men. In short, women had access to firearms, but men had far more experience with guns in early twentieth-century America.

71. Fifty-one percent of husband killers shot their victims in the head.

72. For Wiley, see *Chicago Tribune*, August 15, 1899. For other examples of wives firing multiple times, see *Chicago Tribune*, September 7, 1916; *Chicago Defender*, May 18, 1918. For Mitchell, see *Chicago Tribune*, November 25, 1920. For a related study of late twentieth-century homicide, see Carolyn Rebecca Block and Antigone Christakos, "Intimate Partner Homicide in Chicago over Twenty-Nine Years," *Crime and Delinquency* 41 (October 1995): 516.

73. Block and Christakos, in their analysis of late twentieth-century partner homicide, found a similar pattern. See ibid., 512.

74. For Wiley, see *Chicago Tribune*, August 15, 1899; for Burnham, *Chicago Tribune*, December 28, 1912; for Doyle, *Chicago Tribune*, July 3, 1899; for Wall, *Chicago Tribune*, February 9, 1918; for Simpson, *Chicago Tribune*, April 26, 1919.

75. One early twentieth-century Chicago sociologist argued that women who had worked outside of the home tended to be especially independent, which generated "household friction." In his study of family desertion in the city, Earle Edward Eubank contended that "there is no doubt that the entrance of women into wage-earning occupations before marriage tends to make them unfit for married life when they eventually assume its duties; and this in itself may contribute to domestic unhappiness." Eubank, "Study of Family Desertion," 13.

76. For Barker, see *Chicago Evening Post*, July 23, 1903; for Benson, *Chicago Tribune*, November 21, 1914. For the "morally justifiable" quotation, see *Chicago Record*, July 3, 1899. For Snowden, see *Chicago Inter Ocean*, October 4, 1903.

77. See *Chicago Tribune*, April 26, 1919.

78. Three states—New Mexico, Texas, and Utah—codified the unwritten law. Texas's penal code allowed such a justification for homicide until 1973. See Paul Kens, "Don't Mess Around in Texas: Adultery and Justifiable Homicide in the Lone Star State," in *Law in the Western United States*, ed. Gordon Morris Bakken (Norman, OK, 2000), 114. Rana Lehr-Lehnardt, "Treat Your Women Well: Comparisons and Lessons from an Imperfect Example across the Waters," *Southern Illinois Law Journal* 26 (Spring 2002): 402, 427; Henry P. Lundsgaarde, *Murder in Space City* (New York, 1977), 161–166.

79. "Article 567 of the Penal Code," the Texas Court of Appeals explained in an 1885 case, "reads as follows: 'Homicide is justifiable when committed by the husband upon the person of any one taken in the act of adultery with the wife, provided the killing take place before the parties to the act of adultery have separated.'" See Anthony Price v. State of Texas 18 Tex. Ct. App. 474 (Texas, 1885). Also see Louisiana v. Dennison 10 So. 599 (Louisiana, 1892); Rupert B. Vance and Waller Wynne, Jr., "Folk Rationalizations in the 'Unwritten Law,'" *American Journal of Sociology* 39 (January 1934): 483–492; H. C. Brearley, *Homicide in the United States* (1932; reprint, Montclair, NJ, 1969), 51. For modern analyses of the history of the unwritten law in the United States, see Robert M. Ireland, "The Libertine Must Die: Sexual Dishonor and the Unwritten Law in the Nineteenth-Century United States," *Journal of Social History* 23 (Fall 1989): 27–44; Hendrik Hartog, "Lawyering, Husbands' Rights, and the 'Unwritten Law' in Nineteenth-Century America," *Journal of American History* 84 (June 1997): 67–96; Hartog, *Man and Wife in America* (Cambridge, MA, 2000), 219–237; Rosemary Gartner and Jim Phillips, "The Creffield-Mitchell Case, Seattle, 1906: The Unwritten Law in the Pacific Northwest," *Pacific Northwest Quarterly* 94 (Spring 2003): 69–82.

80. Judge McSurely, in fact, sentenced the defendant to prison. His comments were offered to explain why he did not impose the death penalty. See *Chicago Record-Herald*, November 28, 1908. Most of the men who invoked the unwritten law in early twentieth-century Chicago, however, were acquitted. For a few newspaper accounts of trials in which this defense proved successful, see *Chicago Tribune*, August 16, 1913, and June 30, 1917; *Chicago Daily News*, July 18, 1917. For reactions to such honor killings, see *Chicago Record-Herald*, June 9, 1909; *Chicago Inter Ocean*, May 18, 1911; *Chicago Tribune*, August 16, 1913.

81. See Robert M. Ireland, "Frenzied and Fallen Females: Women and Sexual Dishonor in the Nineteenth-Century United States," *Journal of Women's History* 3 (Winter 1992): 95–117.

82. *Chicago Tribune*, February 16, 1918; *Chicago Daily News*, February 16, 1918; *Chicago Evening Post*, February 16, 1918; *Chicago Tribune*, February 17, 1918, and June 28, 1918. A local judge speculated that jurors acquitted Plotka because they "had committed adultery with her in their hearts." See Kavanagh, *Criminal and His Allies*, 155. Also see Raymond B. Fosdick, *American Police Systems* (New York, 1920), 45.

83. *Chicago Inter Ocean*, July 22, 1912.

84. See *Chicago Inter Ocean*, July 22, 1912; *Chicago Tribune*, April 26, 1919; Frederick L. Hoffman, *The Homicide Problem* (Newark, NJ, 1925), 38.

85. For Hopkins, see *Chicago Record-Herald*, March 21, 1905; and *Chicago Tribune*, January 2, 1905.

86. Vance and Wynne, "Folk Rationalizations in the 'Unwritten Law,'" 483–484, 492.

87. Siegel, "Rule of Love," 2151.
88. For a related discussion of the old unwritten law, see Martha Merrill Umphrey, "The Dialogics of Legal Meaning," *Law and Society Review* 33 (1999): 407.
89. For Kersten, see *Chicago Inter Ocean*, March 21, 1905; for Chytraus, *Chicago Record-Herald*, March 21, 1905; for Barnes, *Chicago Record-Herald*, March 21, 1905.
90. For Prindiville, see *Chicago Tribune*, January 16, 1919; for Bell, *Chicago Tribune*, November 3, 1917; for Hoyne, *Chicago Evening Post*, March 16, 1914.
91. For Fleming, see *Chicago Tribune*, December 28, 1912; for Newcomer, *Chicago Inter Ocean*, January 10, 1906. For a discussion of similar modern concerns, see Laurie J. Taylor, "Comment: Provoked Reason in Men and Women," *UCLA Law Review* 33 (August 1986): 1705.
92. For Hoyne, see *Chicago Tribune*, January 17, 1919; for Prindiville, *Chicago Tribune*, January 16, 1919.
93. Of these one hundred three husband killers, nine committed suicide. For a discussion of African-American women and domestic homicide, see Chapter 4.
94. Because nine husband killers committed suicide and thus were not tried, prosecutors dealt with seventy-two cases where white women killed their husbands. Seven of the seventy-two white husband killers were convicted (9.7 percent). Josephine Schmitt, who shot her husband on November 11, 1900, after he taunted her, was convicted and sentenced by Judge Gibbons, but Judge Dunne remitted the sentence and released her.
95. During this period, two husband killers escaped arrest (and thus were never charged or tried) and a third committed suicide.
96. After 1910, as more and more murdering wives invoked the new-unwritten-law defense, the conviction rate for white husband killers dropped to 5.4 percent—compared with 14.3 percent from the period 1875–1910.
97. According to Illinois case law, such homicides should not have been treated as justifiable, since self-defense required "that the slayer endeavored to decline any further struggle before the mortal blow was given." See Illinois v. Forte et al., 110 N.E. 47, 49 (Illinois, 1915).
98. *Chicago Tribune*, September 22, 1913. For similar sentiments, see *Chicago Inter Ocean*, July 22, 1912; *Chicago Evening Post*, March 16, 1914; *Chicago Tribune*, January 23, 1915, September 20, 1916, July 9, 1919, and September 26, 1919.
99. For the prosecutor's statements, see *Chicago Inter Ocean*, January 10, 1906; and *Chicago Tribune*, August 10, 1905. Troupe served eight years in Joliet Penitentiary. See Joliet Convict Registers, Illinois State Archives, Springfield. Some sources identify the defendant as "Virginia," some as "Regina," and others as "Mrs. Troupe." One Chicago journalist argued that many husband killers merely hid behind the veil of the unwritten law. A reporter

for the *Chicago Inter Ocean* suggested that many of these women killed for "gain," particularly for insurance policies and "property rights." See *Chicago Inter Ocean*, July 22, 1912.

100. For the Exlund case, see *Chicago Tribune*, January 17 and 15, 1919. Though sentenced to fourteen years in Joliet Penitentiary, Exlund served five years. See Joliet Convict Registers.

101. *Chicago Inter Ocean*, March 21, 1905. Also see Dodge, *Whores and Thieves*, 61.

102. For interesting discussions of related themes, see Carolyn Strange, "Wounded Womanhood and Dead Men: Chivalry and the Trials of Clara Ford and Carrie Davies," in *Gender Conflicts: New Essays in Women's History*, ed. Franca Iacovetta and Mariana Valverde (Toronto, 1992), 151, 178; Martin J. Wiener, *Men of Blood* (Cambridge, UK, 2004), 130.

103. For the "protective wing" quotation, see *Chicago Inter Ocean*, July 22, 1912. For Darrow, see *Chicago Tribune*, September 26, 1919. For the "dainty hands" quotation, see *Chicago Inter Ocean*, July 22, 1912. For Johnston, see *Chicago Tribune*, August 22, 1920; for Kavanagh and Hoyne, *Chicago Evening Post*, March 16, 1914. Police reformer Raymond B. Fosdick, describing a Chicago trial, attributed the jurors' sympathies to "false sentiment." See Fosdick, *American Police Systems*, 45. For the "public bosom" quotation, see *Chicago Tribune*, July 9, 1919; for Exlund, *Chicago Evening Post*, January 17, 1919.

104. If all homicide cases are included in the calculation (even fatal automobile accidents, abortion-related deaths, and other kinds of homicides that were enforced erratically), the figure climbs from 22 percent to 23 percent.

105. If cases in which the killer committed suicide are excluded, the proportion of women convicted of homicide rises from 16 to 20 percent. These figures, however, exclude infanticides, abortion-related homicides, and related categories of homicide in which law enforcement strategies changed significantly over time. The proportion of white women who were convicted rises from 8 percent to 11 percent if suicides are excluded from the total.

106. *Chicago Evening Post*, November 21, 1914; Annie Hinrichsen, "The Criminal Statistics of Illinois," *Institution Quarterly* 8 (June 1917): 94. Raymond B. Fosdick reached the same conclusion. See Fosdick, *American Police Systems*, 44.

107. See *Chicago Evening Post*, March 14, 1914; *Chicago Tribune*, September 26, 1919. Also see Dodge, *Whores and Thieves*, 102, 109.

108. For Illinois case law on self-defense, see Enright v. Illinois, 39 N.E. 561, 562 (Illinois, 1895); Healy et al. v. Illinois, 45 N.E. 230, 234 (Illinois, 1896); Steiner v. Illinois, 58 N.E. 383, 384 (Illinois, 1900); Foglia et al. v. Illinois, 82 N.E. 262, 264 (Illinois, 1907); Illinois v. Williams, 88 N.E. 1053, 1056 (Illinois, 1909); Illinois v. Forte et al., 110 N.E. 47, 49 (Illinois, 1915); Illinois v. Stapleton, 133 N.E. 224, 226 (Illinois, 1921).

109. *Chicago Tribune*, July 11, 1882.

110. For a discussion of this issue, see Pamela Haag, "The 'Ill-Use of a Wife':

Patterns of Working-Class Violence in Domestic and Public New York City, 1860–1880," *Journal of Social History* 25 (Spring 1992): 447–477. In her book on domestic violence in Boston, historian Linda Gordon argues that particularly after the 1930s women demanded a "right" or "entitlement" to protection from abusive husbands. The surge in husband killing and the new justification for husband killing in early twentieth-century Chicago suggest that the process may have begun earlier for women in the Illinois metropolis. See Gordon, *Heroes of Their Own Lives* (New York, 1988), 258–259; David Peterson del Mar, *What Trouble I Have Seen* (Cambridge, MA, 1996), 132.

111. Siegel, "The Rule of Love," 2151.

112. For a related argument that emphasizes the blending of older and emerging notions of gender roles, see Gwen Hoerr McNamee, "Social Justice and the Chicago Courts: The Work of the Protective Agency for Women and Children, 1886–1905" (paper presented at the annual meeting of the Social Science History Association, Pittsburgh, Pennsylvania, October 26, 2000).

113. According to State's Attorney Maclay Hoyne, "Experience in the Criminal Court building teaches us that while the honest woman, or the average woman, is less prone to commit crime than men, that when a woman does become a criminal, she sinks lower and goes further in brutality and cruelty than the other sex." See *Chicago Evening Post*, March 16, 1914. Local law enforcers investigating a 1912 murder relied on similar views: "That the crime was planned by a woman and executed by a man or men is the belief of the detectives working on the case. The fiendishness with which the crime was committed, the police declare, could only have been planned by a woman." See *Chicago Inter Ocean*, December 22, 1912.

114. Legal scholar William Ian Miller argues that "violence is gendered male" and thus "violent females are considered more deviant than violent males." Miller, *Humiliation* (Ithaca, NY, 1993), 73.

4. "If Ever That Black Dog Crosses the Threshold of My House, I Will Kill Him"

1. John W. Hardy, quoted in Affidavit of Thomas Pearson, October 7, 1909, Petition for commutation of the sentence to imprisonment for life of Andrew Williams, Executive Clemency Files, Illinois State Archives, Springfield.

2. Andrew Williams to G. D. Kenny, Illinois State Board of Pardons, October 4, 1909, Petition for commutation of the sentence to imprisonment for life of Andrew Williams.

3. C. H. Soelke to the State Board of Pardons, September 29, 1909, Petition for commutation of the sentence to imprisonment for life of Andrew Williams.

4. Chicago Police Department, "Homicides and Important Events, 1870–

1920," Illinois State Archives, Springfield. This figure is based on the total number of homicides for the year, including infanticides, abortion-related deaths, automobile accidents, and other kinds of newly "discovered" (that is, newly enforced or newly criminalized) forms of homicide. Williams was one of sixty-nine murderers executed by the State of Illinois between 1875 and 1920, 28 percent of whom were African American.

5. *Chicago Tribune*, September 21, 1906.
6. *Chicago Record-Herald*, February 22, 1906; *Chicago Evening Post*, February 22, 1906; *Chicago Record-Herald*, July 31, 1906; *Chicago Tribune*, September 21, 1906; Maynard Shipley, "Crimes of Violence in Chicago and in Greater New York," *Popular Science Monthly* 73 (August 1908): 129.
7. *Chicago Record-Herald*, January 6, 1908.
8. *Chicago Defender*, August 22, 1914.
9. Upton Sinclair, *The Jungle* (1906; reprint, with an introduction by Jane Jacobs, New York, 2002), 302.
10. Needless to say, the phrase "white Chicagoans" includes a diverse, internally divided pool of people who rarely saw themselves as a part of a single, cohesive group. But in the context of discussions of, or reactions to, African Americans, Chicagoans of European extraction, including both recent immigrants and old-stock native-born Americans, often felt a powerful bond of racial solidarity. Thus, in this particular context, "white Chicagoan" is a meaningful category and an important basis of identity. The homicide of Joseph Schoff revealed this binary framework. On July 30, 1919, during the bloody race riot of that year, Schoff attacked Jose Blanco, a Mexican immigrant whom Schoff believed was African American. In the fight that ensued, Blanco fatally stabbed Schoff. The police report on the homicide recorded that Schoff "mistook Blanco for a negro and attacked him." See Chicago Police Department, "Homicides and Important Events." Similarly, the coroner's inquest report noted that the "deceased mistaking the said Jose Blanco, a Mexican, for a negro . . ." Schoff, in other words, could conceive of only two racial categories. See Cook County Coroner, *Race Riots: Biennial Report [of the Cook County Coroner], 1918–1919 and Official Record of Inquests on the Victims of the Race Riots of July and August 1919* (Chicago, 1920), 31–32. For a detailed analysis of this issue in early twentieth-century Chicago, see Thomas A. Guglielmo, *White on Arrival* (New York, 2003), 26–30. Guglielmo draws a distinction between "color" and "race," and as a result he discusses, for example, the "Color Riot of 1919" (39–43). For related analyses, see David R. Roediger, *The Wages of Whiteness* (London, 1991); Noel Ignatiev, *How the Irish Became White* (New York, 1995); Matthew Frye Jacobson, *Whiteness of a Different Color* (Cambridge, MA, 1998).
11. George Kibbe Turner, "The City of Chicago: A Study of the Great Immoralities," *McClure's Magazine* 28 (April 1907): 580. *Chicago Defender*, August 22, 1914. Chicago Commission on Race Relations, *The Negro in Chicago: A*

Study of Race Relations and a Race Riot (Chicago, 1922), 631, 346. Such carefully constructed images served to underscore the superiority and "civilized" nature of whites. See Gail Bederman, "'Civilization,' the Decline of Middle-Class Manliness, and Ida B. Wells's Antilynching Campaign (1892–94)," *Radical History Review* 52 (Winter 1992): 13.

12. St. Clair Drake and Horace R. Cayton, *Black Metropolis* (New York, 1945), 184. Also see Thomas Lee Philpott, *The Slum and the Ghetto* (New York, 1978), 185.

13. Capone placed the property in his mother's name, and during the late 1920s Theresa Capone signed the covenant when the neighborhood association organized to protect the area "against undesirables." See Philpott, *Slum and Ghetto,* 199.

14. Chicago Commission on Race Relations, *The Negro in Chicago,* 192–194; William M. Tuttle, Jr., *Race Riot* (New York, 1975), 173–176; Allan H. Spear, *Black Chicago* (Chicago, 1960), 210–222.

15. Drake and Cayton, *Black Metropolis,* 178. See also Chicago Commission on Race Relations, *The Negro in Chicago,* 122–133; Carl Sandburg, *The Chicago Race Riots* (New York, 1919), 14–15; Tuttle, *Race Riot,* 159; James R. Grossman, *Land of Hope* (Chicago, 1989), 178. For an important analysis of firebombings and related activities during the mid-twentieth century, see Arnold R. Hirsch, *Making the Second Ghetto* (New York, 1983).

16. Spear, *Black Chicago,* 211.

17. Chicago Commission on Race Relations, *The Negro in Chicago,* 328. Also see Vice Commission of Chicago, *The Social Evil in Chicago: A Study of Existing Conditions* (Chicago, 1911), 38; Louise Venable Kennedy, *The Negro Peasant Turns Cityward: Effects of Recent Migrations to Northern Centers* (New York, 1930), 182; Walter C. Reckless, *Vice in Chicago* (Chicago, 1933), 29.

18. Charles Merriam, a political scientist and reformer, recognized this elision. See Charles Edward Merriam, *Chicago: A More Intimate View of Urban Politics* (New York, 1929), 146.

19. Kennedy, *The Negro Peasant Turns Cityward,* 182; Chicago Commission on Race Relations, *The Negro in Chicago,* 328.

20. For a few examples, see *Chicago Herald,* February 20, 1893; *Chicago Tribune,* May 31, 1902; *Chicago Evening Post,* May 31, 1902; *Chicago Tribune,* August 17, 1908. Also see Chicago Commission on Race Relations, *The Negro in Chicago,* 524.

21. E. Franklin Frazier, *The Negro Family in Chicago* (Chicago, 1932), 166.

22. Marcus Kavanagh, *The Criminal and His Allies* (Indianapolis, IN, 1928), 142.

23. Ida B. Wells, *Crusade for Justice: The Autobiography of Ida B. Wells,* ed. Alfreda M. Duster (Chicago, 1970), 284. Wells encountered the same view—and the same figure—a few years later. Ibid., 300.

24. *Chicago Tribune,* May 24, 1905.

25. Chicago Commission on Race Relations, *The Negro in Chicago*, 524.
26. *Chicago Broad Ax*, March 14, 1908.
27. Ophelia Williams, quoting Andrew Williams, in Benedict J. Short [assistant state's attorney] to the Illinois State Board of Pardons, October 2, 1908, Petition for commutation of the sentence to imprisonment for life of Andrew Williams.
28. Many scholars have argued that African-American migrants to the North carried with them a southern "subculture of violence." That is, they contend that southern traditions of honor, power, and dispute resolution, transmitted across space and time to the industrial North, generated high levels of interpersonal violence among African Americans during the course of the twentieth century. For discussions of this argument, see Sandra J. Ball-Rokeach, "Values and Violence: A Test of the Subculture of Violence Thesis," *American Sociological Review* 38 (December 1973): 736–749; Howard S. Erlanger, "The Empirical Status of the Subculture of Violence Thesis," *Social Problems* 22 (December 1974): 280–292; Steven F. Messner, "Regional and Racial Effects on the Urban Homicide Rate: The Subculture of Violence Revisited," *American Journal of Sociology* 88 (March 1983): 997–1007; Raymond D. Gastil, "Homicide and a Regional Culture of Violence," *American Sociological Review* 36 (June 1971): 412–427. For a discussion of some of the ideological implications of this theory, see Richard B. Felson, "Blame Analysis: Accounting for the Behavior of Protected Groups," *American Sociologist* 22 (Spring 1991): 5–23. Among historians of urban violence, Clare V. McKanna, Jr., has particularly relied on the subculture-of-violence theory to explain African-American violence. See McKanna, "Seeds of Destruction: Homicide, Race, and Justice in Omaha, 1880–1920," *Journal of American Ethnic History* 14 (Fall 1994): 65–90; McKanna, *Homicide, Race, and Justice in the American West, 1880–1920* (Tucson, 1996), 45–77. The nature of African-American homicide in Chicago, however, suggests that these residents responded to social and economic problems and pressures in their homes and their neighborhoods rather than to deeply ingrained, Southern folkways. See Jeffrey S. Adler, "'The Negro Would Be More Than an Angel to Withstand Such Treatment': African-American Homicide in Chicago, 1875–1910," in *Lethal Imagination: Violence and Brutality in American History*, ed. Michael A. Bellesiles (New York, 1999), 295–314; Roger Lane, *Roots of Violence in Black Philadelphia, 1860–1900* (Cambridge, MA., 1986). For a different perspective, see Kimberle Crenshaw's discussion of "structural intersectionality" in Crenshaw, "Mapping the Margins: Intersectionality, Identity Politics, and Violence against Women of Color," *Stanford Law Review* 43 (July 1991): 1241–99.
29. Chicago Commission on Race Relations, *The Negro in Chicago*, 440, 442.
30. For data on homicide in early twentieth-century cities, see "Explaining Our Homicide Record," *Literary Digest* 45 (October 19, 1912): 656.

31. These are offender rates; in 1881, 1891, and 1895 the African-American rate was more than fifteen times the white rate.

32. *Chicago Tribune,* November 6, 1913; "Explaining Our Homicide Record," *Literary Digest,* 656.

33. Spear, *Black Chicago,* 6–7; Charles Branham, "Black Chicago: Accommodationist Politics before the Great Migration," in *The Ethnic Frontier,* ed. Melvin G. Holli and Peter d'A. Jones (Grand Rapids, MI, 1977), 219; Douglas S. Massey and Nancy A. Denton, *American Apartheid* (Cambridge, MA, 1993), 20–21. After 1870, African-American residents could vote in Illinois, and state law banned segregation in schools in 1874 and discrimination in public accommodations in 1884. See Philpott, *Slum and Ghetto,* 117.

34. Scholars of lynching have long debated the theory that racial violence increased as the African-American population in a particular area rose— the so-called power-threat hypothesis. See Hubert Blalock, *Toward a Theory of Minority-Group Relations* (New York, 1967), 157–159; John Shelton Reed, "Percent Black and Lynching," *Social Forces* 50 (March 1972): 356–360; Stewart E. Tolnay, E. M. Beck, and James L. Massey, "Black Lynchings: The Power Threat Hypothesis Revisited," *Social Forces* 67 (March 1989): 605–640. A related theory suggests that discrimination also varied with population levels. See Stanley Lieberson, *A Piece of the Pie* (Berkeley, CA, 1980), 61.

35. Branham, "Black Chicago," 215.

36. By contrast, for the years 1875–1890, 46 percent of white killers were in their twenties, and the average white killer was nearly thirty-one years old. For homicides committed by whites, 25 percent were the result of drunken brawls; and 26 percent of white homicides occurred between acquaintances.

37. For Williams, see *Chicago Times,* October 7, 1884; for Alexander, *Chicago Times,* January 23, 1884.

38. *Chicago Times,* February 24, 1877.

39. Giles Hunt, for example, "was frequently known to avoid a quarrel by refusing to resent an insult." See *Chicago Times,* October 7, 1884.

40. *Chicago Times,* August 2, 1881.

41. *Chicago Herald,* September 29, 1891; *Chicago Daily News,* September 28, 1891; *Chicago Tribune,* September 29, 1891.

42. *Report of the Population of the United States at the Eleventh Census: 1890, Part 1* (Washington, DC, 1895), 884.

43. Vice Commission of Chicago, *The Social Evil in Chicago,* 38–39; Reckless, *Vice in Chicago,* 25, 29; Sophonisba P. Breckinridge, "The Color Line in the Housing Problem," *Survey* 9 (February 1, 1913): 575; Drake and Cayton, *Black Metropolis,* 47, 55; Kevin J. Mumford, *Interzones* (New York, 1997), 38.

44. For example, see *Chicago Times,* September 3, 1876.

45. For a superb discussion of this transformation, see Grossman, *Land of Hope.*

46. Ibid., 13–97.

47. Kennedy, *The Negro Peasant Turns Cityward,* 34.

48. Otis Dudley Duncan and Beverly Duncan, *The Negro Population of Chicago* (Chicago, 1957), 34, 39.

49. Duncan and Duncan, *The Negro Population of Chicago*, 35.

50. Grossman, *Land of Hope*, 150; *Fourteenth Census of the United States: Population, vol. 2* (Washington, DC, 1923), 291.

51. Newspaper headline quoted in Chicago Commission on Race Relations, *The Negro in Chicago*, 530. Also see Philpott, *Slum and Ghetto*, 159; Grossman, *Land of Hope*, 168.

52. Chicago Commission on Race Relations, *The Negro in Chicago*, 331.

53. In 1908, journalist Ray Stannard Baker observed that "the more Negroes the sharper the expression of prejudice." See Baker, *Following the Color Line* (1908; reprint, New York, 1964), 111.

54. These figures are drawn from Duncan and Duncan, *The Negro Population of Chicago*, 93. In *Black Chicago*, Allan H. Spear offers lower figures. He indicates that in 1920 Chicago had 10 census tracts that were over three-quarters African American and 135 with no African-American residents. Spear, *Black Chicago*, 145, 146.

55. Tuttle, *Race Riot*, 163. For the boundaries of the Black Belt, see Chicago Commission on Race Relations, *The Negro in Chicago*, 107. A second, smaller African-American section developed on the city's West Side.

56. John Landesco, "Organized Crime in Chicago," in *The Illinois Crime Survey*, ed. John H. Wigmore (Chicago, 1929), 959.

57. Breckinridge, "The Color Line in the Housing Problem," 575.

58. H. L. Harris, Jr., "Negro Mortality Rates in Chicago," *Social Science Review* 1 (March 1927): 58, 60.

59. Vice Commission of Chicago, *The Social Evil in Chicago*, 38–39; Breckinridge, "The Color Line in the Housing Problem," 575; *Chicago Daily News*, December 22, 1916; Reckless, *Vice in Chicago*, 1, 29, 194.

60. *Chicago Daily News*, December 22, 1916.

61. W. P. O'Brien, quoted in Herbert Asbury, *Gem of the Prairie: An Informal History of the Chicago Underworld* (1940; reprint, with an introduction by Perry R. Duis, DeKalb, IL, 1986), 311.

62. *Chicago Daily News*, December 22, 1916; Chicago Commission on Race Relations, *The Negro in Chicago*, 328.

63. *Chicago Record-Herald*, August 17, 1908.

64. McDonald was arrested, tried, and acquitted. See Chicago Police Department, "Homicides and Important Events"; *Chicago Tribune*, March 12, 1908.

65. For Hohing, see *Chicago Tribune*, July 3, 1917, and *Chicago Defender*, July 7, 1917. For Ashmore, see *Chicago Tribune*, May 24 and July 12, 1917; Chicago Police Department, "Homicides and Important Events."

66. Chicago Commission on Race Relations, *The Negro in Chicago*, 430–432; Tuttle, *Race Riot*, 119; Spear, *Black Chicago*, 40; Grossman, *Land of Hope*, 128; Philpott, *Slum and Ghetto*, 118.

67. *Chicago Broad Ax*, May 6, 1905.

68. *Chicago Tribune,* May 22, 1905.

69. Ibid.

70. For a provocative discussion of a related issue, see Frantz Fannon, *The Wretched of the Earth* (New York, 1963). For discussions of weapons, violence, and street life, see Lane, *Roots of Violence in Black Philadelphia,* 136–139; Robert J. Cottrol and Raymond T. Diamond, "The Second Amendment: Toward an Afro-Americanist Reconsideration," in *Gun Control and the Constitution,* ed. Robert J. Cottrol (New York, 1994), 415–427.

71. Twenty-seven percent of the African Americans who committed homicide in 1905 killed whites.

72. The 43 percent figure is for homicides with African-American offenders. The African-American homicide victimization rate for 1905 rose by 34 percent over the 1904 level. The white homicide rate increased by 28 percent during 1905, and the white domestic homicide rate rose by 107 percent—less than half the rate of increase for African-American domestic homicide.

73. *Chicago Tribune,* August 11, 1896.

74. *Chicago Broad Ax,* May 27, 1905.

75. See Wells, *Crusade for Justice,* 302; Harris, "Negro Mortality Rates in Chicago," 70.

76. Organizations such as the Phyllis Wheatley Club and the Lincoln Law and Order League were particularly active in this crusade. See *Chicago Record,* June 19 and 22, 1897; *Chicago Record-Herald,* August 24, 1908. Also see Grossman, *Land of Hope,* 123–160; Philpott, *Slum and Ghetto,* 165–166; Anne Meis Knupfer, *Toward a Tenderer Humanity and a Nobler Womanhood* (New York, 1996).

77. Reverend H. E. Stewart, quoted in *Chicago Record-Herald,* August 24, 1908.

78. Stewart, quoted in *Chicago Tribune,* August 17, 1908; *Chicago Defender,* May 9, 1908.

79. See Paul Frederick Cressey, "Population Succession in Chicago: 1898–1930," *American Journal of Sociology* 44 (July 1938): 68–69; Tuttle, *Race Riot,* 159; Grossman, *Land of Hope,* 259–265.

80. *Chicago Broad Ax,* May 27, 1905.

81. Ferdinand L. Barnett, quoted in *Chicago Tribune,* July 4, 1917.

82. For a discussion of this phrase and this issue, see Tuttle, *Race Riot,* 159, 226.

83. The killer, a nineteen-year-old Greek immigrant named George Miller, insisted that Tucker had misunderstood him, though African-American residents often battled with Greek immigrants, particularly in the Greek restaurants along State Street. For the Miller homicide, see *Chicago Inter Ocean,* April 7, 1900; *Chicago Tribune,* April 7, 1900. For conflict between Greek and African-American Chicagoans, see Ida B. Wells, "Letter to the Editor," *Chicago Defender,* July 25, 1914.

84. *Chicago Tribune,* September 25, 1917.

85. *Chicago Defender,* September 29, 1917.

86. For Wilson, see *Chicago Inter Ocean*, May 13, 1901, and *Chicago Tribune*, May 13, 1901. For Taylor, see *Chicago Tribune*, May 22, 1905, and *Chicago Broad Ax*, May 27, 1905.

87. For example, see *Chicago Broad Ax*, May 27, 1905; *Chicago Defender*, March 18, 1911; Chicago Commission on Race Relations, *The Negro in Chicago*, 345, 622.

88. *Chicago Broad Ax*, May 27, 1905.

89. On July 27, 1919, a local law enforcer, Daniel Callahan, failed to intercede in the earliest moments of the conflict, as white beachgoers stoned Eugene Williams. See Chicago Commission on Race Relations, *The Negro in Chicago*, 4–5; Tuttle, *Race Riot*, 7.

90. For a description of one such law-enforcement effort, see *Chicago Tribune*, May 23, 1899.

91. *Chicago Inter Ocean*, March 4, 1911; *Chicago Tribune*, March 4, 1911; *Chicago Evening Post*, March 8, 1911; *Chicago Defender*, March 18, 1911.

92. Quantitative data provide some indication of the discrimination endured by African-American Chicagoans during the late nineteenth and early twentieth centuries. African-American men were convicted at twice the rate of white men and executed at nearly three times the rate of white men. Similarly, when an African-American resident killed a white resident, the offender was executed in 7 percent of the cases. No white Chicagoans were executed for killing African-American Chicagoans.

93. Harris, "Negro Mortality Rates in Chicago," 70. In the mid-1930s many Chicago hospitals still refused to treat African-American residents, even when they had life-threatening injuries. See interview with Thomas Ellis, in Timuel D. Black, Jr., *Bridges of Memory: Chicago's First Wave of Black Migration* (Evanston, 2003), 27.

94. Harris, "Negro Mortality Rates in Chicago," 70.

95. Chicago Commission on Race Relations, *The Negro in Chicago*, 1–52.

96. In no other year did interracial violence account for the majority of African-American homicides.

97. *Thirteenth Census of the United States: Population*, vol. 1 (Washington, DC, 1913), 278, 439. *Fourteenth Census of the United States: Population*, vol. 2, 473. See also Frazier, *The Negro Family in Chicago*, 72.

98. This reflected the combination of a low birth rate as a result of poor health, an African-American stillbirth rate more than double that of white residents, and an infant mortality rate 60 percent higher. See Harris, "Negro Mortality Rates in Chicago," 58, 66; Chicago Commission on Race Relations, *The Negro in Chicago*, 159; Lieberson, *Piece of the Pie*, 194–195. Cultural factors probably also influenced the child homicide rate, for the child homicide figures were far lower than demographic patterns would predict. The number of African-American children who were homicide victims, however, was so small that it is impossible to calculate accurate African-American child-homicide rates.

99. Also see Cynthia Grant Bowman and Ben Altman, "Wife Murder in Chicago, 1910–1930," *Journal of Criminal Law and Criminology* 92 (Spring–Summer 2002): 759–760, 769.

100. For Rollins, see *Chicago Inter Ocean*, July 19, 1904; *Chicago Evening Post*, July 18, 1904; *Chicago Tribune*, July 18, 1904. For Francis, see *Chicago Tribune*, October 28, 1905; for Ewing, *Chicago Record-Herald*, August 7, 1907.

101. *Chicago Broad Ax*, March 14, 1908; *Chicago Tribune*, September 25, 1908.

102. Ophelia Williams, quoting Andrew Williams, in Benedict J. Short to the Illinois State Board of Pardons, October 2, 1908, Petition for commutation of the sentence to imprisonment for life of Andrew Williams. For Bishop, see *Chicago Defender*, April 12, 1919.

103. By comparison, 38 percent of white killers and 34 percent of white wife killers between 1890 and 1920 were unskilled.

104. Board of Pardons to Governor Charles S. Deneen, [undated] Recommendation of the Board of Pardons, Petition for commutation of the sentence to imprisonment for life of Andrew Williams.

105. Ibid.

106. Benedict J. Short to the Illinois State Board of Pardons, October 2, 1908, Petition for commutation of the sentence to imprisonment for life of Andrew Williams.

107. Thomas Hardy, quoted in Affidavit of Thomas Pearson, October 7, 1909, petition for commutation of the sentence to imprisonment for life of Andrew Williams. In 1872 Mayor Joseph Medill, a Republican and the owner of the *Chicago Tribune*, appointed Chicago's first African-American policeman. At the time of the Williams murder, Thomas Hardy was one of approximately fifty African Americans in a Chicago Police Department with about four thousand policemen. See Harold F. Gosnell, *Negro Politicians* (Chicago, 1935), 247–253; W. Marvin Dulaney, *Black Police in America* (Bloomington, IN, 1996), 19–21, 117; Wesley G. Skogan, "Chicago since 1840," (typescript; Urbana, IL, 1976), 91.

108. Board of Pardons to Governor Charles S. Deneen, [undated] Recommendation of the Board of Pardons, Petition for commutation of the sentence to imprisonment for life of Andrew Williams.

109. C. H. Soelke to the State Board of Pardons, September 29, 1909, Petition for commutation of the sentence to imprisonment for life of Andrew Williams.

110. Board of Pardons to Governor Charles S. Deneen, [undated] Recommendation of the Board of Pardons, Petition for commutation of the sentence to imprisonment for life of Andrew Williams.

111. Andrew Williams to G. D. Kenny, Illinois State Board of Pardons, October 4, 1909, Petition for commutation of the sentence to imprisonment for life of Andrew Williams.

112. Board of Pardons to Governor Charles S. Deneen, [undated] Recommen-

dation of the Board of Pardons; and Andrew Williams to Governor Charles Deneen, April 27, 1909; both in Petition for commutation of the sentence to imprisonment for life of Andrew Williams.

113. Alzada P. Comstock, "Chicago Housing Conditions, 6: The Problem of the Negro," *American Journal of Sociology* 18 (September 1912): 255; *Chicago Defender*, October 19, 1912; Breckinridge, "The Color Line in the Housing Problem," 575; Chicago Commission on Race Relations, *The Negro in Chicago*, 162–163; Sandburg, *The Chicago Race Riots*, 39; Tuttle, *Race Riot*, 163; Spear, *Black Chicago*, 23–24. Segregation increased the cost of housing for African-American residents by forcing these Chicagoans to compete for a small component of housing stock—thus imposing an artificial limitation on the real estate market.

114. Kennedy, *The Negro Peasant Turns Cityward*, 164.

115. Chicago Commission on Race Relations, *The Negro in Chicago*, 155.

116. *Chicago Defender*, June 30, 1917.

117. Between 1890 and 1910, 52 percent of African-American uxoricides were sparked by jealousy-inspired charges, compared with 26 percent for white uxoricides.

118. Comstock, "Chicago Housing Conditions," 256; Breckinridge, "The Color Line in the Housing Problem," 575; Chicago Commission on Race Relations, *The Negro in Chicago*, 155, 158, 341; Harvey Warren Zorbaugh, *The Gold Coast and the Slum* (1929; reprint, with an introduction by Howard P. Chudacoff, Chicago, 1976), 148; Frazier, *The Negro Family in Chicago*, 163; Kennedy, *The Negro Peasant Turns Cityward*, 164.

119. See Claudia Goldin, "Female Labor Force Participation: The Origins of Black and White Differences, 1870 and 1880," *Journal of Economic History* 37 (March 1977): 100.

120. African-American women had long worked outside of the home, even after they married. See ibid., 87–108.

121. *Fourteenth Census of the United States: Population, vol. 4*, 801. For a similar pattern at the national level, see Teresa Amott and Julie Matthaei, *Race, Gender, and Work* (Boston, 1991), 166. Also see Goldin, "Female Labor Force Participation," 94.

122. For data on marital dissolution in Chicago during this period, see Ernest Mowrer, *Family Disorganization* (Chicago, 1927), 95, 119.

123. St. Clair Drake and Horace P. Cayton observed that "lower-class men are thus in a weak economic position vis-a-vis their women and children." See Drake and Cayton, *Black Metropolis*, 583.

124. In 1907, the African-American spousal homicide rate was 20 per 100,000 residents.

125. The Chicago Commission of Race Relations noted the same "curious fact." See *The Negro in Chicago*, 331.

126. For a perceptive discussion of the making and remaking of Chicago's Afri-

can-American community during this period, see Grossman, *Land of Hope*, 123–160.

127. During the 1920s Chicago's African-American population more than doubled, and the African-American homicide rate surged once again. This huge influx of newcomers, which began during the late 1910s, may have recreated the instability and conflict of the turn of the century. According to H. C. Brearley, Chicago's African-American homicide rate exceeded 100 per 100,000 residents in 1925—nearly ten times the white rate. See Brearley, *Homicide in the United States* (1932; reprint, Montclair, NJ, 1969), 218.

128. The comparable rate for African-American men dropped by 48 percent. These figures are rough approximations. Because I did not have sex-specific, race-specific population figures for every year, I estimated, using linear extrapolation. As a consequence, the denominators in my calculation of rates are not precise, and so the homicide rate presented in this sentence is an estimate.

129. For discussions of the "large share of female offenders," see Chicago City Council, *Report of the City Council Committee on Crime of the City of Chicago* [*The Merriam Report*] (Chicago, 1915), 51; Arthur V. Lashly, "Homicide (in Cook County)," in *The Illinois Crime Survey*, ed. John H. Wigmore (1929; reprint, Montclair, NJ, 1968), 625.

130. This figure does not include infanticides.

131. Criminologists examining the late twentieth century also noted this trend. See Coramae Richey Mann, "Black Female Homicide in the United States," *Journal of Interpersonal Violence* 5 (June 1990): 184.

132. L. Mara Dodge found a similar pattern. See Dodge, *Whores and Thieves of the Worst Kind* (DeKalb, IL, 2002), 99.

133. Demographic conditions partially account for the absence of child victims, as Chicago's African-American community included a very low proportion of young residents. But cultural factors, specifically attitudes toward children, played a larger role. The infanticide pattern is especially surprising, since infanticide was typically committed by poor women and African-American women were very poor. It is possible that law enforcers simply failed to investigate infanticide cases in the Black Belt. While it is likely that the police were less inclined to consider these cases, the absence of any infanticide reports or child-killing cases remains remarkable, particularly since the police investigated child and infant deaths in immigrant communities.

134. When white women killed between 1910 and 1920, 61 percent of the victims were men.

135. Bowman and Altman, "Wife Murder in Chicago," 768–769, 777n184.

136. *Chicago Evening Post*, November 21, 1914; *Chicago Tribune*, November 21, 1914.

137. Scholars analyzing late twentieth-century domestic violence found a similar

pattern. See Ann Goetting, "Homicidal Wives: A Profile," *Journal of Family Issues* 8 (September 1987): 33.

138. For a discussion of the relationship between social isolation and violent self-help, see M. P. Baumgartner, "Violent Networks: The Origins and Management of Domestic Conflict," in *Aggression and Violence: Social Interactionist Perspectives*, ed. Richard B. Felson and James T. Tedeschi (Washington, DC, 1993), 214.

139. Chicago City Council, *Report of the City Council Committee on Crime*, 51.

140. For Smith, see *Chicago Defender*, May 18 and September 7, 1918. For the "cool and deliberate" description, see *Chicago Defender*, August 4, 1917, and May 18, 1918. For Smith's comments over her husband's body, see *Chicago Defender*, September 7, 1918; for her words to Franklin, see *Chicago Defender*, May 18, 1918. In spite of a history of abuse at her husband's hands, Smith was convicted and sentenced to an indeterminate prison term; she served two years at the Joliet Penitentiary. See Joliet Convict Registers, Illinois State Archives, Springfield.

141. Of the African-American husband killers who were arrested, 41 percent were convicted, compared with 11 percent of white husband killers. Excluding the two white women found to be criminally insane and a third whose sentence was remitted, two white husband killers received one-year prison terms and two received fourteen-year sentences. By comparison, 55 percent of convicted African-American husband killers received sentences of fourteen years or more (for murder); and 33 percent received "indeterminate" sentences (for manslaughter) and served, on average, fourteen months in prison.

142. Drake and Cayton, *Black Metropolis*, 582.

143. For the African-American population between 1890 and 1920, I relied on the figures in Skogan, "Chicago since 1840," 19.

144. For a detailed discussion of perceptions of African-American Chicagoans during this period, see Chicago Commission on Race Relations, *The Negro in Chicago*, 436–519.

145. See, for example, Turner, "City of Chicago," 580.

146. For a fuller discussion of the "intersectionality" of African-American violence, see Crenshaw, "Mapping the Margins," 1245–46.

147. Ibid., 1258.

148. See Andrew Williams to G. D. Kenny, Illinois State Board of Pardons, October 4, 1909, Petition for commutation of the sentence to imprisonment for life of Andrew Williams.

5. "The Dead Man's Hand"

1. Reporters for both the *Chicago Inter Ocean* and the *Chicago Tribune* called these four cards the "dead man's hand" or the "death hand." The journalist for the *Tribune* contended that Lubio recognized the significance of the

cards, asserting that they offered the saloonkeeper "warning he was about to be attacked a moment before he was shot." See *Chicago Inter Ocean*, February 18, 1911; *Chicago Tribune*, February 18, 1911. The "dead man's hand" was probably a reference to the cards held by Wild Bill Hickok when we was shot by Jack McCall on August 2, 1876, in Deadwood, South Dakota. Hickok's hand, however, according to legend, had two black aces and two black eights, not jacks and eights. The *Chicago Inter Ocean* contended that "holding two black jacks and two black eights" was "known among gamblers as the 'dead man's hand.'" The *Chicago Tribune* suggested an ethnic variation, noting that this particular cluster of cards "was what Italians call the 'death hand.'"

2. For details of the murder, the Dizederos, and Wallen, see *Chicago Inter Ocean*, February 18, 1911.For the arrival of Tierney, see *Chicago Tribune*, February 18, 1911. For Lubio's wife, see *Chicago Evening Post*, February 18, 1911.

3. This figure is based on the total number of homicides for the year, including infanticides, abortion-related deaths, automobile accidents, and other kinds of newly "discovered" (that is, newly enforced or newly criminalized) forms of homicide. Police records identified the victim as Vincenzio Luboy, rather than Vincenzo Lubio. See Chicago Police Department, "Homicides and Important Events, 1870–1920," Illinois State Archives, Springfield.

4. "Race Suicide for Social Parasites," *Journal of the American Medical Association* 50 (January 4, 1908): 55.

5. *Thirteenth Census of the United States: Population, vol. 1* (Washington, DC, 1913), 439; *Fourteenth Census of the United States: Population, vol. 2* (Washington, DC, 1923), 291.

6. For "lodestone," see George W. Steevens, *The Land of the Dollar* (1897; reprint, Freeport, NY, 1971), 152. Steevens went on to lament that Chicago was also the "sink into which drain their dregs." For "laboring population," see Charles J. Bushnell, *The Social Problem at the Chicago Stock Yards: A Contribution to the Study of Democratic Progress in Industrial Centers* (Chicago, 1902), 119. Collins quoted in *Chicago Record-Herald*, July 31, 1906.

7. To be more precise, the city's homicide rate rose by 46 percent between 1900 and 1920, while its foreign-born population increased by 37 percent.

8. For "crimes of violence," see Maynard Shipley, "Crimes of Violence in Chicago and in Greater New York," *Popular Science Monthly* 73 (August 1908): 129. James Edgar Brown quoted in *Chicago Record-Herald*, July 31, 1906.

9. George Kibbe Turner, "The City of Chicago: A Study of the Great Immoralities," *McClure's Magazine* 28 (April 1907): 591.

10. Steevens, *Land of the Dollar*, 152.

11. *Thirteenth Census of the United States: Population, vol. 2*, 512; *Fourteenth Census of the United States: Population, vol. 2*, 291; *Report of the Population of the United States at the Eleventh Census: 1890, Part 1* (Washington, DC, 1895), 671–672.

12. Similarly, 47.5 percent of married women in Chicago in 1920 were foreign born. See Day Monroe, *Chicago Families: A Study of Unpublished Census Data* (1932; reprint, New York, 1972), 22, 281.

13. Steevens, *Land of the Dollar,* 144–145.

14. Charles J. Bushnell, "The Social Problem of the Twentieth Century in America," pamphlet (Tiffin, OH, 1904), 5.

15. Thomas A. Guglielmo, *White on Arrival: Italians, Race, Color, and Power in Chicago, 1890–1945* (New York, 2003), 16, 21; Rudolph Vecoli, "Chicago's Italians Prior to World War I" (Ph.D. diss., University of Wisconsin, 1963); Vecoli, "The Formation of Chicago's Little Italies," *Journal of American Ethnic History* 2 (Spring 1983): 5–20; Humbert S. Nelli, *Italians in Chicago, 1880–1930* (New York, 1970), 22–54.

16. See Guglielmo, *White on Arrival,* 21.

17. Collins quoted in *Chicago Record-Herald,* July 31, 1906. Thorpe quoted in *Chicago Evening Post,* February 22, 1906. James Edgar Brown quoted in *Chicago Tribune,* September 21, 1906. Turner, "The City of Chicago," 590–591.

18. The Bertillon system measured and catalogued in police files the physical features of criminals, such as the size of the feet and the shape of the head.

19. J. M. Lavin quoted in *Chicago Tribune,* March 3, 1908; Belfield in "Race Suicide for Social Parasites," 55.

20. U.S. Congress, Senate Committee on Immigration [Dillingham Commission], *Report of the Immigration Commission: Immigration and Crime* [vol. 36], 61st Cong., 3rd sess. (Washington, DC, 1911), 1. The Chicago City Council Committee Report on Crime quoted this passage as well. *Report of the City Council Committee on Crime of the City of Chicago* (Chicago, 1915), 52.

21. U.S. Congress, Senate Committee on Immigration, *Report of the Immigration Commission: Immigration and Crime,* 2, 144. See also "Criminality of Italians," *Literary Digest* 40 (March 26, 1910): 582.

22. Jane Addams, "The Objective Value of a Social Settlement" [1892], reprinted in *The Social Thought of Jane Addams,* ed. Christopher Lasch (Indianapolis, 1965), 50.

23. See William I. Thomas and Florian Znaniecki, *The Polish Peasant in Europe and America* (1927; reprint, New York, 1958), 2:1753–75; William I. Thomas, with Robert A. Park and Herbert A. Miller, *Old World Traits Transplanted* (1921; reprint, with an introduction by Donald R. Young, Montclair, NJ, 1971), 10–11.

24. Shipley, "Crimes of Violence in Chicago and in Greater New York," 130.

25. Police records did not systematically record the place of birth of Scandinavian killers or victims. Coroner's reports, however, often provided aggregate data on victims. Although the coroner's population estimates were at odds with the figures calculated by census takers, data from the coroner's annual tallies provide some foundation for estimating homicide rates among

Swedish and Norwegian immigrants. See, for example, Cook County Coroner, *Biennial Report of the Coroner of Cook County* (Chicago, 1915), 109.
26. Jane Addams, 1911, quoted in Vecoli, "The Formation of Chicago's Little
Italies," 10.
27. *Chicago Tribune,* December 2, 1905, and July 2, 1917; Harvey Warren
Zorbaugh, *The Gold Coast and the Slum* (1929; reprint, with an introduction
by Howard P. Chudacoff, Chicago, 1976), 171.
28. These figures are for homicide victims. See Cook County Coroner, *Cook
County Coroner's Quadrennial Report for the Years 1908–1911* (Chicago, 1912),
29–30; Cook County Coroner, *Biennial Report of the Coroner of Cook County*
(Chicago, 1914), 88, 120.
29. These figures are for homicide victims. See Cook County Coroner, *The
Race Riots: Biennial Report [of the Cook County Coroner], 1918–1919 and Official Record of Inquests on the Victims of the Race Riots of July and August 1919*
(Chicago, 1920), 108.
30. For a thoughtful exploration of the "pornography of violence," see Karen
Halttunen, *Murder Most Foul* (Cambridge, MA, 1998), 60–90.
31. "Revenge Rules Little Sicily," *Chicago Tribune,* June 24, 1914. "Just Another
Shooting in Little Italy," *Chicago Tribune,* December 29, 1916. Marello murders in *Chicago Inter Ocean,* February 2, 1912. For the 1904–1912 figure, see
Guglielmo, *White on Arrival,* 78.
32. My coding protocol was very conservative. In many instances, I had evidence about the ethnic or racial background of the killer or the victim but
not both; in other instances, the evidence suggested but did not prove that
both came from the same ethnic or racial background. Thus, for 58 percent
of the homicides in the data set, I could not determine whether the killing
occurred within or across group lines. For Italian homicides, the sources
provided direct evidence of intragroup homicide in over 81 percent of cases.
The figure for African-American homicides was the second highest, at 72
percent. The Dillingham Commission also found unusually high rates of
intragroup crime among Italians. See U.S. Congress, Senate Committee on
Immigration, *Report of the Immigration Commission: Immigration and Crime,*
286. See also E. H. Sutherland, "Murder and the Death Penalty," *Journal of
the American Institute of Criminal Law and Criminology* 15 (February 1925):
525.
33. Allan H. Spear, *Black Chicago* (Chicago, 1960), 15; Thomas Lee Philpott,
The Slum and the Ghetto (New York, 1978), 137; Stanley Lieberson, *A Piece of
the Pie* (Berkeley, 1980), 263, 267.
34. Turner, "The City of Chicago," 580.
35. See, for example, *Chicago Record-Herald,* April 28, 1910; *Chicago Tribune,*
June 24, 1914.
36. *Chicago Tribune,* March 5, 1910.

37. For "characteristic Italian murder," see *Chicago Times*, February 14, 1887; for 1910 investigator, *Chicago Evening Post*, March 5, 1910; for "murderous certainty," *Chicago Times*, September 14, 1885; for "carving bee," *Chicago Inter Ocean*, August 16, 1886. For a related analysis, see Thomas W. Gallant, "Honor, Masculinity, and Ritual Knife Fighting in Nineteenth-Century Greece," *American Historical Review* 105 (April 2000): 359–382. For "anger in his heart" quotation, see *Chicago Tribune*, December 15, 1919; for Volini, *Chicago Record*, May 29, 1899.

38. Between 1875 and 1910, nearly 30 percent of homicides with Italian killers occurred during drunken brawls, compared with 20 percent for all Chicago killers. For a discussion of the immigrant community, see Guglielmo, *White on Arrival*, 15.

39. For example, see Turner, "The City of Chicago," 580.

40. The figure for the entire city was 11.2 percent.

41. The scholars associated with the Chicago School of urban sociology explored in great detail the ways in which big-city life undermined "traditional" forms of social control. For example, see Robert E. Park, "Community Organization and Juvenile Delinquency," in *The City*, ed. Robert E. Park, Ernest W. Burgess, and Roderick D. McKenzie (Chicago, 1920), 99–112.

42. According to M. P. Baumgartner, "as the degree of support available to the wife increases, the likelihood of violence against her decreases." See Baumgartner, "Violent Networks: The Origins and Management of Domestic Conflict," in *Aggression and Violence: Social Interactionist Perspectives*, ed. Richard B. Felson and James T. Tedeschi (Washington, DC, 1993), 213.

43. *Chicago Record-Herald*, April 14, 1909.

44. *L'Italia*, April 1, 1911, translated by the Chicago Foreign Language Press Survey (Chicago Public Library Omnibus Project, WPA, Chicago, 1942).

45. Vecoli, "Chicago's Italians Prior to World War I," 115.

46. For the sociologist's quotation, see Zorbaugh, *The Gold Coast and the Slum*, 168. For "a Sicilian never forgets," see *Chicago Times*, July 5, 1879.

47. *Chicago Tribune*, January 18, 1912; *Chicago Evening Post*, January 17, 1912.

48. The average age of an Italian family killer was slightly under thirty, while the citywide average was thirty-four.

49. Vecoli, "Chicago's Italians Prior to World War I," 115; Thomas et al., *Old World Traits Transplanted*, 10.

50. For details of the case and the trial, see *Chicago Record-Herald*, March 8, June 9, and June 30, 1909. For Pacellano's words after his arrest, see *Chicago Tribune*, March 8, 1909. The prosecution produced witnesses who testified at the trial that Pacellano's sister had moved "willingly" to New York City and that "Serino had not taken the young wife to a disorderly resort"; see *Chicago Record-Herald*, June 30, 1909.

51. *Chicago Tribune*, August 19, 1918.

52. For the use of the term "ambushed," see *Chicago Evening Post*, January 17, 1912.

53. Zorbaugh, *The Gold Coast and the Slum*, 169.

54. Ibid., 175. For data on ethnicity and desertion in early twentieth-century Chicago, see Earle Edward Eubank, "A Study of Family Desertion" (Ph.D. diss., University of Chicago, 1916), 16; Ernest R. Mowrer, *Family Disorganization* (Chicago, 1939), 94. For a related discussion, see Virginia Yans-McLaughlin, *Family and Community* (Ithaca, NY, 1971), 222. For a discussion of honor and violence, see Anton Blok, "The Enigma of Senseless Violence," in *Meanings of Violence*, ed. Goran Aijmer and Jon Abbink (New York, 2000), 23–38.

55. These active, tenacious kin networks may have made Italian wives relatively less vulnerable to domestic violence. See Baumgartner, "Violent Networks," 222, 227.

56. For Laporta, see *Chicago Tribune*, December 15, 1913; for Montalvano, *Chicago Inter Ocean*, March 22, 1914; for DiAgnostino, *Chicago Daily News*, January 11, 1915; for the 1916 observation, *Chicago Tribune*, December 27, 1916.

57. I coded a homicide as a "Black Hand" killing if police records indicated it was or if newspaper accounts, court records, or other sources revealed that the police viewed the crime as a Black Hand murder. In cases where subsequent evidence pointed to other motives, I changed the coding to reflect the new explanation. In short, I relied on the often loose definitions and categorizations of contemporary law enforcers.

58. See Humbert S. Nelli, *The Business of Crime* (New York, 1976), 47–100; Guglielmo, *White on Arrival*, 77. The *New York Times* account of the Hennessy murder ran under the headline "Crimes of the Mafias." See *New York Times*, October 20, 1890.

59. See, for instance, *New York Times*, March 20, 1891. For a description of the mob violence, see Nelli, *The Business of Crime*, 60–66.

60. On March 14, 1891, the *Chicago Tribune* reported that "an immense crowd" of New Orleans residents "may lynch the Mafia thugs." Similarly, the account of the lynching ran under the headline "Mafia Murderers Slain." See *Chicago Tribune*, March 15, 1891.

61. *Chicago Tribune*, March 18, 1891.

62. *Chicago News Record*, October 6, 1892; *Chicago Tribune*, October 6, 1892.

63. Regarding the Mersineo case, some newspaper accounts identified the shooter as Shalo Knosho. See *Chicago News Record*, October 3, 1892. For an account identifying Mersineo as the killer, see *Chicago Tribune*, October 6, 1892. According to police records, Martino survived the shooting. Instead, Charchiro died. See Chicago Police Department, "Homicides and

Important Events." For Wheeler's words, see *Chicago News Record,* October 6, 1892; for the inspector and Durante, see *Chicago Tribune,* October 6, 1892.

64. See *Chicago Tribune,* April 14, 1909; Arthur Woods, "The Problem of the Black Hand," *McClure's Magazine* 33 (May 1909): 40–47; Arthur H. Warner, "Amputating the Black Hand," *Survey* 12 (May 1909): 166–167; Gaetano D'Amato, "The 'Black Hand' Myth," *North American Review* 187 (1908): 543–549. The *New York Times* ran stories with titles such as "'The Black Hand' Death Threat" (February 29, 1904), "Black Hand in Passaic" (August 21, 1904), "Black Hand in Allegheny" (August 24, 1904), "Black Hand in Greenwich" (August 31, 1904). Also see Nelli, *Italians in Chicago,* 134.

65. Guglielmo, *White on Arrival,* 182n18.

66. Quoted in John Landesco, "Organized Crime in Chicago," in *The Illinois Crime Survey,* ed. John H. Wigmore (Chicago, 1929), 936.

67. Landesco, "Organized Crime in Chicago," 947.

68. For example, see *Chicago Tribune,* May 8, 1909.

69. Landesco, "Organized Crime in Chicago," 938; *Chicago Evening Post,* November 19, 1907; *Chicago Tribune,* June 24, 1909.

70. D'Amato, "The 'Black Hand' Myth," 548; "Italian Crime in America," *Literary Digest* 29 (August 27, 1904): 246.

71. *Chicago Tribune,* May 8, 1909; February 16, 1916.

72. Landesco, "Organized Crime in Chicago," 870–872.

73. For an example of a homicide in which the police suspected Black Hand involvement, see the newspaper coverage of the murder of Joseph Fillipelli, on April 12, 1909—*Chicago Evening Post,* April 13, 1909; *Chicago Tribune,* April 13 and 14, 1909; *Chicago Record-Herald,* April 14, 1909.

74. *Chicago Daily News,* December 22, 1900.

75. *Chicago Inter Ocean,* January 7, 1910.

76. For information on the first letter, see *Chicago Evening Post,* January 6, 1910; *Chicago Tribune,* January 7, 1910. For the bomb, see *Chicago Inter Ocean,* January 7, 1910. For Sinene's sense of the "hand of death," see *Chicago Inter Ocean,* January 7, 1910; *Chicago Evening Post,* January 6, 1910. For suspicions about Sinene's past, see *Chicago Tribune,* January 7, 1910; *Chicago Evening Post,* January 6, 1910; *Chicago Inter Ocean,* January 7, 1910.

77. *Chicago Inter Ocean,* January 7, 1910. In 1909, Mayor Fred A. Busse had assigned Schuettler to investigate organized crime in the city. See Landesco, "Organized Crime in Chicago," 874.

78. Quoted in Landesco, "Organized Crime in Chicago," 942.

79. *Chicago Evening Post,* December 29, 1915.

80. Thomas et al., *Old World Traits Transplanted,* 11.

81. *Chicago Tribune,* June 24, 1914.

82. Thomas et al., *Old World Traits Transplanted,* 10–11; *Chicago Tribune,* April

2, 1911; Grace Peloubet Norton, "Chicago Housing Conditions, 7: Two Italian Districts," *American Journal of Sociology* 18 (January 1913): 510; *Chicago Tribune,* January 23, 1914; *Chicago Tribune,* February 16, 1916; Zorbaugh, *The Gold Coast and the Slum,* 170–171; Landesco, "Organized Crime in Chicago," 946.

83. *Chicago Tribune,* April 2, 1911.

84. Landesco, "Organized Crime in Chicago," 938–939; *Chicago Tribune,* February 16, 1916.

85. *Chicago Record-Herald,* June 2, 1915, cited in Landesco, "Organized Crime in Chicago," 940.

86. Carter H. Harrison, *Growing Up With Chicago* (Chicago, 1944), 222.

87. *Chicago Tribune,* February 16, 1916.

88. For the Shippy quotation, see *Chicago Evening Post,* November 19, 1907; for Schuettler, *Chicago Evening Post,* April 13, 1909.

89. *Chicago Tribune,* March 5, 1910.

90. *Chicago Evening Post,* March 15, 1911. Chicago law enforcers probably followed the lead of the New York police, who had established an "Italian Squad" a few years earlier—though the New York experiment failed when Black Handers in Palermo assassinated Lieutenant Joseph Petrosino, the head of the city's Italian unit. See Warner, "Amputating the Black Hand," 166.

91. Quoted in Thomas et al., *Old World Traits Transplanted,* 248.

92. *Chicago Tribune,* April 12 and October 28, 1916; *Chicago Evening Post,* March 15, 1911.

93. *Chicago Inter Ocean,* February 20, 1911. *Chicago Tribune,* April 2, 1911; January 23, 1914; June 30, 1918.

94. Thomas et al., *Old World Traits Transplanted,* 248.

95. For "hoax," see *Chicago Record-Herald,* April 14, 1909. For "imagination of reporters," see Giovanni E. Schiavo, *The Italians in Chicago* (1928; reprint, New York, 1975), 125. For Sabetta, see *Chicago Record-Herald,* March 26, 1910, quoted in Landesco, "Organized Crime in Chicago," 943; for Barasa, see *Chicago Record-Herald,* April 14, 1909.

96. *Chicago Tribune,* November 19, 1907; *Chicago Evening Post,* November 19, 1907; *Chicago Tribune,* February 3, 1908; *L'Italia,* April 1, 1911, translated by the Chicago Foreign Language Press Survey; Nelli, *Italians in Chicago,* 134–135. Residents established the organization in 1907, though it did not become active in the battle against the Black Hand until 1910. See Landesco, "Organized Crime in Chicago," 937–938.

97. *Chicago Tribune,* March 15, 1911. See also Landesco, "Organized Crime in Chicago," 945; Guglielmo, *White on Arrival,* 79.

98. Landesco, "Organized Crime in Chicago," 937–938, 947; Nelli, *Italians in Chicago,* 134, 154.

99. Thomas et al., *Old World Traits Transplanted,* 248.

100. Landesco, "Organized Crime in Chicago," 856–857; Nelli, *The Business of Crime*, 77–78.
101. Landesco, "Organized Crime in Chicago," 937.
102. *Chicago Tribune*, June 23, 1914.
103. *Chicago Tribune*, May 8, 1909; *Chicago Evening Post*, May 11, 1909.
104. For the "wall of silence" phrase, see *L'Italia*, December 9, 1919, translated by the Chicago Foreign Language Press Survey.
105. *Chicago Tribune*, March 15, 1911.
106. *Chicago Record-Herald*, April 28, 1910.
107. Testimony of E. J. Raber, Assistant State's Attorney, to the Governor, October 15, 1920, Report of the Division of Pardons and Paroles of the Department of Public Welfare on the Application of Frank Campione, Thomas Errico, and Nicholas Viana for Commutation, Illinois State Archives, Springfield.
108. Jane Addams, *The Second Twenty Years at Hull-House: September 1909 to September 1929* (New York, 1930), 244.
109. *Chicago Daily News*, September 27, 1915.
110. *Chicago Daily News*, October 26 and 27, 1915; *Chicago Tribune*, October 27, 1915.
111. The tradition of personal vengeance, where fathers and brothers interceded against those who had seduced, "wronged," or "ruined" their daughters or wives, reduced the autonomy of women and imposed deadly penalties on men who engaged in illicit sexual behavior.
112. For the White Hand president quotation, see *Chicago Tribune*, March 15, 1911. For Marcadnano, see *Chicago Tribune*, March 14, 1911; for Delgila, *Chicago Evening Post*, September 27, 1920. For the injured murderer, see Landesco, "Organized Crime in Chicago," 945. For the journalist's comments on "the code," see *Chicago Tribune*, June 30, 1918.
113. *Chicago Tribune*, November 20, 1916.
114. *Chicago Tribune*, December 19, 1909.
115. James R. Howe to Governor Frank O. Lowden, September 18, 1920, Application for the Commutation of Nicholas Viana, Executive Clemency Files of Frank O. Lowden, Illinois State Archives, Springfield.
116. This figure does not, obviously, include homicides in which the killer committed suicide. Moreover, it does not include automobile homicides, infanticide cases, medical malpractice cases, or other socially constructed forms of homicide—a distinction explored in detail in Chapter 6.
117. According to John Landesco, during the Beer Wars of the 1920s, "the gang code of silence and personal vengeance rather than legal redress was so compelling that of the two hundred fifteen murders of gangsters during the four years of armed strife, only a handful of arrests and no convictions were secured by law enforcement agencies." See Landesco, "Organized Crime in Chicago," 930.

118. Ibid., 942.

119. *L'Italia,* April 1, 1911, translated by the Chicago Foreign Language Press Survey. I was unable to verify this figure, which is not entirely surprising in view of the imprecision of the "Black Hand" label.

120. I calculated this figure using police records. See Chicago Police Department, "Homicides and Important Events."

121. See Vecoli, "Chicago's Italians Prior to World War I," 115.

122. Pockets of early twentieth-century Chicago society, in short, operated beyond the effective reach of state institutions or state control. Such a relative absence of state authority encouraged aggressive self-help and violence as a form of "social control." See Donald Black, "Crime as Social Control," *American Sociological Review* 48 (February 1983): 41. Norbert Elias argued that interpersonal violence falls as the state assumes a monopoly on violence. See Elias, *The Civilizing Process: The History of Manners* (1939; reprint, New York, 1978), 201–202; Jonathan Fletcher, *Violence and Civilization* (Cambridge, UK, 1997), 31–39.

123. For a discussion of the "reciprocal exchange of violence," see Black, "Crime as Social Control," 35.

124. Guglielmo, *White on Arrival,* 51; Nelli, *Italians in Chicago,* 39–54.

125. For the impact of increasing racial tensions—or, as Guglielmo puts it, increasing "color" tensions—see Guglielmo, *White on Arrival,* 43.

126. For the "sensation mongers" phrase, see Henry M. Hyde's analysis of newspaper coverage of the Black Hand in the *Chicago Tribune,* June 23, 1914.

127. These figures are based on data for 1910–1913. See Wesley G. Skogan, "Chicago since 1840" (typescript; Urbana, IL, 1976), 19; Cook County Coroner, *Cook County Coroner's Quadrennial Report for the Years 1908–1911,* 29–30; Cook County Coroner, *Biennial Report of the Coroner of Cook County* (Chicago, 1914), 88, 120.

128. Chicago School sociologists reached the opposite conclusion. Robert E. Park argued, "It is probably the breaking down of local attachments and the weakening of the restraints and inhibitions of the primary group, under the influence of the urban environment, which are largely responsible for the increase in vice and crime in great cities." Park, "The City: Suggestions for the Investigation of Human Behavior in the Urban Environment," in *The City,* ed. Robert E. Park et al., 25.

129. *Chicago Inter Ocean,* March 30 and May 18, 1911.

130. These figures are culled from coroners' reports for the 1910–1913 period. See Cook County Coroner, *Cook County Coroner's Quadrennial Report for the Years 1908–1911,* 29–30; Cook County Coroner, *Biennial Report of the Coroner of Cook County* (Chicago, 1914), 88, 120.

131. Cook County Coroner, *Biennial Report of the Coroner of Cook County* (Chicago, 1915), 109.

132. Ibid.

133. Cook County Coroner, *Race Riots: Biennial Report [of the Cook County Coroner], 1918–1919*, 108.

6. "A Good Place to Drown Babies"

1. Each source spelled the surname of the participants differently. Police records listed the killer and the victim as "Furganich." The *Chicago Record-Herald* identified them as "Furnajik," while the *Chicago Tribune* listed them as "Fieaich." See Chicago Police Department, "Homicides and Important Events, 1870–1920," Illinois State Archives, Springfield; *Chicago Record-Herald*, June 19, 1913; *Chicago Tribune*, June 19, 1913. For information about Maggie's mental state and the agent's visiting the home, see *Chicago Record-Herald*, June 19, 1913. The *Tribune* identified the daughter as Elizabeth, whereas the *Record-Herald* called her Margaret; see the June 19, 1913, editions of both newspapers. For Elizabeth's starting for shore, see *Chicago Record-Herald*, June 19, 1913. In the *Chicago Tribune* account, Patrolman Alfred Kayes rescued Elizabeth. For Maggie's description of Lake Calumet, see *Chicago Tribune*, June 19, 1913.

2. This figure is based on the total number of homicides for the year, including abortion-related deaths, infanticides, automobile accidents, and other kinds of newly "discovered" (that is, newly enforced or newly criminalized) forms of homicide.

3. City officials defined an "infant" as a child under the age of one.

4. *Report and Handbook of the Department of Health of the City of Chicago for the Years 1911 to 1918, Inclusive* (Chicago, 1919), 1454.

5. *Chicago Tribune*, May 11, 1914; May 18, 1918.

6. Historians have produced an important body of literature on this topic. See Morton Keller, *Regulating a New Society* (Cambridge, MA, 1994), 78–79, 109; Lawrence M. Friedman, *Total Justice* (New York, 1985), 45–79; Michael Willrich, *City of Courts* (New York, 2003), 59–115, 320; Barbara Young Welke, *Recasting American Liberty* (New York, 2001), 35–39; John Fabian Witt, *The Accidental Republic* (Cambridge, MA, 2004), 37.

7. For example, see *Chicago Record-Herald*, February 21, 1903. Between 1875 and 1900, prosecutors secured convictions in 27 percent of drunken-brawl homicide cases.

8. *Chicago Record-Herald*, December 27, 1904; Chicago Police Department, "Homicides and Important Events."

9. For analyses of this process, see Robert Silverman, *Law and Urban Growth* (Princeton, NJ, 1981); Randolph E. Bergstrom, *Courting Danger* (Ithaca, NY, 1992); Welke, *Recasting American Liberty;* Witt, *The Accidental Republic.*

10. See Sam B. Warner, "Changes in the Administration of Criminal Justice during the Past Fifty Years," *Harvard Law Review* 50 (February 1937): 586;

Keller, *Regulating a New Society*, 159; Kermit L. Hall, *The Magic Mirror* (New York, 1989), 187; Martin J. Wiener, *Men of Blood* (Cambridge, UK, 2004), 15–20.

11. The criminal court jury, however, acquitted Doherty. See Chicago Police Department, "Homicides and Important Events."

12. Bergstrom, *Courting Danger*, 183.

13. *Chicago Tribune*, September 18, 1914.

14. Jury decisions and awards suggest that these ideas about government responsibility, personal liability, and the need to protect the public extended beyond middle-class policy makers and law enforcers. See Bergstrom, *Courting Danger*; Welke, *Recasting American Liberty*; Witt, *The Accidental Republic*.

15. Peter M. Hoffman, *Biennial Report of the Coroner's Office, Cook County, Illinois, 1912–1913* (Chicago, 1914), 65.

16. For the "auto slaughter" phrase, see *Chicago Tribune*, May 22, 1908.

17. Perry R. Duis, *Challenging Chicago* (Urbana, IL, 1998), 49.

18. For the turn-of-the-century and the 1908 figures, see Lyle Benedict and Ellen O'Brien, "Deaths, Disturbances, Disasters, and Disorder in Chicago: A Selective Bibliography of Materials in the Municipal Reference Collection of the Chicago Public Library" (pamphlet; Chicago, 1996), 8. For 1920 and 1924, see Homer Hoyt, *One Hundred Years of Land Values in Chicago* (Chicago, 1933), 205, 485.

19. Hoyt, *One Hundred Years of Land Values*, 485.

20. Duis, *Challenging Chicago*, 50; Hoffman, *Biennial Report of the Coroner's Office, Cook County, Illinois, 1912–1913*, 65; Judge Sheridan E. Fry, "The Automobile Court of Chicago," in Peter M. Hoffman, *Biennial Report of the Coroner of Cook County* (Chicago, 1915), 29. For early efforts at regulation, see Paul Barrett, *The Automobile and Urban Transit: The Formation of Public Policy in Chicago, 1900–1930* (Philadelphia, 1983), 60–65.

21. Hoffman, *Biennial Report of the Coroner's Office, Cook County, Illinois, 1912–1913*, 65; Clay McShane, *Down the Asphalt Path* (New York, 1994), 198; Stefan A. Riesenfeld, "Comment: Criminal Law: Homicide Committed through the Operation of a Motor Vehicle While Intoxicated," *California Law Review* 24 (July 1936): 572.

22. Duis, *Challenging Chicago*, 57.

23. For a discussion of these issues, see Barrett, *The Automobile and Urban Transit*.

24. Duis, *Challenging Chicago*, 56. For data on automobile fatalities at the national level, see Paul C. Holinger, *Violent Deaths in the United States* (New York, 1987), 70–83, 211–213.

25. For example, see Arthur R. Reynolds, *Vital Statistics of the City of Chicago for the Years 1899 to 1903 Inclusive* (Chicago, 1904), 64; Charles J. Whalen, *Bien-*

nial Report of the Department of Health of the City of Chicago for the Years 1904–1905 (Chicago, 1906), 270.

26. *Chicago Record-Herald,* June 23, 1909.

27. *Report of the Department of Health of the City of Chicago for the Years 1926 to 1930 Inclusive* (Chicago, 1931), 1136.

28. *Chicago Tribune,* May 11, 1914. In the New York metropolitan area, automobile fatalities also topped horse-drawn wagon fatalities for the first time in 1912. See *New York Times,* February 2, 1913.

29. *Report of the Department of Health of the City of Chicago for the Years 1926 to 1930 Inclusive,* 1136.

30. *Chicago Tribune,* January 1, 1921.

31. For example, see City of Chicago, Police Department, *Annual Report for the Year Ending December 31, 1920* (Chicago, 1921), 36.

32. For "something's got to be done," see *Chicago Tribune,* June 24, 1917. For the same phrase from Hoffman, in a slightly different context, see *Chicago Daily News,* January 24, 1916. A photograph of Hoffman, pointing sternly to the camera and proclaiming "I am trying to make this county safe," adorned the cover of the coroner's biennial report for 1918–1919. See Hoffman, *Biennial Report [of the Coroner of Cook County], 1918–1919 and Official Record of Inquests on the Victims of the Race Riots of July and August, 1919* (Chicago, 1920). For "human life is too valuable," see *Chicago Tribune,* June 24, 1917; for his 1912 pledge, see *Chicago Evening Post,* August 24, 1912. Hoffman's motives were complex. By all indications, he wanted to reduce the number of accidents in the city, a theme at the core of the annual reports issued by his office. Hoffman, however, used this topic to enhance the power and professional authority of his office. He may have been influenced by other considerations as well: his critics charged that Hoffman's financial interests in a company that produced automobile lights contributed to his zeal for public safety. Other public officials used the effort to save Chicagoans from "auto slaughter" as a campaign issue during local elections. But most reform movements during this era attracted diverse groups of supporters who embraced a wide range of motives. For a discussion of Hoffman's financial interests, see *Chicago Evening Post,* March 21, 1913. For the use of the issue to secure elected office, see *Chicago Evening Post,* October 29, 1920.

33. For McWeeny, see *Chicago Record-Herald,* November 23, 1912; for Fairbank, *Chicago Inter Ocean,* June 30, 1912.

34. *Chicago Tribune,* January 1, 1921.

35. *Chicago Tribune,* October 23, 1915; *Chicago Daily News,* October 22, 1915. For a similar sentiment from New York law enforcers, see "A Conviction for Automobile Manslaughter," *Literary Digest* 38 (June 12, 1909): 1003.

36. Hoffman, *Biennial Report of the Coroner's Office, Cook County, Illinois, 1912–1913,* 63.

37. See, for example, *Chicago Evening Post,* July 23, 1913; *Chicago Tribune,* May 23, 1914, and December 25, 1915.

38. *Chicago Tribune,* October 19, 1916.

39. Illinois v. Clink, 216 Ill. App. 357 (Illinois 1920).

40. According to the *Chicago Tribune* on May 3, 1913, the Illinois state's attorney's office reported that the Lindbloom case marked the first murder conviction for an automobile homicide in the United States.

41. Joliet Convict Registers, Illinois State Archives, Springfield.

42. For details of the incident, see *Chicago Record-Herald,* May 3, 1913; *Chicago Tribune,* May 3, 1913. For the death of Weiss's daughter and Malato's statements, see *Chicago Tribune,* May 3, 1913.

43. For a related analysis, see Herbert Wechsler and Jerome Michael, "A Rationale of the Law of Homicide," *Columbia Law Review* 37 (May 1937): 703.

44. For the Cooper quotation, see *Chicago Record-Herald,* May 3, 1913. For discussions of the definition of murder, see Wechsler and Michael, "A Rationale of the Law of Homicide," 701–761; Edwin R. Keedy, "History of the Pennsylvania Statute Creating Degrees of Murder," *University of Pennsylvania Law Review* 97 (May 1949): 759–777.

45. *Chicago Record-Herald,* May 3, 1913. Fourteen years was a common sentence for those convicted of murder during this period.

46. For the "speed fiends" characterization, see *Chicago Tribune,* June 24, 1917. Not surprisingly, Hoffman used the phrase. Explaining the low conviction rate, a legal scholar suggested that homicide did not seem to be "the right label" for traffic fatalities. See Stefan A. Riesenfeld, "Negligent Homicide: A Study in Statutory Interpretation," *California Law Review* 25 (September 1936): 8.

47. Joliet Convict Registers.

48. When a grand jury did not return a bill of indictment, the verdict typically appeared in police records as "no bill." During the mid-1920s, barely 15 percent of automobile homicide cases resulted in criminal trials. See Arthur V. Lashly, "Homicide (in Cook County)," in *The Illinois Crime Survey,* ed. John H. Wigmore (Chicago, 1929), 602.

49. This figure includes cases in which a coroner's jury ruled the death a homicide but the driver was never apprehended.

50. For the "speed maniac" phrase, see Hoffman, *Biennial Report of the Coroner's Office, Cook County, Illinois, 1912–1913,* 65. For "death-dealing 'joy riders,'" see *Chicago Inter Ocean,* October 16, 1910. Police officials and coroners sometimes termed automobile fatalities homicides because drivers left the scene of the accidents, thus confirming their disregard for human life. In over a third of automobile homicides, the driver was never arrested.

51. Illinois v. Falkovitch, 117 N.E. 398, 399 (Illinois, 1917); R. Waite Joslyn, *Criminal Law and the Statutory Penalties of Illinois,* 2nd ed. (Chicago, 1920), 89, 90.

52. Culver and Chicago Title & Trust Company v. Harris, 211 Ill. App. 474, 476 (Illinois, 1918).

53. Illinois v. Adams, 124 N.E. 575, 577 (Illinois, 1919).

54. Illinois v. Kuchta, 129 N.E. 528, 529 (Illinois, 1920). A thirty-year-old box-maker, Kuchta was speeding, driving on the wrong side of the street, and allegedly intoxicated when his vehicle struck Sauter. See *Chicago Tribune,* November 18, 1918; *Chicago Evening Post,* November 18, 1918.

55. Illinois v. Falkovitch, 117 N.E. 398, 402; Illinois v. Adams, 124 N.E. 575, 577. For a related process in civil litigation, see Barbara Y. Welke, "Unreasonable Women: Gender and the Law of Accidental Injury, 1870–1920," *Law and Social Inquiry* 19 (Spring 1994): 376.

56. Illinois v. Adams, 124 N.E. 575, 577.

57. See Illinois v. Camberis, 130 N.E. 712, 716 (Illinois, 1921).

58. For an analysis of this process, which unfolded over the course of nearly two decades, see Riesenfeld, "Negligent Homicide," 1, 8. Riesenfeld argues that the "creation of this new crime" "gave the jury the alternative to convict of a lesser crime in the automobile cases, thus avoiding acquittals or contradictory verdicts."

59. Writing in 1937, legal scholar Livingston Hall reported that "the crimes of murder, manslaughter, and assault and battery are being used in an attempt to control the reckless use of dangerous instrumentalities which modern inventions have entrusted to unskilled hands." See Hall, "The Substantive Law of Crimes, 1887–1936," *Harvard Law Review* 50 (February 1937): 642.

60. For the Malato quotation, see *Chicago Tribune,* May 3, 1913. For related discussions of the impact of gendered and patriarchal constructions of the law, see Welke, "Unreasonable Women," 369–403; Welke, *Recasting American Liberty,* 42–80; Keller, *Regulating a New Society,* 78.

61. During the mid-1920s, the proportion of automobile fatalities treated as homicides rose to 19 percent. See *Report of the Department of Health of the City of Chicago for the Years 1926 to 1930 Inclusive,* 679; Lashley, "Homicide (in Cook County)," 602.

62. *Chicago Inter Ocean,* October 16, 1910; Illinois v. Camberis, 130 N.E. 712, 716. The "joy rider" label and imagery influenced legal discussions for decades. See Hall, "Substantive Law of Crimes," 635.

63. *Chicago Inter Ocean,* October 16, 1910, and May 11, 1910; *Chicago Record-Herald,* May 11, 1910; *Chicago Tribune,* May 12, 1910.

64. For McWeeny, see *Chicago Record-Herald,* November 23, 1912; for Hoffman, *Chicago Tribune,* June 19, 1917.

65. For Fotzke, see *Chicago Evening Post,* January 28, 1919, and *Chicago Tribune,* January 29, 1919. For Camberis, see Illinois v. Camberis, 130 N.E. 712, 713.

66. By contrast to automobile homicides, fatal automobile accidents disproportionately occurred on Mondays and during the early evening. See Horace Secrist, "Automobile, Motor-Truck, and Motor-Cycle Street Accidents in

Chicago," *Journal of the American Statistical Association* 16 (December 1919): 515–516.

67. For discussions of the threat to children, see *Chicago Tribune*, May 18, 1918, and July 23, 1920; Hoffman, *Biennial Report [of the Coroner of Cook County], 1918–1919 and Official Record of Inquests*, 80. For the same issue in New York City, see *New York Times*, January 3, 1912; McShane, *Down the Asphalt Path*, 176; Viviana A. Zelizer, *Pricing the Priceless Child* (Princeton, NJ, 1985), 33–35. The threat to women was framed more implicitly, with coroners and prosecutors tending to pursue cases in which the victims were women and then introducing evidence about the respectable, matronly demeanor of these victims. Helen O'Connell, for example, was crossing Twelfth Street with her "small son" when Samuel Adams struck and killed her. See Illinois v. Adams, 124 N.E. 575, 576.

68. *Chicago Tribune*, October 5, 1920.

69. Nineteenth-century standards for negligence had often been measured against the care that an "ordinary man," a "reasonable man," or a "free man" would exercise. See Bergstrom, *Courting Danger*, 61; Welke, *Recasting American Liberty*, 82.

70. Welke, "Unreasonable Women," 369–403; Welke, *Recasting American Liberty*, 55–61, 123–124; Keller, *Regulating a New Society*, 78.

71. *Chicago Tribune*, May 18, 1918.

72. Hoffman, *Biennial Report of the Coroner of Cook County* (Chicago, 1915), 11–28.

73. Illinois v. Schwartz, 131 N.E. 806, 808 (Illinois, 1921).

74. Illinois v. Adams, 124 N.E. 575, 577.

75. For a related discussion, see Roger Lane, "On the Social Meaning of Homicide Trends in America," in *Violence in America*, ed. Ted Robert Gurr (Newbury Park, CA, 1989), 67.

76. This figure was calculated using the total number of homicides for the period, including automobile homicides, abortion-related homicides, infanticides, medical malpractice cases, and the like.

77. To calculate the level of increase produced by automobiles, I compared the adjusted homicide rate with the sum of the adjusted homicide rate and the automobile homicide rate. For the figure on the number of automobiles registered in the city, see Hoyt, *One Hundred Years of Land Values*, 485. For the figure on traffic citations, see Wesley G. Skogan, "Chicago since 1840" (typescript; Urbana, IL, 1976), 91. For the number of fatal automobile accidents, see *Report of the Department of Health of the City of Chicago for the Years 1926 to 1930 Inclusive*, 1136.

78. For a discussion of the process through which policy makers, often relying on "sociological jurisprudence," used the criminal justice system to address larger social problems, see Willrich, *City of Courts*.

79. Cook County Coroner, *Cook County Coroner's Quadrennial Report for the Years 1908–1911* (Chicago, 1912), 7; Cook County Coroner, *Coroner's Annual Report for A.D. 1907* (Chicago, 1907), 5.

80. In Illinois, abortions were illegal and abortions in which the woman died were murder, "unless the same were done as necessary for the preservation of the mother's life." See *Hurd's Revised Statutes of Illinois,* quoted in Vice Commission of Chicago, *The Social Evil in Chicago* (Chicago, 1911), 341; Ossian Cameron, *Illinois Criminal Law and Practice* (Chicago, 1898), 5.

81. *Chicago Times,* December 17–18, 1888.

82. *Chicago Daily News,* July 24, 1899; *Chicago Record-Herald,* March 5 and March 13, 1905; Hagenow v. Illinois, 59 N.E. 242, 244 (Illinois, 1900); Illinois v. Hagenow, 86 N.E. 370, 373–374 (Illinois, 1908).

83. *Chicago Tribune,* June 1, 1915, and October 17, 1909.

84. I use the term "discover" in the manner employed by sociologists studying moral panics. See, for example, Stephen Pfohl, "The 'Discovery' of Child Abuse," *Social Problems* 24 (February 1977): 310–323. Also see Leslie J. Reagan, *When Abortion Was a Crime* (Berkeley, CA, 1997), 15.

85. *Chicago Record-Herald,* April 7, 1906; *Chicago Tribune,* December 7, 1918.

86. *Chicago Tribune,* December 7, 1915.

87. Illinois v. Hobbs, 130 N.E. 779, 783 (Illinois, 1921).

88. Cook County Coroner, *Cook County Coroner's Quadrennial Report for the Years 1908–1911,* 22; Hoffman, *Biennial Report of the Coroner of Cook County,* 92; Hoffman, *Biennial Report [of the Coroner of Cook County], 1918–1919 and Official Record of Inquests,* 78; Reagan, *When Abortion Was a Crime,* 76.

89. For example, see *Chicago Tribune,* September 30, 1915.

90. Hagenow v. Illinois, 59 N.E. 242, 244.

91. Illinois v. Hagenow, 86 N.E. 370, 373.

92. Illinois v. Hagenow, 86 N.E. 370, 373.

93. *Chicago Tribune,* May 10, 1909.

94. For "no evidence of pneumonia," see *Chicago Daily News,* August 5, 1915; for other examples, see *Chicago Tribune,* August 6 and October 5, 1915.

95. For the Lawlynowicz case, see *Chicago Tribune,* September 12, 1915; *Chicago Daily News,* September 11 and 30, 1915; for the "prize herd" quotation, see *Chicago Daily News,* September 11, 1915.

96. For Jones, see *Chicago Tribune,* October 2, 1915; for the county coroner, see Cook County Coroner, *Coroner's Annual Report for A.D. 1907,* 5.

97. This figure is based on the homicide cases identified in Chicago Police Department, "Homicides and Important Events." Leslie J. Reagan found a similar pattern. See Reagan, *When Abortion Was a Crime,* 40.

98. *Chicago Inter Ocean,* August 5, 1900. For a similar set of circumstances, see Illinois v. Hagenow, 86 N.E. 370, 372.

99. *Chicago Times,* July 10, 1887; *Chicago Tribune,* March 6, 1906; Samuel

Paynter Wilson, *Chicago and Its Cesspools of Infamy* (Chicago, 1909), 161; *Chicago Tribune*, September 30, 1915; *Chicago Evening Post*, October 1, 1915. See also Reagan, *When Abortion Was a Crime*, 102–104, 108.

100. For the "illegal practitioners" phrase, see *Chicago Tribune*, May 6, 1906; for "abortionist's scalpel" and Rockwell, *Chicago Tribune*, September 30, 1915; for Woodruff, *Chicago Evening Post*, October 1, 1915; *Chicago Daily News*, October 1, 1915; for "hideous practice," *Chicago Tribune*, December 7, 1915.

101. For the "butchery" characterization, see *Chicago Tribune*, October 2, 1915. For those against vice and white slavery, see Vice Commission of Chicago, *The Social Evil in Chicago*, 223; and Reagan, *When Abortion Was a Crime*, 85, 91. For those concerned about "race suicide," see Reagan, *When Abortion Was a Crime*, 85, 92, 108.

102. For the Committee on Criminal Abortion, see Reagan, *When Abortion Was a Crime*, 82. For the "check this evil" quotation, see *Chicago Tribune*, April 7, 1906; for "menace to the maintenance," *Chicago Tribune*, December 7, 1918.

103. Reagan, *When Abortion Was a Crime*, 80–112.

104. For the services provided by midwives, see Grace Abbott, "The Midwife in Chicago," *American Journal of Sociology* 20 (March 1915): 684; Reagan, *When Abortion Was a Crime*, 70. For midwives' appeal to immigrants, see Abbott, "The Midwife in Chicago," 691; Reagan, *When Abortion Was a Crime*, 73. For their charges, see Reagan, *When Abortion Was a Crime*, 74.

105. *Chicago Tribune*, April 7 and 8, 1906; Reagan, *When Abortion Was a Crime*, 81–89.

106. For Hagenow's "specializing" in "women's troubles," see Illinois v. Hagenow, 86 N.E. 370, 373–374. For her advertisements, fortune, and friends, see *Chicago Tribune*, March 3, 1906. For the tally of her fatalities and indictments, see *Chicago Tribune*, March 17, 1905; and Reagan, *When Abortion Was a Crime*, 77, 284n108. For the four indictments in seven years, see *Chicago Record-Herald*, March 3, 1906. Twice Hagenow was acquitted; one case was "stricken off" by the trial judge; and once she was convicted. See *Chicago Record-Herald*, March 3, 1906; *Chicago Inter Ocean*, March 4, 1906; Chicago Police Department, "Homicides and Important Events." For details of the autopsies, see Hagenow v. Illinois, 59 N.E. 242, 244; for Morrow's testimony, see Illinois v. Hagenow, 86 N.E. 370, 375. For "most notorious," see *Chicago Evening Post*, November 30, 1907; for the state's attorney's words, see Illinois v. Hagenow, 86 N.E. 370, 380. For Hagenow's use of money and powerful friends, see *Chicago Tribune*, March 3, 1906. Hagenow served less than a year of a one-year-to-life sentence for the death of Marie Hecht and less than eight years of a twenty-year sentence for the death of Anna Horvatich; see *Chicago Tribune*, March 17, 1905, and March 3, 1906; *Chicago Evening Post*, November 30, 1907; Joliet Convict Registers.

107. *Chicago Tribune*, March 3, 1906.

108. This figure was calculated using the total number of homicides, includ-

ing automobile homicides, abortion-related homicides, infanticides, medical malpractice cases, and the like.

109. Abortion-homicide cases fell sharply after 1917, dropping by nearly two-thirds in 1918. This decrease reflected the waning of the physicians' and moral reformers' campaigns against midwives and abortion. For a discussion of this process, see Reagan, *When Abortion Was a Crime*, 108–110, 117.

110. For general proportions of infant deaths, see *Report of the Department of Health of the City of Chicago for the Years 1926 to 1930 Inclusive*, 683. For the 1900 figures, see Reynolds, *Vital Statistics of the City of Chicago for the Years 1899 to 1903 Inclusive*, 104; Benedict and O'Brien, "Deaths, Disturbances, Disasters, and Disorder," 2–3.

111. *Report and Handbook of the Department of Health of the City of Chicago for the Years 1911 to 1918, Inclusive*, 1240, 1244, 1268, 1316, 1340, 1364, 1388.

112. For an intriguing discussion of this issue, see Martin Daly and Margo Wilson, *Homicide* (New York, 1988), 61–72.

113. For local baby farms, see *Chicago Evening Post*, August 5, 1902; *Chicago Record-Herald*, May 23, 1903; *Chicago Record-Herald*, August 10 and 11, 1903. For broader discussions of baby farms, see Linda Gordon, *Heroes of Their Own Lives* (New York, 1988), 43–46; Zelizer, *Pricing the Priceless Child*, 176.

114. *Chicago Record-Herald*, August 11, 1903.

115. L. Mara Dodge also found that prosecutors devoted little attention to infanticide. See Dodge, *Whores and Thieves of the Worst Kind* (DeKalb, IL, 2002), 98–99.

116. *Chicago Tribune*, August 30, 1914.

117. Hoffman, *Biennial Report of the Coroner of Cook County*, 51.

118. For the 1902 case, see *Chicago Inter Ocean*, August 10, 1902. For the 1906 cases, see *Chicago Record-Herald*, April 17, 1906; and *Chicago Evening Post*, September 7, 1906. For other cases, see *Chicago Record-Herald*, December 12, 1906; *Chicago Tribune*, August 23, 1914; *Chicago Daily News*, February 13, 1918. For the 1917 case, see *Chicago Tribune*, November 17, 1917.

119. Chicago Police Department, "Homicides and Important Events"; City of Chicago, Police Department, *Annual Report for the Year Ending December 31, 1918* (Chicago, 1919), 25; City of Chicago, Police Department, *Annual Report for the Year Ending December 31, 1919* (Chicago, 1920), 28.

120. For "beautify her complexion," see *Chicago Tribune*, May 30, 1902; for Johnson's dismissal of the neighbors, see *Chicago Inter Ocean*, May 30, 1902. Police records and newspaper accounts provided hints about the theories of investigators. The "mysterious" nature of Thompson's death led the physicians who performed the postmortem examination to verify the victim's "good character." In other words, they first determined that Thompson had not died from the effects of a botched abortion. When this possibility was eliminated, Johnson's "treatment" became the focus of the criminal investigation. See *Chicago Tribune*, May 30, 1902.

121. For other examples, see *Chicago Tribune,* March 22, 1918.

122. For Errant, see *Chicago Tribune,* October 8, 1911; for Weikus and Keriz, *Chicago Evening Post,* August 27, 1920; for officials' efforts to "hold to the grand jury," *Chicago Tribune,* December 30, 1919; for the health commissioner's quotation about wood alcohol, *Chicago Evening Post,* December 27, 1919. For "cocaine poisoning," see City of Chicago, Police Department, *Annual Report for the Year Ending December 31, 1914* (Chicago, 1915), 17; *Chicago Tribune,* August 7, 1914, January 1 and May 18, 1916, and March 23, 1917.

123. For the Robertson quotations, see *Chicago Tribune,* October 2 and 7, 1920.

124. The "crude homicide rate" includes the newly criminalized or newly enforced forms of homicide.

125. Edith Abbott, "Recent Statistics Relating to Crime in Chicago," *Journal of Criminal Law, Criminology, and Police Science* 13 (November 1922): 355.

126. For the drop in deaths from alcoholism, see *Report of the Department of Health of the City of Chicago for the Years 1926 to 1930 Inclusive,* 1140. For the average age at death and accidental death rate, see ibid., 683 and 1136.

127. Children were particularly quick to adjust to these hazards. See Zelizer, *Pricing the Priceless Child,* 51.

128. Keller, *Regulating a New Society,* 153.

129. To calculate this figure, I compared crude homicide levels for the 1900–1920 period with adjusted homicide levels for the same period. In other words, the figure measures the proportion of cases added to the homicide total as a consequence of the broadening scope of law enforcement efforts.

7. "A Butcher at the Stockyard Killing Sheep"

1. For the events leading up to the shooting, see Testimony of Charles C. Williams and Testimony of James C. O'Brien, June 19, 1919, Hearing on the Application of Earl Dear for Commutation of Sentence, Executive Clemency Files of Governor Frank O. Lowden, Illinois State Archives, Springfield. For the shooting itself, see Testimony of John Haupt, Coroner's Inquest, January 20, 1918, in Application of Earl Dear for Commutation of Sentence. For details of Wolfe's wounds, see Testimony of W. H. Burmeister, Coroner's Physician, Coroner's Inquest, January 20, 1918, in Application of Earl Dear for Commutation of Sentence. For the apprehension and Wolfe's identification of the suspects, see Testimony of John A. Quinn, Chicago Police Detective, Coroner's Inquest, January 20, 1918, in Application of Earl Dear for Commutation of Sentence. For the death of Wolfe, details of the trial, and the "beast of prey" quotation, see *Chicago Tribune,* January 20, 1918; Emory J. Smith, "Motion to the Supreme Court of the United States regarding Illinois v. Earl Dear, June 2, 1919," in Application of Earl Dear for Commutation of Sentence; miscellaneous newspaper clippings ("Demands Noose for Earl Dear"), Application of Earl Dear for Commutation of Sentence. For the "butcher" quotation, see Emory J.

Smith, "Motion to the Supreme Court of the United States regarding Illinois v. Earl Dear, June 2, 1919," in Application of Earl Dear for Commutation of Sentence.

2. This figure is based on the total number of homicides for the year, including abortion-related deaths, automobile accidents, and other kinds of newly recognized (or newly criminalized) forms of homicide. See Chicago Police Department, "Homicides and Important Events, 1870–1920," Illinois State Archives, Springfield.

3. George Kibbe Turner, "The City of Chicago: A Study of Great Immoralities," *McClure's Magazine* 28 (April 1907): 590.

4. *Chicago Tribune,* May 11, 1914.

5. *Chicago Tribune,* August 29, 1913.

6. For an examination of the process through which traditionally masculine behavior was redefined as deviant, see Martin J. Wiener, "The Victorian Criminalization of Men," in *Men and Violence,* ed. Pieter Spierenburg (Columbus, OH, 1998), 197–212.

7. Wesley G. Skogan, "Chicago since 1840" (typescript; Urbana, IL, 1976), 90–91.

8. This information was culled from annual coroner's and health department reports. For a perceptive analysis of the link between drowning and self-control, see Roger Lane, *Violent Death in the City* (Cambridge, MA, 1979), 48–51.

9. For a discussion of this process, see Roy Rosenzweig, *Eight Hours for What We Will* (New York, 1983).

10. For employment patterns, see Lizabeth Cohen, *Making a New Deal* (New York, 1990), 13–16. For a discussion of the impact of supervised employment on violent behavior, see Lane, *Violent Death in the City,* 121–129. For data on the number of students in Chicago's public schools, see Skogan, "Chicago since 1840," 96.

11. This figure is based on the adjusted, rather than the crude, homicide rate. The calculation excludes automobile accidents, abortion-related deaths, infanticides, and other newly enforced or newly criminalized forms of homicide. When these forms of homicide are included in the calculation (in other words, when the figure is based on crude homicide rates), the rate of increase rises to 124 percent.

12. Skogan, "Chicago since 1840," 24–25.

13. Cohen, *Making a New Deal,* 16.

14. James R. Barrett, *Work and Community in the Jungle* (Urbana, IL, 1987), 19.

15. "Blue Monday" referred to the weekly cycle of work and leisure in which the effects of weekend inebriation undermined productivity on Mondays. See Herbet G. Gutman, *Work, Culture, and Society in Industrializing America* (New York, 1966), 37.

16. Skogan, "Chicago since 1840," 31.

17. Homer Hoyt, *One Hundred Years of Land Values in Chicago* (Chicago, 1933), 490; Skogan, "Chicago since 1840," 31.

18. Hoyt, *One Hundred Years of Land Values*, 493.

19. Henry Barrett Chamberlin, "The Proposed Illinois Bureau of Criminal Records and Statistics," *Journal of the American Institute of Criminal Law and Criminology* 12 (February 1922): 520.

20. For the proportion of murder victims, see Edwin H. Sutherland, *Criminology* (Philadelphia, 1924), 65.

21. *Chicago Tribune*, March 8, 1875.

22. Eric H. Monkkonen found a similar pattern in late nineteenth-century New York City. See Monkkonen, *Murder in New York City* (Berkeley, CA, 2001), 107–108.

23. Ibid., 107; Roger Lane, *Roots of Violence in Black Philadelphia, 1860–1900* (Cambridge, MA, 1986), 104.

24. For descriptions of such violence, see *Chicago Tribune*, November 14, 1879; *Chicago Times*, August 4, 1880.

25. William N. Gemmill, "Crime and Its Punishment in Chicago," *Journal of the American Institute of Criminal Law and Criminology* 1 (July 1910): 200.

26. *Chicago Tribune*, March 4, 1875.

27. The proportion for the late 1910s was roughly comparable to the figure for the late twentieth century. See Richard Block and Carolyn Rebecca Block, "Homicide Syndromes and Vulnerability: Violence in Chicago Community Areas over Twenty-Five Years," *Studies in Crime and Crime Prevention* 1 (1992): 67; Carolyn R. Block and Richard Block, *Patterns of Change in Chicago Homicides* (Chicago, 1980), 13; Monkkonen, *Murder in New York City*, 108; Richard T. Wright and Scott H. Decker, *Armed Robbers in Action* (Boston, 1997), 7; Marc Riedel, "Stranger Violence: Perspectives, Issues, and Problems," *Journal of Criminal Law and Criminology* 78 (Summer 1987): 227.

28. See, for example, Petition of Harvey Van Dine for Commutation of Death Sentence, Illinois Board of Pardons, April 20, 1904, Illinois State Archives, Springfield.

29. For the availability of firearms, see *Chicago Daily News*, March 20, 1900; *Chicago Tribune*, October 21, 1905. For a discussion of automatic guns, see Petition of Harvey Van Dine for Commutation of Death Sentence, April 20, 1904. For Burke, see *Chicago Daily News*, October 25, 1915.

30. Sam Cardinelli, the leader of one holdup gang, for example, provided the "machine" and the driver for his teams of robbers. See Testimony of E. J. Raber, Assistant State's Attorney, to Governor Frank O. Lowden, October 15, 1920, Report of the Division of Pardons and Paroles of the Department of Public Welfare on the Applications of Frank Campione, Thomas Errico, and Nicholas Viana for Commutation, Executive Clemency Files of Frank O. Lowden, Illinois State Archives, Springfield. For descriptions of robbery homicides in which the holdup men relied on getaway automobiles, see

Chicago Daily News, September 20, 1915; *Chicago Evening Post,* February 24, 1919, and May 19, 1920.

31. For the "machine" reference, see Testimony of E. J. Raber, Assistant State's Attorney, to the Governor, October 15, 1920, Report of the Division of Pardons and Paroles of the Department of Public Welfare on the Application of Frank Campione, Thomas Errico, and Nicholas Viana for Commutation. For "automobile bandits," see, for example, *Chicago Evening Post,* September 20, 1915; see also Perry R. Duis, *Challenging Chicago* (Urbana, IL, 1998), 59. For "chugging automobile," see *Chicago Daily News,* April 21, 1917. For "90 per cent," see *Bulletin of the Chicago Crime Commission,* April 2, 1923, quoted in Frederic M. Thrasher, *The Gang* (1927; abridged, with an introduction by James F. Short, Jr., Chicago, 1963), 309–310. Marcus Kavanagh, *The Criminal and His Allies* (Indianapolis, 1928), 349. John Landesco, "Prohibition and Crime," *Annals of the American Academy of Political and Social Science* 163 (September 1932): 129. Also see Roger Lane, "On the Social Meaning of Homicide Trends in America," in *Violence in America,* ed. Ted Robert Gurr (Newbury Park, CA, 1989), 69.

32. For 1915, see *Report of the City Council Committee on Crime of the City of Chicago* [Charles Merriam, Chairman] (Chicago, 1915): 88. For 1917, see Sutherland, *Criminology,* 36. For 1918, see Raymond B. Fosdick, *American Police Systems* (New York, 1920), 18; "America's High Tide of Crime," *Literary Digest* 67 (December 11, 1920): 12.

33. Turner, "The City of Chicago," 590. For other assessments of urban crime, see "New York's Crime Wave," *Literary Digest* 42 (April 1, 1911): 611; "Cities Helpless in the Grip of Crime," *Literary Digest* 73 (April 22, 1922): 10. For insurance rates, see *Chicago Daily News,* February 28, 1918; Edwin W. Sims, "Fighting Crime in Chicago: The Chicago Crime Commission," *Journal of the American Institute of Criminal Law and Criminology* 11 (May 1920): 22–23; Henry Barrett Chamberlin, "Crime as a Business in Chicago," *Bulletin of the Chicago Crime Commission* 6 (October 1, 1919): 6; *Chicago Tribune,* December 10, 1920. For the 1917 robbery murder, see *Chicago Evening Post,* August 28, 1917. For the plea of the Chicago Association of Commerce, see Sims, "Fighting Crime in Chicago," 21; for Kimball, see *Chicago Daily News,* February 28, 1918.

34. Between 1910 and 1920, 43 percent of Chicago homicides occurred on the streets. By comparison, between 1890 and 1910, 30 percent of the city's homicides occurred on the streets.

35. The proportion of robbery homicides committed by strangers in the late twentieth century was close to 80 percent. See Riedel, "Stranger Violence," 232.

36. In late twentieth-century cities, the figure was roughly comparable to the 1920 figure. See ibid., 228–230.

37. Testimony of Henry Barrett Chamberlin to Governor Frank O. Lowden,

October 15, 1920, Report of the Division of Pardons and Paroles on the Department of Public Welfare, on the Application on Frank Campione, Thomas Errico, and Nicholas Viana for Commutation. Chamberlin, "Crime as a Business," 1.

38. Letter from Trial Judge Oscar Hebel to Governor Frank O. Lowden, September 20, 1920, Report of the Division of Pardons and Paroles of the Department of Public Welfare on the Application of Frank Campione, Thomas Errico, and Nicholas Viana for Commutation.

39. Chamberlin, "Proposed Illinois Bureau," 52.

40. For the Stein robbery, see *Chicago Daily News*, May 19, 1917. For the Cardinelli gang, see Illinois v. Cardinelli, 130 N.E. 355, 357 (Illinois, 1921); Testimony of E. J. Raber, Assistant State's Attorney, to the Governor, opposing clemency, October 15, 1920, Report of the Division of Pardons and Paroles of the Department of Public Welfare on the Application of Frank Campione, Thomas Errico, and Nicholas Viana for Commutation; *Chicago Tribune*, June 25, 1919. For Errico, see Testimony of Henry Barrett Chamberlin to Governor Frank O. Lowden, October 15, 1920, Report of the Division of Pardons and Paroles on the Department of Public Welfare, on the Application on Frank Campione, Thomas Errico, and Nicholas Viana for Commutation.

41. For information on the number of participants and victims, as well as the "calculations" quotation, see *Chicago Tribune*, August 31, 1903. For the amount stolen in the robbery, see Thomas S. Duke, *Celebrated Criminal Cases of America* (San Francisco, 1910), 428. For the ten days of planning, see Petition of Harvey Van Dine for Commutation of Death Sentence, Illinois Board of Pardons, April 20, 1904. For information on Edmond, see *Chicago Inter Ocean*, August 21, 1903. For "amazing knowledge," see *Chicago Record-Herald*, August 31, 1903; for the gang's nickname, see Herbert Asbury, *Gem of the Prairie* (1940; reprint, with an introduction by Perry R. Duis, DeKalb, IL, 1986), 224. For the gang's knowledge of the security system and layout, see *Chicago Inter Ocean*, August 31, 1903; Petition of Harvey Van Dine for Commutation of Death Sentence, April 20, 1904, Illinois Board of Pardons.

42. For Martin, see *Chicago Tribune*, August 31, 1903. Turner, "The City of Chicago," 590.

43. Testimony of Henry Barrett Chamberlin, October 15, 1920, Report of the Division of Pardons and Paroles of the Department of Public Welfare on the Application of Frank Campione, Thomas Errico, and Nicholas Viana for Commutation. For a discussion of the strategies of late twentieth-century robbers, see Wright and Decker, *Armed Robbers in Action*, 96.

44. *Chicago Daily News*, quoted in "Increase of Crime in Chicago," *Literary Digest* 27 (December 19, 1903): 858.

45. Assistant State's Attorney James C. O'Brien, quoted in unidentified newspaper clipping, Application of Earl Dear for Commutation of Sentence; *Chicago Tribune*, June 14, 1896.

46. *Chicago Times-Herald,* October 19, 1895; *Chicago Tribune,* June 14, 1896.
47. For the 1897 quotation, see George W. Steevens, *The Land of the Dollar* (1897; reprint, Freeport, NY, 1971), 150. For "cleaning up Chicago," see *Chicago Record-Herald,* August 24, 1907. For Shea, see *Chicago Tribune,* January 6, 1899; for Shippy, *Chicago Record-Herald,* August 24, 1907; for Kostner, *Chicago Tribune,* December 26, 1920.
48. For Baumgartner, see *Chicago Tribune,* April 19, 1915; for Sullivan, *Chicago Daily News,* April 10, 1915. Contemporary reformers expressed concern about such "justifiable and excusable homicides" by policemen. See Edith Abbott, "Recent Statistics Relating to Crime in Chicago," *Journal of Criminal Law, Criminology, and Police Science* 13 (November 1922): 356–357.
49. *Chicago Times-Herald,* October 19, 1895. *Chicago Record,* November 20, 1893. For examples of the resulting domestic violence, see Daniel McCarthy's statement to the Chicago Police Department, May 16, 1896, Petition for Commutation of the Sentence of Daniel McCarthy, Executive Clemency Files of Governor John Tanner, Illinois State Archives, Springfield; *Chicago Tribune,* November 17, 1900.
50. For example, see *Chicago Evening Post,* October 24, 1904.
51. For the Morgan quotation "Then they came toward me," see *Chicago Record,* September 12, 1894. *Chicago Tribune,* September 11, 1894. For Morgan's quotation "My gun was lying on the bar," see *Chicago Record,* September 12, 1894. For the Harrity case, including the quotation "Throw up your hands," see *Chicago Tribune,* December 30, 1894. For "carries a medal," see *Chicago Record,* December 31, 1894. For "No you don't" and the death of Harrity, see *Chicago Tribune,* December 30, 1894. For McGrail's "wish," see *Chicago Record,* December 31, 1894.
52. Of the twenty-four, five were killed by policemen and two by watchmen.
53. Just 6 percent of robber killers were brought to trial. Of these, six of them—or 2.5 percent of the killers of holdup men—were convicted, and in these six cases either watchmen shot indiscriminately or the robbers died at the hands of accomplices.
54. Letter to Governor Frank O. Lowden, July, 1920, Statement of the Division of Pardons and Paroles of the Department of Public Welfare, on the Application of Frank Campione, Thomas Errico, and Nicholas Viana for Commutation.
55. For a related discussion, see Wright and Decker, *Armed Robbers in Action,* 107.
56. For Kniering, see *Chicago Record-Herald,* October 24, 1904; *Chicago Evening Post,* October 24, 1904; *Chicago Tribune,* October 24, 1904. For Loberg, see *Chicago Evening Post,* December 23, 1920; *Chicago Tribune,* December 23, 1920; *New York Times,* December 23, 1920.
57. Harvey Van Dine, for example, filed the number off of one of the weapons he used. Petition of Harvey Van Dine for Commutation of Death Sentence, April 20, 1904.

58. For the Cardinelli gang, see Testimony of E. J. Raber, Assistant State's Attorney, to Governor Frank O. Lowden, October 15, 1920, Report of the Division of Pardons and Paroles of the Department of Public Welfare on the Applications of Frank Campione, Thomas Errico, and Nicholas Viana for Commutation; Illinois v. Cardinelli, 130 N.E. 355, 357; Thrasher, *The Gang*, 297. For the 1903 gang, see Asbury, *Gem of the Prairie*, 224. For the "young fellows" quotation, see Testimony of Henry Barrett Chamberlin to Governor Frank O. Lowden, October 15, 1920, Report of the Division of Pardons and Paroles of the Department of Public Welfare on the Applications of Frank Campione, Thomas Errico, and Nicholas Viana for Commutation. Also see *Report of the City Council Committee on Crime of the City of Chicago*, 165. For "boy bandits"/"baby bandits," see *Chicago Evening Post*, February 24, 1919; Illinois v. Cardinelli, 130 N.E. 355, 357; "Increase of Crime in Chicago," 858. For the quartet, see *Chicago Inter Ocean*, August 4, 1904.

59. For Healey, see *Chicago Daily News*, February 4, 1916; for the crime writer quotation, see Samuel Paynter Wilson, *Chicago and Its Cess-Pools of Infamy* (Chicago, 1909), 92. For the 1905 lieutenant, see *Chicago Tribune*, March 20, 1905. For the Joliet information, see Joliet Convict Registers, Illinois State Archives, Springfield. This figure is more suggestive than definitive, since it compares robber-killers with robbers who were arrested, tried, and convicted. For "inexperienced thieves," see *Chicago Tribune*, March 6, 1908.

60. Petition of Harvey Van Dine to Governor Richard Yates for Commutation of Death Sentence, April 20, 1904, Illinois Board of Pardons; Sophie E. Van Dine to Governor Richard Yates, undated [April 1904] Petition of Harvey Van Dine for Pardon or Commutation of Sentence, Illinois Board of Pardons.

61. Petition of Harvey Van Dine for Commutation of Death Sentence, April 20, 1904, Illinois Board of Pardons; Van Dine quoted in Asbury, *Gem of the Prairie*, 226.

62. Testimony of Henry Barrett Chamberlin to Governor Frank O. Lowden, October 15, 1920, Report of the Division of Pardons and Paroles of the Department of Public Welfare on the Applications of Frank Campione, Thomas Errico, and Nicholas Viana for Commutation; *Chicago Tribune*, May 1, 1920.

63. For the typical organization of gangs, see Letter of Edward F. Dunne, December 1, 1920, Report of the Division of Pardons and Paroles of the Department of Public Welfare on the Application of Nicholas Viana for Commutation. Dunne called Sam Cardinelli a "Fagan" [*sic*]. For another reference to "modern Fagins," see Thrasher, *The Gang*, 188. For the role of the older criminal and their being in pool halls, see Testimony of E. J. Raber, Assistant State's Attorney, to Governor Frank O. Lowden, October 15, 1920, Report of the Division of Pardons and Paroles of the Department of Public Welfare on the Application of Frank Campione, Thomas Errico,

and Nicholas Viana for Commutation; Illinois v. Cardinelli, 130 N.E. 355, 357; Thrasher, *The Gang*, 297. For "crime schools," see Thrasher, *The Gang*, 188.

64. For Shippy, see *Chicago Record-Herald*, January 4, 1908. Kickham Scanlan quoted in Chicago Commission on Race Relations, *The Negro in Chicago* (Chicago, 1922), 346. Harvey Van Dine quoted in Asbury, *Gem of the Prairie*, 226. For Zager, see *Chicago Tribune*, May 1, 1920; for a related discussion, see Jack Katz, *Seductions of Crime* (New York, 1988). For Viana, see William Colvin to Governor Frank O. Lowden, July 1920, Report of the Division of Pardons and Paroles of the Department of Public Welfare on the Applications of Frank Campione, Thomas Errico, and Nicholas Viana for Commutation; T. Frank Laramie and James R. Howe to the Illinois Board of Pardons, September 21, 1920, Application of Nicholas Viana for Commutation of Death Sentence; for Raber, see Testimony of E. J. Raber, Assistant State's Attorney, to Governor Frank O. Lowden, October 15, 1920, Report of the Division of Pardons and Paroles of the Department of Public Welfare on the Application of Frank Campione, Thomas Errico, and Nicholas Viana for Commutation.

65. For Levi, see *Chicago Tribune*, November 18, 1918. For the "smart guy" quotation, see *Chicago Tribune*, November 16, 1919. For Viana, see Testimony of E. J. Raber, Assistant State's Attorney, to Governor Frank O. Lowden, October 15, 1920, Report of the Division of Pardons and Paroles of the Department of Public Welfare on the Applications of Frank Campione, Thomas Errico, and Nicholas Viana for Commutation. For Fanter, see *Chicago Tribune*, April 3, 1915.

66. For an excellent analysis of this theme, focusing on New York City during the 1950s and 1960s, see Eric C. Schneider, *Vampires, Dragons, and Egyptian Kings* (Princeton, NJ, 1999). Also see Wright and Decker, *Armed Robbers in Action*, 55–56.

67. Youth gangs, often masquerading as "athletic clubs," sometimes assaulted African-American residents during this period. "Ragen's Colts," who played a prominent and grotesquely violent role in the Race Riot of 1919, were especially "notorious" in this regard. See Chicago Commission on Race Relations, *The Negro in Chicago*, 14, 54–55. For an analysis of early twentieth-century gang wars, see William Foote Whyte, "Race Conflicts in the North End of Boston," *New England Quarterly* 12 (December 1939): 623–642.

68. James Formby quoted in Asbury, *Gem of the Prairie*, 223. For a related analysis, see Katz, *Seductions of Crime*, 174, 178. For "spicy risk," see *Bulletin of the Chicago Crime Commission*, October 6, 1920, quoted in Abbott, "Recent Statistics Relating to Crime in Chicago," 353. For a provocative examination of thrill killing, see Katz, *Seductions of Crime*.

69. William I. Thomas, with Robert A. Park and Herbert A. Miller, *Old World*

Traits Transplanted (1921; reprint, with an introduction by Donald R. Young, Montclair, NJ, 1971), 71–72.

70. Chamberlin, "Crime as a Business in Chicago," 3–4; Thomas et al., *Old World Traits Transplanted,* 71–72.
71. Thomas et al., *Old World Traits Transplanted,* 71; *Chicago Tribune,* October 23 and December 29, 1911.
72. Thrasher, *The Gang,* 77; Illinois v. Garippo, 127 N.E. 75, 77 (Illinois, 1920).
73. See Illinois v. Garippo, 127 N.E. 75, 76; Clifford R. Shaw, *The Jack-Roller* (1930; reprint, with an introduction by Howard S. Becker, Chicago, 1966).
74. Charles C. Arado, "Vignettes of the Criminal Court, 1: Abandoned Colored Defendants Charged with Murder," *Journal of the American Institute of Criminal Law and Criminology* 23 (May–June 1932): 77–78. For a similar assessment, see Chicago Commission on Race Relations, *The Negro in Chicago,* 440.
75. Scholars studying modern robbery and robbery homicide have found similar patterns. See Wright and Decker, *Armed Robbers in Action,* 7.
76. For the Lipschultz case, see *Chicago Tribune,* October 16, 1910; *Chicago Record-Herald,* October 15, 1910; *Chicago Evening Post,* October 15, 1910. For Theiner, see *Chicago Evening Post,* August 29, 1918; *Chicago Tribune,* August 29, 1918. For Calber, see *Chicago Tribune,* November 27, 1916.
77. *Chicago Tribune,* December 27, 1916.
78. For a discussion of this "Americanization" process, see Humbert S. Nelli, *The Business of Crime* (Chicago, 1976), 136, 199–202. Also see Landesco, "Prohibition and Crime," 125–126.
79. For the Beer Wars, see Landesco, "Organized Crime in Chicago," 923, 930–931. For the 1926 figure, see Arthur V. Lashly, "Homicide (in Cook County)," in *The Illinois Crime Survey,* ed. John H. Wigmore (Chicago, 1929), 610–611. For a description of the St. Valentine's Day Massacre, see Nelli, *The Business of Crime,* 166–167.
80. For data of the homicide rates of Chicago and other cities, see H. C. Brearley, *Homicide in the United States* (1932; reprint, Montclair, NJ, 1969), 209–216.
81. *Pittsburgh Dispatch* quoted in "Cities Helpless in the Grip of Crime," 10.

Conclusion
1. H. C. Brearley, *Homicide in the United States* (1932; reprint, Montclair, NJ, 1969), 209–216. See also Frederick L. Hoffman, *The Homicide Problem* (Newark, NJ, 1925), 97–100; Kenneth E. Barnhart, "A Study of Homicide in the United States," *Birmingham-Southern College Bulletin* 25 (May 1932): 10–15.
2. For example, see Cook County Coroner, *Cook County Coroner's Quadrennial Report for the Years 1908–1911* (Chicago, 1912), 22–23; Peter M. Hoffman, *Biennial Report of the Coroner of Cook County* (Chicago, 1915), 78; *Report of the*

Department of Health of the City of Chicago for the Years 1926 to 1930 Inclusive (Chicago, 1931), 1136–41.

3. These figures are based on the adjusted, rather than crude, homicide numbers and exclude infanticides, abortion-related deaths, automobile accidents, and other kinds of homicides that were socially constructed.

4. For a discussion of this powerful but uneven process, see Peter N. Stearns, *Battleground of Desire* (New York, 1999), 55–186.

5. Lincoln Steffens, "Chicago: Half Free and Fighting On," *McClure's Magazine* 21 (October 1903): 563.

Appendix

1. Chicago Police Department, "Homicides and Important Events, 1870–1920," Illinois State Archives, Springfield.

2. *Report of the Department of Health of the City of Chicago for the Years 1926 to 1930 Inclusive* (Chicago, 1931), 1138.

3. For homicide tallies, see *Chicago Inter Ocean*, September 28, 1910; *Chicago Tribune*, September 28, 1910, and November 6, 1913; *Chicago Evening Post*, December 23, 1915. For a discussion of the capture-recapture method that I employed, see Douglas Eckberg, "Stalking the Elusive Homicide: A Capture-Recapture Approach to the Estimation of Post-Reconstruction South Carolina Killings," *Social Science History* 25 (Spring 2001): 67–91.

4. The number of individual homicides reported in local newspapers typically far exceeded the annual homicide totals reported in the same newspapers.

5. *Chicago Tribune*, October 7, 1890; *Chicago Herald*, October 7, 1890; *Chicago Times*, October 7, 1890.

6. *Chicago Herald*, October 8, 1890; *Chicago Tribune*, October 8, 1890.

7. *Chicago Tribune*, October 11 and 13, 1890.

8. For some subsets of the data, I added variables and additional columns, providing me with larger case files and the ability to analyze the evidence in greater detail.

9. Police and coroners' annual reports often provided aggregate-level data on the nativity and the racial backgrounds of homicide victims. For African-American and Italian victims, the case-level data matched the aggregate-level totals in the police and coroners' reports.

10. For a thoughtful perspective on this issue, see Robert R. Dykstra, "Body Counts and Murder Rates," *Reviews in American History* 31 (December 2003): 554–563.

11. For the "barnacles and boat" metaphor, see John H. Langbein, "Albion's Fatal Flaws," *Past and Present* 98 (February 1983): 120.

Acknowledgments

The cliché in acknowledgments—one I have used myself—is that writing is a solitary venture, but the author benefited from the help of others. For this project, however, neither the research nor the writing was a solitary enterprise. I received assistance and support at every stage—from granting agencies and institutions, from archivists, librarians, and research assistants, and especially from colleagues and friends.

A research grant from the Harry Frank Guggenheim Foundation launched my work on homicide and afforded me the luxury of reading broadly and across disciplines about aggression and violence. I also received research support from both of my academic homes, the Department of History and the Department of Criminology, Law and Society, and from the College of Liberal Arts and Sciences at the University of Florida. Michael Ebner, on behalf of the Chicago Historical Society's Urban History Seminar Series, and Leigh Bienen, of the Northwestern University College of Law, invited me to Chicago to discuss my research and provided audiences that posed thoughtful questions and offered stimulating comments. Like every historian, I depended on the skill, knowledge, and hard work of archivists and librarians, and I am particularly indebted to the late Archie Motley of the Chicago Historical Society, Kim Efird and Charles Cali of the Illinois State Archives, and Marvin Crabb of the Microform Center at the University of Florida's Smathers Library. The staffs of the Inter-Library Loan Office at the University of Florida, the Municipal Reference Collection at Chicago's Harold Washington Library, the Cook County Circuit Court Archives, and the Cook County Medical Examiner's Office provided professional assistance, including the clerk in the Medical Examiner's Office who identified herself as the "cremation lady." Nor could I have completed this project without the conscientious, diligent help of research assistants, and I am pleased to convey my gratitude to Donna Jacklosky, Erin Lane, Jennifer Matheny, Marcus Nenn, Amy Reckdenwald, Debra Rhoad, and Sarah Ryan. The early fruits of the research for this project appeared in journal articles, and I would like to thank the *Journal of Social History*, the *Journal of Urban History*, the *Journal of Interdisciplinary History*, the *Journal of Criminal Law and Criminology*, and *Social Science History*. Finally, it has been a joy to work with the editorial staff at Harvard University Press, particularly Kathleen McDermott.

As I undertook the research and presented my initial findings, I discovered a wonderful community of scholars studying violent behavior. Many of these historians, legal scholars, criminologists, and sociologists gather at annual meetings of the Social Science History Association. Members of the Association's crime–law network listened, year after year, as I presented papers based on the research for this book; and their comments, critiques, and suggestions were, without exception, constructive and collegial. One of the pleasures of this project was coming into contact with this intellectual community, in which scholarship is treated as a cooperative venture and in which personal and professional generosity is the rule. For their willingness to share their time, ideas, data, insights to conceptual and theoretical issues, and solutions to methodological problems, I am grateful to Dougie Eckberg, Mark Haller, Peter Hoffer, David Johnson, Bill Miller, Stan Nadel, Pieter Spierenburg, and Marty Wiener. Leigh Bienen, Cynthia Grant Bowman, Elizabeth Dale, Sean McCrohon, and Chris Slobogin also provided a great deal of help. I am fortunate to have a group of friends who were willing to put their own scholarship aside and read the manuscript (most of them also read drafts of conference papers, articles, and chapters); this book has benefited enormously from the perceptive comments and the extraordinary generosity of Leonard Beeghley, Carolyn Conley, Tom Gallant, Matt Gallman, Roger Lane, Bob McMahon, Eric Monkkonen, and Randy Roth.

Closer to home, friends have helped in other ways. Dave Colburn provided a captive audience of sorts, as I blathered on about Chicago homicide while we jogged around Westside Park every other day; sometimes I wondered if he was running faster and faster in order to escape another tale of murder in turn-of-the-century Illinois. I took egregious advantage of other good friends as well. I am grateful for the forbearance of the Thursday Night Margarita Group, whose members—Bev Sensbach, Jon Sensbach, and Luise White—also listened to me chatter about murder in Chicago, even as they tried to unwind from work and patiently waited for me to pass the salsa or—more important—the pitcher of frozen magaritas. Old friends, particularly Mark Hirsch, Laurie McDade, David Hannah, and Sue Anderson, provided support of various kinds, for which I am truly appreciative. My golden retrievers deserve mention as well; they were close, very close, to this project, consistently wedging themselves under my desk, around my chair, against my legs, and, during thunderstorms, onto my lap as I sat in front of my computer. For their efforts, they have been and will continue to be lavishly rewarded—with gourmet dog treats. My family will not receive any gourmet treats, though they have been unflaggingly supportive. I thank them for more things than I could possibly list.